JACOB M. SCHLESINGER

SHADOW SHOGUNS

The Rise and Fall of Japan's Postwar Political Machine

STANFORD UNIVERSITY PRESS
STANFORD, CALIFORNIA

Stanford University Press
Stanford, California

First published in 1997 by Simon & Schuster
Reprinted with a revised Conclusion by
Stanford University Press, 1999
Printed in the United States of America

Last figure below indicates year of this printing:
10 09 08

For Louisa,
and for Sonia Ann

Contents

A Note to Readers

In Japanese, a person's family name appears first and the given name second. The American media generally reverse the order, using the family name last, in the manner of English names. For example, the Japanese press writes of Tanaka Kakuei, the American press of Kakuei Tanaka. The text of this book follows the rule of the American press. In the endnotes and bibliography, Japanese authors are also listed in the American style. However, the Japanese titles of books and articles are cited exactly as they were published.

Similarly, the official transliteration of many Japanese words requires macrons, which indicate elongation of a syllable. Under this rule, Ichiro Ozawa should be Ichirō Ozawa. Macrons are not used in the text of this book, but they are used for Japanese sources cited in the notes and bibliography.

Introduction

JAPAN'S rich and powerful flocked to Tokyo's stately Aoyama Funeral Hall on December 25, 1993. Their Cadillacs, Mercedeses, and chauffeured limousines lined the streets. The reigning prime minister, as well as all seven living former premiers, were solemnly escorted to their assigned seats inside, where the sweet mourning smells of chrysanthemums and incense mingled.

Japan's commoners arrived by foot, by subway, by overnight bus from the hinterland. Some in black suits, others in construction workers' garb, still others in wheelchairs or with baby carriages in tow, they formed a line that stretched outside the hall's steel gates, up the sidewalk a full city block, around a bend, and far onto the overgrown path that lay among the gravestones of Aoyama cemetery.

They came by the thousands, Japan's mighty and its masses, for the funeral of Kakuei Tanaka, the most commanding Japanese politician of his generation, who had died of pneumonia at the age of seventy-five. The mourners were not just bidding farewell to the man but were marking the ceremonial end of an era. For Tanaka, who had shown an impeccable sense of timing in life, also did so in death. His passing coincided with the demise of the national machine he had built, an organization that had presided over—and profited handsomely from—Japan's ascendance from the rubble of World War II to economic superpower.

WHEN MY NEWSPAPER dispatched me to Tokyo in 1989, I felt as if I had been sent to the new center of the universe. It was a time when many Americans harbored great uncertainties about our country's economic viability and our future—doubts magnified by Japan's simultaneous stunning success. Japan's economy was growing twice as fast as America's; its companies were taking over strategic industries, from automobiles to computer memory chips, and were buying up American landmarks and icons, from Rockefeller Center to Columbia Pictures. As the Soviet Union began falling apart, Japan became our greatest rival.

What made Japan's ascent so unnerving to the United States was not just the notion that the Asian nation might eclipse America's industrial might. Tokyo seemed to be doing so by providing a different, perhaps better, alternative to the American political-economic model, especially for Asia's other rapidly developing nations. While Japan was ostensibly a free-market democracy, its politics and its economics appeared cleverly planned and intertwined, somehow impervious to the messiness of competition and conflict so common in the West. A symbol of this harmonious continuity was the Liberal Democratic Party, or LDP; while free parliamentary elections took place, from 1955 on only this probusiness, probureaucracy party ever won. Those best convinced of the potency of cooperation within, and between, Japan's government and business worlds dubbed the whole concoction "Japan Inc." The term connoted a system that ran cleanly and efficiently, more like a corporation than an elected government. In the mythology that evolved, Japan Inc. was both superhuman and ahuman. It had no dynamic personalities, but was managed by a mysterious horde of interchangeable blue-suited automatons.

By the time I left Tokyo in 1994, however, the Japanese juggernaut had stalled. The economy had fallen into its deepest recession since the war. Politics was wracked by sensational scandals. The people's trust in long-successful institutions waned, while the famous unity of the leadership was shattered amid bitter disputes. The establishment's arrogant assumptions about its immortality had been jolted in 1993, when the Liberal Democratic Party lost power after thirty-eight years in control.

The remnants of any global appeal of the Japan Inc. model disappeared in the summer of 1997, when a similar political/economic crisis spread throughout Asia: first in Thailand, then in Indonesia, then in South Korea. In each case, the story was eerily familiar: the close ties between government and business, once hailed as brilliant coordination, had been exposed as corrupt, inefficient, and ultimately unsustainable, derided as "crony capitalism." The Asian financial meltdown was triggered, in part, by Japan's own long-term stagnation. The region's troubles, in turn, aggravated Japan's ongoing struggles. At the same time, Tokyo's once-proud elite continued to stumble into scandal. In early 1998, it was the revered Finance Ministry that was jolted by a series of arrests. The LDP, which had managed to claw its way back to power in 1996, suffered another stunning electoral defeat in July of 1998, and its future once again looked doubtful.

The questions raised during Japan's difficulties through the 1990s have forced a rethinking of Japan's recent history, and an intense debate about its future course. In retrospect, how smooth and effective was Japan's management of its political economy? What kind of model did Japan represent? Was it one of careful bureaucratic design, distinct from Western models? Was it culturally specific? Or was it the predictable—and ephemeral—product of unique circumstances? How destructive have the recent upheavals been to Japan's old order? Will elements of a distinctly Japanese system survive?

This book argues that the past was not so neatly crafted as it had appeared and that the old order cannot be put back together again. The starting premise is that the Japanese system was never so superhuman nor so mysterious as it had appeared. It was a smoothly run machine, all right. But it was a political machine—much like New York City's Tammany Hall or Huey Long's apparatus in Louisiana, one that would be quite familiar to students of American history. Japan's machine did, in some respects, manage economic policy with remarkable consensus and efficiency. Yet the costs required for holding the system together were huge, in the form of blatant favoritism, monumental amounts of pork, and gold-plated corruption. In many ways, Japan Inc. was a gaudy, inefficient mess.

This is the story of Japan Inc. as political machine. It chronicles the political culture of a nation obsessed with economic advancement and the distortions to democracy and capitalism that accompanied what the world called Japan's economic "miracle." It is about the ambitions of colorful, domineering politicians—the dynasty of machine bosses known as "shadow shoguns"—who skillfully rigged the seemingly faceless, selfless system for their own gain.

It is a very human story, spanning three political generations.

The founder was Kakuei Tanaka, the charismatic son of a dissolute horse trader whose fiery populism made him, for a time, the nation's most beloved politician. The second generation was the political odd couple of Shin Kanemaru, a gruff, incoherent brawler known as "the Don," and Noboru Takeshita, the wily fixer. The third generation was Ichiro Ozawa, the favored scion of the machine "family"—trained as Tanaka's political "son" and, through a complicated network of marriages, kin to Kanemaru and Takeshita. The four men managed to impose and maintain crooked boss control from the early 1970s to the early 1990s over a national legislature governing a country of 100 million people. The ruling LDP and opposition parties, the national bureaucracy, and major corporations were all subject to their manipulation. The Tanaka cabal rarely claimed titular authority, preferring to influence Japan's official leaders from behind the scenes. As "shadow shoguns," the bosses could skirt the constraints of public scrutiny and accountability. Indeed, the machine was able to survive numerous money scandals, including Tanaka's own arrest and conviction for taking bribes.

The Tanaka machine was the natural outcome of its time, an era when the entire nation unified around, and reveled in, the pursuit of prosperity. Many of the elements that gave rise to America's political machines in the late nineteenth and early twentieth centuries were also prominent in postwar Japan: an impoverished, recently enfranchised electorate that was less concerned about the lofty, unfamiliar principles of democracy than about access to the largess of the state; an absence of controversial issues, which allowed the government to attract a wide alliance of supporters and to focus on the nuts and bolts of local administration instead of wider public policies; and the dominance of one political party, which enabled a machine to count on ongoing power. Corruption was of little concern to the voters as long as they got their cut.

Cold War–era America also helped foster the Tanaka machine by virtually dictating to Tokyo its foreign policy in the wake of Japan's World War II defeat. In so doing, Washington removed from Japanese politics the difficult issues of global stability and security. The absence of such questions created an environment conducive to a machine, by elevating to supreme importance the more mundane matters of government favors and public works. The Tanaka machine, in turn, shaped a style of diplomacy that would come to irritate American leaders in later years. Japan's notoriously frustrating trade barriers were often the result of a political system designed to cater only to narrow domestic special interests. Japan's inability to solve swiftly its banking crisis—a main source of the world's economic turmoil in 1998—became another symbol of the old order's failings. And despite the country's new rank as a global economic power, Japan's political rulers had no ability or experience to address their world responsibilities.

Having been nurtured under special conditions, the machine could not last when its environment changed in the late 1980s and early 1990s. And as the machine became threatened by external forces, internal pressures naturally mounted. Political unity was not inherent in the culture, but was the lucky outcome of sustained peace and prosperity, when there was ever-expanding wealth to share. When signs of trouble emerged—and when the machine had grown too big to satisfy all of its members adequately—the group turned out to be not a cabal of automatons after all, but an organization all too vulnerable to the normal human weaknesses of ambition and jealousy.

Sensing the precarious state of the machine, boss Ozawa turned against his "family" in 1993 and declared himself an anti-LDP, anti-machine "reformer." While his crusade has had its setbacks, he launched the process that will, over time, fundamentally change Japan's policies and its politics. The first step of that process was to shatter the assumption of eternal harmony of Japan's political elite and to show that it is possible to divide the best and brightest politicians into opposing camps. Thus, after a quarter century in which Japan's democracy was defined by the Tanaka machine's consensus, the country's politics are now being shaped by a more open competition for power, money, and ideas.

PART ONE

KAKUEI TANAKA: MAN OF THE PEOPLE, MAN OF MEANS, 1918–1976

When the Japanese empire formally disintegrated in August 1945, Kakuei Tanaka was in an awkward spot.

He was a twenty-seven-year-old businessman in the colony of Korea, overseeing construction of an aircraft parts factory for the now-defeated imperial forces. There were more than 6 million Japanese—nearly half, like him, civilians—spread across Asia, dispatched over three decades to build and defend what had become the "Greater East Asian Co-prosperity Sphere." Overnight, the masters were stripped of their authority, and they found themselves trapped among their liberated—and hostile—subjects. The new mission of these humiliated colonialists was, somehow, to find a way home.

Many were subjected to rape, torture, hard labor, starvation, disease, public humiliation—traumas the Japanese themselves had inflicted when they were in charge. The escape from Korea would take more than a year for thousands of the fleeing empire builders, and many had to do it by foot through dangerous mountain terrain, camping outside in the rain and snow. Survivors would later describe it as a living hell.

Tanaka somehow was able to orchestrate a smoother retreat. He and a half-dozen fellow Japanese executives managed to get on a train to Pusan just three days after the official August 15 Japanese surrender and were given the royal treatment for a night at the Japanese Army's officers' quarters. Most of their compatriots lucky enough to reach Pusan so quickly were then kept languishing in crowded, disease-infested camps for weeks. Tanaka caught defense ship No. 34, a naval ferry to the northern tip of Japan's main island, on August 20. The craft was filled with women and children; in later years he would impishly credit a clerical error: he was listed on the ship's roster as Kikue, a woman's name, not his own unmistakably masculine Kakuei. Others suspect he bribed his way aboard.

The rough seas and steady drizzle deepened the journey's gloom. Yet Tanaka seems to have traveled in style, a calm executive on a routine business trip, oblivious to the surrounding mayhem. "He came to make formal greetings," the ship's chief engineer would later recall. "I thought it odd that somebody would do that, but here was this strange man with a little mustache giving me his calling card. He was accompanied by a man carrying a bag as if it were very important." A small child died on the trip, and Tanaka gave the mother 300 yen in consolation, three times the chief engineer's monthly salary. Ten days after the surrender, Tanaka was safely back in Tokyo.

Tanaka not only survived but actually thrived from his Korean ordeal. Before the war's end, his company had been paid 15 million yen—a sum today worth more than 7 billion yen, or $70 million—to build the factory which, due to what might be called a change in market conditions, he never had to complete. Tanaka later implied in his memoirs that he had not profited from the venture, claiming that he had gallantly promised his Korean employees that he would donate the assets "to the new Korea." He didn't explain, though, whether he ever actually followed through on that pledge. Business associates say he pocketed the money. As an unexpected bonus, the returning Tanaka found that, despite heavy American bombing of Tokyo, much of his property there—his office, his home, even a fish shop he had bought in a distress sale from its fleeing owners—was largely intact. Amid the ruins, he was a newly wealthy man.

August 1945 is a good moment to begin the story of Kakuei Tanaka. For all of the tragedy and trauma of the war, this was an oddly optimistic period for many survivors, a chance to make a fresh start, to build a different, better nation. As much as any public figure, Tanaka would come to symbolize and shape the time and place known as "postwar Japan." And his magnificent entrance onto that stage—his plucky, lucrative return from Korea—presaged the style with which he would make his mark. He had an uncanny knack for turning adversity into advantage.

CHAPTER ONE

FROM PENURY TO PARLIAMENT

TANAKA is a significant figure in Japanese culture not just because of his achievements but because of his roots.

Prewar Japan was a nation governed by a well-bred, well-heeled elite, a country of haves and have-nots. The pressure and tensions resulting from this disparity were major causes, historians believe, of Japan's ruinous military crusade. "Postwar Japan," in contrast, was supposed to be different, a land of equality and opportunity. Tanaka's humble origins seemed to affirm the broader transformation; tales of his youth are staples of Japanese political lore, his country's equivalent of the Lincoln log-cabin legend.

Most of what is known of Tanaka's early days and family history comes from his own detailed, nostalgic renditions, widely published and broadcast by Japan's mass media. As Kakuei tells it, the Tanaka clan fared decently enough until the early twentieth century, when his father, Kakuji, developed delusions of grandeur. The Tanakas had the modest distinction of being one of the eighteen original families of Futada, a farming village founded around the fifteenth century. Futada was in Niigata Prefecture in the heart of Japan's "snow country," a northwestern pocket of the main island of Honshu. Because of the long, harsh winters, this was considered one of the poorest, bleakest regions of Japan. But Futada was relatively prosperous for its surroundings, benefiting from its location as a convenient stop for travelers heading to and from the local feudal castle, and later from a patch of oil discovered amid its lush fields and forests. By the time Kakuei was born on May 4, 1918, the farming and drilling town had grown to about two hundred households.

Kakuji's mother was the daughter of a village elder, and his father was a respectable carpenter who built schools, local government offices, and Shinto shrines. Kakuji's wife came from a business family, of sorts, that ran an inn catering to itinerant blind female musicians, who were famous for performing along the Japan Sea coast. With forests and rice paddies stretching nearly four square miles and his own sundry animal trades, Kakuji was somewhat better off than his neighbors. He certainly had enough to support his brood, which would grow to six daughters and one son.

But the restless Kakuji wanted something better. He talked of one day moving beyond the remote outpost wedged between the Japan Sea and the Mikuni mountain ranges, where his family had been stuck for half a millennium. Perhaps he would strike it really rich; maybe he could set up a large ranch in the vast northern plains of Hokkaido.

Unfortunately, Kakuji's ambitions surpassed his brains, luck, and drive. One year he sold the family forests and borrowed heavily to import three cows from Holland. He staked 45,000 yen on the hunch, more than the family could make in a century of rice harvests. But two Holsteins were dead on arrival, driven mad by the hot, rough ocean journey. The third collapsed on the Tanaka family lawn as the town veterinarian struggled in vain to save it. Kakuji then switched from Dutch cows to Australian racehorses but misjudged their value and had to sell them at a loss. Another summer, a drought dried up Kakuji's expensive carp pond.

Despite his increasingly precarious financial state, Kakuji disdained manual labor. Kakuji instead preferred to drown his cares in sake and to cover his losses by trading and betting on horses. "My father used to drink from early in the day," Kakuei would recall years later. "In the spring, he would place straw mats all over the garden at our house and have a drinking party with his horse-trader colleagues. He didn't behave well when he got drunk." The boisterous Kakuji would also invite the police, who granted the horse licenses, and even the elementary school teacher, to join his bouts at the local tavern.

That was when Kakuji was home. Mostly he abandoned his family for months at a time, following his steeds to racetracks all over the country. Once, the family received an urgent telegram directly from the betting grounds; it was from Kakuji desperately seeking a bailout. To his only son fell the shameful task of begging neighbors for money to help cover the bum wagers.

If Kakuei's main birthright from his father was the capacity to dream and to scheme, his mother instilled in him the drive actually to fulfill those visions. She worked slavishly to salvage a modicum of respectability for the Tanakas. A familiar image in the community was the slight Fume (pronounced "FOO-meh") alone in the Tanaka rice paddies, stooping to pull out the stalks, or trudging more than a mile up a mountain road carrying other farmers' rice stalks on her back to earn extra cash. On the way, when she passed houses of families to whom her absent husband was in hock, she would pause, take off her shoes and socks, fold her hands together, and bow in apology.

Fume Tanaka was the prototype of the long-suffering, iron-willed Japanese wife. After marriage, she moved into her husband's household, and for years she felt like an outsider. Once, when Kakuei pinched money from his grandfather, she hysterically cried that she would tie both herself and him to the railroad tracks in penance. Her mother-in-law had been known as one of the town's three great beauties and was considered too fragile to help with the household chores.

Kakuei would always describe Fume with a mixture of affection and awe. She was laboring in the fields when he woke in the morning, sewing when he went to bed at night, still working whenever he got up in the middle of the night. Yet she never complained or asked others, even her children, for help. "Although my mother was gentle and quiet, she was the most fearsome person to me," Tanaka later recalled.

Life in 1920s rural Japan was, in many ways, primitive. Houses were built of weak, flammable wood and straw. Sanitation and medical facilities were poor or nonexistent. Japan's national mortality rate was the highest of any developed nation—from disease, heavy work, natural disasters. In some farming regions, one in five babies died in their first year. Kakuei had an older brother who died in infancy. Two of his sisters would pass away before reaching the age of twenty. Kakuei himself caught diphtheria when he was two and was nearly killed by the high fever. At four, he was buried by an avalanche of snow off the roof of his house; when his grandmother tried to dig him out, she struck his head with the spade, leaving him scarred for life.

Yet Kakuei portrays his youth as charmed. Pale and thin, the only boy, with two older and four younger sisters, he was spoiled rotten, never expected to do housework or tend to the fields. He was frequently allowed to ride horses and play tennis. He didn't fare as well with the neighborhood children, who often attacked him, even the girls. His stammer made him easy prey, and he was often forced to return taunts with his fists. His whole life, he boasted of how he had adored school and excelled in his studies. He overcame a stutter by starring in the school play. His elementary school teacher and principal would remain among his closest mentors and supporters throughout his life.

But his father's losing streak meant Kakuei couldn't afford to continue his education past the age of fourteen, and he was then pressed into a stint of hard labor. As depression darkened the countryside, the government tried to create jobs for struggling farmers; one such project involved working on the road in front of the Tanaka house. In the summer of 1933, Kakuei got a new pair of Japanese-style split-toe worker boots, and he pushed mud and stones in a handcart thirteen hours a day under the hot summer sun.

That experience distinguished Kakuei from most politicians of his generation, and throughout his career he invoked it in empathy with his working-class supporters. A well-worn part of his repertoire was the story of the veteran worker who told him in the midst of their toils that everybody looks down on manual laborers, "but we are the sculptors of the earth." "I certainly learned not to be afraid of labor," Kakuei would say, "thanks to this."

It wasn't, however, a particularly long experience. At the end of July, the supervisors doled out the pay, and the underaged Kakuei was shocked to find he had been given the women's rate, two thirds what grown men got. He quit in a huff, declaring, "I've studied enough about manual labor."

In later years, when asked what she had envisioned for her son, Fume Tanaka said she had hoped he could someday become a ticket puncher on the regional Echigo train line. For someone who spent her life in the insecurity of Futada's muddy rice paddies, watching the regular train go by, that must have seemed like a steady, respectable job. But Kakuei himself had much bigger plans. After quitting the road project, he managed to get himself a job in the county seat as a government official overseeing public works—including the project he had quit. Shortly before his sixteenth birthday, he struck out on his own, to seek his fortune in Tokyo.

His mother gave him a small sum of money and a long list of advice: don't drink too much, don't own horses, don't boast, don't rest until you've worked, don't ever forget what you borrowed even if you forget what you lent. And "if you are driven to do wrong in order to live there," she urged, "come back home." As for the money, she told him to tuck some in his waistband because "if you die in an accident and you have no cash, people will laugh at you."

A crowd of forty villagers, led by the mayor, gathered at the station that March morning to see their native son off. En route he stopped overnight in the town of Takasaki, where his father was playing the horses. His father took most of the money that Fume had given her son.

Tanaka's journey was part of a widespread exodus to the big cities, spurred by the economic and demographic calamities that rocked Japan's countryside in the late 1920s and early 1930s. The global depression slashed the value of silk, the main cash crop of Japan's farmers. In 1930, a national bumper harvest drove down rice prices, while a crop failure the next year brought widespread starvation. The year Tanaka set out, 1934, rural cash incomes were less than half the level of a decade earlier.

Tokyo was the place to go, along with the other bustling urban centers such as Osaka and Fukuoka to the west. Fueled by Japan's military buildup and the nation's growing heavy industries such as metals and machinery, the cities were expanding rapidly and starving for labor. Tokyo's population was more than doubling, and nearly half of that growth was the result of in-migration from rural areas. For these children of the farms, their new world was starkly different from anything they had ever seen. The drab, quiet rural culture had barely been touched by Japan's modernization drive, launched in the late nineteenth century. The cities, meanwhile, were rapidly westernizing, with blazing neon lights; noisy, crowded roads; glittering department stores; and dance halls filled with flapperlike *"mo-ga"* (modern girls) and their *"mo-bo"* (modern boy) dates. The sophisticated city slickers disdained their new country-bumpkin neighbors. "They constantly shift their little brown eyes in a sinister manner," a city doctor wrote of Japan's peasants, "with a dumb smirk on their lips."

From the moment he set foot in Tokyo, the naïve Tanaka stumbled into that culture chasm. After arriving at the train station, he tried to go to the office of a friend's relative, who had agreed to take care of him for a while. He hopped into a cab, and the driver, perhaps sensing a good target, took an hour to make what should have been a fifteen-minute ride. The cabbie then demanded 5 yen, the total amount in Tanaka's purse, and when the country boy resisted, the driver threatened to take him to the police box conveniently located across the street.

So it went. People laughed at his mountain accent, and he couldn't follow the fast-speaking bus conductors. One night, short of cash, he sought some easy money at a board game he passed on the street, a sort of three-card monte of the day. Tanaka was suckered in by winning the first round; then he lost several in a row. He told the hustlers he couldn't pay, and they dragged him into a back alley and took the watch his sister had given him as a farewell gift.

When Tanaka showed up at the house of a prominent businessman—a man he had been told back home would give him an apprenticeship—an elegant woman greeted him by saying, "My master will not see anybody at his house," and slid the door shut. He could barely understand her refined speech. "Tokyo," the dejected Tanaka muttered to himself as he stumbled away, "is a tough town."

Despite the setbacks, he chose to stay, receiving temporary lodging from the hometown friend's relative. Life didn't get any easier. He could find jobs but had a hard time keeping them. He quit his first employer, a small construction company, after an argument with a supervisor. In a fury, Tanaka marched across a row of costly roofing tiles, smashing them as he went. "Immediately, I jumped onto a bicycle and ran," he wrote of the incident. "Naturally, now that things had turned out this way, I was ready to leave the company." He then worked briefly at an insurance industry newspaper, followed by a stint delivering imported glass to department stores and an abbreviated assignment at a small architectural company tucked away on the second floor of a house.

Tanaka was not discouraged by his unsteady employment. Work was not his goal but a means to an end. His main ambition was to get a higher education in Tokyo, and his jobs were merely a way of paying the tuition. He started his studies shortly after arriving in the city, and as he changed employers one after the other, he kept up his night school studies in architectural drafting and engineering. He threw himself into building this new life with the same drive his mother applied to supporting her family. After putting in a twelve-hour workday, he would rush to class on his bicycle, once getting hit by a train on the way. To stay awake during the three-hour lectures, he would jab his hands with a knife or a pencil.

At the age of nineteen, three years after arriving in Tokyo, Tanaka had learned enough to set up his own architectural firm. It was a one-man operation that handled everything from measuring and drawing plans and specifications to applying for construction permits, selecting a contractor, and supervising the final building work. "If a job was supposed to take three months, he would make his men do it in one and a half," a Tanaka biographer wrote. "If work was going slowly, he'd pick up a saw and pitch in. When he ran out of lumber . . . he'd buy old houses and dismantle them."

Tanaka's plans and dreams, like those of all Japanese citizens in the late 1930s, were ultimately fused into the nation's lunge toward war. The decade began with a series of frightening acts of violence: attempted coups against the Japanese government, political assassinations in Tokyo, an army run amok in Manchuria. By 1939, those events were leading to total mobilization for a fatal showdown with the West. No business transaction, no personal relationship, no simple daily routine would remain untouched. Every industry and neighborhood was forced to join local citizen associations charged with enforcing discipline in their ranks in support of the war effort. Under the banner of "National Spiritual Mobilization," supplies and food were rationed.

Millions of young men were drafted. Tanaka's turn came in March 1939, and he was shipped to Manchuria to join the cavalry. He worked as a clerk in personnel and in the post office, never seeing combat. The most immediate threat to Tanaka seems to have come from superiors easily irked by the cocky recruit.

Trouble began the evening he arrived in the mud-covered barracks, when the new troops were ordered to empty their wallets. Tanaka was carrying a small photo of the American actress Deanna Durbin."Who is this?" the sergeant demanded. "She's my kind of woman," Tanaka answered. "I'm hoping to have such a woman for my wife." The reply drew a hard blow from one of the nationalistic officers.

The next day, he was smacked on both cheeks for wearing the wrong shoes and failing to salute a superior. Tanaka had taken to wearing a mustache, a sign of the success and prominence he had achieved back in Japan. As a lowly grunt in Manchuria, he was slapped because "I wasn't substantial enough to grow a mustache" and was ordered to shave it off. At night, the older soldiers took turns giving Tanaka "a lesson" in the barracks with their fists. "What am I doing wrong?" he would cry out. "You've got a bad attitude," he was told as they hit him some more.

It was a tense time in a dangerous place. Japan's brutal advances in Manchuria in the early 1930s triggered the chain of events that led to Tokyo's withdrawal from the League of Nations in 1933 and, eventually, to the fraying of its ties with the United States. Manchuria was central to Japan's imperialist designs; the Japanese government was urging its citizens to move there as colonists, to expand the empire, to secure raw materials, and to reduce poverty and overpopulation at home.

Throughout their occupation of Manchuria, Japanese troops were threatened by local bandits, warlords, and revolutionaries. In July 1938, just before Tanaka arrived, Japanese and Russian troops clashed over the border. Shortly after Tanaka reported for duty, tensions with the Soviets flared up into a full-scale battle. The Japanese were routed in the four-month conflict, with more than 17,000 troops dead or missing. Japanese soldiers who survived these ordeals were soon dispatched to bloody battle throughout China and battlefields farther south. For those who stayed behind in Manchuria, worse was to come. Near the end of the Pacific war, they were attacked by American bombers, and shortly before hostilities ceased, Soviet troops invaded.

So it was almost certainly Tanaka's good fortune that, about a year after arriving in Manchuria, he contracted a near-fatal combination of pneumonia and pleurisy. He was shipped back to Japan, where he struggled for life in a military hospital. The army was preparing to send out the routine death telegram to his parents, and the doctor took the inventory of his possessions that was usually performed on corpses. But Tanaka beat the odds and pulled through, and on October 5, 1941, he was discharged. Just two months later, the emperor's forces would launch their surprise attack on Pearl Harbor, converting their Asian battleground into a full-blown and disastrous war with America. It was, Tanaka learned, a conflict better served as an entrepreneur than a soldier.

Immediately after Tanaka's discharge from the military, he eagerly resumed the task of building his fortune as a wartime construction tycoon. His new company had already started to flourish as a regular subcontractor to one of the pillars of the Japanese military-industrial complex, the Riken Industrial Group, which was, among other things, the center of Japan's own unsuccessful attempt to create an atomic bomb. Riken was founded by Masatoshi Okochi, the businessman Tanaka had come to Tokyo to work for in 1934 but whose maid had turned the country boy away. Ultimately, Okochi had taken a liking to the brash teenager and become his mentor and patron, giving Tanaka's fledgling enterprise more work than it could handle. "I was involved in the business and construction plans of all the factories," Tanaka wrote thirty years later. "I still remember even the layout of the main machinery in the factories."

Another key move was his marriage. Hana Sakamoto was the daughter of Tanaka's new landlady. She was a homely woman seven years his senior, married once before and with a small daughter. Though Tanaka wrote suggestively about many women from his youth, Hana wasn't one of them. She "kindly looked after me while I was busy," he said, and he described her only as "small and quiet."

Less than six months after meeting, Tanaka and Hana Sakamoto married in March 1942. Tokyo's mood being dampened by the war's severity, they skipped a formal ceremony. On their wedding night, Hana asked for just three simple promises: that he never throw her out, that he never kick her, and that, if he ever got the chance to visit the Imperial Palace, he take her along. If he fulfilled those promises, she said, she'd "endure anything." She apparently didn't ask for fidelity, and over the years he was open about not giving it.

But what Hana may have lacked in sizzle, she made up for in other ways. "When I got married, I was 24 and my wife 31," Tanaka later explained. "As I worked hard day and night and Sundays and holidays, I needed a woman like her, not a younger one, for my wife." More significantly, her father—who had died a few months earlier—had run a construction firm with important government connections. Though the family company, Sakamoto-gumi, was virtually defunct when Tanaka took it over, it was apparently crucial to his plans. Under the strict wartime rationing rules, the government was shutting down construction firms that hadn't netted a certain level of revenues in the previous three years. Tanaka had been in Manchuria during that time, but with the Sakamoto venture, he automatically exceeded the minimum revenue required to stay in business. As a bonus, he inherited a prominent client list.

Tanaka also bought a lumber company and built himself a new headquarters. As the imperial forces poured more and more resources into their increasingly futile and fatal attempt to protect the empire, Tanaka Doken, or Tanaka Construction, was there to draft and build. While Japan's forces were beating a slow, painful retreat across the Pacific, Tanaka Construction was quickly becoming the fiftieth largest construction company in Japan.

In early 1945, the Allied air force intensified their firebombing raids on Tokyo and other industrial centers, attempting to smash Japan's war machine. Most of Tokyo burned down, including two thirds of Riken's buildings. With more than 80 percent of the military's crucial factories located on the Japanese mainland—now an easy target for enemy bombers—frantic planners hatched a risky scheme to move factories to the colonies.

Few companies volunteered for the work, which offered huge potential rewards yet held even larger risks. The shortage of ships, in fact, blocked most industries from ever carrying out the relocation plans. Tanaka asked to handle Riken's transfer of a massive piston ring factory from central Tokyo to Taejon in southern Korea. With some liquor, he was able to persuade the captain of a military ship to take his equipment across the Japan Sea. Tanaka did start the project, even venturing close to the hazardous Soviet border to buy timber, but he hadn't gotten very far when Japan surrendered. This was the project that was discontinued so abruptly, netting Tanaka that 15-million-yen windfall. It had proved a risk worth taking.

THE TOKYO Tanaka returned to was in ruins. Whole neighborhoods had been reduced to rubble and ash by the American air raids and the resultant fires, which raged through row upon row of the wood-and-paper houses. Three million Japanese had died, 10 million were unemployed, and 15 million were homeless. Food shortages had created a thriving black market and threatened mass starvation. "It was the time when a man would kill his brother in a quarrel over a piece of potato; and a son would batter his father to death for a small rice ball," according to a lengthy retrospective by a leading Japanese newspaper, conveying the panic of the time.

The despair was deepened by anxiety about what would come next. Japan had just lost a vicious war that it had provoked, and now it was being occupied by a half-million American soldiers. Revenge—looting, rape, mass executions by firing squad—was widely feared and expected. In the weeks leading up to Japan's defeat, U.S. troops had fought a ruthless battle on the island of Okinawa. There, Japanese soldiers had told women that those captured by the Americans would be killed, flattened under bulldozers, raped, "and reraped." As the mainland Japanese knew, many Okinawans had chosen suicide over surrender.

But when General Douglas MacArthur arrived at Atsugi Air Base near Yokohama on August 30, 1945, he promised a dictatorship that would be benign—one that would not exact reprisals but would swiftly remake Japan into a peaceful, stable society. The general vowed to "sever for all time the shackles of feudalism and in its place raise the dignity of man under protection of the people's sovereignty." He was giving Japan democracy.

Japan had in fact had a democracy of sorts before the war, but it had been limited in many ways. The first parliamentary elections had been held in 1890, but suffrage had been restricted at first to only the wealthiest few. The elected House of Representatives had been given only limited power, mainly over the government budget. It had had no legal control over other major government institutions, such as the appointed House of Peers, the bureaucracy, the imperial household, and, most important, the military. In the late 1910s and 1920s, Japan had seemed to experience a flowering of democracy. In 1918, the year Tanaka was born, the country had had its first party-led cabinet with its first elected prime minister. In the 1920s, universal male suffrage had been introduced. But even then, many government leaders had been wary of democracy, worried that it would undermine national unity by giving voice to dissent. They had also felt that discussion of popular sovereignty would threaten the sovereignty of the emperor. In 1932, the slaying of the prime minister by young military officers and fanatical supporters had marked the end of party-led cabinets. While Parliament had stayed open and elections had been held throughout the war, Japan had been run by a series of "national unity" governments subject to army and navy decree. Civil rights had been suppressed.

Attempting to correct the "flaws" of Japan's prewar political system, MacArthur's staff wrote a new constitution for Japan that strengthened the power of the elected legislature, making it the supreme government organ. He also gave women the vote, incorporated a "Bill of Rights," and included a near-utopian guarantee of the economic right to make a decent living. The document also had an unprecedented "peace clause" by which Japan forswore the right to wage war or even maintain an army. Teams of American "democracy instructors" fanned out across the country to instruct Japanese citizens on how to use their new rights.

The objective of most Occupation reforms, according to one

press release from MacArthur's office, was to "blast from their entrenched positions all those who planned, started, and directed the war, and those who enslaved and beat the Japanese people into submission." To further these goals, the Americans launched a series of radical economic reforms, forcing landlords to turn property over to tenant farmers and giving workers the right to organize and strike. The Occupation also "purged" more than 200,000 government, military, and business leaders, barring them from public office and the executive suite. The sweeping action drew sharp criticism, even from the Occupation staff. Such a purge, Brigadier General Courtney Whitney warned, would leave Japan with a government "of interpreters and mistresses."

Indeed, the Occupation's actions unleashed a torrent of democratic excitement. A multitude of parties, from the Socialists to the Liberals to the Great Japan Charcoal Production Party, contested the first postwar election for the national Parliament (known as the Diet), which took place in April 1946. People who could never have contemplated a political career before—such as Tanaka—joined the fray. Nine of every ten candidates had never held any political office. "Anyone could be a candidate," Tanaka recalled. "This election was a dogfight symbolizing the disorder of Japanese politics right after the war."

TANAKA'S OWN political career started in November 1945 in a dingy restaurant in a bombed-out Tokyo district just ten weeks after the war's end. He had been summoned by Tadao Oasa, a wily veteran fixer in the wartime legislature. The meeting took place in a *ryotei*, a type of pricey traditional Japanese restaurant that had once been, and would again become, the symbol of exclusive power in Japan: a well-appointed, discreet sanctum where important political deals were cut. At the time, even the *ryotei* were in ruins. "There was no sign of life; it looked empty," Tanaka wrote. "Oasa-san was in a bleak Western-style room that had no furniture, not even a carpet. He was sitting on the only chair at the far end of the room."

Tanaka's ticket to the new world of power was his wealth. Oasa was trying to put together a party to contest the upcoming elections, but it was hard to come by funding, especially from the devastated industrial combines that had underwritten politics before the war. The Progressive Party was so strapped, in fact, that it was choosing its leader not by a vote of party members but by a straight fund-raising contest: whichever candidate could raise 3 million yen, a staggering sum at the time, would win.

"Do you mind contributing some money?" Oasa asked. Tanaka, flush from his wartime profits, "pleasantly agreed." Soon after Oasa's man won the party leadership, the adviser summoned Tanaka once again, this time to ask Tanaka himself to run as a Progressive Party candidate in the upcoming parliamentary elections in the Niigata district representing his hometown. Tanaka once again consented.

Tanaka had long claimed electoral ambitions, yet he was not a natural politician. He showed up for one of the first candidates' forums looking every bit the thriving business magnate—"I had a haircut, changed my underwear, and wore a morning coat"—while the other candidates appeared before the rough-hewn country crowd in muddy boots and workers' garb. They laced their speeches liberally with cries of "We farmers and laborers." When Tanaka's prattle about "policy platforms which would revive our fatherland with the spirit of democracy" was interrupted by catcalls, the nervous stutter of his childhood returned.

He knew next to nothing about issues. "I had not even read the constitution," he said with a laugh years later. Nor did he know the basics about the electoral system. Tanaka's pedigree didn't help; the hometown Futada crowd laughed him off as a mama's boy, the son of a deadbeat. He'd lay down straw mats to seat several hundred people, but manage to draw only a dozen.

Tanaka had been assured by Oasa that his election was a sure thing. "Just spend 150,000 yen and let me handle it," the well-connected adviser had told him. "Just get on the *o-mikoshi* for a month and you'll surely win," Oasa promised, referring to the portable shrines paraded around during festivals. Instead, like the teenager who had lost his watch to Tokyo street gamblers a decade earlier, Tanaka the political novice got hustled. Some of his supporters took campaign monies to frolic with geisha. Three political veterans who had promised to manage crucial parts of the Niigata district for him decided to run as candidates themselves—apparently using his funds as seed money. With neither popular appeal nor organization, Tanaka got hammered, finishing eleventh out of thirty-seven candidates.

That first election, though, was just a beginning. Rather than creating a new democratic order right away, the American meddling unleashed a long period of chaos, with political alliances forming and dissolving rapidly in a vain attempt to find a new political center. It took forty days of arguing and bargaining before a government emerged after the 1946 election. That one lasted less than a year, and new elections were called for April 1947.

This time, Tanaka was ready. He set up branch offices of Tanaka Construction in the two biggest cities in the district and hired a hundred "company employees" to "handle my campaign directly." He made over his image, going out during the day in traditional workingman's gear and carrying a simple bag lunch of rice balls. He was now portrayed in the local press as a man "with young energy and vigor" who "sometimes campaigns in nine places in one day."

That second election, too, saw a great turnover. Half the winners had never held office before. Tanaka was now among them. On election day, he collapsed from exhaustion. "I was sleeping all day in my home. . . . Suddenly the paper screen door slid open and my elder sister poked her face in," he wrote. " 'Hey, you've won! You've become a member of Parliament!' She was almost shouting, but my ears were uncertain whether it was a dream or reality. Then I fell asleep again and kept sleeping for several hours."

In his first two campaigns, Tanaka did not seem to have much in the way of a coherent political philosophy or platform. He had cast his lot with the Progressive Party, which, to judge by its candidate rolls, was in fact the most reactionary in the elections. It was largely made up of politicians who had supported the war—"a gathering place for the tainted," one Japanese political historian called it—and was hit hardest by the American purges; of the original 274 candidates slated to run in the election, only 14 were cleared. His slogan was "Shout of the Young Blood," but it wasn't clear what exactly he was shouting for. Another Tanaka motto was "A True Brave Man of Sincerity."

Tanaka did make one prominent pledge to the long-suffering voters of the snow country: "Hey, everybody, let's cut down the mountains at the border, then the winter winds from the Japan Sea will blow straight through to the Pacific and we'll no longer have snow! We won't have to suffer anymore!" He vowed to take the excess soil and "fill in the sea" so people could walk to a nearby island.

At the time, the pledge drew attention more for its apparent eccentricity than for its substance. But the promise, in essence, became Tanaka's chief doctrine for the rest of his career and a philosophy that would guide Japan's conservative mainstream for nearly forty years: the use of massive government funds to move mountains, bend rivers, pave rice paddies. Years later, it would be roundly derided as crass, corrupt pork-barreling, a debasement of the 1945 democracy, with all its high hopes, to a soulless shell in which political discourse was merely an accounting of highways, dams, tunnels, and bridges. In its time, however, it was a resonant, revolutionary manifesto.

CHAPTER TWO

SNOW COUNTRY

THE CRUCIBLE for what came to be known as "Tanaka-style politics" was Niigata Prefecture, his birthplace and electoral district. Echigo, as the region was known in feudal times, is a jinxed stretch of land on Japan's west coast, encircled by soaring mountain ranges on three sides and the Japan Sea on the fourth. Across the sea lies Siberia. Each year, harsh Russian winds push through clouds, which release their heavy load of snow when they reach the wall of mountains. The first flakes fall in October; the last don't melt away until June. In between, the drifts can reach fifteen feet.

For centuries, snow—its presence and the annual struggle to endure it—has defined the life, the architecture, the dress, the culture, the very mentality of the people of Niigata. Even the tight accent of the region is supposedly shaped by the cruel climate, as generations learned to speak without opening their mouths.

After a negligible spring, a short summer, and an early-autumn rice harvest, the townsfolk begin the onerous task of bracing for the blizzards—boarding up houses, wrapping living trees and shrubs in protective cover, storing enough food to last through the months of seclusion. When Tanaka was a child and his home village was distant from any commercial center, many locals had to reach the train station early each morning to conduct their day's business. To ensure passage for the whole community, each house was responsible for clearing a path through the snow to the next house, all the way to the station. "People used to get to the station by five A.M., so each morning we had to shovel a hundred-meter path to our next-door neighbor," Tanaka once reminisced. "My mother used to wake up at three A.M. and dig."

Like an ice curtain cutting off the rest of the world, the storms doomed the region to an eerie annual isolation. Even during the balmiest days of summer, the mountainous terrain made many Niigata villages difficult to leave or to visit; the winter snows closed them off completely. Some towns were called "remote islands on land." The isolation was especially treacherous for anyone unlucky enough to fall ill a mountain away from the nearest doctor. "Getting sick in the winter meant facing death," the local paper quoted a town elder as saying. "Pregnant women died; old people died without adequate treatment. What was hard was that we couldn't do anything for the innocent cildren who died when their colds developed into pneumonia." The psychological toll, too, was great. "Blizzards rage day after day and we are unable to clear away the snow that blocks our windows and plunges homes into blackness," local author Bokushi Suzuki wrote in *Tales of the Snow Country,* an early-nineteenth-century book that brought the region's plight to national attention. "People's spirits sink dangerously." "Until cherry blossom season, we had to spend all our time at home," Tanaka said more than one hundred years later. "There was no other way than to wait patiently for spring."

The gods, of course, were largely to blame for Niigata's plight. But the injuries of fate were aggravated by the insulting attitude of the humans inhabiting the rest of the Japanese isles. In ancient times, "To mention Echigo or Sado, the large, not-far-distant island, was to bring a shudder," writes Anne Walthall, a historian of Japan. "These were places of exile for men who had committed heinous crimes against the state. Isolated and feared, Echigo was terra incognita, a place of strange customs and stranger creatures."

In modern times, Echigo, which had become Niigata, was alternately exploited and ignored. As Japan began to industrialize in the late nineteenth century, Niigata and its neighboring districts along the Japan Sea coast came to be known as *"ura Nippon."* The phrase means "hidden Japan" or the "backside of Japan." That was not just a geographic description but a clear expression of inferiority to *"omote*

Nippon," or "the face of Japan," the much richer Pacific coast region dominated by Tokyo. The engines of Japan's famously accelerated economic development—the factories, the shipyards, the banks—were concentrated largely in the central Pacific regions. The Japan Sea coast was, in the first half of the twentieth century, relegated mostly to farming. Even after the stunning growth of the 1960s "Japanese miracle," three fourths of Japan's industrial production remained in *omote Nippon,* while *ura Nippon* lagged behind.

The national government encouraged this imbalance by earmarking public monies mainly for Pacific coast regions. "We people who live in the unblessed snow country are always neglected by the central government," a politician from a prefecture bordering Niigata complained in a formal petition to the cabinet in 1930. "If the government feels that it is unnecessary to consider the interests of the snow country Japanese simply because it still regards them as ignorant and phlegmatic, then the future of Japan is at risk. . . . The snow country people . . . are also Japanese citizens." Niigata's leaders argued that, given government funding for roads, railroads, tunnels, and dams, the prefecture would become less remote from the rest of the country and factories might even locate there. But their pleas for assistance were usually rejected during the first half of the century, since Tokyo considered the requested work too expensive and inefficient. Even communities hit by heavy blizzards were denied emergency aid to remove the snow, the Tokyo bureaucrats arguing that the drifts would simply melt in the spring anyway. Some desperate villages launched pitiable attempts to spur development on their own. The men of Ojiya, for example, starting in 1938, took four years to scratch a tunnel through the middle of Mount Amagoi in order to connect their community with neighboring towns. One worker died in a landslide in the process. Even after it was finished, the tunnel had no light and was small—only two people walking abreast could pass at a time.

Niigata did have an important role to play in Japan's development drive. Like an internal colony, it was plundered for raw materials—the big industrial combines colluded to hold down prices on sugar, sake, silk, charcoal, and other rural commodities—and manpower. It was partly because Niigata's economy was so dependent on the depressed agricultural sector that the prefecture's hundreds of thousands of residents sought work elsewhere in the 1920s and 1930s. Many joined an annual migration known as *dekasegi,* leaving during the snowy half of the year, when work and food were particularly scarce at home. An important task for many town offices was finding their citizens migrant work elsewhere; those workers then sent part of their incomes home to help support their families.

Tanaka's personal experience as a migrant—studying and choosing his own work—was fortunate compared with that of many of his compatriots. Most Niigata men became domestic coolies, taking on the backbreaking, low-paying jobs around the country that other Japanese shunned: pulling rickshas, brewing sake, building roads, assembling weapons, and, later, making the inexpensive goods that Japanese companies would export to the world. "Who has supported Japan's rapid growth from behind the scenes?" lamented Kiyoshi Okabe, a farmer-poet from the "remote island" of Sumon. "The largest number of migrant workers have been used in the big cities of *omote Nippon*. We built the subways and buildings, bullet trains and highways, but we have never received the benefits."

The young girls of Niigata were famous nationwide for their diligence in factory work, especially spinning and weaving, and company representatives came each year to recruit, asking fathers to sign away their daughters for a season or even years at a time. Working conditions for these migrant laborers from *ura Nippon* were notoriously bad, akin to those in Britain's Dickensian textile mills. Some girls never made it to the factories, their recruiters instead forcing them into brothels. "It is reasonable to say that Niigata's special products," noted a petition filed by protestors in the 1920s to the local government, "are licensed prostitutes, male bathhouse attendants, and factory girls."

Back home in Niigata, this mass desertion was ripping the social fabric apart. The annual labor migration meant that broken families, the fathers gone six months out of each year, were an accepted way of life. Children away at school would board at their dormitories until the snow receded enough for them to come home. The incidence of child abuse and suicide was high. The steady emigration was demoralizing. In many towns, only the very old and very young remained.

Niigata's economic and social problems were exacerbated by the oppressive tenant farming system that plagued most of rural Japan. The agricultural depression in the 1920s and 1930s worsened the plight of farmers nationwide as landlords sought to boost their falling revenues by hiking usurious rents ever higher. Across the country, farmers rose up in protest, and Niigata was in the forefront. In one of the most prominent insurrections, an eight-year campaign of rallies, riots, and rent strikes was waged in Kizaki Village, near the city of Niigata. The movement turned violent in 1930, with farmers attacking landlords' homes. Children joined the demonstrations, boycotting public schools and forming their own "proletarian school."

Both before and after the war, Niigata's adverse conditions made its politics ripe for radical agitators. In the 1930s, its most popular politician was Shoichi Miyake, a firebrand organizer and member of Parliament for the Japan Labor-Farmer Party. He had been the leader of the tenant revolts and had been jailed half a dozen times for his various protests. When he was free, policemen would monitor his rallies. Miyake's humility and penury were legendary. He traveled the region on his rusting bicycle organizing farmers and campaigning for office, sporting his trademark hunting cap. He was so poor that creditors seized his futon. Farmers, lacking money to give to his parliamentary campaigns, donated handfuls of rice, radishes, and pickled vegetables.

Miyake's crusading was stunted by the war, but after Japan's surrender, he quickly resumed his work on behalf of Niigata's destitute. He was aided by the American Occupation, which made land reform a centerpiece of the program to remake Japan; Miyake helped weak, uneducated tenant farmers handle the procedures for claiming the property the Americans had ordered landlords to relinquish. By then, Miyake had joined Japan's ascendant Socialist Party, and he framed his activism within a broader ideological context. He argued that capitalism was a corrupt, exploitative system. His party endorsed "class struggle," and he told snow-country voters that the answer to their difficulties was a "socialistic agricultural policy."

But in the postwar period, a new rival arose who had better offers to Niigata's poor than the Socialist abstractions: Kakuei Tanaka. Under Japan's unusual multiseat district system, both men could win seats in the national Parliament from the Niigata Third District. Unlike American congressional elections, in which each district sends only one representative to Washington, each of Japan's parliamentary districts elected an entire delegation to Tokyo, the size of the delegation varying by district. In the Niigata Third District, for example, the top five vote getters in an election won. Throughout the 1950s, 1960s, and 1970s, both Miyake and Tanaka captured legislative seats. But Tanaka became the more popular, and it was his platform, a radicalism of the Right, that prevailed.

Though he was a successful businessman and a candidate endorsed by a national conservative party, Tanaka had much in common with Miyake. A school dropout with a disreputable father, Tanaka was considered a coarse outsider by the local conservative elite dominating Niigata's cities. In the 1952 election, the most prominent business and government figures in Tochio City, for example, were openly supporting a well-connected anti-Tanaka conservative. Fearing harassment, Tanaka's backers were afraid to walk Tochio's main streets. And after Tanaka's local speeches, no Tochio restaurant or inn would serve him or his supporters.

So, like the Socialists, Tanaka sought backing at first among the poorest farmers in the countryside. He started hunting for votes in the outposts, places that had never seen a politician before. Tanaka used them as bases, slowly working his way into the cities. One Japanese journalist compared the strategy to Mao Zedong's early guerrilla tactics of winning over the Chinese peasants. "Young Tanaka was a politician who would walk, climb, and crawl" to remote villages "with no traffic access," recalled Koichi Honma, Tanaka's local organizer for forty years.

A newspaper account of the January 1949 election campaign describes how four candidates traveled from one debate to another during a blizzard. Three gave up the journey while "only one courageous one trudged along the railroad tracks across a bridge," the article reported about Tanaka. "A train came from the opposite side, and he hung from the bridge to save himself. He arrived in time for the meeting."

Tanaka's pitch, like that of the Socialists, evolved into one of class warfare. But instead of pitting the masses against the capitalists, he stoked the smoldering resentment of *ura Nippon* against *omote Nippon*. "Our younger brothers and sisters go to Tokyo, then come back and take away our rice and vegetables," he often preached. "The eldest son and his wife stay back and protect the household, doing manual labor. But ultimately," he'd say, "the anger explodes!"

That difference in rhetoric spawned a divergence in strategy. The Japanese Left retained the politics of protest, but the farmers wanted something more practical. Kinjiro Hiraishi of Koshiji Village, for example, had worshiped the Socialists for their help in winning tenants land. But at a 1954 party meeting, he wanted to know: "Will the party's total platform ever be realized?" "There are two kinds of policies: one for today and one for the future," a senior Socialist politician lectured. "The Socialist platform is the latter—policies to be implemented in ten or twenty years, not now." Hiraishi had actually been hoping to get immediate funds to repair a crumbling bridge. "Mr. Hiraishi," the MP chided, "you need to study more."

Tanaka, by contrast, championed the politics of petition—for new infrastructure, to be funded by the Pacific coast oppressors, as a sort of restitution for a century of exploitation. "Niigata has a large population and plenty of food, so why do we need to do migrant labor?" Tanaka thundered in an early campaign speech. "It is because we lack roads and bridges that Niigata is underdeveloped."

In 1953, he formed the Etsuzankai, the "Association for Crossing the Mountains"—a poignant expression of the region's yearning to overcome its surroundings. The group drew young idealists with the rallying cry of "Developing Niigata, Our Home." In effect, the Etsuzankai's platform was to realize the crazy scheme Tanaka had advocated in his first stumpings: to tear down the imprisoning mountain ranges—at least figuratively—by ripping holes through them with tunnels and paving them with roads. For centuries, the people of Niigata had simply accepted the natural world they had been given. The Etsuzankai's philosophy was that, with enough bulldozers and concrete, they could bend nature to their will.

To Tanaka, the contractor turned politician, Niigata was not a wasteland but an untapped opportunity—one big, empty building site. As if he were the chief architect of his district, MP Tanaka would scour the area for projects to propose. He traveled Niigata, seeking out places such as Koshiji that wanted public works funds but couldn't get help elsewhere. In 1949, in Horinouchi Town, Tanaka took over a "political salon" that had been lobbying unsuccessfully since before the war to get a national railroad station. He met with the citizens of Nigoro Village, whose only route to the nearest big city was a long, winding footpath over a mountain range. Tanaka personally surveyed the area many times with Nigoro's mayor, wearing worker's boots for the long climb up the craggy path. They would sit in the wilderness and build a fire to cook the fish they'd brought along while Tanaka gazed down into the valley and chose the best spot for a paved road.

He sometimes personally drew up his own detailed blueprints. "Tanaka is so great," a supporter marveled during one of his local swings. "He remembers all the details of the roads and bridges that even we, the residents, don't know."

In Tokyo, Tanaka tirelessly begged and badgered national political and bureaucratic leaders to back the plans, while better-known Niigata politicians simply made requests and meekly accepted the regular refusals. When landowners in Shimoda Village had a problem with land prices, they first went to their longtime MP, Shiro Watari. "He is a very gentle man," the petitioner fretted about Watari after the complaints went nowhere. "Although he has approached the Agriculture Ministry, he has talked to only the midlevel staff." The petitioner concluded, "A proverb says 'A drowning man will grasp at straws.' " In this case, the straw was Tanaka, the pol so derided by the traditional conservative voters. After Tanaka was approached by the voters, he went straight to the number two man in the bureaucracy. "My wife is in trouble because the boss of my ardent young supporters . . . insists on staying at my house to discuss this problem," Tanaka told the official. Soon after, a black limousine from the Agriculture Ministry showed up in the distant paddies, carrying an official to investigate the matter.

When another group of local officials wanted Tanaka's help in getting a slice of a river development project, he rallied the group to threaten to bolt the national conservative party if their request was ignored. He led a procession of constituents into the hallowed halls of the Construction Ministry and proclaimed loudly to the relevant official, "Hey, chief, this is my election campaign, please build the new riverbank!" During one intense debate about a road-funding bill, Tanaka had a desk set up for himself inside the Finance Ministry. When, predictably, bureaucrats listened impassively and declared that a project Tanaka wanted wasn't in the plan, the politician retorted, "It's politics that makes possible the impossible." With enough persistence, he often prevailed.

Tanaka quickly developed a reputation as *the* Niigata politician for public works. Another conservative MP, unable to get funds for a tunnel, retired and turned his support group over to Tanaka in its entirety; soon afterward, the tunnel won approval. In 1958, Kashiwazaki City's chamber of commerce backed Tanaka in an explicit attempt to help develop the city. The leaders of Irihirose Village canvassed their community to get votes for Tanaka, believing that a high support rate would bring them projects. "This village gave me seventy percent votes. I can never neglect it," Tanaka would say, and he showed his appreciation by making National Route 252 bend through the town.

Other right-wing politicians shunned pleas from supporters of the Socialists, their ideological enemies. Tanaka, the pragmatist, told a Socialist seeking help with an irrigation project, "I don't mind if you are a Socialist or whatever—if you are petitioning on behalf of

Mitsuke City's forty thousand people, I will help you as much as I can." Even Miyake, Tanaka's Socialist rival, started sending backers to ask Tanaka for lobbying help, urging that Tanaka could probably be more successful on their behalf than he himself could.

In the 1950s and early 1960s, national money showered down on long-ignored Niigata like the annual snowstorms. Train lines were extended and tracks upgraded for faster service; funds came through for the first major highway ever to bore through the Mikuni Mountains, linking Niigata to Tokyo; vast tracts of land were reclaimed for farming. Life improved steadily. The construction brought high-paying jobs to the region and, by creating a decent infrastructure, eventually made the area more practical for factories. The annual migration from *ura Nippon* to *omote Nippon* decreased. Within a decade, Niigata's sense of remoteness dissipated, and the country seemed to join the rest of Japan. The overnight trip to Tokyo could now be done in a day. The big-city visits that had required four-hour walks along perilous ridges could now be done safely by car in a mere half hour.

It is impossible to say precisely how much of this was really Tanaka's doing. During that period, the Japanese government, aided by the World Bank and other foreign lenders, spent billions of dollars to rebuild the nation after the war's devastation. Japan's economic growth spurt, which began in the 1950s, made even more government funds available. But Tanaka clearly affected the shape of many projects. For example, the national bureaucrats wanted to build Highway 17 in a straight line from Tokyo to Nagaoka, a large city in Tanaka's district. Tanaka persuaded them to weave it through several small towns in the prefecture—even getting funds for two bridges to take the road back and forth over a river just to favor more communities.

And, deserved or not, he got credit for luring many of those projects to the region in the first place. With each new public works announcement for the district, Tanaka's popularity soared. His political backers came from all corners. The previously apolitical shopkeepers of Ojiya joined the Etsuzankai after a widened road boosted their business. The leftist Japan Farmers' Union branch in Koshiji—the village where the Socialists had snubbed the bridge request as too nearsighted—simply converted itself into the local Etsuzankai division. "We need to have our village improved while we're alive," explained a Koshiji Communist who also joined the Etsuzankai. Many Socialists said they didn't want to join Tanaka's conservative political party, but they did want to join his Etsuzankai.

By 1952, Tanaka had become the highest vote getter in his district, his 62,000 votes besting Miyake's by a margin of 10,000. In 1958, Tanaka won 86,000 votes, 30 percent more than any other candidate in the district had ever garnered. To some voters, he had transcended politics to become a quasi deity. In 1964, a shrine in Ojiya City placed a bust of Tanaka on its grounds. "In the chaotic period of postwar Japanese politics," the black marble plaque reads, "he poured his heart into the development of *ura Nippon*."

CHAPTER THREE
KAKU-SAN VERSUS THE ELITE

THE CONTEST in Niigata between the prodevelopment Tanaka and the Socialist Miyake was played out in similar fashion across the nation in the 1950s and 1960s.

Early postwar Japan was a country that had neither come to grips with its painful past nor reached consensus over its future path. Debates raged over fundamental issues: capitalism versus socialism, rearmament versus pacifism, membership in the American anti-Soviet camp versus neutrality or a pro-Soviet tilt. When the United States ended its seven-year occupation in 1952 and granted Japan independence, the democracy that the Americans had worked to instill seemed fractious and fragile. Mass rallies, general strikes, brutal police crackdowns, even politically inspired acts of rail sabotage were a way of life. Violence often spilled onto the floor of Parliament, where courtly debates between MPs degenerated into brawls.

In 1955, the divisions hardened. Until then, Japan's postwar Parliament had been a confusing whirl of governments, of parties appearing, disappearing, merging, and splitting apart. (The Progressive Party, for example, which had endorsed Tanaka in his first election, was defunct by his second election, and in the early 1950s he ran as a member of the conservative Liberal Party.)

No clear-cut, long-term stable majority existed. In October 1955, the main parties of the Left, buoyed by steady gains at the polls and hopes of taking power, combined into a new Socialist Party. They held one third of the seats in Parliament.

The business world, spooked by the prospect of a unified, ascendant anticapitalist movement, pressured the disparate forces of the Right to unite. It wasn't easy. The two main conservative blocs, the Liberal Party and the Democratic Party, did not get along well. They had some policy disagreements over issues such as the rate at which the country should rearm and the degree of independence from the United States that Japan's foreign policy should have. But mainly there was bad blood from years of personal animosities and slights. One elder of the Liberal Party and one veteran of the Democratic Party "had not even shared a cup of tea . . . for over a period of thirty years," one of those politicians wrote in his memoirs, telling of a mutual disdain that dated back to their memberships in different competing parties before the war. "Even when we would run into each other at a bar . . . our sense of rivalry was so fierce that we would sit with seats between us, one trying to outdrink the other."

Three dozen top executives representing a broad cross section of the economy demanded that the grudges be set aside. Some endorsed a resolution called the "Emergency Request Regarding the Stabilization of the Political Situation." And the industrial barons backed up their pleas with financial threats. By the mid-1950s, the large business associations were providing about half of the disparate conservative camps' campaign financing; they threatened to withhold monies if their demands weren't heeded and promised to give more funds if the politicians complied. In November 1955, the Liberals and the Democrats joined hands to create the Liberal Democratic Party.

The LDP was large enough to control the government through the rest of the 1950s. But that did not ensure political stability. The nation was still split over many issues, most sharply over foreign policy. The Socialists favored an unarmed, pacifist Japan. The LDP—despite internal disagreements over the details—backed a rebuilding of the military and a strong anti-Communist line. The tensions came to a head in 1960, when the LDP sought Parliament's ratification of a security treaty with the United States. Under the pact, the government reaffirmed the right of American troops, who had stayed after the Occupation ended, to continue using Japan as a main Asian military base. Leftist MPs staged a sit-in to prevent the LDP majority from approving the treaty. On May 19, police stormed Parliament to break up the blockade. A month later, hundreds of thousands of protesters flooded Tokyo's narrow, winding streets, snake-dancing in unison and hoisting strident banners while their leaders barked shrill slogans over loudspeakers. Demonstrators tried to invade Parliament. The police fought back. Hundreds of people were injured, and one, crushed to death, became a martyr. It was Japan's worst political crisis since gaining independence.

In the wake of the security treaty crisis, the LDP took a new course with the intent of solidifying its control and becalming the country. A new party leader, a career Finance Ministry technocrat named Hayato Ikeda, was made prime minister with the blessing of Japan's business leaders. Like Tanaka in Niigata, Ikeda's platform for Japan promoted economic development above all else.

The LDP's "GNP-ism," as the new conservative ideology came to be known, consisted of two main planks. The first was Ikeda's alluring pledge that, if the LDP were to stay in power, the personal income of every Japanese citizen would double in a decade. The second was a retreat into isolationism, an attempt to paper over the country's irreconcilable differences on diplomacy by simply avoiding the question. This "absence of diplomacy" did not mean repealing the controversial U.S.-Japan security treaty but rather using it as a protective shell for Japan's withdrawal from world affairs. Under this arrangement, the United States paid for and provided most of Japan's defense. In return, Japan agreed to remain a staunch, though passive, member of the Western anti-Communist Cold War alliance. Throughout the 1960s, Japan was "more a trading company than a nation-state," as one American scholar put it.

Ikeda's wealth-generating plan mixed conventional macroeconomic policies—increased government spending and low interest rates—with extra goodies for big voting blocs such as farmers. The government also fostered strategic industries such as steel and computers by using heavy bureaucratic guidance, as well as tariffs, quotas, and informal import prevention policies. And while Japan kept many of its markets shut to imports, the United States, as part of the Cold War bargain, kept world markets open to Japanese products; exports became an engine for Japan's growth.

Ikeda's income-doubling pledge came true—and earlier than promised. By 1967, per capita income in Japan was twice the 1960 level, marking one of the greatest "economic miracles" the world had ever seen. What made it all the more miraculous was its breadth.

In most countries, rapid growth creates vast disparities between rich and poor, a condition that in turn breeds social tension; in 1960s Japan, nearly everybody shared the wealth, thus diminishing the potential for these strains. In an often-cited 1964 survey, fully 90 percent of the Japanese said they considered themselves "middle class." A "Japanese-lantern-shaped society" was one common description of the income curve—a wide middle with virtually no top or bottom.

In the early 1950s, the average Japanese family was still preoccupied with securing *i-shoku-ju,* a word covering the three main necessities of clothing, food, and shelter. By the early 1960s, most households had within reach the "three sacred treasures" of a car, color TV, and air conditioner. (The phrase was a playful allusion to the "imperial treasures" of mirror, jewel, and sword.) The once-ubiquitous street beggars had virtually disappeared, and practically everybody had a job. Indeed, factories were producing at such a furious pace that workers often went six months at a time without a single day off, sleeping in company dorms and eating in company canteens.

Economic success became a unifying national goal just as Asian conquest had been a generation earlier. The 1960s brought one triumph after another. In 1963, the International Monetary Fund declared that Japan had once again become a "developed" country. The 1964 summer Olympics, hosted in Tokyo, were transformed from an athletic competition into a proud showcase of the nation's progress. Workers rallied frantically to overhaul the capital, to widen roads, improve sewage, build hotels—in short, to modernize Tokyo, much of which was still ramshackle twenty years after war's end. The world's fastest trains, the "bullet" trains, came on line in time for the event. The Japanese celebrated the gold medals their compatriots won in those games; they also celebrated that year when the nation entered the leading club of the global economic elite, the Organization for Economic Cooperation and Development (OECD). At decade's end, they were still cheering when Japan became the third largest economy in the world, lagging behind only those of the two great protagonists of the Cold War, the United States and the Soviet Union. By 1965, Japan's chronic trade deficit with its American patron had disappeared, and from then on, it ran constant surpluses. Peering thirty years ahead, the great American futurist Herman Kahn declared, "The 21st century is Japan's."

All this was accompanied, especially in the early 1960s, by a sudden, new domestic tranquillity, and the Liberal Democratic Party, the overseer of this prosperity and peace, thrived. A month after Ikeda took office, one newspaper poll reported that for the first time since the country had regained independence, a Japanese leader had the support of a majority of the Japanese people. In November 1960, Ikeda's LDP won a smashing victory in national parliamentary elections, taking 296 of 467 seats, or nearly a two-thirds majority. Despite early worries about its fragility, the party stayed united—and firmly in power—throughout the 1960s. The electorate, meanwhile, proved to be impervious to Marxist dogma: the violence of the Left turned most voters off, while the cornucopia provided by the Right drew them in. As the decade drew to a close, the Liberal Democratic bandwagon was still rolling strong. After the December 1969 elections, the party had 303 seats in Parliament, its largest number since the party's founding; the opposition Socialists, meanwhile, held on to only 90 seats, the party's worst drubbing in more than a decade.

THE LDP'S RISING TIDE lifted Kakuei Tanaka's boat. "I will be a Parliament member in my twenties, a cabinet member in my thirties, and the prime minister in my fifties!" he boasted to a hundred voters gathered during his first campaign in 1946. Tanaka accomplished the first goal the following year, with his election at the age of twenty-eight. He then quickly ingratiated himself with the leading conservative politicians of the day through his fund-raising prowess and impeccable political instincts—compiling detailed national district-by-district election strategies and helping mediate peaceful settlements among clashing egos. He was readily accepted as a founding member of the Liberal Democratic Party in 1955.

Two years later, Tanaka fulfilled his second ambition when he became minister of posts and telecommunications at the age of thirty-nine, the youngest cabinet member since 1898. In the early 1960s, his ambition continued to outpace precedent, as he became the youngest-ever finance minister, one of the most powerful positions in government, and then held a series of important party posts, serving as chief strategist for the LDP's 1969 national electoral landslide. He was fifty-one years old at that time and began plotting for his ultimate ambition—becoming the leader of all Japan.

Despite Tanaka's rapid climb up the national political ladder, however, that last rung was still a very long reach. For although the LDP establishment had found Tanaka useful, it had never fully accepted the rough-hewn country bumpkin without a high school diploma as a member of the club. A quarter century earlier, General MacArthur's idealists had aspired to make Japan into a broad-based democracy, more progressive in many ways than America's. They had achieved some noteworthy successes, vastly expanding the voting rolls, drawing women into politics for the first time, fostering a labor movement—and opening the corridors of power to people such as Tanaka who would certainly have been excluded under the prewar system. Yet the inner sanctum remained off limits to all but a homogeneous few. Japan's conservative leadership was made up largely of men from wealthy, connected families who had graduated at the top of their classes in the leading national universities and then joined the best bureaucracies before entering politics. Career politicians who had not had access to this select breeding were treated as second-class citizens.

Even Shigeru Yoshida, the man the Americans had worked with most closely in their democratizing efforts, represented the view that a well-educated, well-heeled elite should run the country. He was acceptable to the United States because of his early, forceful advocacy for ending World War II, a courageous view that had landed him in jail under the military government. But he was hardly a firebrand advocate for a new social order, and during his seven years as prime minister between 1946 and 1954, he frequently fought with MacArthur to preserve the old ruling class. Yoshida had been adopted by a wealthy merchant shortly after birth in 1878, graduated from Tokyo Imperial University, married the daughter of one of Japan's prominent statesmen, and pursued a successful career as a civil servant in the prewar Foreign Ministry. As Japan's democratically elected leader, Yoshida maintained his aristocratic demeanor—with his rimless glasses and expensive cigars—and a faith in his own superior intellect. The young Tanaka, with his unerring nose for power and his compelling charm, managed to win his way into Yoshida's good graces. But Yoshida mainly chose to mentor those with a pedigree like his, whom he plucked straight from the civil service ranks and gave plum political jobs. These men, known as the disciples of the "Yoshida School," all shared a certain noblesse oblige and a disdainful distance from the masses at whose behest they theoretically served.

The ex-bureaucrats' grip on power seemed to tighten in 1957 when—after a brief interregnum of professional politicians at the helm—Nobusuke Kishi became the LDP's choice for prime minister.

To leftist critics of postwar Japanese conservatism, Kishi was a particularly galling illustration of the old elite's unabashed resilience. He had, after all, been the point man in General Hideki Tojo's cabinet for mobilizing Japan's wartime economy and had been jailed by the Americans as a "Class A" war criminal. When he rammed the U.S.-Japan security treaty through Parliament in 1960, a critic said the "insolence typified the worst aspects of prewar bureaucracy." Though the fallout from the ensuing riots brought Kishi's personal demise, the ex-bureaucrats continued to dominate the LDP.

Kishi's successor, Hayato Ikeda, was no populist, his promises of "income doubling" notwithstanding. He had been a willing architect of early-1950s austerity policies and had won notoriety for remarking that bankruptcies were inevitable, saying, like Marie-Antoinette, that poor Japanese families unable to afford rice should instead "eat barley." In 1952, he was forced to resign as industry minister for remarking that "it cannot be helped" if a few small business owners were "driven to suicide."

In his new role of promising plenty, the bespectacled Ikeda still maintained a nonpolitical, technocratic style, preferring to stay above the fray rather than excite the populace. In the highly charged atmosphere of 1960, he managed to turn his bland, uninspiring manner into a political plus with his slogan, "The Politics of Low Posture." More concerned with finance than philosophy, he was known for carrying a radio at all times to catch the latest stock prices. France's Charles de Gaulle supposedly dismissed Ikeda as a mere "transistor salesman."

Ikeda's successor, Eisaku Sato, was the perfect man to sustain this exclusive line. The descendant of samurai, he was a younger brother of Kishi (who had been adopted into another family in his youth and changed his surname), a Tokyo Imperial University grad, and a career civil servant in the Ministry of Transport. Sato remained in office for seven years and eight months, from 1964 to 1972, which is still a record for continuous longevity and attributable, most Japanese believe, to his doing or saying little of note. As a young train stationmaster, he had carefully rehearsed the remarks he would have to deliver to a meeting on box lunches. After years as a politician, he was still painfully stiff whenever forced to address an assembly. Never convivial, he preferred to spend his late-night hours alone in the prime minister's residence playing solitaire. When he did go drinking, "there's no way of knowing whether Mr. Sato is enjoying himself," a fellow pol cracked. He disliked the glad-handing, the crowds, and the open debate of democratic politics. Not surprisingly, Sato never won more than a 40 percent approval rate.

Sato lowered the pulse of Ikeda's "low posture" with his trademark "politics of waiting." This quintessentially bureaucratic style often meant delaying for months—years, even—before taking action on a specific problem. The oft-invoked wisecrack was that he "would tap his way across a stone bridge to be sure it was safe." "The fact is," Sato himself once noted unapologetically, ". . . that I am rather dull. . . . I think, however, that there ought to be something dull about any man."

There was nothing dull or bureaucratic about Tanaka. By the time he became a national figure in the late 1950s, he had, of course, left his humble farm-boy roots far behind. He hobnobbed with the rich and powerful as devotedly as did any major politician. But he continued to court the common people and to cultivate his image as one of them. Japan's first true, successful populist, he immediately embraced—rather than scorned—the full potential of postwar democracy. "Everybody! Politics is life, the life of the nation itself!" he would croon to the large crowds that came to hear him. He made a point of crediting the voters for each success, stroking the people of Niigata in 1962 by saying, "It's you, not the prime minister, who made me finance minister." The cheering mobs, in turn, celebrated with fireworks, confetti, and a locally composed "Song to Welcome Finance Minister Tanaka." On the street and in newspaper headlines, he was often addressed without the formalities of title or even last name, simply as "Kaku-san."

He was Japan's acknowledged master of moving crowds, artfully playing the nostalgic raconteur, the cutting stand-up comic, the stern teacher. Tanaka's strong mountain dialect, his rapid-fire rambling, and his leaps from one half-finished topic to the next made the actual content difficult to follow. But his raspy Louis Armstrong voice flowed in singsong rhythms from low growls to high squeaks, while his body rocked and his arms gestured frenetically, making his stump speeches spellbinding performances that induced nods, laughter, and tears.

Tanaka's staples were the importance of old-country values and common sense, frequently portrayed in caustic contrast to the logic of the educated urban elite, who often tended to be embarrassed by the "uncivilized" customs of an earlier age. Below his Western tie and business suit, he wore wooden clogs, called "geta." At fancy hotel banquets, Tanaka sent aides scurrying to find rice balls wrapped in seaweed while other guests dined on fine steak. "Japanese intellectuals disdained anything traditional," Shigezo Hayasaka, one of Tanaka's closest aides, later explained. "But Kakuei valued it. He was a politician who embodied the old sentiments." Tokyoites should send their children to the farms to "come close to the insects and animals," Tanaka urged in speeches. "Nowadays, ask a child in Tokyo 'Where do you find a grasshopper?' and he will say, 'The department store.' What utter nonsense!" Tanaka roared to his audience's laughter.

During a radio interview when he first became a cabinet member in 1957, Tanaka broke into *naniwabushi,* maudlin ballads popular in the late nineteenth century but considered déclassé by "modern" Japanese. Choosing a song of two Robin Hood–like gangster families, he bellowed about "gold coins flying around the gambling den." The straitlaced opposition parties raised a fuss in Parliament about "the minister encouraging gambling." Tanaka was unfazed. "I don't care how harshly intellectuals attack me," he retorted. "I'm thinking of how to catch the honest feelings of the public. Don't you think the people like to listen to *naniwabushi*?" Later, in 1962, as finance minister, Tanaka had to travel to Washington to try to raise funds in the American capital markets for the financially strapped Japanese government. He delighted his American investment-banker hosts—and unnerved his Japanese bureaucratic handlers—with an after-dinner rendition of an old-fashioned song about a poor man who dreams of success.

Most Japanese politicians kept their personal lives private. Tanaka, on the other hand, regularly drew from his well of hardships; his folksy autobiography, *My Personal History,* became a best-seller in the mid-1960s. His family became a sort of national sitcom, flavoring not only his own speeches but the weekly magazines and the feature television shows. In this saga, Tanaka was forever trying to please his elderly mother, Fume, in the countryside, and to tame his rebellious, American-educated daughter, Makiko, in Tokyo. Reporters could always get a good story by visiting Mama Tanaka in Niigata, where, well into her eighties, she was still pickling vegetables for her son and urging him to "take a rest," come home, and join her in the fields. Or they could talk to the twenty-something Makiko, who nagged her father in public for his smoking and drinking and who once interrupted him during a meeting with a foreign dignitary to explain, "I think my father is a wonderful man, but his greatest shortcoming is that he is talkative."

For his Everyman persona, Tanaka accentuated his rough edges.

He sweated profusely, the result of a chronic thyroid condition, and sat through meetings wiping himself with a handkerchief and vigorously plying a folded paper fan. He unabashedly delighted in vice, drinking heavily—"Unless I have two glasses of whiskey in my office every day, my blood pressure won't go down," he'd say. "I expand my veins by using alcohol"—and frequenting racetracks. He outdid his sharpie father, amassing a large stable of racehorses and tagging all of them with variations of his daughter's name. "You think my speech is vulgar because I say 'asshole' and 'shit,' right?" Tanaka once baited a journalist. "But that makes me closer to people."

He was not, however, a rube. Despite his lack of a college degree, Tanaka developed a reputation for brilliance. He had a prodigious memory for names, dates, and figures and peppered his speeches with long lists of economic statistics and impromptu calculations. A voracious reader, he claimed to have digested on his own the important Japanese works of literature, major studies of Japanese law, and "the complete works of world literature—before I was sixteen." A higher education, he argued frequently, was a waste of time: "It is nothing special to graduate from a college law department with top grades; an ignorant, illiterate old lady can recite a sutra [a sacred Buddhist scripture] smoothly." He had huffily refused, he liked to say, when a university had offered him an honorary degree. His education was the real-world training of a self-made businessman. "A man who has never been stripped bare becomes nervous," he said. "I have been."

With every brusque gesture, Tanaka's short, husky body reinforced his no-nonsense image. He walked fast, talked fast, and fidgeted constantly when forced to sit still. He greeted people by abruptly raising his right arm and quickly cut them off with grunts of *"Yossha, yossha,"* an informal "Okay, okay." "Don't idle away the time with silly topics like the weather," he admonished visitors. "Just get to the point." "I once refused my girl," he told an interviewer, "only because she was late for the date." When Tanaka took up golf in middle age, he started by ordering an aide to bring him "twenty-five pounds" of books, studied them day and night for three months, then hit five hundred balls a day at a driving range under the tutelage of a pro for the next three months. He ran from hole to hole, playing four and a half rounds some days, and set himself an annual quota of games.

Like his populist image, all of this, too, was calculated to contrast Tanaka with the bureaucrat-politicians, who were regularly portrayed as quiveringly cautious. Whereas Sato's slogan was "The Politics of Waiting," Tanaka's mantra was "Decision and Action." His nickname became "the computerized bulldozer."

Indeed, Tanaka had little patience for the Japanese style of timidity, deference to seniority, tedious deliberation, and conflict avoidance. In one of his first acts as postal minister in the late 1950s, he ordered the powerful Japan Postal Workers' Union to remove its huge plaque from the front of the ministry building, declaring, "It's rude to post a bigger plate than the landlord's." He fired top labor leaders and punished more than twenty thousand workers for conducting union business during working hours. (Ever the politician, however, he offered one of the axed union executives a job as his aide.) Tanaka held that position for only eleven months in the late 1950s due to the rocky politics of the time, but he is also widely credited with having cut through a large knot of red tape to accelerate the arrival of the mass television age. For four years after broadcasting began in Japan, only a few stations had licenses—until Tanaka overruled the ponderous ministry staff and gave out forty-three new permits in one weekend. "This is the time to make history in Japan's electronic waves," he declared, ordering the technocrats to change their plans. The following year the number of television sets passed that of radio receivers for the first time.

Unhindered by the usual concerns for precedent, Tanaka was not hesitant about forging new roles for government. In 1965, fear spread that a collapse of the securities sector would ruin the economic boom. After a tense all-night meeting with the nation's top economic bureaucrats, Finance Minister Tanaka engineered a special central bank loan for one of Japan's "Big Four" securities companies—the only time in postwar history that the Bank of Japan has extended credit to a company other than a bank.

He did not shy away from a fight, whether political or physical. In 1958, when leftists tried to block legislation expanding the powers of the police, Tanaka personally led the charge of LDP politicians past the gang of burly Socialists inside Parliament. In 1969, when student radicals were shutting down universities, Tanaka—secretary-general of the LDP at the time—helped ram legislation to suppress the uprisings through Parliament. Most top LDP leaders—including Prime Minister Sato—were wary about pushing the controversial measure in the face of bitter opposition protest. As the elderly chairman of Parliament hesitated to call the vote, a red-faced

Tanaka barked, "I'm going to beat that old man up." He stormed into the chairman's chambers screaming, "Ring the bell [to start the session], you old fogey!" The vote was held, and the measure passed.

Such moves often drew laurels from the public and the press. The mass-circulation *Mainichi* newspaper, in an article typical of the time, praised Tanaka in July 1971, upon his appointment as minister of trade and industry, for his "dynamism and quick thinking." He is, the article continued, "a man of action . . . expected by the nation . . . to solve [the] thorny problems facing present-day Japan." Yet that same style set a lot of the country's old guard on edge. To them, his populism was crass, his "decision and action" rash.

Practically each promotion Tanaka received drew opposition from older LDP politicians, bureaucrats, and business leaders. When the suggestion was floated that Tanaka be made finance minister, Prime Minister Ikeda at first resisted, snidely dismissing the upstart, according to an aide, as "a man of the rickshaw class." (Another account has Ikeda deriding Tanaka as "a horse dealer's son.") Tanaka did prevail, but the chairman of the powerful Keidanren big-business federation publicly protested the choice. Bankers expressed "unease" with his "very shallow acquaintance with the finance world." "His voice cuts like a dagger," and "when he starts talking, it looks like his mouth will not stop," the *Asahi* newspaper said of the new finance minister. "His youth and energy" make him a "reckless runner." The finance bureaucrats, the newspaper noted, viewed their new boss as "different"—and these were not people who viewed diversity as a good thing.

Nevertheless, Tanaka did come to play an increasingly important political role throughout the 1960s. His "open and extroverted personality" was credited with helping "popularize the image" of the long-running Sato cabinet, which, as one newspaper observed in 1970, "if anything, is obscure." Prime Minister Sato himself once described Tanaka as "like a right hand to me." Even Sato, however, saw his helpful underling as a parvenu unfit to lead the nation. When he finally decided to retire in 1972, Sato favored as his successor yet another prominent representative of the bureaucratic line, Takeo Fukuda.

Tanaka should have posed no challenge to Fukuda. In a system that placed high priority on seniority and pedigree, Fukuda was older and much better bred: at the time the eleven-year-old Tanaka had been nearing the end of his formal schooling at a lowly Niigata elementary school, Fukuda, at age twenty-four, was completing his education by receiving a ceremonial silver watch as the top graduate of the 1929 class of Tokyo Imperial University's law school, the institution specifically created to train the nation's civil servants. While Fukuda was learning how to shape government economic policy in the 1930s as a rising star in the Finance Ministry, Tanaka was doing manual labor in Tokyo at an engineering company that was friendly with Fukuda and later became one of Fukuda's main political backers. Years later, Fukuda still talked of Tanaka as a sort of hired hand. Tanaka's blatant politicking grated on Fukuda; when the two men, as cabinet ministers, went to dinner, "Tanaka even gave a tip to the man who looks after customers' shoes," Fukuda haughtily observed. "I would never do that."

Fukuda, like Sato, came across to the general public as bland and arrogant. His sparse hair and gaunt frame connoted the frugality that guided his personal life and political outlook. Whereas Tanaka reveled in the bawdy Japanese folk traditions that repulsed Japan's upper crust, Fukuda partook in such delicate "high arts" as the ancient tea ceremony. Fukuda liked to play the tightwad, fighting new government spending on social programs. "The nation's economic circles [also] prefer . . . Fukuda to Tanaka as Sato's successor," a political columnist for the *Mainichi* newspaper wrote. Fukuda was expected to follow "the policies of Sato without a sudden diversion." Tanaka, on the other hand, "is considered an unpredictable man, and even dangerous." By the old rules, there would have been no contest.

CHAPTER FOUR

BUILDING A NEW JAPAN

But by 1972, the rules were changing rapidly and Sato's grasp was slipping. If the 1960s were Japan's celebration of economic advancement and the victory of conservatism, the 1970s quickly became an era of concern about the "distortions" of that near-freakish growth—and the shocking apathy of the ruling elite toward those problems. "The super-express *Nippon* rushes at full speed down the 'Prosperity' line," a leading newspaper wrote in early 1971, conveying the mood of the times, "carrying one hundred million passengers who, men and women alike, are crying hysterically and jostling one another in the overcrowded coaches. The train never stops; its mechanical and hand brakes are not functioning properly. This is today's Japan in miniature." In November 1970, popular novelist Yukio Mishima stunned the nation by committing hara-kiri—fatally slashing his own abdomen with a dagger, then having a loyal retainer cut off his head—after exhorting hundred of soldiers to stage a coup d'état. Most Japanese, of course, considered Mishima's politics beyond the fringe. But he did strike a chord with his rambling suicide note: "Japan has never enjoyed such economic prosperity . . . as in this postwar period. . . . This has led to neglect of the very foundation of the state, and the people have lost their spirit."

■

The postwar industrial boom, concentrated heavily in the major urban areas, had created an "overpopulation-underpopulation" crisis: crammed cities and dying countrysides. Less than a generation earlier, fully half of all Japanese had lived in rural areas. But the economic growth had forced manufacturers to scour the farms for labor, and they had literally hired whole school classes at a time away from their homes. By 1970, fewer than one in five Japanese remained in the villages; about half were squeezed into the megalopolis stretching from Tokyo to Osaka.

This human tidal wave overwhelmed the limited capacities of Tokyo. Houses were shoddy, tiny, and scarce, sewage disposal antiquated or nonexistent. The narrow streets suffered the world's worst traffic jams with cars crawling two miles per hour at rush hour, while white-gloved "pushers" crammed as many commuters as possible into trains. Though incomes rose, so did a frightening uncertainty, for the impersonal cities supplied neither the protections of the countryside nor the social safety net of other developed nations. Even though Japan's economy had grown larger than those of France and Germany, it spent proportionately less on welfare than did those two European nations.

Meanwhile, those left behind in the rural areas saw their communities vanish. Poverty and disease largely disappeared, and farmhouses now enjoyed the modern amenities of electricity and television, but the city's excitement and high-paying jobs still encouraged young people to leave their sleepy countryside homes. The "grandpa-grandma-mom farm" was the 1960s pop cliché describing who was left to tend the fields; by 1971, only 30 percent of farmers were men under the age of sixty. Village schools closed for lack of students, and annual festivals were curbed or canceled because nobody remained to carry the portable shrines. By the early 1970s, the government officially designated more than one thousand villages as "underpopulated."

Japan's new status as an economic giant was also stained by its accompanying reputation as one of the world's worst polluters. Tokyo's smoggy skies got so bad that residents near certain busy intersections accumulated more lead in their blood than factory workers did, wore masks to walk outside, and had to wash down their houses four times a day. From the late 1960s through the early 1970s, Japan experienced a half-dozen separate world-infamous industrial pollution scandals. In one case in the city of Yokkaichi, Japan's first large-scale petroleum combine brought a "fatal asthma" to people living nearby. In other scandals, factory chemicals poisoned the nearby water supplies, causing cracking of residents' bones, uncontrollable muscle convulsions, and other unspeakable human sufferings, deformities, and death. In each of these cases, the tragedy begat treachery because the government, seemingly worried only about protecting industry, ignored the public cries for help. Official negligence, in the late 1960s and early 1970s, forced the grotesquely disfigured victims into lengthy court battles—and onto the front pages. "The technocrat . . . takes the most haughty authoritarian attitude toward the people," one of Japan's most noted scholars of the problem wrote. "Can we expect Japan's State monopolistic capital with its technocrats, its riot police and kept scholars really to solve this dangerous crisis?"

As the Japanese public began to question the benefits of growth, the other main pillar of postwar conservative doctrine—Japan's alliance with the United States—started trembling from the "Nixon shocks" of the summer of 1971. For the first quarter century following World War II, the trans-Pacific partnership had rested on a simple quid pro quo: Japan would stay in the American-led anti-Communist camp, while the United States would provide unwavering support to Japan's defense, democracy, and capitalism. But when Japanese capitalism proved surprisingly robust—to the point of creating huge trade surpluses with the United States—the American president suddenly announced a new, more hostile economic policy. The first "shock" included a 10 percent tax on imports and the threat of invoking Trading with the Enemy Act sanctions against Japanese textiles. The second "shock" was the sharp turn in American foreign policy that took place when Richard Nixon initiated a rapprochement with Communist China. Friendly ties between Washington and Beijing, Japanese leaders feared, would considerably diminish the strategic importance of Tokyo.

America's new aloofness toward Japan was accentuated by the manner in which these radical shifts were handled. Nixon neither consulted with, nor notified, the Japanese prime minister in advance. (Sato was reportedly playing golf when he learned that Nixon's China bombshell would be announced within minutes; the Japanese premier's characteristically detached response was "Is that so?") The bewildered Sato came under harsh attack for being dangerously ignorant of the fundamental changes swirling about Japan. "I have done everything they [the Americans] have asked," a tearful Sato later told a visiting diplomat. "They let me down."

The pervasive, unnerving sense of instability was heightened by the return of the noisy mass protests that had largely subsided after the 1960 unveiling of the income-doubling plan. As in the United States and Europe, university students waged a fierce antiauthoritarian campaign in the late 1960s and early 1970s, protesting everything from the nation's pro-U.S. foreign policy to what they considered "outdated" lectures and "remote" professors. At Tokyo University, breeding ground of the elite, and other schools, students occupied buildings for months, tried professors in twenty-hour kangaroo courts, and barricaded faculty meetings, letting only limited food and drink reach the prisoners. Those uprisings spawned more extremist offshoots, such as the notorious Red Army, which hijacked planes, "captured" a resort town, and shot police at point-blank range. The contentious U.S.-Japan security pact came up for review in 1970, and though it was easily renewed, 2 million treaty opponents joined rallies around the country, more than had filled the streets a decade earlier.

Within months of the LDP's great 1969 landslide victory, the conservative party appeared weak. The LDP's indifference to the country's mounting social problems made it especially vulnerable in the cities. Leftist governors and mayors around the country offered their citizens the government-sponsored medical care the national government resisted. The Communist Party lured small-business owners with innovative credit programs and saw its support double in major urban centers in just five years, from the late 1960s to the early 1970s. In local elections in 1971, progressives won control of three of Japan's largest cities. In addition to the traditional leftist opposition posed by the Communists and different Socialist parties, a new political party formed by a militant Buddhist sect, called "Komeito," or "Clean Government Party," made heavy inroads among the urban dispossessed.

By the spring of 1972, after nearly eight years in office, Prime Minister Sato's popularity had plunged below 20 percent, the worst figure ever for a Japanese leader. In mid-June, on the final day of Parliament under his reign, the premier was humiliated when opposition parties killed two major pieces of economic legislation. By that time, Sato was so thoroughly defeated that he couldn't even "exit honorably," as he had desired; at a June 17 press conference formally announcing his retirement, Sato chased away the reporters, screaming before a national television audience, "Get out! I hate the biased newspapers!"

The feeling was mutual. There was a strong backlash in the press, and among the Japanese as a whole, against the country's politico-bureaucratic leadership. "We are sick and tired," a popular newspaper columnist wrote in the summer of 1972, "of dull, safe-driving bureaucrats—of cold authoritarianism and of government by high-handed officials." "The 'Yoshida School' [of bureaucrat-politicians] can no longer tide over the situation," a Japanese magazine argued. "Sato's 'politics of waiting' are no good. A man of decision must replace him."

That was Tanaka's opening. In Sato's final months in office, the flailing premier had no choice but to lean more and more heavily on his chief fixer. In July 1971, Sato sacked his trade minister and gave Tanaka the job; in just three months, "the computerized bulldozer" was able to resolve the textile trade dispute with the United States that had festered for more than two years. "He's got enough guts to speak out on Japan's problems and policies," an admiring trade bureaucrat cooed, noting that when issues arose, Tanaka dealt with them "the very next day." The internal tensions within the struggling LDP heightened, and when a rump bloc stopped the cabinet from meeting in early 1972 as a protest against national budget plans, it was Tanaka who was sent to negotiate a settlement. "Any troubles that occur in the party are taken to Mr. Tanaka," the *Asahi* newspaper observed, "in the belief that 'he will take care of [them] somehow.' "

Tanaka spoke out with growing frequency about the "various contradictions [that] have surfaced amidst the affluence" of the income-doubling decade. In June 1972, he published a 220-page manifesto for a radical redirection of economic policy titled *Building a New Japan: A Plan for Remodeling the Japanese Archipelago.* The book painted a grim picture of Tokyo as an "asphalt jungle which decayed the minds and hearts of its inhabitants," a place where "cherry blossoms are dying" and "children must play on the steps of an apartment house or dodge cars in the back streets," where their parents own cars only for display "because of the difficulties and dangers of driving" them and are "not likely able to fulfill the life-long dream of owning a house . . . even if they are willing to settle for a site two to three hours away" from work. Japanese cities are like "the physically handicapped," Tanaka wrote. "There are better new towns built in the Jakarta suburbs than in Japan."

Tanaka's prescription was to "replace the pursuit of growth with the utilization of growth"—not to curb the expansion but to redirect it. The government, he argued, should act like a massive dam to "boldly reverse this torrential urban concentration" toward the dying countryside—away from *omote Nippon* and, not surprisingly, into his native *ura Nippon.* He called for literally "scrapping the existing industrial areas in Tokyo, Osaka and elsewhere" by spending huge sums of government money to relocate industries to rural areas.

Supplementing this lofty rhetoric, the book offered an oddly detailed blueprint of Tanaka's ideal Japanese city, an industrial-residential complex with a population of no more than 250,000. Tanaka, the ex-contractor/architect, included a specific diagram of this model city and listed the types of parking facilities that would be built, the number and functions of different highway lanes, and the categories of recreational centers (especially bowling alleys) to be allotted to each town. "There will be at least 8 yards between buildings across a street," he wrote with certainty. The goal, he concluded grandiloquently, was "a society where every home is filled with laughter, where senior citizens live peaceful, restful lives, where the eyes of youth shine bright with the light of hope."

While Tanaka's descriptions of Japan's problems were spot on, his solutions, by any detached analysis, were strange. His ideas rapidly caught fire, though, and *Building a New Japan* instantly became the best-selling book in Japan. In a nation with little tradition of political rhetoric—where politicians and bureaucrats preferred to settle matters behind closed doors with little regard for public opinion—here was a serious politician who actually made a direct appeal to the people. "Sato never advanced any such comprehensive collection of policies," even a harsh critic of Tanaka's proposals conceded. "Indeed, part of the popularity [of Tanaka's book] is undoubtedly a reflection of the popular reaction to Prime Minister Sato's stern and unpopular silence."

Tanaka moved with equal dexterity to answer public cries for a bold new diplomacy. Japan's postwar foreign policy had focused nearly exclusively on the United States and mimicked the American rejection of Mao Zedong's Communist control of the Chinese mainland. But that twenty-five-year disruption in Sino-Japanese relations was a mere moment of history in two millennia of ties. Though the relationship had often been marred by violence, hatred, jealousy, and fear, Japan considered its links with China an integral element of the nation's body politic. Politicians from both the Left and Right denounced the absence of Tokyo-Beijing diplomatic relations imposed by America's simple-minded anti-Communist stance as a painfully unnatural state.

Nixon's epic eight-day "journey of peace" to China in February 1972 intensified support in Japan for a similar overture. And as the United States became a more uncertain ally and trading partner for Japan, China—with its huge population, large potential market, and rich supply of raw materials—seemed to offer a valuable counterweight. Over the summer, numerous Japanese business delegations rushed to the mainland to propose development projects. Sato remained paralyzed, unwilling to deviate from earlier policies in any significant way, and maintained Japan's hostile stance. Fukuda, his heir apparent, backed him. Tanaka, meanwhile, won plaudits from several other senior LDP politicians by signaling, after Nixon's trip, that he supported a thaw.

All of this was, of course, part of Tanaka's campaign to become prime minister in 1972. "It is finally the year for battle," he told his aides at a New Year's gathering in early January of that year. With a calligrapher's brush, he stroked his first poem of the year: "Men, like plants, compete to win success in the spring."

At first, neither Sato nor Fukuda took Tanaka seriously. In Japan's clubby politics, public campaigns for higher office were low-key affairs. Prime ministers and cabinets had, by and large, been chosen discreetly from a small circle of party elders and business leaders, and there was no reason to think this time would be any different. The very act of campaigning was unseemly—Sato never made a formal, public endorsement of Fukuda, while Fukuda dismissed pleas by nervous backers to seek the office more actively. "Beyond the party is the state," he sniffed. "Tanaka has raised an army," an observer put it. "Fukuda has entrenched himself in his castle."

But the smug old guard eventually realized that Tanaka was winning support, helped by rank-and-file fears that, lacking a fresh popular appeal, the LDP was in serious trouble. Sato and Fukuda were repeatedly shocked by each of Tanaka's blatant moves, and the lame-duck premier turned angry, dressing down Tanaka while disciplining the LDP members who pledged support to him. (One Sato loyalist berated them as "traitors who defy the wishes of the prime minister.") Strains emerged within the party as many politicians were torn by longtime loyalties to both camps. One entered the hospital pleading illness rather than declare his allegiance.

Failing to persuade Tanaka to step aside in favor of the senior Fukuda, Sato had no choice but to put the matter of his succession to an open party vote. Dropping his stately pride, the prime minister personally made a barrage of phone calls the night before the contest, begging partisans to "vote for Fukuda, no matter what." Nearly five hundred LDP delegates gathered the morning of July 5 to settle what had, by that point, been openly tagged the "Kaku-Fuku War"; because of the LDP's majority in Parliament, the winner would automatically become prime minister.

Four candidates entered the race, none winning the necessary majority on the first ballot. Tanaka and Fukuda took the top two slots in a virtual tie. A runoff between them was held immediately, and the long tally began again, the delegates walking one by one to the front of the hall to cast their votes. As the ballots were counted, Tanaka sat silently, eyes closed and arms folded. He sweated, and back home in Niigata, his octogenarian mother wiped the television screen with her handkerchief as if to clean her son's face. Shortly after noon, the chairman announced the results: "Kakuei Tanaka, 282 votes! Takeo Fukuda, 190 votes!" At fifty-four years of age, Tanaka had become the youngest prime minister since the war and the only one without a university degree. The hall erupted into raucous cheers.

A flushed Tanaka rose from his seat and cut short the applause with a sharp raise of his right hand. Unsmiling, he told the delegates, "There is a mountain of difficult problems that must be resolved immediately. I will carry out the responsibility of solving them." He bowed and the delegates raised their arms, roaring "Banzai!"

The long-suffering people of Niigata, ignored for a century by the central powers, celebrated the selection of their first-ever prime minister with a frenzied lantern parade, snaking through the streets on the stiflingly hot summer night. They sent up a thousand balloons, accompanied by a full rainbow of fireworks. A horde traveled by bus to Tokyo—via the Highway 17 that Tanaka had brought to the region—to congratulate their native son; the stately banquet hall reserved for the victory party in Tokyo had to set up tents in the garden to handle the overflow turnout.

Within ten days, the "commoners' prime minister" opened an unusual "dialogue with the people," not just meeting with the LDP and its traditional backers but holding high-profile sessions with the opposition parties and their supporters as well. He told surprised labor leaders, "I, too, am a workingman." Tanaka averted a government workers' strike by ordering a large pay hike and helped settle a bitter, three-month-long seamen's walkout. Within a month, he established a commission to start translating his best-seller *Building a New Japan* into concrete legislation. From streamlining red tape to compensating air pollution victims, "Everyday new ideas and directives have been issued from the Prime Minister's Office," one newspaper reported breathlessly.

Less than three months later, Tanaka took his most daring gambit, voyaging to Beijing in September to establish formal diplomatic relations with Communist China. The leaders of the main opposition parties joined the delegation that saw Tanaka off from Tokyo's Haneda Airport, an unprecedented display of postwar national unity. His arrival in Beijing was also replete with the symbols of healing: for the first time since the war, the Chinese government permitted Japan's "Rising Sun" flag to be flown and its national anthem played. (Just before the Japanese delegation's plane touched down, though, the People's Liberation Army sang a hearty chorus, penned by Mao, about the bloody battles with the invading Japanese in the 1940s.) During the six-day visit, Tanaka presented Zhou Enlai with a poem he had written on Sino-Japanese relations, and the two leaders chatted about everything from Confucianism to the rheumatism they both suffered. The new Japanese premier—who had last seen the mainland thirty years earlier as an occupying soldier—soberly recalled Japan's wartime atrocities and then, turning to the future, negotiated a "treaty of peace and friendship." Tanaka and Zhou signed the pact in an emotional ceremony, not with Western pens but with Asian brushes. Mindful of the ambitious agenda awaiting him back home, Tanaka told Zhou that his visit to the Great Wall "has given me great confidence that I can remodel the Japanese islands."

Japan's premier returned to a "Tanaka boom" sweeping his country. Polls taken in the wake of the China visit showed that a record-high 62 percent of the people—including half the Socialists' regular voters and a third of the Communist stalwarts—backed the Tanaka cabinet. Hundreds of experts and academics appealed to be part of the "Building a New Japan" commission, while the opposition parties scrambled to draft their own "remodeling" plans. A half-dozen prominent business titans called on Tanaka at the prime minister's office, issuing a hopeful plea for him to "regain the people's faith" in politics and to "create national solidarity." The boom's echoes reverberated overseas. *The New York Times* praised Tanaka's "archipelago-remodeling" plan as "a sweeping essay urging an economic and social revolution like Franklin D. Roosevelt's." "No American party leader has come up with anything like it," gushed American columnist Max Lerner, who hailed Tanaka as "a new figure on the world scene at a time when Japan is recognized as a new major world power." "Very forceful, very direct, very attractive, very blunt-spoken" was how Nixon's national security adviser, Henry Kissinger, sized him up.

Tanaka's aura flowed less from what he actually did than from what he was perceived to represent. He seemed to offer a new face for Japan in the world—not an anonymous suit easily mistaken for a transistor salesman, but finally someone who could stand as an equal to a Nixon or a Mao. (Japanese commentators saw significance in the fact that Tanaka's first summit with Nixon, held in August 1972, was in Hawaii, three thousand miles closer to Tokyo than to Washington, and that, during his visit to China, Tanaka walked one turret farther at the Great Wall than Nixon had.) The China ploy appeared to signal a new international role for a Japan that had long been reduced to the status of America's lackey. The Japanese press trumpeted reports of a "Tanaka shock" hitting Washington. Tanaka's Beijing visit, crowed the *Tokyo Shimbun* newspaper, marked "the beginning of a new 'independent' diplomacy for Japan." Tanaka's rags-to-riches story was seen as the belated flowering of Japan's postwar democracy, the symbol of a new "egalitarian society" freed from the stifling bonds of old school ties. The *Yomiuri* newspaper, Japan's largest daily, asserted that Tanaka was "the most powerful person in Japan ever to have so little distance between himself and the masses."

CHAPTER FIVE

THE POLITICIAN AS ENTREPRENEUR

THAT WAS, HOWEVER, just one side of the Tanaka story: Tanaka was also the most powerful person in Japan to keep so little distance between the pursuit of public good and his own personal enrichment —and with such blatant disregard for the commonly accepted ethical and legal boundaries separating the two. In the early 1970s, the Japanese people were so desperate for a "contemporary hero," as that same *Yomiuri* front-page story labeled the new premier, that they were willing—for a while—to overlook his faults. But Tanaka's attempt to juggle two such contradictory personae—the idealistic torchbearer of Japanese democracy and its mocking, cynical profiteer —was an extremely precarious stunt.

In reality, politics was just one part of the complex, interlocking empire of power and money that Kakuei Tanaka had built between 1945 and 1972. As he climbed steadily to the premiership, Tanaka had also become president of several different companies and taken advisory roles and ownership stakes in others. In his district's biggest city, Nagaoka, he had converted some of the choicest real estate along the Shinano River into a sprawling compound of Tanaka-related firms.

Tanaka's personal lifestyle took on all the opulence that usually accompanies such business success. Beginning in the 1950s, he started to build a sprawling estate that eventually was valued at more than $8 million and covered two acres in the tony Tokyo neighborhood of Mejiro. The compound was graced with landscaped gardens, a tulip field, and a pond filled with carp worth $3,000 each. He acquired three villas in the wealthy resort town of Karuizawa, the Nantucket of Japan, and in the early 1960s "purchased" a beautiful geisha, buying her a large house and supporting the two sons he fathered by her. The year Tanaka became prime minister, he reported a total income of 86 million yen (well over $200,000), five times the official premier's pay. Critics said that his spending habits indicated a much higher unreported total.

It would be impossible to separate "public servant Tanaka" from "tycoon Tanaka." Each relied heavily on, and contributed handsomely to, the other. Tanaka's construction company, after all, had opened the door to politics for him in the first place, since he had used the profits to curry favor with conservative bigwigs and had then had his employees run his first campaigns. Soon after, he had found an even better confluence of his political and business interests when he became president of a struggling local train company. The Nagaoka Railroad, as it was known, was one farming community's lifeline to urban markets. Its failure would be a severe economic blow to Tanaka's district; whoever saved it, therefore, would be a hero.

That tiny railroad became the foundation of Tanaka's local power base. As the company's dynamic, youthful chief executive, he rallied his executives to work long hours at reduced pay to build a new, modern rail system. When five of the six new trains broke down in tests just hours before the system's planned public opening in late 1951, Tanaka pushed the glum company to take its last chance. At two A.M., the sixth train successfully chugged down the line. Meanwhile, as the railroad's representative in Parliament, Tanaka secured the crucial funds to pay for the project from the national government's Japan Development Bank. When the new electric-powered train made its maiden journey, large crowds, heedless of dark clouds above, thronged every crossing along the twenty-five-mile track, waving Japanese national flags and cheering as the cars sped by. The company sponsored "Tanaka Cup" baseball games and fishing contests to spread his name. In the 1952 parliamentary election campaign, stationmasters and ticket punchers urged passengers to vote for their boss. Tanaka handily won, boosting his vote total by 50 percent over the previous election.

Over the next decade, he and some cronies bought control of another railroad and did a hostile takeover of a bus company. In addition to helping Tanaka expand his operations into a major new transportation service, the bus company was a desirable acquisition because its ousted chairman had backed a rival Niigata politician and had taken to hanging anti-Tanaka posters. Tanaka consolidated the businesses into a company called Echigo Kotsu, or Echigo Transport, which developed into the dominant public transportation network in Tanaka's constituency. He then engineered an informal union between Echigo Transport and his political support group, the Etsuzan-kai, which ran, among other things, his local campaigns and his district constituent services. The two organizations had the same executives and shared a headquarters, as if both were wholly owned subsidiaries of a sort of Tanaka Inc.

As he assembled this politico-business conglomerate, Tanaka would profess that his role models were two of Niigata's most beloved politicians: Mitsugu Okamura, who, on entering Parliament in 1894, had owned mountains, forests, and acres of rice fields; and Kan-ichi Otake, who had also become an MP in 1894 and who headed a family that had ruled sixty communities for thirty-two generations. Japan had adopted a limited parliamentary government a few years earlier, and these men were part of a class of politicians, especially common in the countryside, who filled the role of the old feudal system's domainal lords, taking personal responsibility for the well-being of their subjects. Okamura used his fortune to try to build a railroad that could alleviate the isolation of the snow country; Otake personally planned and paid for the damming and dividing of a river to prevent destructive floods. Such men were called "well-fence politicians," because a well and a fence were said to be all that was left of their clans' once-vast properties. At the end of Okamura's life in 1922, according to local legend, his holdings had dwindled to a few paintings, and those remained only because his family, fearing starvation, had hidden them from the railroad-obsessed patriarch. Otake died heavily in debt, unable to fix the leak in his roof.

In 1961, the people of Niigata erected a commemorative bust of Okamura at a train station, and it was Tanaka who was invited to inscribe the plate and deliver the evocative dedication. "Both men [Okamura and Otake] endeavored devotedly for the development of our home province, taking no account of their own interests . . . nay, throwing away all their property," he recalled. "Once I became a politician, I aspired to be like my great predecessors." But Tanaka managed to invert the Okamura-Otake formula: The more he did for the people of Niigata, the richer he got.

Tanaka tended to concentrate his entrepreneurial energies in fields such as construction, building supplies, transport, and real estate that benefited from the public works he was channeling, as a politician, into Niigata. The new roads he lobbied for proved a boon to his bus company, while the construction boom increased the value of the Niigata property he owned. Tanaka's firms also relied heavily on government contracts—and, apparently, on inside information about future national budgets. In 1953, he used his position as an MP to help bring a large-scale government-funded hydroelectric power project to his district and, separately, secured national monies to rebuild a train line. That same year, one of his companies just happened to begin producing gravel. Parliament Member Tanaka got votes for enriching the district, while supplier Tanaka monopolized the lucrative gravel contracts for both projects. Tanaka also won passage of a popular law requiring the government to clear the heavy snows from highways—and then set up a road-clearing service that won much of the work.

In the 1960s, "Tanaka Inc." moved heavily into Japan's thriving real estate market, this time working through a series of "ghost companies," mysterious firms with no phone numbers, staff, or offices, and often no formal link to Tanaka. But the ties were obvious: the registered executives and owners were his close friends and relatives—even his chauffeur—while the listed headquarters of one such venture, called Tokyo New House, was smack in the middle of a garden on Tanaka's compound. Whoever ran them, the companies had an uncanny knack for snapping up cheap Niigata property that, unbeknownst to the old landowners, was about to soar in value, thanks to soon-to-be-announced public works projects. In 1961, a "Tanaka family" company bought some undeveloped swampland; then the government decided to build a school on that very location, paying 20 percent above the total purchase price for just a small portion of the land. In the mid-1960s, Tanaka's associates offered farmers what seemed, at the time, a good price for a worthless, flood-prone riverbed. Shortly after they secured all the property, the national government disclosed plans to build a dike, then a highway, right through the plot. In less than a decade, the acquisition appreciated in value two hundred times. The Tanaka team hit jackpots again with the bullet train and the nuclear power plant that came to the region. It was, as one observer put it, "modern alchemy."

Tanaka's frequent accomplice in such wizardry was the murky mogul Kenji Osano, who, like Tanaka, had overcome humble roots to win the grudging acceptance of the Establishment. The son of a tenant farmer, Osano had made a killing selling auto parts to the Japanese military during the war, and then to the American forces in peacetime, and was a main fixer in the currency black markets that thrived under both. In the days following Japan's surrender, when many people were scavenging the ruins of Tokyo for sustenance, Osano ostentatiously kept piles of cash in his house. "This is the time for land," he told an associate, flashing a grin. "I will buy every hotel, inn, and summerhouse in Japan." Just two weeks after Japan's surrender, he snapped up his first luxury inn. He then bought his way into the destitute aristocracy, paying a 4-million-yen dowry to marry the daughter of a former earl. Osano suffered a temporary setback in 1948, when the U.S. Occupation jailed him for embezzling scarce gasoline. But by the mid-1980s, he had gone on to amass a conglomerate with stakes in seventy companies from airlines and bus lines to hotels and golf courses, with total assets estimated at more than $18 billion. He cornered the Waikiki Beach hotel business in the 1970s, becoming one of the first in a line of Japanese real estate investors to draw American protests of "economic invasion." When Osano died at age sixty-nine in 1986, he left an estate of 16 billion yen, or $100 million, the fourth largest ever recorded in Japan. (Experts suspected that, as a cutthroat strategist to the end, he had hidden trillions more to spare his heirs inheritance taxes.)

Osano's ruthless tactics and gruesome countenance—sunken eyes, fleshy nose, swollen lips, and protruding bald pate—earned him the tabloid sobriquet "Monster." Tanaka, though, referred to him as a "sworn friend." They had met as young men in 1947, when a prophetic mutual acquaintance decided to introduce "the biggest politician in Japan" to "the biggest businessman in Japan." "We'd go drinking" was how Osano described their relationship years later. But their ties developed much further than that. Osano was a frequent investor, lender, adviser, and purchaser in Tanaka's complicated financial schemes. Tanaka, meanwhile, was a valuable friend in a high place. When Tanaka was finance minister in 1963, Osano secured a special waiver to Japan's strict capital-export limits, allowing him to buy his first Hawaii hotel. Tanaka's ministry also sold government-owned Tokyo real estate to Osano for a pittance. Osano, who reaped a handsome profit reselling the land on the open market, returned the favor, buying a near-bankrupt company from businessman Tanaka at far above the market value.

Osano was a heavy donor to Tanaka's political campaigns. During his summit meeting with Nixon in Hawaii, Tanaka stayed in an Osano hotel, and later he gave his pal a plum spot on the management committee of the national telephone monopoly. Wags snidely referred to Tanaka's premiership as the "Tanaka-Osano Trading House."

Associates often warned Tanaka that he was risking political—and legal—trouble by so blithely blurring the line between doing good and doing well. "Tanaka is somebody who walks on the fence of prison," Shigeru Yoshida, the doyen of early postwar politics, quipped. Tanaka himself never seemed perturbed by such perceptions, once telling a group of legislators, "You can't be called a man if you are afraid of going to jail once or twice."

He had, in fact, landed there in 1948—during his first parliamentary term—for taking a bribe from the coal industry to oppose state control of the mines. At least, that's how prosecutors had seen things when they had charged him. Tanaka did not deny the facts: he had voted against the bill and taken the money. But he maintained his innocence, arguing that the two actions were unrelated. "The one-million-yen check I accepted from the mine operator was an advance payment on construction work [by Tanaka Construction]," he told the authorities. Refusing to concede even the appearance of an ethical problem, Tanaka unapologetically filed his reelection papers from the Tokyo Detention House. Upon his release ten days before the vote, he told constituents, "My conscience is perfectly clear." He won the election and, though convicted by one court in 1950, won his appeal the following year.

Over the next twenty years, Tanaka and his Etsuzankai support group had, by one estimate, nearly a dozen more "brushes with the law," most involving "misuse of public office." In 1955, two Tanaka underlings were arrested for embezzlement and misappropriation from the public railroad Tanaka had saved with such fanfare a few years back. In the early 1960s, clouds appeared over contract awards for a new highway and a series of dams that Tanaka had brought to the district, once again landing close Tanaka backers in jail. In each case, Tanaka himself was also investigated personally, though he was never charged with any crimes.

As he rose to national prominence, suspicion of wrongdoing trailed Tanaka like a shadow. In 1966, he was forced to resign as national secretary-general of the Liberal Democratic Party over accusations of cronyism in the bargain-price sale of public lands. Even at the peak of the "Tanaka boom," rumblings arose about his business ethics. In late 1972, the opposition parties managed to turn Prime Minister Tanaka's geisha turned mistress into a miniscandal—not because of his marital infidelity but because she was apparently serving as a front for some of his funny-money land deals. A few months later, a Communist MP alleged during parliamentary proceedings that Tanaka had leaked advance information about government projects to land-investing friends, drawing a furious outburst from the red-faced Tanaka.

Each of these "incidents," as the Japanese press calls scandals, blew over quickly, slowing Tanaka's skillfully navigated power drive only slightly. Many of the charges were dismissed in their time as reckless rhetorical grenades from the Left; instead of investigating the Communist's suspicions, for example, Parliament suspended the accuser for twenty days for spreading malicious slander. The lesson Tanaka seemed to derive from that long experience of dodging allegations was that he would always beat the rap. But he was wrong. Those scandals were the persistent early-warning symptoms of a serious, career-threatening ailment.

THE NITTY-GRITTY of governing is always more formidable than the heady promises of campaigning, as Tanaka learned shortly into his term as prime minister. The centerpiece of his domestic agenda—the grand scheme to redirect industry—quickly collapsed under the weight of short-term economic crises. In 1973, business conditions, policy missteps, and then the Arab oil embargo pushed Japan's annual inflation rate to 30 percent, among the worst in the industrialized world. The "crazy prices" touched off the first widespread consumer panic since the dark days just after the war, as housewives, fearing shortages, stampeded stores for everything from heating oil to detergent to toilet paper. The bright neon lights of Tokyo's Ginza shopping district, an emblem of the nation's thriving commercial culture, were dimmed to conserve scarce energy. A communal gloom settled in over the nation; the hottest novel of Tanaka's reign, turned into a blockbuster movie, was *The Sinking of Japan*.

The times called for austerity. But Tanaka had built his whole career around the simple formula of winning votes by showering constituents with government largess, and he clung stubbornly to his sanguine pledge for more and better growth. He exacerbated inflationary pressures by pushing through a giant increase in public spending and a deep tax cut. His blind obsession with "archipelago remodeling" turned irritating. The people wanted a "firm determination to put down inflation and control disruptions of their economic life," one newspaper editorial pleaded after yet another oblivious policy speech by the prime minister; they certainly didn't want "another lecture, no matter how well intentioned, about why the construction of more bullet-train lines and three . . . bridges is necessary to sustain Japan's economy and population ten years from now." By early 1974, Tanaka's grandiose "remodeling" brainchild was widely derided as "the grand illusion of economic development," and he was forced to drop it.

The hopes Tanaka stirred for a more independent, Asian-oriented diplomacy were also soon dashed. Barely a year after his warm welcome in China, he was disgraced in Southeast Asia, where smoldering anti-Japanese sentiment—the aftermath of Japan's World War II military invasion, stoked by recent economic incursions—mixed dangerously with unstable politics. In Thailand, a mob paraded his effigy, labeled "Tanaka, Ugly Economic Imperialist," outside his hotel. In Indonesia, he was a virtual prisoner inside the Presidential Palace for three days as demonstrators outside smashed Japanese cars, pushed them into canals, and torched the Toyota distribution center. The Indonesian police killed eleven rioters during the visit, which the Japanese leader had to cut short by fleeing Jakarta early one morning by helicopter.

Japan's domestic politics, too, proved far more sticky than Tanaka had imagined. Despite his popularity, he was unable to stanch the conservatives' early-1970s decline. In elections for the lower house of Parliament in December 1972, Tanaka's stumping tours drew unusually large, enthusiastic throngs. But his Liberal Democratic Party still suffered heavy losses and fell to its lowest strength since its founding; the Communists, meanwhile, who kept promising more social services, especially for urban small businesses, continued their surge, nearly tripling their legislative power. In the 1974 elections for Parliament's upper house, the LDP clung to a bare three-seat majority. Squabbles also flared up within the party. A group of young right-wing politicians, furious about Tanaka's continued overtures to Communist China, formed the "Blue Storm Society." Members joined the group by taking a gangster-style blood oath, and they sometimes acted like mobsters

—in one intraparty debate, the upstarts toppled desks, smashed glasses, and hurled sushi.

Tanaka did not handle these stark realities of office well. His temper grew short. "Some call him mini-Hitler now," one newsmagazine reported. He got easily flustered in parliamentary debates and frequently made embarrassing gaffes requiring retraction. Unable to boost the LDP's strength through elections, Tanaka rashly tried to overhaul the entire electoral system. So blatant a power grab drew protests even from within his own party; after the ensuing commotion virtually shut down Parliament for a month, he was forced into a humiliating retreat. Under the strain, Tanaka's health deteriorated. An ear infection sent him to the hospital for a week in December 1973. He came out with a bad case of facial neuritis that left his right cheek frozen for three months. When he spoke, his words were slurred and his face twisted into grotesque contortions. Many people saw more than a medical explanation: "His face shows the uneasy state of his mind," a housewife was quoted as saying, "which is the result of his policy failures."

Popular disappointment was especially perilous for a politician such as Tanaka. He had, after all, ridden to power on mass expectations that his commoner's touch, combined with the no-nonsense efficiency of a self-made businessman, would succeed where distant bureaucrats had failed. His spotty record after two tough years in office inevitably led to a reassessment of that image.

The turning point came in the summer of 1974. At the time, industry leaders were extremely worried about the Left's electoral advances and the implications for Japan's fundamentally probusiness stance. Tanaka's advisers proposed what seemed like a logical, mutually convenient solution: just as Tanaka's Echigo Transport conglomerate ran his campaigns back in Niigata, corporations should "buy" candidates, then "sell" them to the voters. Major banks, automakers, and steel producers, even cosmetics companies, signed on to sponsor specific conservative politicians. In one instance, the twenty-seven companies of the large Mitsubishi group rallied to raise funds and votes among its 300,000 employees for one LDP candidate, while the seventy-five-year-old chairman of Mitsubishi Electric Corporation personally jetted around the country, coordinating the campaign.

The strategy backfired. The brazen collusion between big business and top politicians provoked an outpouring of denunciation against "money-power politics" gone too far. The Mitsubishi stooge lost. Furthermore, the outrage alerted Tanaka's rivals to the force of the issue—as well as to his vulnerability on that score. One of the first to pick up the cudgel was Takeo Fukuda, who was still sore about losing, two years earlier, the premiership he considered his entitlement and eager to unseat the man who had swiped it. During the 1974 national parliamentary election campaign, Fukuda seemed less intent on helping the LDP than on undercutting the party president. "The trend of money-based politics is too strong," he taunted at one campaign stop. "Politics must be conducted cleanly." Fukuda and two other senior politicians quit Tanaka's cabinet with much fanfare after the election, claiming shock at the premier's free-spending political style and raising a new banner: "Reform the LDP." This time, the charges started to stick. The attacks intensified through the summer, until Tanaka's name became all but synonymous with "money-power politics." America's Watergate scandal, which forced Richard Nixon from office that August, invited Nixon-Tanaka comparisons and fueled the crusade by heightening sensitivity to corruption in high places.

Inspired by the investigative journalism that had toppled a sitting U.S. president, a respected Japanese intellectual magazine called *Bungei Shunju* assembled a crack team of twenty researchers to get to the bottom of Tanaka's "gold-studded background." The detailed exposé, published in early October under the title "A Study of Kakuei Tanaka: His Money & His Men," ran an exhaustive forty pages. The articles provided intricate details of Tanaka's properties, his past scandals, his "ghost companies," his constant conversion of power into profit. Much of the report was actually a rehash of old allegations or unconfirmed innuendo—the authors typically cited "standard rumor" on reports that "Tanaka spent as much as 25 million yen to completely renovate his house in Niigata with precious cypress wood." But it was the first time any publication had presented the whole rather incredible record in one account, and it effectively cast Tanaka in a new, harsher light, arguing that his political career had been one long confidence game. "Was there a connection," the magazine suggested at one point, "between his political enthusiasm and his passion for more land?"

Tanaka's response only worsened matters. The first time he was cornered into commenting on the magazine exposé—at a luncheon speech to foreign journalists—he turned pale and stormed out of the session. He seemed genuinely unable to understand why his behavior might be considered improper. He did not—could not—dispute most of the facts that had been published. But as with his run-in with the prosecutors over the 1948 coal bribery case, he insisted that somehow his two careers should be judged separately—even though he himself clearly ran them together. "It is regrettable that the article mixed up my business dealings with my politics," he grumbled at a press conference devoted to answering the charges. Echoing Nixon's "I am not a crook" refrain, he repeated over and over, "I have done nothing illegal."

Those were hardly reassuring words. Merely "to stay out of legal prosecution is not enough," the *Mainichi* newspaper retorted. "Moral integrity is a key for political leaders to gain people's confidence." "He should have been critical enough of himself to realize that, for a politician at the pinnacle of power, the public and private phases of his life were the same," the *Yomiuri* newspaper lectured.

A couple of years earlier, Tanaka's protestations might have gotten a sympathetic public hearing, but in 1974 the Japanese people were no longer in a tolerant mood. Two years of rampant inflation had done more than erode incomes; they had undermined the common assumption that the fruits of Japan's postwar growth were being divided fairly. The conviction that Japan was a "lantern-shaped society" with its 90 percent middle class had been a crucial foundation of support for the LDP. Now the middle-class housewives who had been reduced to brawling with neighbors for an extra roll of toilet paper resented the sectors that were profiting—the large trading companies, for example, that were widely suspected of jacking up prices, even when shortages did not exist, to reap a windfall from the panic buying.

By failing to slam a lid on prices, the man chosen as the "people's prime minister" now seemed to side with the LDP's fat-cat contributors. When Tanaka promised during one parliamentary address "to conduct the affairs of government so that social justice will be attained—so the honest will not be cheated," he was hooted down with jeers. Then the mob turned on Tanaka's personal wealth. Protesters outside his Tokyo home wielded papier-mâché knives and chanted, "Let's kill Tanaka's [$3,000] carp and eat them."

The thing that really stuck in the collective Japanese craw was Tanaka's extensive real estate portfolio, laid bare in great detail in the *Bungei Shunju* report. The early-1970s hyperinflation had hit the land market particularly hard, making homeownership all the more unthinkable for millions of Japanese. It was bad enough when people realized that Tanaka's "archipelago-remodeling" plan, by touching off a speculative stampede in anticipation of major new government projects, had been a major cause of the skyrocketing real estate prices. But, as the magazine exposé pointed out, it was altogether unforgivable that the prime minister and his pals had profitably played that market. Tanaka was no longer the "commoners' premier"; he was just another member of the odious nouveau-riche cabal of parasitic speculators. Because Tanaka had raised hopes so much, this was more than disappointing; it was betrayal. His public support rating, once a record-high 62 percent, plunged to a record-low 12 percent.

By November 1974, events were spinning completely beyond Tanaka's control. "Tanaka's money veins" dominated the front pages. Opposition politicians trooped to Niigata to conduct an investigation of his ill-gotten lands. Tanaka faced open mutiny in his own party: an LDP "League for Party Reconstruction" openly clamored for a formal inquiry, while, behind the scenes, Fukuda and other Tanaka rivals were actively scheming to bring the premier down. Amid the mayhem, Tanaka had no choice but to accept the scheduling of embarrassing parliamentary hearings on his personal finances; a date was set for later that month with a close Tanaka aide slated to testify first.

Tanaka tried to divert attention with a two-week diplomatic foray, but he himself was plainly rattled by the growing din at home. During a state banquet in Australia, he drank glass after glass of wine; in between his numerous trips to the bathroom, he lectured the Australian prime minister with wild gesticulations, forcing his rattled host to dodge Tanaka's flailing fork and knife. Tanaka was exhausted, his aides said. His blood pressure and his sugar count shot up, while his eyes often seemed to bulge out of his head.

First thing on the morning of Tuesday, November 26, Tanaka went to the Buddhist altar in his Tokyo home and told his ancestors he was going to make "an important decision" later that day. Outside, he encountered dozens of reporters, some of whom had been waiting since five A.M. "I am in a serene state of mind," he told them. After a cabinet meeting, Tanaka's spokesman read to the press a brief statement titled "My Determination." "I have not rested even a day since I left my hometown without a single yen in my pocket," the pronouncement said. As a politician, "I did my best to . . . improve the people's livelihood with a sense of decision and action." But "political confusion . . . has resulted from my personal problems," he acknowledged. There was no choice: "I have decided to resign as prime minister and president of the Liberal Democratic Party."

"I must have been possessed by some evil spirit," he told associates that night. "There is an evil spirit you cannot control." It was a demon that would haunt Tanaka for the rest of his life.

CHAPTER SIX
ARRESTED

FOR A TIME, though, Tanaka apparently thought he could exorcise the demon. An old Japanese proverb states that no scandal lasts longer than seventy-five days, and indeed, barely two months after his ignominious resignation, reports surfaced of a planned comeback. He kept his seat in Parliament and his membership in the party, and the various official investigations into the scandals were all petering out without punishment—without his even being questioned by the authorities. The probe into one suspicious land deal was dropped after the relevant documents mysteriously disappeared from the Construction Ministry's files. A criminal case, meanwhile, did lead to the conviction of two Tanaka business associates in late 1975, but they pleaded guilty without a trial, a move widely suspected as being an attempt to end the matter quickly and protect the boss. In the end, the only penalty Tanaka faced for all the fuss was a bill, reportedly for 40 million yen, in back taxes.

The disgraced leader and his backers started openly wielding influence again, advising the new prime minister, Takeo Miki, on parliamentary strategy and helping smooth over various crises such as a public workers' strike. Japan's political commentators, as if they were Kremlinologists, sought a deeper significance in Tanaka's every move. Some saw signs, for example, of rehabilitation in his appointment as chair of the funeral committee for former Prime Minister Eisaku Sato in mid-1975, one of Tanaka's first public appearances since his fall. "He is still young," a politician loyal to the charismatic Niigata politician crowed, noting that the fifty-seven-year-old Tanaka was eleven years younger than Prime Minister Miki and thirteen years younger than archenemy Fukuda, who was still angling for the top job. "The day will again come when his vitality and ability will be needed to get things done."

Then "Tanaka's money veins" sprang a new scandal, one far more serious than the manipulation of provincial marshland—graver, in fact, than any postwar political corruption case.

The "Lockheed Incident," as it is now called in Japanese history books, first surfaced in Watergate-obsessed Washington, where investigators wading through the records of Nixon's slush funds stumbled on evidence that U.S. corporations had given shady contributions to foreign politicians as well. By the time the inquiry was through, more than five hundred U.S. companies had admitted making questionable payoffs to win business all over Asia, Europe, and the Middle East. One of the most active was the Lockheed Aircraft Corporation, America's biggest defense contractor and a major civilian manufacturer. Lockheed's confession of having paid $55 million in such overseas "donations" single-handedly touched off political upheavals in the Netherlands, Germany, and Italy. But nowhere did the revelations stir up as much turmoil as in Japan.

In February 1976, Lockheed president A. Carl Kotchian told a U.S. Senate committee hearing that he had personally arranged for bribes to "high government officials" in Tokyo to win a hotly contested contract, worth $430 million, to sell wide-bodied jets to a leading Japanese commercial airline. He did not name names or provide much detail. But that was enough to launch a public frenzy in Tokyo. Within two weeks, Parliament was holding special hearings that drew huge national television audiences. By month's end, nearly four hundred government agents had raided twenty-nine locations seeking evidence. The U.S. government, wary of fomenting political instability in a close ally, declared it would keep crucial documents related to the matter confidential—until March, after Prime Minister Miki wrote an emotional personal letter to President Gerald Ford pleading that, if the scandal were covered up, it would destroy democracy in Japan.

In late June, the Japanese authorities started rounding up the perpetrators. In one day, four executives from two corporations involved in the affair were arrested. Two weeks later, two more suspects were detained. By July 20, a dozen men, mainly corporate officials, were behind bars for their alleged involvement in the complex scheme. But the country was still waiting for the other shoe to drop—no politician had yet been touched.

At 6:30 A.M. on July 27, the dragnet finally reached the wooden front gate of the Tokyo estate of a "high government official": former prime minister Tanaka. He said he had not slept well that night, waking four hours earlier with a premonition that something bad would happen that day. Now two representatives of the Tokyo prosecutors office were politely presenting themselves to one of his servants, saying they would like to escort Mr. Tanaka to their office for a few questions. He put on his standard dark blue suit with a light blue necktie and sat between the two men in the backseat of their black sedan.

Upon arrival, the tanned politician offered a wan smile and wave to the gathered reporters. The session lasted barely more than an hour. The interrogators were deferential but resolute: "We are very sorry to have to investigate a person who was once prime minister of Japan, but we must ask you to tell the truth in order to find out the truth," one prosecutor began. Tanaka denied any involvement in the matter. "Please take care of yourself," an inquisitor said gently as the interview ended. "Thank you," replied Tanaka with a wave. "Thank you. Thank you." He was then formally arrested and ignominiously dragged to the same dreary Tokyo Detention House where he had been incarcerated twenty-eight years earlier in the coal bribery affair. That day, he was charged with violating the Foreign Trade and Exchange Control Law by taking money illegally from foreigners. The bribery indictment came a few days later; if convicted, Tanaka would face a five-year jail term. While Tanaka sat in the "pig-box," as Japan's criminals call a detention cell, a team of prosecutors spent eleven hours scouring his home and carting out box upon box of documents.

If it hadn't been for the gravity of the matter, the case would actually have seemed somewhat humorous, like an amateur production of a cloak-and-dagger B movie. The sordid affair, prosecutors charged, had started in August 1972, just six weeks after Tanaka had become prime minister. Hiro Hiyama, president of the Marubeni Corporation general trading company, which Lockheed had hired as its official sales agent in Japan, had come calling early one morning to congratulate the premier on his recent victory. As the new head of the government, Tanaka had a lot on his mind: he was leaving the next week for a summit with President Nixon to try to patch up the fraying alliance, planning his historic trip to China, and starting to implement his daring economic reconstruction plan. But Hiyama wanted to take just a moment of his time with a more mundane matter: if Tanaka could just make sure that All Nippon Airways (ANA) bought Lockheed planes, he'd get a cut of 500 million yen, worth $1.6 million at the time. Tanaka supposedly gave his trademark reply of approval, *"Yossha, yossha,"* and it was agreed. The entire meeting lasted but a few minutes.

Tanaka is said to have called the ANA president later that month to urge the Lockheed purchase. In a particularly shameful twist, the prosecutors charged, he dragged in U.S.-Japanese tensions to earn his bribe, claiming that Nixon had personally requested that ANA buy Lockheed aircraft as a way of cutting Japan's trade surplus. In October, ANA finally got the message and made the right choice. But after winning the bid, Lockheed president Kotchian had second thoughts about making the payoff. The Marubeni president, through an underling, told him it was "very serious": if Lockheed reneged on the deal, it would never sell so much as another monkey wrench in Japan again. And Marubeni's Hiyama would have to leave Japan for good.

Lockheed delivered the cash in four installments in 1973 and 1974. Each time, the company's Tokyo manager handed over to a Marubeni official a cardboard box stuffed with piles of yen. (One Japanese commentator scoffed that the box was a typically uncouth American touch; a Japanese briber, he said, would surely have wrapped the money carefully in a tasteful cloth bundle.) In return, Marubeni would give Lockheed a typed receipt, signed by a trading company executive, saying "I received 150 pieces" or, one time, "I received 100 peanuts"—a "piece" or "peanut" being the not-so-subtle code for one million yen. A Marubeni man would then take the valuable box to a prearranged rendezvous spot—one time a street behind the British Embassy, other times a public phone booth or a hotel parking lot—where Tanaka's waiting limousine would pick up the package.

"The nation was shocked," the *Yomiuri* newspaper blasted the day after the arrest, "to learn that a man of his rank had accepted dirty money from a foreign business corporation. . . . Kakuei Tanaka has the dubious distinction of being the first prime minister in history to sell out the nation for private gain." He was, indeed, the first Japanese premier ever to face criminal charges for abusing his position. Newspapers rushed out extras. When the news broke, trading on the busy Osaka Stock Exchange came to a temporary, stunned halt. Crowds gathered in a downtown park to demand a full airing of the scandal and punishment of those involved. THE PEOPLE OF THE NATION, one handwritten placard declared, CANNOT BE DECEIVED. An unarmed, middle-aged drifter was apprehended after scaling the wall into Tanaka's private garden; he had wanted to personally urge the politician to commit hara-kiri, or ritual suicide. Marubeni, too, drew scorn for its role. Local governments all over the country canceled contracts with the trading house. Marubeni employees complained that their children were being harangued by classmates for having family ties to "the bad, bad company"; one such child got stuck with the schoolyard nickname "Lockheed."

The most bizarre response came from a young porno movie actor dressed in full kamikaze regalia, complete with a rising-sun headband, who dive-bombed a rented Piper-Cherokee airplane smack into the home of a Japanese consultant to Lockheed. The suicide mission was apparently intended to protest the shame the affair had brought upon the nation; the pilot's final words, shrieked over the plane's radio, were *"Tenno heika BANZAI!"* (Long live the emperor!). The target of his attack, a well-known fixer named Yoshio Kodama, escaped unscathed. But when Kodama tried to check into a hospital for treatment of a chronic illness, an angry mob forced him to turn around and go home. Later, four armed ultrarightists took over the headquarters of Keidanren, the national big-business trade group, and held four staffers hostage for more than ten hours. "The Lockheed scandal has rocked the nation's free-society system to its roots," their manifesto protested.

People were furious, not only because of the obvious dishonor of having a prime minister on the take but because the Lockheed affair, as it turned out, had stained much of the Japanese power structure. While Tanaka was at the center of the caper, he was by no means the only one implicated. A total of eighteen men were eventually arrested. Two were respected leaders of the big-business world: the presidents of the Marubeni trading company and All Nippon Airways. Two were conservative politicians who, like Tanaka, were arrested for taking bribes. There were four "gray" politicians—MPs who, Lockheed said, had received money but who were never indicted. (Lockheed's executives, meanwhile, were given immunity from prosecution in Japan in return for their testimony.) The scandal's fallout even forced the president of NHK, Japan's leading television broadcast system, to resign his post; a public uproar ensued after he paid a friendly personal condolence call to Tanaka after the arrest. Then there was the eccentric district judge in Kyoto who somehow came up with the idea of making a midnight phone call to Prime Minister Miki in which, impersonating a prosecutor, he urged a stop to the arrest of politicians. He later offered mental instability as a motive and had to relinquish his position.

One notably disturbing facet of the scandal was the exposure of the clout of Kodama, a notorious underworld boss. The American aircraft company said it had paid Kodama $6 million for his services as a special agent supplementing Marubeni's role. No evidence surfaced that Kodama had ever dealt directly with Tanaka on the issue. But he seems to have been able to pull a number of other important strings in the business and political world in order to, as Kotchian put it, "establish a climate in which our product would be properly received." Kodama had apparently pulled off such fantastic feats as engineering a scandal to oust an ANA executive who favored a competitor over Lockheed. He had also introduced Lockheed executives to magnate Kenji Osano, who was both Tanaka's "sworn friend" and ANA's tenth largest shareholder—and who, after receiving more than a million dollars from Lockheed, was willing to lobby both.

That a man such as Kodama had such valuable connections was a national disgrace. His ideology tended toward ultranationalism and militarism; his modus operandi was blackmail, intimidation, and violence. Before the war, he had been jailed for, among other things, plotting a failed "state massacre" to assassinate a large part of the business and political establishment. After the war, he had been imprisoned again, as a suspected "Class A" war criminal. In between, he had made a fortune procuring strategic raw materials in China for the Imperial Navy—or rather, stealing the minerals, then selling them to his government at a huge profit.

Kodama had used part of his booty to help fund the new postwar conservative parties, thereby gaining pull with politicians. He had been a prison buddy of one future LDP prime minister, Nobusuke Kishi, and a close friend of other party bosses. Kodama also wove into and out of the worlds of *yakuza* gangsters and extreme rightists, serving as a broker between those groups and the mainstream conservatives. He could do useful things that, officially, the government could not. In 1939, Japan's Foreign Ministry had sent him to Hong Kong to round up bodyguards for a Chinese leader collaborating with Japan; in 1960, he had organized a private army of nearly fifty thousand gangsters, rightists, and others to help police a planned state visit by American President Dwight D. Eisenhower. (Despite Kodama's extra security force, leftist riots over the U.S.-Japan security treaty had forced Eisenhower to cancel the trip.) Kodama also managed to frighten anybody, including top political and business leaders, who crossed him—such as the time he sent a messenger to ask an MP, at sword point, to halt a certain line of questions in Parliament. The very night before the Lockheed scandal surfaced, several LDP politicians attended a swank banquet thrown in Kodama's honor, and for a full week after Kodama's name had been linked to the Lockheed affair, his friends in the police supposedly kept his whereabouts a secret.

The implication was becoming clear: perhaps Tanaka was not a monstrous aberration, as many Japanese had liked to believe when his money scandals had surfaced a couple of years earlier. Maybe he was, in fact, a fitting captain for a ship of state rotten to the core. "The whole LDP and its traditional practices are under indictment," a senior conservative MP stated tearfully on the floor of Parliament after Tanaka's arrest. "All of the evils accumulated under the conservative party system during the past 30 years are now out" in the open, the *Mainichi* newspaper moaned. Tanaka's detention, it continued, "warned us to make a soul-searching reappraisal of postwar political history." Americans evidently saw the Japanese power structure as both rigged and buyable. "I think you should recognize," Lockheed's Kotchian told the assembled senators in that February 1976 hearing, justifying his dubious behavior, "that the Japanese establishment, if you want to call it that, is a fairly close-knit group of individuals, both in business and government." To enter that group, he explained, "you need some help." That the revelations had first come out in the United States—Japan's closest ally and its mentor in democracy—only heightened the embarrassment. "I thought [such] rampant bribery was seen only in underdeveloped countries," sneered Senator Frank Church, who was leading the congressional investigation.

It was all the more excruciating, of course, for Tanaka himself. RAGS TO RICHES TO JAIL was how one headline pithily traced his tragic arc. For twenty-one days after his arrest, Tanaka was confined in the detention house, where, like the murderers, bombing suspects, and other common criminals in that holding facility, he was stuck in a six-foot-by-nine-foot concrete cell adorned with collapsible desk and toilet—quite a comedown from his twenty-five-room mansion. He was fed a breakfast of cheap rice mixed with cheaper barley, a meal that "even a beggar hardly eats these days," one press account noted with vengeful glee. He was strip-searched upon incarceration and thereafter denied a watch and a belt to hold up his pants, routine precautions against prisoner suicide. Though famous for his profuse sweating, Tanaka was given only a bamboo hand fan to cut the sweltering Tokyo summer heat in his un-air-conditioned cell and allowed just one bath every five days. After the daily seven A.M. morning roll call, he would roll up his own bedding, then endure hours of prosecution grilling lasting well into the night.

When Tanaka was finally released for a near-record bail of 200 million yen—he managed to raise the money in just ten minutes—he found his world shattered. The press had dropped the honorific "san" after his name, now referring to him either as "Suspect Tanaka" or just plain "Tanaka." His longtime chauffeur, prodded by prosecutors to supply damaging information, had driven into the woods and asphyxiated himself with a hose attached to his car's tailpipe. Tanaka was forced to resign from the LDP. It was widely presumed that he would also relinquish control of the faction of MPs who had followed him and that, though he did not quit Parliament, he would do so soon.

The ritual public humiliation peaked in January 1977, with the opening of Tanaka's trial. A thousand people braved a cold morning rain to compete for the fifty-two spectator tickets assigned by lottery. "Your Honor, I swear that I have nothing to do with this case," began Tanaka's emotional half-hour declaration of innocence. By the last ten minutes, the well-known jut-jawed visage had dissolved into a stream of tears, the rapid-fire voice into halting, choked-up sobs. When the man once dubbed a "mini-Hitler" did manage to see and speak clearly enough to proceed, his hands—famed for their firm, sharp gestures—trembled to the point that he could not read the statement they held. "I am suffering even more than if I were put to death," he wailed. "My terrible misfortune has damaged the reputation of Japan. . . . I deeply apologize to the people."

Japan, it seemed, would never be the same again. "The foundations of this establishment-oriented society have been permanently shaken," a correspondent for *The New Yorker* magazine argued in a lengthy analysis of the Lockheed case and its fallout. "The case has passed beyond scandal into self-exploration and a search for new answers and motivations." Optimists thought the exposure and prosecution of such blatant corruption would cleanse the system, the *Mainichi* newspaper calling the event a "springboard" to "create a better and healthier political atmosphere." Many forecast the end of two decades of conservative one-party rule. The party started to fracture, with a half-dozen young, popular MPs quitting in disgust and forming their own reform party. At the very least, Tanaka, the figure who had dominated Japanese government since the early 1970s and come to symbolize "money-power politics," was surely crushed.

"This is an opportunity to strengthen democracy in Japan and build a foundation for political reform," declared Prime Minister Miki, who bravely overcame powerful opponents to push full prosecution of the case. The "Lockheed Incident" indeed turned out to be a momentous turning point for Japanese democracy—but not in the ways that anyone had expected or desired.

PART TWO

THE "SHADOW SHOGUN OF MEJIRO": BUILDING A NATIONAL MACHINE, 1976–1985

FOR SEVEN YEARS, from 1977 to 1983, Kakuei Tanaka's courtroom nightmare persisted. Every Wednesday morning, he was summoned to drab Room 701 of the Tokyo District Courthouse and forced to sit, silent and fidgeting, at a bare hardwood table a few feet below three stern, robed judges. He was told when to rise and when to sit, forced to listen as a team of young prosecutors unveiled more and more intricate details of his alleged crimes. Journalists and spectators packed the small gallery; consistently among them was an anonymous elderly man with long white hair who, like an eccentric prophet, would mutter indistinguishably while shaking a finger at the famous defendant. Security in the halls was unusually tight, with throngs of guards and plainclothes policemen and metal detectors tuned so sensitively that coins set them off. Outside the building crowds gathered, some merely to witness the spectacle of the former premier's arrival and departure, others—usually right-wing thugs with ear-splitting loudspeakers—to berate him.

In January 1983, the state finally wrapped up its case with a 560-page closing statement, read out from morning to night by a tag team of four prosecutors. They demanded that Tanaka be found guilty, fined 500 million yen, and sentenced to the maximum five years of hard labor in prison, a punishment, they said, befitting a man who had "seriously damaged popular trust in the political and administrative establishments."

But for the rest of each week during that seven-year stretch, at his estate just a half-hour drive from the courthouse in his dark blue Chrysler sedan, Tanaka cut quite a different figure. Other than on those Wednesday mornings when the master of the house was otherwise engaged, a stream of visitors started entering the Tanaka residence at 7:30 A.M., and by the end of each day as many as three hundred had passed through. In the morning, they were generally rough-skinned farmers and other constituents who had traveled by overnight train from the countryside; in the afternoon, top pols, business executives, senior government officials in blue suits. They sought everything from a sample of Tanaka's handwriting or a job for a son to his backing in an election, his help brokering the deregulation of Japan's telecommunications industry, or a decision on which construction company would build what dam. "Visiting Tanaka at his home gave power to politicians, businessmen, and bureaucrats," a Tanaka acolyte said. "You could become a cabinet minister by visiting Tanaka. You could not become a cabinet minister if he disliked you." In 1983, Tanaka boasted to one visitor that a dozen important policy decisions were at that moment awaiting his approval. He obliged everybody the best he could, jotting down memos for aides to follow up, making a quick phone call, occasionally handing out bills from his wallet. For his Niigata constituents, he ended the sessions by posing for a quick snapshot in the garden.

The meetings tended to last at most five to ten minutes each, after which Tanaka would push down the head of a small gold turtle engraved with birds, stars, and flowers that rang a bell to summon the next guest. The waiting area often got so crowded that visitors had a hard time finding a seat or even a place to stand, and the overflow would spill over onto the grounds; at the end of 1981, a new hall with a seating capacity of two hundred was added to the main house. Outside the estate's tall gates, an ever-present crowd of reporters, including cameramen tiptoeing on ladders trying to get a glimpse inside, stood watch to see who came. In Niigata, these visits were officially called the "Mejiro pilgrimage," named for the neighborhood where Tanaka lived, and Tanaka once jokingly compared his residence to Asakusa, one of Tokyo's busiest temples: "Some people are encouraging me to become a religious guru, enshrining a deity like Benten," the Japanese goddess of good fortune.

Despite the taint of a criminal corruption trial—and, oddly, in many ways, because of it—Tanaka in 1983 remained the most important politician in Japan. He could never become prime minister again as long as the bribery allegations hung over him. But only Tanaka himself was allowed to sit in the chair at Mejiro known as "the prime minister's seat." And he managed to become more powerful, even, than when he had been prime minister; more powerful, certainly, than the hapless series of men who succeeded him in that job, whom he virtually hired and controlled at will. Rather than suffering the expected expulsion from the nation's power structure, Tanaka used his unparalleled might to forge that structure into his own national political machine.

From the time he had first entered Parliament in the 1940s, Tanaka had devoted himself to studying and exploiting the weaknesses of Japan's postwar democratic system. From 1976 to 1983, the years between his arrest and the verdict in his trial, he masterfully converted major components of that system—the voters, the Liberal Democratic Party, the opposition parties, the elite bureaucracy, business—into interconnected gears running a continuous "conveyor belt" (Tanaka's own words) of money and power. The man who had once been the "commoners' prime minister" was transmogrified into, as the press started calling him, the "Shadow Shogun of Mejiro."

CHAPTER SEVEN

BACK TO THE SNOW COUNTRY

THE STORY of Tanaka's remarkable resilience begins, like that of his original rise, in the mountainous snow country along the Japan Sea. This was where he had had to lay the foundation for his national political organization: without the solid support of Niigata's voters, Tanaka's career would have been over; with it, he could never be completely destroyed, no matter how much the rest of the country reviled him.

At first, much of the Tokyo elite celebrated the Lockheed scandal as Tanaka's political death knell. Perhaps some assumed that he would be so ashamed, he would simply retire in disgrace. But Tanaka decided instead to face "the stern judgment of the public," leaving his fate up to the voters in his district. The first test of his populist strength as an accused felon would come barely four months after his arrest, in parliamentary elections set for December 5, 1976. "The battle of the century is about to open," the head of his Etsuzankai support group wrote in an appeal launching the campaign. "Keep the fort secure!"

It had been thirteen years since Tanaka had bothered to campaign in his district at all, but in his 1976 "revival operation" he invoked the exhaustive guerrilla tactics of his earliest elections, once again plunging deep into the tiny mountain villages no other politician would approach. It was an odd spectacle: in 1947, the young, unknown candidate had traveled this rough terrain alone by foot; now, as a former prime minister, he sped through in a mud-caked limousine, a full entourage of aides, bodyguards, and journalists in tow. (The flaccid entourage had some trouble keeping up: one group of out-of-town reporters gave up the chase at a narrow mountain trail, and a Tokyo newspaper's car tumbled more than seven feet off the road when the driver misjudged a sharp turn.) No crowd was too small for Tanaka's "street preaching," sometimes delivered to just a dozen elderly farmers. No staging was too humble, as he mounted podiums holding his own umbrella to fend off the heavy wet flakes of early winter. After retiring to his inn late each night, Tanaka would pore over detailed written reports of that day's crowds, adjusting his strategy accordingly for the next day. By the time the three-week official campaign period had ended, the candidate had logged well over 1,500 miles crisscrossing the district and delivered more than 500 speeches, sometimes 40 in a day. He shook so many hands that, at times, blood spots seeped through his white gloves, the traditional Japanese electioneering garb worn to signify purity.

Tanaka's audacity drew a chorus of tirades. "I do not think it appropriate for Tanaka to run," said Niigata's governor. "We will not ask for his help on important issues anymore." Local schoolteachers had been mortified when Tanaka's Etsuzankai support group had sent a letter to his prison cell urging him to become a candidate again; the educators had asked for a retraction, fearing the message would damage children's trust in democracy. The sharpest harangues came from Tokyo, with the national newspapers uniting in denunciation. TANAKA MAKES WRONG MOVE, grumbled the headline of a *Yomiuri* newspaper editorial after Tanaka announced plans to seek reelection. "Some nerve!" scowled the *Mainichi* newspaper. "He has no sense of shame at all." Since Tanaka refused to leave politics gracefully, an *Asahi* columnist exhorted Niigata's voters to "defeat the Etsuzankai logic" and kick him out. The national leader of the Socialist Party took the unprecedented step of kicking off his countrywide stumping tour in Tanaka's district. "He must stop," the leftist cried.

Tanaka deftly turned all this to his advantage. After all, he had spent thirty years indoctrinating his constituents in the belief that they were oppressed by the Tokyo establishment. Now Tanaka's arrest and the subsequent attacks were portrayed as part of the same plot, an attempt to crush the one man who had stood up for the snow country against the Pacific coast cabal. The Etsuzankai's campaign leaflets depicted their leader's scandals as an "inhuman . . . frame-up" by the "degree-holding elite because [Tanaka] is not a university graduate." One handbill canonized Tanaka as a modern-day Nichiren, the thirteenth-century monk exiled to the Japan Sea for his controversial religious beliefs who had launched one of Buddhism's most enduring sects. "People over there have never seen the snow," Tanaka bellowed with disdain at one campaign stop. "They have been under sunshine for a hundred years." "There" was the capital city across the mountain range, and "snow" meant not just nature's hardships but the indignities and neglect heaped on top by the national government.

In the days leading up to the election, Tanaka's campaigners set a vote goal: "If we cannot collect 100,000, I will apologize to Tanaka *sensei* by committing hara-kiri," one booster pledged, affixing to the politician's name the honorific term—literally "teacher"—used for MPs. Pundits said he would do well to draw that many votes. But when the results came in on the night of December 5, even Tanaka's most enthusiastic proponents were stunned: the candidate had won 168,522 votes, more than triple the tally for his nearest competitor in his district and the third highest of any politician anywhere in the country. As a defendant under indictment, Tanaka saw his vote count drop less than 10 percent from the previous election in 1972, when he had been the new prime minister and at the peak of his national popularity. "Tanaka *sensei*, banzai! Lockheed means nothing!" came the shouts in front of a construction company, the local campaign headquarters. At the raucous celebration party, supporters humbly approached the magisterial victor, asking forgiveness for not delivering even more ballots from their families and promising to do better the next time. Tanaka faced the voters of Niigata twice more during his criminal trial, in 1979 and 1980; he would prove to be similarly triumphant, both times winning well above 100,000 votes and finishing far ahead of all competitors.

Tanaka often said that these results "purified" him of wrongdoing, as if the voters had carefully weighed the facts of the case and found him not guilty and as if that verdict should supersede whatever ruling would someday come from the court. But that wasn't quite accurate. One poll taken during the 1976 election showed that even among Etsuzankai members, only 8 percent thought Tanaka was innocent. And the campaigns were hardly thorough, open airings of the charges. Tanaka's standard 1976 stump speech, for example, deftly reduced the awkward matter of his arrest to an opening quip: "This was a cold summer for you"—an allusion to an unseasonable cool spell that had damaged the local crops—"but it was a bit hot for me." Or he would sometimes apologize, as he did in his statement announcing his campaign, not for any wrongdoing but for "having greatly inconvenienced the people." When an occasional heckler tried to broach the scandal, the domineering politician sneeringly dismissed the issue as irrelevant: "There I was talking about the future of Japan and he has to say, 'What about Lockheed?' "

Tanaka was right: his scandals were irrelevant to the campaigns. He had built his unshakable electoral rampart on one basic premise: that the fledgling democracy that had evolved in Niigata in those postwar years had little to do with morality, ideology, or other ethereal issues. The vote, for many, had become a kind of currency, to be paid to the candidate who brought home the most tangible benefits. Before Tanaka's arrest, no politician had delivered more profits to the impoverished region than he had, and many of the votes he received during his trial were his remuneration. "By your help twenty years ago, we built this place," one man volunteered shyly after a Tanaka campaign speech outside a fruit-packing station, drawing a hug from the candidate. Tanaka may have been a criminal, but he was Niigata's criminal. The mayor of one small hamlet compared Tanaka to the father of a poor family, the voters to the progeny: if the parent had not robbed, the mayor said, the children would have died.

More important, Tanaka persuaded the voters that, despite his legal troubles, he would continue to help them out. His best applause lines on the stump, delivered with shaking fist and sharp voice, were pledges such as "If a tunnel is constructed, it will enable you to commute on a snow-free road" or "If Route 353 is built, large factories will come seeking water and land!" As he would note, "This cannot happen in just any prefecture. . . . This can only be done in the course of [one politician's] consistent planning over thirty, thirty-five, forty, fifty years." "Our voters are told to exercise sound judgment and put an end to his career," mused one Niigata resident. "But do people with sound judgment really slit their own throats?"

Tanaka bestowed favors upon his flock by implementing an elaborate, machinelike process. Any constituent with practically any need could always turn for help to the politician or his Etsuzankai association. In its early years, the Etsuzankai had frequently gotten into trouble for illegally plying voters with food and drink. After the group had dropped such "obvious methods" of luring support, it had continued, as one critic pointed out, to base its appeal on "assisting people to make a profit." The Etsuzankai secretariat—working, under the benevolent photographic gaze of the politician as a young man, in the Nagaoka headquarters of Tanaka's Echigo Transport company—arranged for school admissions, marriages, and jobs, keeping detailed records of the requests and responses in a thick ledger. In a second volume, they registered area weddings and funerals, then sent out congratulatory cards or memorial wreaths in the boss's name to every possible ceremony, sometimes accompanied by a small cash gift. The group's office building doubled as a community center; the auditorium, equipped with a movie projector and a karaoke machine, was available for local social events. The Etsuzankai also acted as a sort of travel agency, specializing in "Mejiro pilgrimage" tours to Tokyo. "I learned from the Boy Scouts that traveling and eating together will create friendships," the organizer explained. In addition to the stop at Tanaka's estate, these three-day excursions included visits to the national Parliament and the Imperial Palace, and an evening at the theater.

While his staff took care of favors back in Niigata, in Tokyo Tanaka personally handled constituents' requests daily during those revolving-door meetings at Mejiro. Nothing was too inconsequential for his attention: When a small businessman wanted to buy the land on which an abandoned post office stood, Tanaka called the top-ranking postal bureaucrat and arranged a meeting. One poor Niigata teenager struggling to make a living in the capital came in one day, peddling newspapers; while all the other Niigata MPs had refused, noting that they already had subscriptions, Tanaka took out a second and urged the kid to persevere. Forty years later, the former delivery boy's eyes still welled up with tears as he recounted the gesture.

For all of this, Tanaka was a pragmatic politician, not a philanthropist. He could not rely on gratitude alone but needed a fail-safe system to make sure that those who backed him reaped the benefits and those who reaped the benefits backed him. For example, the Etsuzankai had a special auxiliary, the "True Hearts Circle," just for the thousands of people who got jobs through the group's good graces; the "True Hearts" were then encouraged to take vacation time during elections in order to campaign for Tanaka.

Meanwhile, the trillions of yen in national tax money that Tanaka raised for Niigata public works were essentially channeled not through the authorizing government agency but through the Etsuzankai. It was the Etsuzankai that decided which projects would qualify for funds, over time developing a special dispersal routine: early each year, the group's precinct leaders would submit requests to the town councils, which would sort them out and pass them on to the county leaders, who would refer the top priorities to the Etsuzankai secretariat. Then, each summer, before the Tokyo bureaucrats drew up the nation's annual budget, Tanaka's handpicked viceroy, Taiji Yamada—a trusted aide since joining Tanaka Construction just after the war—took a month to survey the Niigata domain, anointing projects for funding that year. Trailed by a retinue of fifty or so local functionaries, Yamada was greeted wherever he went with extravagant ceremonies performed by fawning villagers. The people in the valley village of Ojiya, trapped every winter behind a snow-buried mountain, wanted a new tunnel to ease their plight. One year, they gathered the best cedar from their forests, took three days and nights to assemble a large arch at the village border, then hired a professional calligrapher to adorn it with a sign beckoning WELCOME, YAMADA SENSEI, SECRETARY TO PRIME MINISTER. As Yamada's entourage neared, a horn used to herald festivals blared, and all but the invalids among Ojiya's two hundred citizens flocked to greet him. At a banquet, Yamada was given the seat of honor, and, one by one, community leaders knelt before him to fill his cup with sake. In election years, communities often competed with one another to show the highest pro-Tanaka voting rates in order to win such projects; it also helped if they chose an Etsuzankai official as mayor.

Public works projects represented Tanaka's greatest economic contribution to Niigata over the years. While rising in national politics, he was careful never to lose sight of the local vision he had offered in his first campaigns: of rectifying the historical exploitation suffered by Niigata, of transforming the region from a de facto colony into an industrial hub. Following on those first projects he had won in the 1940s, Tanaka literally reshaped the landscape of his district, turning useless flood zones into arable land and impassable land into concrete roads, adorning desolate rice paddies with endless train tracks that rose above the lush green crops like a new kind of vine. "In twenty years," he would boast, "we have somehow accomplished sixty percent of the things [Niigata] has longed for for more than a thousand years." Recounting how his earliest roads and tunnels had helped stem the tide of migrant workers out of Niigata, he vowed that, with even more spending, "there will be a flow [of workers] *from* Tokyo *to* Niigata." When Tanaka was urged, upon becoming prime minister, to refrain from enriching his own district and to worry more about the whole nation, he cried out in protest, "This is the last thing I can stop!" Indeed, the gush of national tax monies from Tokyo to the Japan Sea continued to swell during his premiership, after he resigned that post in disgrace, and—just as he promised during his 1976 campaign—after his arrest. By 1983, the year the Lockheed prosecution was concluding its case against Tanaka, Niigata was receiving more public works funding from the national budget than any of Japan's forty-six other prefectures. On a per capita basis, the snow country got two and a half times the national average in such monies, three times more than it paid out in taxes.

Over time, the projects paid for with that money became more and more grandiose. In the 1940s, Tanaka had fought to get narrow, single-lane mountain trails paved; by the early 1980s, he had managed to confer on his district two national superhighways, a high-speed bullet-train line, Japan's largest atomic energy complex, a new international university, and a government-designated "technopolis" to attract futuristic industries. Some projects seemed designed to be as ridiculously garish as possible to astound the locals—and nettle the rest of the country—with towering pork-barrel monuments to Tanaka's ineradicable clout. The supplicants of Ojiya, for example, got a tunnel with a brightly lit highway to run through the passageway; the total government tab for the thoroughfare, which averaged traffic of one car every ten minutes, was 1 billion yen—or 17 million yen ($73,000) for each of the sixty families who benefited. In many locations, the shabby prior structure was left standing next to its replacement—for example, a narrow, winding road, covered by a flimsy metal overhang to keep off the snow, by a concrete tunnel–protected highway—to serve as an ever-present reminder of the magnitude of improvement.

Tanaka's most brazen show of influence was the high-speed rail line, inaugurated in 1982, that linked his district to Tokyo. When Japan's national railway launched the sleek bullet train in 1964, the world's fastest, 130-mile-per-hour system became a proud symbol of the nation's burgeoning, ultraefficient, high-technology might. Naturally, the bureaucratic planners chose to deploy this new asset where it could be built the most cheaply and quickly and serve the most riders—along the level terrain running among the dense population and industrial centers along the Pacific coast of *omote Nippon.* The mountainous *ura Nippon* backwater was not a priority until Tanaka, as a high-ranking LDP officer in the late 1960s, met with top railway officials and insisted, "Let's do bullet trains all over Japan"; he then grabbed a pencil and sketched on their map a red line straight from Tokyo to Niigata. With that, the bullet train was transformed into a new type of symbol: of bloated, politically driven waste.

The Niigata bullet-train line took eleven years and 1.7 trillion yen to build. At 6 billion yen per kilometer, it was purportedly the most expensive train line in the world, helping to plunge the entire Japanese national railway system into debt. More than one third of the line was built underground, boring through the world's longest tunnel. The construction cost was also boosted by the curious selection of station sites. Of the original eight stops, four were concentrated in Tanaka's district, while the rest were scattered among two other prefectures. Of those four in Tanaka's electorate, two were just fourteen miles apart, less than the gap preferred by the bureaucrats to maximize speed and efficiency. One station was inexplicably plunked down in the sleepy hamlet of Urasa, population 15,000. "The length of the platform nearly exceeds the length of the downtown," one visiting journalist observed, adding that the state-of-the-art station hovered over the town's dilapidated wooden buildings "like a mother spaceship landing on an alien planet."

As a final flourish, Tanaka ostentatiously branded many of these projects, lest there were any doubt that these were his personal legacies. In front of the Urasa station, for example, was erected a twelve-foot-tall, black, full-head-to-toe-length statue of the politician, right arm raised in his trademark wave, standing on a seventeen-foot-tall brown stone pedestal, a bright light illuminating the giant in the otherwise desolate darkness. The "Kan-etsu" superhighway was built with an interchange to Tanaka's hometown of Nishiyama, the former Futada; at the exiting tollbooth, tourists were given a map with directions to the Tanaka family home.

The Etsuzankai—founded in the 1950s as an idealistic, loosely organized political movement to develop an impoverished region—had evolved into a highly sophisticated political machine. The myriad independent local branches had been merged into a hierarchical pyramid, with Tanaka and his Echigo Transport at the top and successive tiers matching the layers of local government in the district.

The base consisted of more than three hundred neighborhood organizations, some representing as few as five families. This allowed information and requests to rise smoothly from the bottom of the pyramid to the top and marching orders and favors to flow quickly back down. Launched with just 80 members, the Etsuzankai's ranks had swelled to 98,000 by the early 1970s, or nearly 20 percent of the district's eligible voters. (In Japan's multiseat electoral system, in which each district elected up to six members, a 15 percent vote rate was more than enough to guarantee election.) Its *Monthly Etsuzan* newspaper had a circulation of more than fifty thousand. Sprouting from such deep roots, the group thoroughly infiltrated the Niigata power structure: twenty-six mayors of the thirty-three municipalities in Tanaka's district were affiliated with the Etsuzankai, as were nearly half of all members of city councils and the prefectural legislature. Etsuzankai director Koichi Honma—a sober, rail-thin man who had worked for Tanaka since 1946—came to be known by the 1970s as Niigata's "shadow governor." The Etsuzankai's influence even crossed party lines: while controlling the local Liberal Democratic Party, the group also helped elect a Socialist mayor in Nagaoka; the Nagaoka government then bought land from a Tanaka-affiliated company for a hefty price. In addition, the Etsuzankai "virtually controls . . . agricultural committees, popular welfare committees, election management committees," the *Asahi* newspaper reported in the mid-1970s. Local PTAs, too, were run by Etsuzankai members. The law enforcement agencies weren't impregnable either; one Niigata district prosecutor was persuaded to quit his job to work for the Etsuzankai and later joined Tanaka's Lockheed legal defense team.

To outsiders, it may have seemed incomprehensibly perverse that a man like Tanaka, so thoroughly stained by scandal, could continue to score one electoral landslide after another. But to those in Niigata, there was no other logical outcome. Tanaka's Etsuzankai had come to so dominate the district's affairs—political, business, social—that the locals had a saying, conceived only partly in jest: "Those who do not join the Etsuzankai are not even human." In the first issue of *Monthly Etsuzan* after Tanaka's arrest in 1976, forty-three voters wrote essays about their feelings toward their political boss. "Tanaka *sensei* is the politician who loves his homeland and works to improve our living," remarked the head of the Etsuzankai's Women's Communications Committee. "We will believe and support Tanaka *sensei* no matter what." By 1983, as Tanaka's criminal trial was winding down, nothing had changed:

according to a poll, 75 percent of the people of Niigata thought the region had profited from Tanaka, and, more significantly, 65 percent thought he was indispensable to their future welfare. (Half the respondents also chose him as the native son they were most proud of; the late Admiral Isoroku Yamamoto, who had led the successful naval attack on Pearl Harbor in 1941, finished a distant second with 22 percent support.) "It is the destiny of someone born in the snow country," Tanaka himself offered by way of explanation for his electoral wizardry. Niigata "will field me as candidate for election until I die."

CHAPTER EIGHT
BAGS OF MONEY

TANAKA'S NIIGATA ORGANIZATION was, in many ways, similar to the great political machines that dominated much of America's urban North and rural South from the late 1800s through the mid-1900s. Matthew Quay, a leading Pennsylvania Republican at the turn of the century, simplified his state's elections by transforming them into a well-defined routine of procuring votes in exchange for jobs and other favors. Public works were a key plank in the platform of Chicago mayor Richard Daley, who earned the moniker "Dick the Builder" in the 1950s for his heavy spending on O'Hare Airport, bridges, streetlights, sewers, and the like. Huey Long masterfully manipulated poor Louisianans' feelings of oppression at the hands of rich, powerful outsiders to secure the governorship in 1928. Allegations of corruption didn't hurt the popularity of James Michael Curley, who in 1903 won a seat as Boston alderman the very day he entered prison. But those politicians' jurisdictions were limited to their cities and states; Tanaka was able to move beyond his local fiefdom to impose his will, and his way, on his whole country.

Tanaka's national power base was a group of conservative parliamentarians who innocuously called themselves the "Political Friends Society," a name later formally changed to "The Thursday

Club." This clique was more commonly and accurately dubbed "Tanaka's *gundan,*" or "army corps," because its members loyally followed their shogun into his aggressive battle for control of the ruling Liberal Democratic Party and Japanese politics in general. Tanaka's primary goal after his arrest was simple: to make the *gundan* as large as possible. He calculated that an indomitable bloc of votes in the legislature would give him the clout necessary to dictate events. "Politics is power, power is numbers" was his ruthlessly simple mantra.

Thus, Tanaka's first challenge in Nagatacho (Tokyo's Capitol Hill) after his arrest was, as it had been in Niigata, to somehow win converts to his cause despite his obvious liabilities.

Rather than beginning his attempted comeback by repenting of his troublesome addiction to money, Tanaka sought to regain his clout by hooking the entire establishment on ever-higher, more potent dosages of the same opiate. His wealth proved to be one of his greatest lures to fellow politicians.

This was no small irony: Japan's reformers had hoped that the exposure of Tanaka's myriad financial shenanigans would eradicate the odious "money-power politics" he had come to represent. Yet these idealists, Tanaka knew, were naïve. His methods were just a rational manifestation of a system prone to corruption, and all the moralistic hand-wringing—even when backed by prosecutorial might—hadn't changed the rudiments of that system.

JAPAN'S POSTWAR DEMOCRACY was shaped by a confluence of factors that put politicians into an awkward dilemma: their access to respectable sources of funds was sharply constricted, while at the same time their dependence on money was amplified. The government salary for MPs was set far below what was realistically needed—at about one third, by some estimates—to cover just a bare-bones office staff and basic expenses. The major national political parties donated little to their own candidates; under Japan's unusual multiseat district electoral system, politicians from the same party competed directly against one another, forcing the national organization to avoid showing favoritism among the candidates it had endorsed. Meanwhile, in those early days, an electorate unschooled in participatory democracy was reluctant to contribute time or cash to campaigns.

At the same time, money took on a disproportionate weight in the manner by which politicians won office. Many voters based their support on what specific benefits their representatives could provide: sometimes that meant outright vote buying; more often, it involved the kind of costly favors that Tanaka's Etsuzankai provided so well in Niigata. Candidates found it hard to appeal to the public with other, nonfinancial approaches. They could not rely much on voters' party loyalty—the way an American congressman, for example, can always count on a certain bloc of ballots simply because he is a Democrat—because, again, the electoral system pitted LDP candidate against LDP candidate. Tight campaign restrictions made it difficult for politicians to persuade voters with ideas or rhetoric. Door-to-door canvassing and newspaper advertising were prohibited, while mailings and handbills were severely restricted; all political activity, including campaign speeches, was confined to a short period immediately before elections.

Thus, the raising and dispensing of funds—legal, extralegal, illegal—took on great importance in defining Japanese politics. In 1948 and 1954, major financial scandals helped bring governments down. When the LDP was founded in 1955, the imperatives of funding helped to dictate its basic structure and governing principles. The party was divided into a half-dozen official "factions," each headed by a senior politician whose main responsibilities included providing aid to his faction's members. Political finances developed their own slang, with 100 million yen known as a "bullet." Party leadership contests literally became bidding wars: "The reason we lost," one unsuccessful candidate in the 1960 intraparty vote said, "was that we ran out of money."

While everybody accepted the logic of that mammon-centered culture, most politicians were somewhat embarrassed by it. At times they professed shock, as in the early 1960s, when the LDP felt compelled to establish a much-publicized, yet ineffectual, commission to help "purify" politics. Or they tried to treat the role of money as a dirty little secret. Two distinct classes of leadership evolved in the LDP in the 1950s and 1960s, the bagmen and the statesmen; the former were expected to remain largely behind the scenes, supporting the latter. One money handler with misplaced ambitions of crossing that line and becoming prime minister himself was dismissed with the cutting quip "You can't put the septic tank into the *tokonoma*"—the prized display space in a Japanese home. So when MPs with higher aspirations climbed the national ladder, they tended to turn over the grubby chores of fund-raising and spending to underlings. During his term as prime minister from 1964 to 1972, for example, Eisaku Sato willingly shared the purse strings of his faction of LDP MPs—with Tanaka.

Tanaka, in contrast, openly embraced the pecuniary side of politics from very early in his career. He himself boasted that he had won his first cabinet post in 1957 "by money," telling supporters that he had given Prime Minister Kishi a small backpack stuffed with 3 million yen in bills. Perhaps because he was unencumbered by pretensions of purity, Tanaka could interpret the intermingling of money and power more pragmatically than his colleagues could. He saw that money was not incidental to politicians, but essential—that MPs were so desperate for cash that their loyalty could be bought, and that it was folly for any leader to shunt aside the critical task of paying followers. That was exactly how Sato had lost the allegiance of his faction members to Tanaka in 1972. After he became prime minister, Tanaka jealously maintained personal control of payouts to his minions. That was also one way that he kept their loyalty despite his troubles. In the weeks after his arrest, when his future seemed in doubt, one of the first things Tanaka reportedly did to keep his faction members in line was to hand three million yen, or $10,000, to each and to promise to sell his beloved Mejiro estate if necessary to keep up such support.

Tanaka took great care to establish himself not just as a reliable source of political funds but as the most generous, once joking, "I am called the governor of the private Bank of Japan." While all factions provided members with stipends during the country's traditional summer *o-chugen* and New Year's *o-seibo* gift-giving seasons, as well as at election time, knowledgeable observers said that Tanaka's *gundan* always received the largest—by estimated ratios ranging from three to twenty times, depending on the intensity of the political competition. In parliamentary elections held during the early 1980s, Tanaka paid members to join his *gundan,* drawing several conservative politicians away from rival LDP factions by offering more campaign funds. "Perhaps you need this," Tanaka said to one candidate who had already signed a pledge to join another conservative bloc, handing over a cloth bundle. It was filled with cash. The pol changed his mind and joined the *gundan.* Sometimes Tanaka completely underwrote a candidate's campaign expenses. "When I said I hadn't gotten the money together, Kaku-san said, 'I'll cover all you need,' " recalled Tai Morishita, a businessman, explaining how he had ended up a member of Parliament's upper house. "I heard more than three hundred million yen was needed for this. . . . Because of that, I am a Tanaka-faction member."

While much of Tanaka's money was aimed at drawing members of Parliament into his fold, he also used the cash strategically, to win support on specific issues. His spending spree to become prime minister in 1972, for example, went well beyond his faction and spread throughout the LDP, shocking even the party's most jaded veterans. One respected magazine, quoting a named source, reported that Tanaka had paid 700 million yen (more than $2 million) to swing a critical bloc of forty votes. Another LDP elder reportedly received from Tanaka a large metal suitcase that he believed was stuffed with cash, though he later claimed to have returned it unopened. "There were rumors of so much money changing hands," groused Takeo Fukuda, Tanaka's rival in that contest, "that I seriously considered dropping out." Tanaka was said to have shelled out up to $16 million, five times Fukuda's war chest, in a race decided by five hundred electors—more than half of what Richard Nixon had spent on his entire national presidential bid in 1968. As premier, Tanaka continued to push the use of money in Japanese politics to new limits. Official corporate contributions to the LDP doubled during his term, and even so, he apparently ran the party's finances into the ground; his successor as prime minister and party president, Takeo Miki, found the LDP's main safe empty except for IOUs indicating debts totaling 10 billion yen.

The Tanaka political apparatus was so flush that, as one senior LDP official cracked, the denials of knowledge about the Lockheed bribe were entirely believable because "the money flows by [Tanaka] so continually that he probably didn't even know where the five hundred million yen came from." "It's not that Tanaka made the standard twice" the old level of payments but "that he raised it by one digit," Kiichi Miyazawa, a leader of the "intellectual" school of politicians who disdained Tanaka's style, estimated years later. "And because factions are fighting one another for election, if the Tanaka faction is oiled by money, then I should do the same thing for my people." Besides, Miyazawa, added, "he was so *blatant*."

Tanaka took great delight in shocking his more fastidious colleagues. He did not quietly transfer his political wealth but ostentatiously doled it out in the form of stacks and stacks of cash. "Distribute this at once," he ordered party officials during a tight mid-1970s election campaign as he casually tossed a large bag onto the table. Opening the sack, they found bundles of 10,000-yen notes.

"How much is there?" a wide-eyed pol asked. "One hundred million yen," the boss replied. When the wife of a young politician stopped by Mejiro, Tanaka slipped packets of money into her kimono. Attempting to persuade a well-known television announcer to run for office in the mid-1970s, Tanaka took the prospective candidate into his home, where a pile of cardboard boxes sat next to "a safe twice as big as a TV set," as one of the meeting's participants recalled. Tanaka brought a box to the reluctant recruit, pulled off the lid, took out the yen, and stacked them on a table. "You can't be a politician if this amount of money makes you nervous," he counseled.

Yet behind that crass exterior, Tanaka was actually sophisticated in his payoffs. He elevated the practice of handing out money, as his close aide Shigezo Hayasaka described it, "to the level where we may call it artistic." Even rivals such as Miyazawa acknowledged that it wasn't Tanaka's indiscriminate scattering of bills that attracted followers but the way he skillfully blended that "with an insight into human psychology." Tanaka's donations were psychological minuets, skillfully drawn-out seductions. "The most difficult thing for an ordinary man is to accept money from others," Tanaka once explained to Hayasaka as he gave him stacks of cash, ranging from one million yen to three million yen, neatly wrapped in paper. "If you act superior when you are giving [money] to the candidates . . . then even if you give one million yen or two million yen, its value will disappear. You must bow deeply, and politely ask them to accept."

Tanaka understood that any reluctance to accept money might be even greater if he, so tainted, were the donor. So he sometimes initiated the offer at a time when it would be difficult to refuse, perhaps offering condolence money at a funeral. He would ask nothing in return, at least not the first few times. He would start small and build up, from 50,000 yen as the first contribution, to 200,000 yen as the second, to 300,000 yen as the third, and so on. The repetition was important, to build dependence and a sense of stability. When an aspiring politician came to seek Tanaka's help, the veteran not only handed over a wad of cash but asked, "When are you coming back?" clearly meaning, "You can get more if you wish next time."

If a politician were particularly hard up, Tanaka would foster deep gratitude by giving more than was anticipated or needed. "I was expecting that Kaku-san was running out of money and he would give me only three million," a struggling pol told Hayasaka. "But you brought me five million yen, and that night I cried in my bed." Another MP, a million yen in debt, went to Tanaka to bail him out. Within hours, he received a package at his home containing *three* million yen and an explanatory note: "(1) Repay your loan of one million yen; (2) Use one million yen to buy delicious food for those who have suffered because of your mismanagement; (3) Keep one million yen on hand in case of another emergency; (4) It is unnecessary to repay me the three million yen." It worked: "Even if you had said bad things about Tanaka before," the MP admitted, "once you had been assisted by him, your talk would be different."

CHAPTER NINE

"POLITICS IS POWER, POWER IS NUMBERS"

Tanaka's shameless moneybags tactics drew the predictable attention and outrage. Yet that tended to obscure the fact that cash was just one inducement in an all-encompassing recruiting strategy. More than any other LDP faction, more than the entire LDP or any other Japanese party, the *gundan* was methodically forged into a unified political bloc. Members worked closely together, played closely together, even mourned closely together. After the death of group lieutenant Noboru Takeshita's father, Tanaka immediately chartered a plane carrying sixty-nine black-clad MPs to the countryside for the funeral. "The Tanaka *gundan*'s speedy response to any ceremonial occasion cannot be matched," noted one report at the time. The knowledge, networks, and experience of all of Tanaka's minions were fused to create a collective power far greater than the sum of the parts. Politicians who joined rival groups had to rely much more on their own aptitude and connections built up over the years; anybody who joined the *gundan* could automatically tap into its clout.

The primary appeal was that Tanaka gave new participants the instant ability to do for their districts what he had done for Niigata: bring home extensive public works and other favors from Tokyo.

This pitch was especially enticing to novice politicians who had no personal track record in processing voter requests. "Even a new guy could say [to constituents], 'Whatever you want, consult me, because I'm in the Tanaka faction,' " says a journalist who spent years covering the *gundan*. When Iwao Matsuda, a bureaucrat, first sought a seat in Parliament, he noted, "I had no base, no single person supporting me." Tanaka dispatched to Matsuda's central Japan district cabinet ministers who were *gundan* veterans. They would call a meeting of businesses "under the jurisdiction of that ministry—people I didn't know at all," Matsuda later explained. "The minister would say what he's going to do" for the district, then point to Matsuda: "This is a nice man, and he's going to become a candidate. Anything you want from me, please ask him. He will do everything for you [in the name of] the minister.' "

Even veteran politicians found long-locked doors suddenly opening for them. Hajime Funada came from a venerable political clan, his grandfather having once served as speaker of Parliament's lower house. Yet when he first entered the legislature as a member of the family faction, "Nobody seemed to listen when I brought up budget requests at the Construction Ministry." After a few years, he entered the *gundan*, and "When I went again as 'Funada of the Tanaka faction,' people became quite helpful." That very year, the minuscule funds allocated to widen a road in his district "almost doubled."

The other significant benefit of the *gundan*'s aggregate muscle made its appearance at election time. The *gundan* offered its members not just money but common campaign office space and experienced staff. The group called on contacts to literally manufacture support groups and find contributors in the candidates' own districts. The most famous senior politicians from the faction would fly around the country making speeches for junior comrades; in one tight contest in a rural area, dozens of veteran MPs were airlifted in to shake hands. Tanaka himself, after three decades in politics ("Sixty percent of my life in the same job," he would say), was a readily tapped fount of valuable wisdom and connections. "I know the complete history of all 130 election districts," he would boast. "I know almost all of the situations, and I have a network of people all over Japan. I can run . . . elections just by using the telephone." After one new politician came in for help, Tanaka immediately called contacts in the candidate's home region. "He told them to turn out one hundred or five hundred votes for me, or they wouldn't get the construction projects they had been expecting," the politician recounted. "I saw the results. . . . People came up to me and said they had voted for me because of a call they got from Tanaka."

Tanaka also took care to give personal tutorials in the art of populist campaigning. "I am sure you are going to win because your father built a foundation for you in your area," Tanaka told Tsutomu Hata, the son of a retiring MP, "but winning is not the final goal. You should visit thirty thousand homes. It is important for you to see the real situation of your area." Kishiro Nakamura worked as an aide to Tanaka before winning a parliamentary seat at the age of twenty-seven; on the stump, he mimicked his mentor precisely, from the way he made eye contact and shook hands to the statistics he crammed into his speeches. That rigorous schooling in the ways of politics continued after the elections. Every summer in the resort town of Hakone, the entire *gundan* would gather for a three-day "training session"; while Tanaka and other specialists lectured, row upon row of sweating legislators endured hard plastic chairs and a poorly air-conditioned hall, diligently scribbling notes on yellow pads.

The *gundan* had one more persuasive recruiting pitch, especially for novice politicians: nearly everyone was welcome. By the mid-1970s, the other LDP factions had become rather exclusive and stagnant, concerned more with protecting veterans than with squandering scarce resources on newcomers. The conservative party had become like an association of fancy department stores satisfied with a stable but small number of high-paying clients. Tanaka's expansionary "power is numbers" strategy required a radical departure. He was a discount retailer, obsessed with rapidly building up sales volume and happily accepting customers who had been rejected by rivals. When Yukio Hatoyama decided to enter politics at the age of thirty-seven, he couldn't get so much as an audience with other top faction bosses. Tanaka called Hatoyama into his office ahead of seventy other people waiting in the antechamber, gave him forty minutes of his time, pulled out a map of Hatoyama's district in the northern region of Hokkaido, and reeled off a series of statistics, including the number of émigrés from Niigata in Hokkaido: "If I support you," Tanaka promised, "you will get those votes and be elected." The other factions even recommended Tanaka to people they had turned down. The young Hata, whom Tanaka had advised to visit thirty thousand homes, had originally sought to enroll in his father's faction but had been discouraged. "We do not have young people in our group, and you might waste your talents," he was told. "It might be better for you to work with Tanaka." In one national election, one in every six *gundan* candidates was a rookie.

That extremely attractive package—ready wads of cash, plentiful public works for the folks back home, election support, training, easy membership—came with one huge catch: the sponsor was an indicted defendant. Even if an office seeker were pragmatic enough to overcome any moral qualms he might personally have about that, there was the danger that his constituents would not feel the same. Outside Niigata, Tanaka had become highly unpopular after his scandals were exposed, widely despised as Japan's most corrupt politician and practically as a traitor to the nation. Candidates who ran with the *gundan*'s backing were branded by campaign opponents as "plutocrats" and "mini-Tanakas." "My biggest sales point—'Please support me because I am so close to Tanaka'—became my worst sales point," recalled Kazuo Aichi, who had been planning to enter politics as a Tanaka faction member just as the Lockheed scandal broke. "My own support group told me to leave him." Tanaka was mindful of the dilemma he posed for fellow politicians: "When I campaign for someone, I warn him in advance that I am drastic medicine. I cannot guarantee only benefits," he once said. "If you are afraid, you had better not come near."

That was the pivotal issue in Tanaka's national comeback crusade: to build up his numbers, to woo politicians to his side, he had to demonstrate conclusively in districts around the country that his backing would draw more votes than it would repel. At first, he seemed to fail that test. In the December 1976 national parliamentary vote, as Tanaka himself was winning his first "purification" landslide in Niigata, nearly a dozen senior members of his faction went down to defeat in other districts. Eight months later, the *gundan* was routed in elections for the upper house of Parliament, with one fifth of its membership losing. In several districts where Tanaka personally wrote supporting letters and made phone calls, his candidate still lost. At that point, the group had only 74 of the LDP's 380 MPs—fewer than its biggest rival. The faction was far smaller than when Tanaka had first taken it over five years earlier, and it appeared to be dwindling fast. "The Tanaka *gundan* . . . is in an extreme downturn," one newspaper reported. "His power is considered to be on the decline."

Then Tanaka's luck turned. In 1979 elections, the *gundan* was able to hold on to all of its seats, despite the fact that the LDP as a whole suffered major losses. In 1980 the *gundan* picked up enough strength at the polls to make it the largest faction in the LDP. In June 1983 upper-house elections, fully 40 percent of the victorious conservative candidates pledged allegiance to Mejiro. These triumphs were partly the result of the sheer organizational proficiency of the *gundan*'s electoral machine. But also, an increasing number of voters around the country, like those in Niigata, were willing to look beyond the cloud of corruption to see the tangible benefits that Tanaka-slate candidates could offer. "I felt some doubt" at first about allying with an accused criminal, Funada later admitted. "But there were many people who felt that I myself had nothing to do with Tanaka's crime, and it was great that I was in a situation where I could do more for them." In 1983, the *gundan* won its first parliamentary seat in Kyoto Prefecture, the nation's cultural capital, long dominated politically by leftist intellectuals. "A man of immediate use to you" was candidate Hiromu Nonaka's slogan. Local officials badly wanted a government-subsidized highway to link their languishing port district with a nearby metropolis. "The line I pursued was far more beneficial than the drawback it involved in ethics," Nonaka observed after his election to the lower house. "Even in Kyoto," a *gundan* aide sent to help with the campaign noted dryly, "everyone has to make a living."

Tanaka became perceived as a campaign asset, not a liability, and conservatives started begging him to come out of hiding and stump on their behalf. "I decided to become the panda for attracting attention," Tanaka roared to more than a thousand partisans who gathered to hear him speak in 1980 for a new LDP candidate. Emboldened by the warm audience response—"With all these people gathered here," he noted at one point from the rostrum, "there has not been any heckling of 'Hey, Lockheed!' "—he rambled on for nearly an hour and a half, ignoring his time limit as well as the arrival of the candidate whom he was there to introduce. A campaign rally in 1983 expected to draw a crowd of eight thousand; when it was announced that Tanaka would be the guest speaker, twelve thousand showed up.

As these electoral patterns revealed themselves, more and more senior pols shed their initial reticence and flocked to the *gundan*. Some quit other LDP factions. One recruit left the New Liberal Club (NLC), the band of conservatives who had renounced the LDP in 1976 to protest the Lockheed scandal. The defector "explained to me that the NLC label has an unfavorable effect on the business of the chief of his support organization," the bewildered leader of the dwindling reformist group reported.

In seven years, the Tanaka variable in Japan's electoral calculus had been transformed: just after his arrest, candidates were afraid to link hands with Tanaka; by the time his trial was ending, they were afraid *not* to. "Even if a politician disliked Tanaka's way of doing things, his constituency would not forgive him for passing up the chance to be part of the faction, for it might bring many concrete benefits," an analyst wrote in a lengthy 1983 magazine article dissecting the *gundan*'s surprising growth. Legislators started jumping onto the bandwagon simply to avoid getting crushed. "It is nearly impossible to turn down an invitation to join the Tanaka family, because they would immediately support an opposing candidate," one young politician noted, as if describing a Mafia protection offer. "If you join the Tanaka faction, you do not need to compete against it."

Those who did have to compete—especially those who had personally crossed Tanaka—were often destroyed. Eiichi Nishimura, a longtime Tanaka ally, fell out of favor with the boss. A swarm of *gundan* men, sent to campaign against the eighty-two-year-old Nishimura, branded him "a man of the past"; their censure became a self-fulfilling prophecy, as he was defeated in 1980 in his attempt to win a twelfth term. A similar fate awaited those politicians who had been most active in pushing for a full investigation of the Lockheed affair. In the seven years after the Lockheed scandal broke, three onetime cabinet ministers who had backed the probe, including the justice minister who had authorized Tanaka's arrest, lost their seats.

As the Tokyo district court contemplated its verdict on Tanaka in the summer of 1983, the *gundan*'s membership had swelled to 118, or more than one in four LDP MPs. That was 60 percent greater than at its nadir just six years earlier, making it one third again as big as its nearest competitor—the largest intraparty bloc ever.

The *gundan* drew strength, though, not just from size but from an ironlike solidarity and a fierce personal devotion to the chief. In the darkest days just after Tanaka's arrest, when affiliation appeared to be a major political onus, only two people quit voluntarily—and both left politics soon afterward. Those who remained willingly endured the strain. When young *gundan* member Ryutaro Hashimoto found a rival faction's MP gloating over Tanaka's arrest, he grabbed the pol by the necktie and threatened to strangle him; it took four MPs to hold the Tanaka disciple down. Keisuke Nakanishi, another follower, was addressed by his constituents with the honorific *"sensei"* appropriate to his status as an elected member of Parliament; at the same time, he happily described himself as Tanaka's "boy-san," a Japanese-English phrase for an errand boy. "I transferred letters from Tanaka [to other politicians]. . . . I connected Tanaka's phone calls. . . . Whenever I had time, I tried to hang around his office." "My hobby is Kakuei Tanaka," one *gundan* leader, Susumu Nikaido, liked to say. At least one aide-de-camp worshiped Tanaka to the degree that he held the boss's very excretions as sacrosanct. "Tanaka was very sensitive," the assistant explained earnestly. "When he went to parties he smoked, and sometimes he coughed something up. If he then passed the tissue to you [for disposal] that meant he considered you close."

Most important, Tanaka could count on total, unquestioning support for his pronouncements. "Even if [members] say 'no' at first, we band together, because I never make a wrong decision" was how Tanaka described the group's operating philosophy. "Our faction will turn right if the boss says 'right' and turn left if he says 'left,' " said Shin Kanemaru, a top lieutenant. Just as Tanaka's maxim had projected, numbers—especially when so staunchly united—translated into magnificent power. "If all these members pull together," he would proclaim, "there is nothing that can stop us."

One of Tanaka's primary goals in amassing his formidable *gundan* was to take over the prime ministership once again. Not officially, of course; he was too soiled for that. But with control of the largest voting bloc in the largest party, he became kingmaker, then parlayed that role into making himself de facto king. "The power structure of the LDP is such that it is impossible for any political leader, no matter how powerful, to form an administration without Tanaka's cooperation," one columnist observed. Indeed, each of the three prime ministers inaugurated during the course of Tanaka's criminal trial—Masayoshi Ohira in 1978, Zenko Suzuki in 1980, and Yasuhiro Nakasone in 1982—owed their exalted position to the *gundan*'s patronage. Ohira and Nakasone in particular faced tough competition in intraparty votes, which they overcame only by relying heavily on the *gundan*'s ballots and its ruthlessly efficient electoral tactics. "The might of the Tanaka *gundan*," Nakasone gushed with appreciative awe shortly after his victory, "has been brought home to me as never before."

As Tanaka's faction grew bigger, the prime ministers became more beholden, and the power sharing—in the form of command over crucial posts—became more and more openly codified. In Ohira's administration in 1978, the *gundan* was given four of twenty-one cabinet posts. In Suzuki's 1980 government, six slots went either to *gundan* members or to MPs who, though having no official factional affiliation, were considered close to Tanaka. Nakasone would ultimately become one of postwar Japan's more forceful leaders. Nevertheless, his 1982 government, with eight Tanaka followers, was aptly dubbed the "Tanakasone cabinet"; there were nearly three times as many *gundan*-affiliated ministers as Nakasone-related ministers—more, even, than Tanaka had put into his own cabinet when he had been prime minister a decade earlier. At different times during these three administrations, *gundan* members were appointed to critical posts that had, as a matter of custom, always gone to the prime minister's own faction including chief cabinet secretary, the equivalent of a combined White House spokesman and chief of staff.

Meanwhile, Tanaka-faction members held a disproportionate number of party positions. They ran nearly half the LDP's policy committees as well as the party's finance bureau; they wrote the rules governing party leadership contests, determined which candidates would receive the official LDP endorsement in parliamentary elections, and held the offices that set the national strategy for those elections. On all significant issues, politicians "immediately ask, 'what does Mejiro think?' " a senior conservative wrote in a magazine article. "There has been no precedent, up until now, for one faction to have such great influence in all the fields of the personnel and financial affairs of the party, and even in the field of parliamentary management," he added. "Today's LDP is showing itself to be completely ruled by Kakuei Tanaka." (While the *gundan*'s numbers helped it dominate key government and party appointments, that dominance, in turn, helped boost the *gundan*'s numbers further, since ambitious politicians tended to flock to the factions that could best offer opportunities for advancement.)

As for Tanaka personally, he took no major post (except, in a cheeky gesture, for a seat on Parliament's Disciplinary Committee, where he could vote on ethics matters). Officially, he was not even registered as the head of his faction, leaving that title to an underling; nor was he a member of the LDP, since he had resigned from the party after his arrest. That did not mean he sat quietly on the sidelines. Rather, no official position could possibly encompass the role he wanted to play. Tanaka regularly phoned the prime ministers with advice and instructions, weighed in on specific budget issues, attempted to set election schedules, and issued his own policy pronouncements. "He is acting," complained one of Ohira's aides, "as if *he* were prime minister."

That probably understated Tanaka's visions of grandeur; the prime ministership itself, he once sneered, was "just a hat." Instead, Tanaka compared himself in one newspaper interview to Deng Xiaoping, the Chinese leader whose modest formal position far understated his omnipotence. To other reporters, he said he was akin to a retired corporate executive who had "retained fifty-one percent of the shares" of his company and was now serving as chairman of the board. "It is natural for big stockholders to choose the company president," he explained—the nation's ruling political party in this case being the company and the prime minister of Japan being the president. "If you [the large shareholder] think that what he [the prime minister–cum–company president] is doing is not good, you just tell him not to do it."

Underscoring his claim to such powers, Tanaka was frequently openly critical and condescending about the performance of the men he was propping up. After Suzuki made a serious blunder in sensitive diplomatic negotiations, Tanaka told a reporter that the premier's overseas trip had come "too soon" after taking office but offered the reassurance that Suzuki "is gradually becoming a prime minister." Nakasone, he complained to a magazine, was developing a reputation "for talking too much and [being] too bossy. . . . I told him . . . 'You should not try to do everything yourself.' " When Nakasone began getting rave reviews abroad for his skillful diplomacy—including the famous "Ron-Yasu relationship" forged with American President Ronald Reagan—Tanaka asserted, "Nakasone may be a first-class geisha dancing on the international stage, but I am the one who molds the clay of this administration."

Tanaka did not reach that distinction without a difficult struggle. As signs of his revival emerged, an alliance of reform advocates and longtime Tanaka adversaries within the ruling party was formed to block him. They called themselves "The Association to Improve the LDP," dedicated to "removing the evils of the 'money-is-everything' party constitution." The ensuing disputes between the pro-Tanaka and anti-Tanaka forces paralyzed Japanese politics for months at a time and nearly shattered the conservative camp. In a

1979 showdown that became known as the "forty-day war," the dissidents prevented Ohira from forming a cabinet for more than a month; one day in the midst of that spat, they literally took over an auditorium at LDP headquarters, barricading the hall with tables and chairs. In 1980, the rump factions—blasting Ohira for, among other things, his dependence on Tanaka and lip service toward "the purification of politics"—took the unprecedented step of siding with the leftist opposition parties in a no-confidence motion. In the summer of 1982, two respected conservatives launched a public campaign decrying Tanaka's revival, publishing articles and giving speeches around the country. "How would you answer a delinquent youth or a robber," one of the crusaders asked rhetorically, "if he argued [in his defense] that Tanaka was still very much an influential figure" despite his arrest? "Tanaka's philosophy amounts to saying, 'If you are numerous, you are powerful and can do anything you please.' "

The *Asahi* newspaper, in an editorial published on November 4, 1982, summarized the essence of the turmoil succinctly: "Politicians are now faced with the fundamental question: Are they going to allow former prime minister Kakuei Tanaka, a man who is on trial, to continue wielding influence or not?"

In principle, everybody was opposed to the empowerment of an accused felon, even those politicians who sided with the *gundan* in those battles. If Tanaka had been brazen enough to force an open "aye" or "nay" vote on his return to power—if he had run for prime minister himself—he would surely have been clobbered; at its peak the *gundan* never commanded a majority of the LDP. But in practice, most everyone accepted his return. The brilliance of his comeback strategy was that he never put the question directly to Ohira, Suzuki, and Nakasone and their respective blocs of followers. Tanaka was going to make each of *them* prime minister by combining his *gundan*'s great numbers with those of their own smaller factions. In fact, the political dynamics were such that Tanaka's backing was the only way any of them could succeed. Confronted with the choice between selflessly sacrificing personal ambition in order to help purge Tanaka or becoming premier with Tanaka's help, each man willingly sold his soul to the devil of Japanese politics. "I want to be prime minister no matter what," Nakasone once said to an aide. In the late 1970s, he had been an outspoken leader of the anti-Tanaka forces, and he explained his 1982 conversion matter-of-factly: "Whenever I collaborate with [inveterate Tanaka rival Takeo] Fukuda, we always lose, but with Tanaka we always win."

In public, Ohira, Suzuki, and Nakasone each felt compelled to pledge that he was somehow keeping his distance from Mejiro, despite the obvious fact that his administration's survival depended completely upon the *gundan*'s support. "I am fully aware that, as a public servant, I must act with prudence in my relations with Tanaka, and he is also fully aware of my position," Ohira insisted. "It is only the newspapers that are playing [Tanaka's influence] up," Suzuki said. "It is not that way, in actual reality." Asked about relinquishing so much power to Tanaka lackeys, Nakasone claimed that there had been "no outside influence" on him, that he had merely "put the right men in the right place."

Few observers of this Faustian drama, however, believed the ritual denials of Tanaka's tightening grip over the ruling Liberal Democratic Party. The newspapers treated him just like any leading government figure, assigning staff to stake out his house, trailing his whereabouts closely, and reporting his every utterance prominently. One newspaper column heralded the "Reign of Kakueiism," while a prominent political commentator declared that the country's prime ministers were, "in a sense, only functioning as Tanaka's disposable bathroom tissue." The Japanese edition of *Playboy* magazine devoted sixteen full pages of its July 1983 issue to a wide-ranging interview with the power behind the conservatives' throne. "We concluded we must see him in person," the editors explained in their introduction, "and find out . . . what he is going to do with Japan."

And it wasn't just the press, as some LDP leaders tried to insist. The man Tanaka claimed as his Asian soul mate, Deng Xiaoping, made sure to take his entourage on a detour to Mejiro during a 1978 state visit to Tokyo; China's paramount leader warmly hugged Japan's "shadow shogun" and invited him to Beijing.

On January 1, 1981, about four hundred visitors thronged to Tanaka's estate for the traditional New Year's homage—triple the crowd that had appeared the previous year and, by one estimate, twice the number that visited the official prime minister's residence on the same day. They were sorted into separate rooms by category: politicians in one, bureaucrats (mainly from the Finance and Construction Ministries) in another, Niigata denizens in a third. After a group of construction workers serenaded the guests with "The Woodmen's Chant," a flushed Tanaka worked the crowd, waltzing from room to room with a glass of his preferred Old Parr scotch in hand, offering toasts, homilies, and economic forecasts.

Two weeks later, when Tanaka collapsed from breathing troubles and high blood pressure, about seventy MPs followed two ambulances rushing to Mejiro. Prime Minister Suzuki, traveling in Indonesia at the time, was not able to come, but he was immediately notified and the acting prime minister went in his place, as well as the government's chief spokesman and the LDP's secretary-general. One legislator, caught in a traffic jam, abandoned his car and sprinted the length of two football fields to see if Tanaka was okay. Many politicians were away visiting their districts when they heard the news and caught the first available planes and trains back to Tokyo to offer encouragement; the young Ryutaro Hashimoto cut short a trip to Canada. The Tokyo Stock Exchange fell and currency markets swooned before it was announced that Tanaka, after receiving minor treatment, was fine. "If Tanaka has health problems," the *Yomiuri* newspaper reported the next day to explain the commotion, "that will inevitably trigger a political shake-up."

CHAPTER TEN

THE LOYAL OPPOSITION

QUESTION: We have heard that your influence spreads even to parts of the opposition parties.

ANSWER: Yes, it depends on the case. . . . I know a man who graduated from Tokyo University, and when he first came to Tokyo, I helped him get set up.

He is now a leader of a [pro-Socialist] labor union. Whenever I visit his city even now, he stops his speech attacking the LDP as soon as he sees my car until it passes him. And he always looks the other way. He never looks at me.

His mother and wife, meanwhile, come to my election offices to cook rice and serve tea.

There are many such examples. You can't ignore these things and think you can do politics; you might as well spit up into the sky.

—*Playboy* magazine interview
with Kakuei Tanaka,
July 1983

IT WAS ONE THING for LDP stalwarts to bolster Tanaka's machine; quite another for the obstreperous opposition's MPs to grease his wheels. Yet Tanaka found a way of traversing the vast ideological divide by making himself useful to them and, as a result, made them useful to him.

It was, on the face of it, an implausible partnership. He was a business magnate. The leading opposition group, the Japan Socialist Party (JSP), was committed to Marxism. He won votes by enriching his constituents. His Socialist foe in Niigata, Shoichi Miyake, condemned this practice, urging farmers not to sell their fields at lucrative prices for new public works projects. "A farmer's viewpoint will change if he feels like a landlord," he declared, putting creed above comfort. (Miyake once championed a hog cooperative to ease the economic sacrifice, but that venture collapsed after the swine didn't reproduce, competing chemical fertilizers made manure sales unprofitable, and the neighboring community complained of the stench.)

Tanaka was the nation's most effective and openly ambitious politician. The Socialists were ambivalent about the very concept of power, especially when won through the ballot box. In 1955—the year the LDP was founded and began its long reign—the JSP resolved, "We must manage the party so as not to fall into a pattern of parliamentary-centeredness and the primacy of elections." Tanaka was the quintessential pragmatist and coalition builder. The Socialists suffered from the common leftist affliction of internecine doctrinal struggles, leading to numerous party defections and expulsions. Tanaka was "money-power politics" incarnate. Attacks on corruption were the campaign staples of all four major non-LDP parties—the Socialists, the Democratic Socialists, the Communists, and the Buddhist-backed Komeito, whose name meant "Clean Government Party."

Yet Tanaka understood that, beneath the rhetoric, opposition politicians were still politicians with certain basic exigencies, from providing constituents favors to raising campaign funds. In fact, their long years in opposition made it difficult for MPs in those parties to fulfill such needs and heightened the importance of developing contacts who could. Tanaka took it upon himself to become just such a contact. Socialists were welcome to send their supporters' petitions to Tanaka associates. Tanaka also volunteered occasional electoral tips, once claiming to be the Komeito's "political coach." He was always on hand to perform other miscellaneous services; when the Komeito went into a panic over a famous critic's scathing book attacking the party, Tanaka used his connections to try, albeit unsuccessfully, to suppress its publication.

With his renowned generosity, Tanaka also "looked after these parties very well," said aide Hayasaka. Sometimes that came in the form of nice presents or parties. "At the end of each year, a special product of Niigata arrived at every member's office in the Parliament building, regardless of whether they were LDP or opposition," a leading Socialist wrote in a newspaper column, adding that the customary LDP-sponsored banquets for the other parties "became particularly lavish in Tanaka's time." Furthermore, Tanaka and his men championed outright cash payments to the leading opposition parties, the scrupulous Communists excepted.

As an LDP executive in the 1960s, Tanaka vastly increased the "parliamentary policy expenses" budget used to ease "negotiations" with opposition parties, and as prime minister he instituted practices such as congratulatory stipends to non-LDP MPs appointed to key parliamentary committees. Sometimes the money was an explicit payoff passed "through an underground sewer," as Hayasaka put it. Often it was cloaked in some disguise, presented as a gift before an overseas journey or as a New Year's gratuity, to avoid the unseemly appearance of a transparty bribe. One Socialist said he had received flowers stuffed with yen notes when his wife fell ill. There were reports of friendly high-stakes mah-jongg games, in which LDP MPs laundered money by intentionally losing to opposition politicians. "The days of Tanaka's cabinet were really terrible, absolutely excessive," one LDP official complained to the *Mainichi* newspaper. "We had meals with the opposition parties, played mah-jongg, and handed over money . . . every night about one to two million yen a person." Whatever form they took, "nobody could deny" payments across party lines, said *gundan* member Hajime Tamura; he not only acknowledged participating but claimed to have tape-recorded the transactions to make sure he had proof.

In exchange for all of this largess, Tanaka secured another lever he could pull to direct Japanese politics. It wasn't as simple as buying off the non-LDP parties: money clearly didn't stop their making a fuss over his scandals. But he did succeed in developing a rapport with the opposition that was far better than that of any other conservative leader. "I have criticized the Socialist Party, but I have never criticized good old Kobayashi," Tanaka said in a speech he was invited to give at a swank 1981 gala (partially funded by the *gundan*) honoring a longtime leftist MP. "Kobayashi, too, is good at criticizing the LDP," Tanaka added, "but he has never criticized me." Komeito's chairman "felt indebted" to Tanaka for his repeated assistance and advice and "felt close to Tanaka as a friend," according to a leading Komeito official.

These were valuable chits to hold in the LDP because, though the opposition parties could never muster enough strength to oust the government, they were masters at harassing it. Throughout the 1950s and 1960s, the opposition parties had employed filibusters, boycotts, and brawls to delay or kill bills. (The fights usually took place over physical possession of the speaker's chair, which was required to open a session; the most famous stalling tactic was the comical "cow walk," in which MPs slowly shuffled to the front of the chamber—sometimes taking half an hour each—to cast their votes.) The 1969 Parliament showed just how effective such diversions could be: the LDP had a solid majority and, through repeated extensions, including six all-night meetings, held the longest continuous session since the war; still, barely half the cabinet's proposals were passed into law, the lowest rate of the postwar period. There was, wrote an American political scientist, "widespread and justifiable concern in Japan and the United States about the viability of parliamentary democracy in Japan."

The conservatives badly needed a conduit for peaceful dialogue with their rivals: to explain the rationale behind legislation, to listen to demands, to negotiate compromises, or, at the very least, to find a less disruptive way of agreeing to disagree. By the late 1970s, the Tanaka faction had become the main such mechanism, the government's chief envoy to the opposition. *Gundan* members were called on to handle informal wheeling and dealing across the parliamentary aisle and were consistently appointed to chair the official committees established to broker multiparty deals. "It will be difficult for the LDP to steer [Parliament] smoothly if it ignores the Tanaka faction," a journal reported in 1979.

That arrangement not only elevated the importance of the *gundan*—by making it indispensable to effective governance—but also represented the ultimate conversion of Japan's political system to its machinelike code of conduct. In part, the more civilized relations that evolved between Right and Left marked a maturation of parliamentary democracy in postwar Japan. Yet in many cases, the legislative process swung to the opposite extreme: where ideological tension had once bogged down the most mundane issues, increasingly Tanaka's own creed of pragmatism and horse trading was improbably applied to the most fundamental philosophical differences. Even the act of protest became routinized: when neither side felt it could give in on an issue, the parties choreographed a confrontation for public consumption, down to the exact count by which a no-confidence motion would lose and the precise minute at which a cow walk would end. A leading *gundan* member recounted, in his memoirs, what he claimed was a typical planning session, held in a swank private restaurant the night before a critical parliamentary hearing:

"Let's decide the script for tomorrow," the LDP representative would say. "Your side is going to oppose us at this point, and probably you'll create a kind of skirmish. But then we'll forcibly open the committee meeting. Then your people will shout for a while and might go wild. How many [people] will you have? Thirty? Maybe we should have thirty, too. Then we will have a kind of sign you can recognize to break it up."

"It's normal," Tanaka explained to an uninitiated aide who was perplexed at the peaceful resolution of one tense showdown. "Everything is coordinated."

CHAPTER ELEVEN

GENERAL HOSPITAL

Tanaka served as Finance Minister for a very long time [in the 1960s]. . . . It was assumed that Tanaka would in no way be equal . . . to the post. However, he ultimately managed to have Finance Ministry bureaucrats at his beck and call. . . .

Here is a story about what happened [years later] when Hideo Bo . . . succeeded [Tanaka] as finance minister. When Bo entered the minister's room, a Finance Ministry leader secretly whispered into his ear: "As you may know, we want you to distribute appropriate midyear and year-end presents, to make management in the ministry smooth. This has been customary practice since Tanaka was finance minister.

"I think that something like cosmetics should be all right for the telephone operators. Neckties for mere clerks, neckties of the Saint-Laurent brand for staff at the subdivision level, and 'separate packages' for the division directors and above." . . .

Bo had never heard the term "separate packages," and therefore he asked, "What does that mean?"

The leader said with composure, "Well, money equal to their bonuses will be all right."

In the Finance Ministry there are more than two hundred officials holding the post of division director or above. Supposing they are given 500,000 yen each on average, that will be more than 100 million yen. It is said that such money is given twice a year—in the middle of the year and at year-end.

In short, Kakuei Tanaka took to buying off the entire Finance Ministry, from top to bottom.

—From a September 1983 speech
by journalist and longtime Tanaka critic
Takashi Tachibana

SUPREMACY OVER POLITICS was necessary, but not sufficient, for the effective operation of Tanaka's national machine. He also required the collaboration of Japan's central bureaucracy, widely considered the most powerful unelected civil service in the free world.

When Japan's rulers replaced feudalism with a cabinet system of government in the late nineteenth century, their first priority was to establish a governing mandarin class; even after the eventual creation of an elected branch, the elite administrators claimed an authority separate from the popular will. "Exalt the Officials, Despise the People" was a common slogan before the war.

Despite General MacArthur's declaration after the war that Parliament would be the supreme unit of government, the ministries found many ways of retaining their independent clout. The bureaucracy prevented American-style patronage, jealously keeping control of personnel matters largely unto itself; in fact, Japan experienced a kind of reverse "spoils system," as a school of ex-bureaucrats turned politicians became the dominant force in the ruling conservative party.

In principle, Parliament was responsible for drafting the laws, the bureaucracy only for their implementation. But MPs, lacking experience and their own policy staffs, typically turned to the highly trained ministries to write legislation for them. Sometimes administrators even wrote, for timorous politicians, the script for the entire public debate, from the cabinet discussion to the interpellation on the floor of Parliament—both the questions to be asked by the opposition and the answers to be given by the ruling party.

The state's substantial power of the purse, meanwhile, resided largely with career Finance Ministry men, who fiercely resisted political "interference" over the size and content of the national budget.

Local governments depended on the central coffers for 70 percent of their spending, and the money generally came with tight strings attached: it was up to Tokyo, for example, to decree not only whether Niigata would get a new bridge but on which riverbank and next to whose rice paddy.

Tanaka's strategy for manipulating the mandarins was a blend of competition and co-option. Striking his populist pose, he constantly railed in public against the bureaucrats, branding them a menace to Japan's fledgling democracy and demanding their obeisance. "I am more afraid of the voters in my district than I am of the bureaucrats," he often taunted. Or he might pause halfway through one of his speeches as cabinet minister and snidely interject, "So far I have been reading what some official wrote for me to say, but from here on I'll say what I really want to."

Unusual among politicians, Tanaka took a keen interest in the arcana of policy, developing his own command of topics from public finance to water supplies. He was known for poring over government documents into the small hours. Drawing from his independent base of knowledge, Tanaka personally drafted twenty-six laws in his first ten years in Parliament (from 1947 to 1957), a record for a Japanese politician, according to his boosters. Many of the young Tanaka's proposals—especially those earmarking revenues for specific purposes, such as gasoline taxes for highway construction—were ardently opposed by career civil servants, who resented the curbs on their otherwise free rein over public funds.

Yet even as Tanaka challenged the bureaucrats, he actively sought friends among them. Like the political opposition, these officials were supposedly impervious to Mejiro's grubby temptations. They were the select, trained at the top universities and anointed for public service, and they considered themselves selfless, impartial, and incorruptible; they felt their duty was to safeguard the national interest against crooked, narrow-minded politicians. Tanaka saw, however, that behind the civil servants' dignified, impassive veneer were the all-too-human foibles—vanity, jealously, ambition, and greed—that were ripe for exploitation.

While holding cabinet posts, Tanaka took care to stroke the considerable egos of the career staff, memorizing their names, birth dates, family backgrounds, and educational records and then sprinkling these minutiae into casual conversations. "When a person is addressed like this by the minister, it elicits emotions" admitted one reputedly unfeeling official. At ribbon-cutting ceremonies for construction projects, Tanaka made sure to single out in his speeches the bureaucrats, normally relegated to anonymity, who had drawn up the blueprints. While boasting publicly that his street smarts equaled any book learning by government officials, in private Tanaka was quick to grovel. "I know I don't have the academic record," a tearful Finance Minister Tanaka once pleaded with an underling, "but I'm reading whatever you give me every day until three A.M." When meeting his staffs for the first time, he would tell them; "I am [merely] a graduate of elementary school, while you represent the genius of all Japan. . . . I am a novice."

For all its might, the bureaucracy was not, Tanaka understood, a unified monolith but a snake pit of petty rivalries. The politician who could skillfully take sides or mediate the raging turf battles would win grateful allies. "The trouble with bureaucrats is their sectionalism," a magazine analysis of Tanaka's hold over the mandarins explained. "The Mejiro machine has come to the rescue by undertaking prompt interest adjustment and decision making. . . . Whenever two ministries [find] themselves at loggerheads, they take the problem to [Tanaka's] residence." The primary index of power for most government agencies was budget size, and Tanaka reliably championed the cause of the less prestigious ministries in their battles for funds. When frugal finance officials tried to constrain government spending on new ports, for example, he intervened on behalf of the disgruntled Transport Ministry. (Transport officials registered their appreciation by building one of the new harbors in Niigata.)

Another chink in the bureaucrats' formidable armor was the customary retirement age of fifty-five. Civil servants, as they carried out their duties, had thus always to be mindful of the need for a second career. Here again, Tanaka enthusiastically extended assistance. He worked to raise the pay for executives at government-funded "public corporations" that served as sinecures for former government officials and supported the creation of new posts. Rather than resisting the influx of career civil servants into politics, he encouraged them and ultimately became their chief sponsor, providing the *gundan*'s unbeatable electoral muscle. In the summer 1983 parliamentary elections, nine victorious Tanaka-slate candidates were former government bureaucrats.

In addition to these numerous indirect courtesies, Tanaka flagrantly attempted to buy outright allies in the civil service, and he found that Japan's bureaucrats—despite their holier-than-pols image

—were just as willing as office seekers to partake of the celebrated Tanaka cornucopia. At one dedication ceremony for a new tunnel, he used half the event's budget to buy expensive kimono cloth for the wives of attending Construction Ministry officials, carefully selecting each cut to suit each woman's age and physique.

When he offered cash, the bureaucrats, like many politicians, justified their acceptance by citing their low salaries. Earlier cabinet ministers had offered small gestures to ease the burden, such as bringing in boxed meals when their minions were working round the clock for days on end. Tanaka "was different," one telecommunications official recalled of Tanaka's term heading that agency, "in that he paid all our expenses. I had never been impressed like that before." Tanaka also initiated the practice of personally covering staffers' expenses for overseas trips, which otherwise were limited to per diems that couldn't meet even the hotel bills, a Finance Ministry leader explained. "He was very considerate, very sympathetic to the low-paid officials," the public servant reminisced fondly. His seasonal gifts at the Finance Ministry became lore: one year he gave every high-ranking official 150,000 yen; it was, however, bestowed not in the prosaic form of cash but as debentures issued by a high-class British clothier. As later finance ministers such as Hideo Bo reportedly discovered, Tanaka set a precedent other politicians felt pressured to match. He was even said to have raised, by a factor of ten, the standard tip given to ministry guards.

Over the years Tanaka meticulously developed what was reputed to be the best network of any politician in Kasumigaseki, the drab Tokyo district housing the leading ministries. The same finance officials who had once greeted the brash parvenu with a snooty wariness ultimately embraced him as an honorary member of their *doki-kai,* the exclusive club of all the men who had entered the ministry in 1941, the year that Tanaka, had he gone to university, would have been able to join. These sterling connections made it easier for Tanaka to influence a wide range of government decisions. Because the bureaucracy had such discretion over government funds, its consent was often vital—sometimes even decisive—for the public works projects that enhanced Tanaka's popularity in his district. When a certain toll road in Niigata was absent from an early draft of the national budget, Tanaka simply phoned a finance official and said, "I'm sorry, this one is missing. Take care of it." The road was built—and the bureaucrat who assisted in the matter later won a seat in Parliament as part of the Tanaka faction. Tanaka could, according to legend, "just walk into a ministry office . . . flick through a towering pile of files on the desk, find the one he was looking for, and place it on the top of the stack. He would then say, 'If you please' and leave," a Japanese biographer wrote. "One word from him, and the entire priority for expenditures would change."

In his first three decades in Parliament, Tanaka was credited with pioneering the way for Japanese career pols' taking an active part in government decisions. His activist term as prime minister from 1972 to 1974 was portrayed at the time as the height of political leadership. It was after his 1976 arrest, however, that he truly made his mark, by transforming what had largely been a personal craft into a comprehensive, standardized system.

The mid-1970s were considered a turning point of sorts in the workings of Japanese governance, a period when the Liberal Democratic Party as a whole, after ruling for twenty years, finally followed Tanaka's model to become more assertive with the bureaucracy. Party committees challenged ministries in originating and altering legislation. There emerged policy "tribes," groups of MPs who developed expertise and cultivated their own mandarin networks in specific areas from agriculture to education. Analysts heralded a new era of "High Party, Low Bureaucracy." Yet, like Tanaka, these "tribesmen" did not usurp the bureaucratic prerogative but rather molded, as two of Japan's leading political scientists put it, an " 'LDP-bureaucracy compound' based on deepening relationships of mutual dependence and involvement."

Of the half-dozen LDP factions, the *gundan* of MPs that Tanaka amassed during his criminal trial was the most industrious in nurturing those precious ties: at one point, according to the most authoritative academic study of the trend, more than half the LDP's policy "tribesmen" were members of his bloc. Tanaka himself was rated the leading "tribesman," or "don," like a Mafia chieftain, as one analyst called him, of four groups: the commerce and industry tribe, the construction tribe, the posts and telecommunications tribe, and the finance tribe. No other politician topped so many lists.

The *gundan*'s strength in maneuvering the bureaucracy derived not just from its depth but from its unusual breadth, or what Tanaka in the late 1970s began calling his "general hospital," staffed with a diverse assembly of "specialists" who, combined, permeated nearly all the important ministries. Far more thoroughly than competing conservative leaders, Tanaka methodically spread his minions over many fields, and his politicians then pooled the resulting fruits with the group. Other blocs tended to be more narrowly focused, limiting the scope of goods they could deliver to members. In the *gundan*, any member wanting a rail line for his constituents, say, could seek help from his transport comrades; a transport specialist could turn to the *gundan*'s agriculture team if he sought an irrigation project. This was integral to the *gundan*'s notable capacity for showering members' constituents with services. "It's hard to maintain votes in your district without having access to various kinds of experts," Tanaka would say. "[In the *gundan*] there are a number of skilled 'doctors,' including me. . . . If you come to the 'general hospital,' . . . everything can be treated."

At the same time as its leader was an accused felon, the Tanaka faction became the nexus for the crafting of numerous critical policies, either in partnership with the relevant ministries or as mediator among feuding bureaucratic camps. As Japan confronted more and more complex issues that cut across traditional ministry lines, the *gundan*'s brains and multifarious contacts regularly made it the leading honest broker, so to speak, in the government. It was the *gundan* that settled a tense standoff over interest rate and tax policies between Finance Ministry and postal officials, who run their own post office savings bank. The *gundan* also set the course for the nation's sweeping telecommunications deregulation. In the rapidly expanding sector of telecommunications in particular, Tanaka and his men were highly influential: the ministry as "the all-expenses-paid geisha of the Tanaka faction," in the words of one critic. Matters such as the privatization formula for the Nippon Telegraph and Telephone Corporation, as well as who would assume the mammoth company's presidency, were left mainly to Tanaka and his followers. "I am," Tanaka brazenly pronounced in an interview discussing the industry, "in charge of everything."

On most issues, in fact, the *gundan* was regularly described by the early 1980s as Japan's most proficient countervailing force to the civil service. "If one is reticent in the face of the bureaucracy, there's no telling how long one will wait," wrote a Japanese academic who studied Tanaka's organization. "When a problem of this sort is taken to the Tanaka faction, the usual outcome is that the Tanaka machine goes into action and promptly disposes of it."

CHAPTER TWELVE

THE PUBLIC WORKS STATE

THE THIRD main cog in the Tanaka machine, meshing with the political world and the bureaucracy, was business. It was a good fit: many companies sought aid or relief from the government and were willing to pay a high price to anybody who could rearrange policies on their behalf. Nobody could work Parliament or the ministries better than Tanaka and his *gundan,* and they needed a steady stream of cash to maintain that ability. "Though Mejiro has not been granted the power of taxation, its style is not cramped," one critic wrote. "The necessary funds are raised by . . . collecting a commission for services rendered."

An interplay between politics and commerce is an inevitable aspect of any capitalist democracy, but the history and habits of the Japanese system tended to intensify the entanglement. The fusion of the public and private sectors was a founding principle of the modern Japanese state in the late nineteenth century; the government literally nurtured the nation's industry from conception, then directed and championed those enterprises. An interventionist philosophy, rather than American-type laissez-faire, continued to guide Japan's rebuilding during the period of rapid growth after the war: everything from importing transistors to opening auto factories required official clearance in the capital; where written regulations did not exist, the central bureaucrats invoked their custom of unwritten "administrative guidance" to intrude on basic corporate affairs. The cozy government-business partnership, often called "Japan Inc.," was admired worldwide as the cornerstone of the country's phenomenal economic prowess. Yet by heightening the importance of the state to companies, this partnership also raised their incentive to buy access to the state's decisions.

In that market, Tanaka was the most aggressive and successful seller. His menu of "services rendered" began with general probusiness policies: backing for a tax cut to stimulate the economy or taking an industry's side in support of, or opposition to, a piece of legislation. Tanaka nobly portrayed these actions as an alliance to preserve the free market: "Companies are founded on liberalism, so it is natural for them to donate money to maintain liberalism," he would proclaim. "I am collecting the national fund which helps patriotic men grow." His detractors sometimes saw a more cynical motive, a kind of legislative protection racket: in the early 1970s, he once proposed a stiff tax on automobiles, sought contributions to the LDP from the threatened auto manufacturers, and, after collecting, watered down the bill.

Tanaka was also willing to go beyond a broad defense of capitalism or an industry to lobby for individual firms. In the simplest cases, he would function as a middleman between bureaucracy and business, attempting to win a slice of the government pie—perhaps a procurement order or a license—for a campaign underwriter. The advantage of being simultaneously a lobbyist and a powerful politician was that he could also bake new pies for his financial supporters: when he was telecommunications minister, he dramatically increased the authorized number of television broadcasters, told the bureaucrats which companies should be allocated the lucrative permits, then took payments from each. There was gold, he perceived, not just in steering government actions but in having access to advance information about such actions; Tanaka's network made him privy at an early stage, for example, to public works plans, which he was suspected of leaking to friendly land speculators.

Tanaka did not limit his "political entrepreneurship" to hustling between the public and private sectors. Because the line separating the two was blurry, he was sometimes able to exert influence in ostensibly private transactions, urging one firm to buy from another or encouraging two companies to cooperate rather than compete. His most famous deal, as described earlier, was the one he brokered in 1972 for the American aircraft maker Lockheed, which paid him a 500-million-yen "commission." The incident was a textbook illustration of how the Japan Inc. model was susceptible to political profiteering: All Nippon Airways (ANA), the company that Tanaka had pressured to buy the Lockheed planes, was privately owned and did not come under his official purview, so technically it had no obligation to comply with his request. Yet ANA competed in a field that was subject to extensive regulation, both formal and informal. The airline's top executives were retired Transport Ministry officials, and they well knew that if Tanaka were rebuffed, he had many buttons he could push to mete out revenge. (The decision was also apparently affected by Lockheed's payments directly to ANA executives, a twist that landed them in the dock along with Tanaka.)

Tanaka's opponents—and, in the Lockheed matter, the prosecutors—branded his behavior a pattern of flagrant corruption. He insisted he had been doing nothing wrong; "I don't want a bribe," Tanaka once protested, according to lore, when trying to swing a government equipment order to a friendly manufacturer. "I just want to receive political donations from the contractor who wins the bid."

Despite Tanaka's arrest, he continued to find new ways of spinning influence into affluence. With the growing power of the LDP's policy "tribes" in the late 1970s, Japanese corporations began heavily funding the MPs in those cliques pertinent to their specific fields—just as, in Washington, defense contractors contribute to Senate Armed Services Committee members and agribusiness to the House Agriculture Committee. In picking committees in Tokyo to infiltrate, Tanaka openly sought to maximize his returns. His *gundan* virtually ignored the tribes specializing in labor, education, and foreign policy, issues of pressing importance to the nation as a whole yet largely irrelevant to industry; instead, he concentrated his men in those policy areas known for drawing the biggest donations and the largest blocs of votes: telecommunications, postal affairs, transportation, finance, health and welfare, commerce, and industry.

He put his greatest effort into the area that offered the greatest rewards: the construction tribe, two thirds of whom were *gundan* members. Indeed, construction—both the industry and the government organs that affected it—became known as Tanaka's "citadel," the best example of how his machine worked.

The construction industry has long been a sponsor of corrupt political machines all over the planet, from Italy to Illinois. Postwar Japan was a natural setting for such collaboration. In the headlong rush to rebuild after the war, construction became the main pillar of the economy. Beginning in the early 1960s, construction spending equaled about one fifth of Japan's gross national product, and by the 1980s, it created nearly one tenth of the country's jobs. So much of that business—from 30 percent to 40 percent a year—was underwritten by the government that many Japanese referred to their country as the "public works state." Indeed, Japan's public works spending as a percentage of GNP was by far the largest in the industrialized world, exceeding America's by a magnitude of four. One analyst asserts that Japan's government spent more on construction than the United States did on defense during the height of the Cold War, making Japan's builders the equivalent of the American military-industrial complex. Paving, erecting, and damming practically became a national obsession: "Asphalt blanketing the mountains and valleys" was the "splendid utopia" cheerily promoted in a Construction Ministry song. Public works also became a rural welfare policy, not just in Niigata but all over the country; in many impoverished regions, government construction was the only sign of manufacturing activity amid the bucolic tranquillity, the local branch of the national Construction Ministry the hub of commerce.

The sheer size of the construction trough was bound to draw politicians, bureaucrats, and businesses together. Politicians required bureaucrats' help in getting building projects and jobs for their districts—signs reading PLEASE BRING PETITIONS IN THE AFTERNOON were posted on the doors of the Construction Ministry's offices to allow the mandarins to do some work each day before dealing with the regular stream of supplicants, usually local officeholders. Politicians also wanted access to the money and employee votes that construction companies could easily deliver; bureaucrats and companies wanted political help in keeping spending high.

But it was also the unusual procedure for doling out those huge sums that created opportunities for Tanaka-style political entrepreneurship. For one thing, Japan made little pretense of awarding contracts through open, competitive bids; the government reserved the right to decide which companies were allowed to apply for a job and had no obligation to disclose its criteria for choosing the winner. The vague, opaque process practically invited political interference, and those officeholders who could make a difference were assured healthy contributions from contractors. There was even a regular phrase connoting a pol's intervention: "the voice of heaven." The going rate for this deus ex machina was reputedly between 1 percent and 3 percent of the contract's value.

Second, collusive bid rigging, or *dango,* was openly rampant. Before nearly every public works project was launched, the contestants convened to decide which company would make the successful bid at what price and to agree on how to parcel out the work; the practice was so embedded in the industry that companies designated special executives who were responsible for their firms' role in the *dango* and printed up *dango* handbooks. Solid political support was required to maintain this custom because it inflated the cost to taxpayers enormously—by anywhere from 16 percent to 100 percent, according to a number of informed guesses—and because the practitioners relied on political protection from law enforcement authorities, since they were clearly committing a crime. Contractors won this support by sharing their illicit profits with sympathetic politicians: construction was consistently among the leading industries in officially reported campaign contributions, and strong evidence suggests that unofficial and illegal donations made it Japan's top political financier. Sometimes, when companies had trouble settling among themselves which firm would receive the job, a pol with credibility in the industry and the ministry might even serve as the *dango* arbiter, receiving a fee for his efforts.

The awesome electoral force of the construction industry was evident as early as the 1950s, when several vice ministers of construction won seats in Parliament, including one who was the nation's top vote getter in the 1959 election; second highest in that contest was Morinosuke Kajima, chairman of one of Japan's largest construction contractors. The financial rewards of political power in that world were made clear by Ichiro Kono, one of the leading postwar politicians, during his stint as construction minister in the early 1960s: his "favored-contractor policy" required companies to pay him gifts to be allowed to place bids; one builder talked of paying a "shoe-removal fee" to get in the door of Kono's house, then a "cushion fee" to get a seat. But it wasn't until Kakuei Tanaka assembled his machine that all the pieces really fit together.

It is worth remembering that Tanaka was a thriving construction magnate first, an MP second, and from his original career he learned firsthand the overlap between the two worlds. He hired influential parliamentarians as his corporate advisers in the 1940s and "spared no means to win government orders," according to one journalistic account. "He wined, dined and provided government officials with money and geisha. If an unobliging official contended that he had no desire to sleep with a woman, Tanaka [suggested] . . . , 'In that case, why don't you sleep with me?' " It was his building fortune that drew conservative leaders to him in the first place, and the funds and employees of his own construction company that carried his first successful campaign.

Although he formally shut down Tanaka Construction in the early 1950s, Tanaka never really abandoned the industry, continuing his participation in a different form. By the 1960s, Tanaka's Etsuzankai support group and the Niigata construction industry had nearly melded together. Building executives took many of the group's leadership slots, and laborers swelled the membership rolls. At election time, contractors converted their numerous branches across the snow country into Tanaka reelection offices while filling the campaign's coffers. And well they should have, since he was credited for single-handedly bringing in most of the construction work that was available in the area—and because the contracts were parceled out mainly to steadfast Etsuzankai member companies. As a result, nearly 70 percent of the prefecture's builders eventually joined the club. Fukuda-gumi, one of Tanaka's staunchest supporters, rode Niigata's 1960s public works boom to grow, in one decade, from a tiny builder into the prefecture's largest nonbanking company. Ueki-gumi, which had backed Tanaka from his first election, raised eyebrows when it won the bid for a major expansion of the Kashiwazaki port; the company had never led such a large project in its sixty-year history, nor had it ever handled port work. Ueki-gumi continued to be awarded prominent jobs, and Tanaka eventually sought direct dividends for his efforts, buying enough stock to make himself Ueki-gumi's fourth largest shareholder by 1979.

In Tokyo during those same years, from the 1940s through the 1970s, Tanaka was creating a parallel national power base. No politician, indeed few bureaucrats, could match his knowledge of, and obsession with, construction policy. He quickly became known as the "builders' MP." The legislation he sponsored dealt exclusively with matters such as rewriting the nation's basic building standards code and the public roads law (Tanaka boasted that he was the first MP to amend the roads law since 1919 and wrote enthusiastically about his proposals in *Doro* [*Road*] magazine) and promoting public housing, electrification, harbors, and dams. He won the eternal loyalty of contractors and construction mandarins for his zealous, at times fanatical, boosterism. In 1956, for example, he led a walkout that managed to delay the opening of Parliament in order to obtain more public works spending. Tanaka had some claim to being the father of the Construction Ministry, as he had vehemently lobbied against plans drawn up shortly after the war to give it a lesser "agency" status with limited functions, pressing instead for full cabinet rank. His much-heralded "Building a New Japan," which launched his campaign for the premiership in 1972, was at heart a contractor's fantasy; the blueprint called for the government to spend up to 550 trillion yen on public works over twenty years, more than triple the total spent over the previous century. Even as the nation's top power broker in the early 1980s, Tanaka remained passionate about the smallest details of building codes. When a newspaper came to speak with him about broad political trends, he somehow meandered into the topic of housing regulations, which he prattled on about at great length:

> For the first category of residential housing, one cannot build higher than ten meters. Ten meters! Ten meters means that even if you do floors at three meters apiece, when you finish the third floor there is only one meter left. You can't do four floors. In order to do the fourth floor, no matter how you do it, you need eleven meters. . . . On top of that, this is wooden construction, you know. With wooden materials, there are the lighting and ventilation considerations. Without lighting and ventilation, the back of the house becomes a problem.

To another visitor about that time, Tanaka confided, "I'm always thinking of architectural plans, like how you lay out entrances, stairs, and elevators."

In the late 1970s and early 1980s, Tanaka's cronies in the industry and the ministry were vital to the expansion of his faction in the ruling conservative party; the *gundan*'s growth, in turn, was fruitful for Japan's contractors. It was the regional branches of national construction companies that allowed Tanaka to create instant campaign organizations—complete with offices, cars, volunteers, and funds—for political neophytes in districts all over the country. He simply "would talk to the construction industry and have them become the support group for new candidates," according to a reporter who wrote extensively about the *gundan*.

Nearly every conservative politician with any background in

the construction industry was drawn to the Tanaka faction. Its ranks included six consecutive ministers of construction and ten of thirteen consecutive construction parliamentary vice ministers; every Construction Ministry bureaucrat who won a seat in Parliament during the period of Tanaka's criminal trial did so as a member of his faction. The *gundan* had cornered the construction tribe to the extent that its members had to cut their specialties finely: one was considered the boss of roads, another the boss of drainage. The *Nihon Keizai Shimbun,* Japan's leading financial newspaper, asserted that eight MPs had the ability to issue "voice of heaven" directives designating exactly which contractor would handle a specific national public works project and that five of these were Tanaka-faction members. In 1983, *gundan* members bullied the Fair Trade Commission, Japan's antitrust watchdog, into dropping a fledgling crusade against *dango;* the MPs threatened, among other things, to use their numbers in Parliament to gut the commission. "A lot of LDP members made demands very loudly, and we were frightened," one FTC staffer later said.

One reason for the *gundan*'s vigor in defense of *dango* was the fact that Tanaka personally sat at the center of the circle. He was so revered and feared within the industry that his approval was sought for every major rigged tender in the country. And when the industry itself could not reach agreement on which company should take the lead on a national dam or a tunnel, it would leave the final decision to Tanaka. Several times each month, the construction industry's national *dango* coordinator visited Mejiro early in the morning to review the latest lists. "Tanaka had his own ideas about which companies should be assigned," recalled a construction executive who participated in some of the sessions. "The last judgment came from Tanaka." One of the lists—a two-page rundown of which companies would build each of forty-eight dam projects over the following years—reached the hands of an opposition politician. The document caused a minor flap in Parliament in 1982, though the revelation didn't seem to force any changes in the contracts or in the practice of *dango* in general. According to numerous Japanese press accounts, for every major construction project consecrated by Tanaka, the winning contractor delivered a payment worth as much as 3 percent of the project's cost; the dams alone, the writer of one report calculated, would have generated fees worth 24 billion yen, or about $80 million at contemporary exchange rates.

"Let's say," a contractor crowed, "that Tanaka-san is running the country as if he were running a construction company."

CHAPTER THIRTEEN

COURT JUSTICE, POLITICAL LOGIC

THE VOTERS. The leading political parties. The bureaucracy. Business. Tanaka devoted his career to finding the weak points in each and exploiting them. In the years after his arrest, he fully integrated his system, as if he had lured the major players of Japanese governance into his own private orchestra and persuaded them to harmonize at the direction of his baton. Yet one institution that remained discordant was the judiciary, which from January 1977 to January 1983 put Tanaka through an exhaustive criminal trial, airing in excruciating detail the charges that he had taken a 500-million-yen bribe from the Lockheed Aircraft Corporation. "Tanaka is at once the seemingly omnipotent kingmaker and the defendant standing trial on criminal charges who risks being stripped of all political fortune," a prominent commentator wrote in a magazine at the end of the trial. "He epitomizes both the zenith and the nadir of human fortune."

In the late 1970s and early 1980s, the Lockheed scandal had driven Tanaka to reach for unprecedented heights of power, yet the taint denied him the legitimacy of his achievement. He could not again become Japan's official leader; he had to be the unofficial "shadow shogun." Tanaka's life had, in a sense, been a tireless quest not just for power but for legitimacy—the struggle of a poor, uneducated horse trader's son to become a respectable member of Japan's ruling class. His desire to clear his name was "an enormous burden weighing on his mind," wrote an aide. "He thought he could not die until it was settled."

Tanaka's lawyers, a legal dream team that included seven former national prosecutors and judges and one retired Supreme Court justice, repeatedly urged him to admit taking the money and to invoke a more narrow, legalistic defense that it hadn't been a bribe since he had had no formal authority over the airline's purchases. But Tanaka, whose greatest strength was his ability to put pragmatism over principle, was, in this instance, uncharacteristically rigid. Confession would be "fine if I were an ordinary person," he lectured his lawyers. "But I was the prime minister of Japan. This would shame the country. Stain history. I have to dispel these false accusations at any cost." Tanaka attempted to invoke the rough justice of his *gundan*, brazenly using his ability to shape cabinets to have a series of allies appointed to the post of justice minister, which technically had authority over the prosecutors and the courts. Again and again, his justice ministers publicly denounced the case being handled by their ostensible subordinates—one declared the prosecutors' tactics "against humanity"—but they had little impact on the proceedings, as Japan's civil servant prosecutors and judges fought to maintain their independence. On rare occasions, Tanaka's role as paramount strongman did affect his trial, as in June 1980, when he was busy brokering the installation of yet another prime minister and asked the court to delay a hearing for "relief from the strained political situation." (The request was granted.) For the most part, however, the 191 hearings continued unimpeded at the steady, slow pace of Japanese justice, under which the court sessions in Tanaka's trial were held just once a week.

The prosecutors took four years to make their case in court, but their argument was relatively simple. They presented detailed testimony from executives of both Lockheed and Marubeni Corporation, the Japanese trading company that had served as Lockheed's sales agent, that payoffs had been made to then–prime minister Tanaka specifically in return for his help in selling aircraft. A turning point came in October 1979—just as "Shadow Shogun" Tanaka was in the midst of a successful battle to prop up the Ohira administration—when former Marubeni chairman Hiro Hiyama took the stand. Hiyama had been alone in the

Mejiro office with Tanaka that fateful day in August 1972 when, the prosecutors alleged, the bribe had been broached. Tanaka had always vehemently denied having had such a discussion, but as the courtroom crowd held its breath, Hiyama said in a quiet voice that he had told Tanaka explicitly in their five-minute meeting that Lockheed wanted to give the premier a 500-million-yen "donation." Hiyama also testified that, after early news of the Lockheed scandal had leaked out three and a half years later, Tanaka's office had contacted Marubeni to try to return the money, an indication that the politician had not had a clear conscience about the cash.

The main defense strategy was denial of the facts as presented by the prosecutors. A number of Tanaka's underlings were dragged into court to claim that they had been with the prime minister's bagman, aide Toshio Enomoto, at the very times when Marubeni officials maintained that they had privately met with Enomoto to hand over the cash. But their alibis quickly disintegrated when several witnesses admitted, upon cross-examination, that their memories were poor and that they had been pressured by Tanaka to testify. The prosecutors then summoned Enomoto's ex-wife, Mieko, who testified that her husband had confided to her that he had taken the bribe, and that she had helped him destroy incriminating evidence. (Mieko's confession became famous in the tabloid press as the "bee sting"; she capitalized on her newfound celebrity by posing nude for the Japanese edition of *Penthouse* magazine and opening a nightclub in Tokyo's Ginza entertainment district.)

Tanaka refused to take the stand but did consent to a brief interrogation by one of the panel of judges. It was late December 1982, a few weeks after the formation of the "Tanakasone cabinet" and the day after the triumphant year-end party of his *gundan*, which was inducting enough new members to boost its rolls to 100. By the morning of the hearing the glow had worn off, and Tanaka appeared, to observers, extremely nervous. Once he had to interrupt the proceedings to run to the restroom; when he returned, a protester from the courtroom crowd stood up and shouted, "This is the last warning, Tanaka: leave politics!" During the prior sessions, Tanaka had stood proud and upright while everybody else in the court had respectfully bowed upon the judges' entrance into the courtroom. This time, the defendant himself paid deep obeisance as he approached the bench, and he addressed the judges with the most polite honorifics. With the other magistrates watching, the chief judge repeatedly asked Tanaka about the most damning testimony.

Again and again the judge cut off the rambling responses while Tanaka took out his handkerchief to wipe the streams of sweat off his face. The prosecutors made their final arguments a month later, in January 1983. The judges were left to deliberate over the summer —Japanese trials are decided by judicial panels, not citizen juries— and they set October 12 as the date they would announce their verdict.

Tanaka's prospects did not look good. One newspaper poll showed that only 4 percent of the Japanese people believed his denials, while 80 percent thought he was guilty. The other Lockheed-related trials had already been completed, and all ten defendants had been found guilty. Just over a week before his judgment day, Tanaka collapsed at his home from high blood pressure: "My eyes stuck out and my face turned ghastly pale," he told friends. "I think I was tired because of all the horseflies and bees biting me." At midnight on October 11, more than a hundred people were lined up outside the courthouse to enter the lottery for spectator seats. By the 8:30 A.M. drawing, nearly four thousand had joined the queue, which snaked a quarter of a mile up and down an overpass and into a nearby park. More than a dozen media helicopters buzzed overhead, while a thousand jostling reporters, photographers, and camera crews greeted the arrival of Tanaka's limousine at 9:30 A.M.

Shortly after entering the courtroom, Tanaka coughed violently three times; while awaiting the announcement, he compulsively checked his watch while fiddling with his paper fan. The chief judge solemnly read out the verdicts and the sentences. All five defendants —Tanaka, his aide Enomoto, and three Marubeni executives including Hiyama—had been found guilty of all charges. The former prime minister, whom the chief judge said had wrought "irreparable damage to the public trust in politics," would be punished the most severely: four years in prison and a 500-million-yen fine. It was the heaviest punishment ever meted out in a Japanese bribery case. Tanaka looked stricken. He buried his face in his hands, then stared silently at the ceiling.

Yet, in an odd way, the court's ruling turned out to be liberating, empowering even. Throughout his career, Tanaka had been treated condescendingly, like an embarrassing dilemma for Japan's establishment, which found his brand of machine politics irresistibly seductive yet crassly corrupt. So they had finessed their dilemma by taking the money and favors but never quite embracing the man or his methods. Some had righteously excoriated him, some claimed not to have known his ways, other downplayed the true extent of his power. Even during those seven years from 1976 to 1983, when Tanaka had been both chief fixer and criminal defendant, the political world could somehow claim that it had not been compromised. He had not conclusively done anything wrong, they said, since he was innocent until proven guilty; he wasn't really the "shadow shogun," they insisted, dismissing that notion as media hype. The guilty verdict shattered these uneasy pretensions. Nobody could feign ignorance of Tanaka's political deviance anymore, since he was now a certified crook. If establishment politicians really were not under his thumb, if they really thought he was guilty, they would have to exile him. But failure to cast him out when his guilt was no longer in question would mean a full endorsement of his methods or a ruling class too weak to reject them. Either way, Tanaka's durability in the face of his conviction proved to be his ultimate victory, an unambiguous public display that Japan's democracy had become Tanaka's machine.

Immediately after the verdict, the awkward question of what to do about Tanaka was forced. The opposition parties demanded the criminal's expulsion from Parliament, and they threatened to block all legislative action until an open vote was held on such a resolution. Tanaka himself was characteristically defiant. Upon hearing the court's ruling, his lawyers filed an appeal and he was released on 300-million-yen bail. As he left the courtroom, Tanaka smiled to the swarm of reporters and raised his hand in his famous wave; inside the car, he sat silently for a while, then muttered, "I won't forgive this." When Tanaka arrived at his Mejiro estate, dozens of cheering and applauding MPs from his *gundan* gave him a hero's welcome reminiscent of a Japanese Mafia ceremony commonly held to greet a mob boss returning home from prison. "If any of you think I am an obstacle," he shouted through a microphone to his flock, "he may quit." Tanaka made it quite clear that he himself wouldn't. In a prepared statement to the nation he announced that, as far as he was concerned, "I will pursue my duties as a member of Parliament as long as I live."

Stuck uncomfortably between the opposition parties and the *gundan*, between conscience and power, was the remainder of the ruling class. Prime Minister Yasuhiro Nakasone, hoping to avoid making the choice, meekly attempted to persuade Tanaka to do the honorable thing and depart from politics voluntarily. Nakasone first sent a politely worded note suggesting that Tanaka resign from his seat temporarily, until the LDP could ride out the storm; a Tanaka aide intercepted the message and returned it. The premier then called a summit with the felon. In that hour-and-a-half meeting at a swank midtown hotel, Nakasone began by discussing Tanaka's health and world affairs, then turned to domestic politics. The conversation, according to a later reconstruction by the *Asahi* newspaper, went like this:

> NAKASONE: It is regrettable that Parliament is stalled. . . . I feel grave responsibility for this. Don't you feel responsibility?
> TANAKA: I feel the same way. Since the verdict, I have been causing the LDP and party members trouble. I apologize.
> NAKASONE: Let us proceed with circumspection in this difficult situation.
> TANAKA: I'm going to act with care.
> NAKASONE: I want to think you will.

In his public account of the session, Nakasone said he had "indirectly advised" Tanaka to resign by "appealing to his feelings."

As long as Nakasone wanted to remain prime minister, there was nothing else he could do, since he was completely dependent upon the *gundan*'s backing for his job. After his halfhearted attempt to force Tanaka's resignation, party executives tried to claim that the Tanaka issue had been solved. Of course it hadn't, and the opposition parties, with the full support of the media, incessantly pressed to bring the "Tanaka issue" to a parliamentary vote. The LDP refused to let the resolution reach the floor. The impasse paralyzed the government for more than a month, and, with no compromise in sight, Nakasone contemplated dissolving Parliament and calling national elections. "The proposition is utterly outrageous," one newspaper editorialized. "Has politics become distorted to the point that a [parliamentary] dissolution is considered just to rescue a man who is under fire for his moral and political responsibilities for being sentenced to four years in prison by a district court?" The answer was "yes." The election was scheduled for December 18, 1983.

Now it was the voters' chance to weigh in. In principle, there was no doubt in the public's mind that Tanaka should pay for his crimes. Polls taken after the verdict showed national sentiment running 80 percent to 90 percent in favor of Tanaka's quitting Parliament. And on election day, the LDP was severely punished for its handling of the affair by losing thirty-six seats, including three held by cabinet members. Yet, as in the immediately prior elections, the matter wasn't so simple as accepting or rejecting Tanaka. Voters may have reviled the sinner, yet they found it hard to reject the sin: with Tanaka's help, his *gundan* members had done quite well for their respective districts over the years, and their constituents were not ready to give up that help. While Tanaka was personally unpopular across the country, his disciples proved resilient. The Tanaka faction slipped by only two seats in the 1983 election. That was by far the best performance of any LDP faction, meaning that the *gundan*'s share of seats within the ruling party—and the power that accompanied those numbers—actually *increased* after the boss's conviction. Among the *gundan*'s new MPs was Tanaka's son-in-law, Naoki Tanaka, who won handily in his first election in Fukushima Prefecture. Naoki, who had the solid backing of his district's construction companies, promised during the campaign to use his connections to increase public works spending in the underdeveloped region.

The only place where voters had a chance to decide Tanaka's fate directly was Niigata, and there he was regarded as a martyr. The region's long history of oppression at the hands of the central government "is still in the people's subconscious and has been kept in cold storage by the snow of long years," a prominent author from the region wrote at the time. "This happened to gush out at this election." Nearly nine of every ten eligible voters in the district braved an election day snowstorm to cast a ballot, compared with a relatively light national turnout of 68 percent. Tanaka won a breathtaking 220,761 of those votes, his highest total in the sixteen elections he had contested; it was 20 percent more than his previous best, more than quadruple that of his closest competitor in his district, more than that of any other politician in any district in the country that year—more, in fact, than any candidate for the lower house of Japan's Parliament had drawn in a decade. Tanaka called the results "a peasant rebellion," and he portrayed the election in high-minded terms as a mandate for his tenacity. "I am grateful for the voiceless voice of the Japanese people that has come my way in these stormy times," he told the press. "I will devote my life to answering this call. The responsibility is graven in my heart."

Shaken by the LDP's disastrous showing at the polls, Prime Minister Nakasone tried to appease Tanaka's critics by issuing a written pledge to "eliminate Kakuei Tanaka's so-called political influence entirely." But the election really heralded the exact opposite: the total evisceration of any possible political challenge to Tanaka's *gundan.*

Right after making his declaration, Nakasone named a new cabinet and again gave the Tanaka faction more posts than any of the intraparty rivals were given. The rush within the LDP to join the *gundan* continued, and less than a year after the verdict, the group had 120 members, reaching a new high of one third of the LDP's strength. The opposition, meanwhile, had been tamed. The New Liberal Club—the small party of young idealists who had left the LDP in 1976 to protest the Lockheed scandal—agreed to rejoin the ruling party in a coalition government. The Socialists claimed still to support a resolution forcing Tanaka to resign, but as a compromise they agreed to participate in the LDP's new parliamentary "political ethics advisory group" chaired by Ichiro Ozawa, Tanaka's favorite among the *gundan*'s younger members. The council's deliberations, which lasted more than a year, were vague and general; Tanaka's name was taboo, and the group ended by proposing only to establish a "political ethics examination council." When one member had the temerity to make a public apology for the group's glaring inaction, Ozawa huffily rebutted his remarks.

In 1984, Tanaka's standing also rose outside Nagatacho, Japan's Capitol Hill. Prominent business leaders sought him out; Soichiro Honda, the maverick founder of the Honda Motor Company, met Tanaka in the summer resort town of Karuizawa for a jovial day of golf. The conservative ex–prime minister became a curious cause célèbre for Japan's human rights advocates, who felt that the Lockheed trial had been an egregious example of government abuse. (Among their complaints, they noted that Tanaka's lawyers had been prohibited from cross-examining Lockheed president A. Carl Kotchian, whose testimony had been crucial to the prosecutors' case.) Three prominent civil liberties lawyers, who had earlier defended radical leftists, joined the defense team for Tanaka's appeal.

The general public did not exactly forgive Tanaka, but it did start to accept him as a kind of pop cult figure. In May 1984, a national television network broadcast a two-hour prime-time special, "Kakuei: One-Man Show," in which he offered a corny stream-of-consciousness reminiscence of his childhood. A feature-length cartoon parody, *Little Kakuei,* opened in movie theaters that September. A growing number of Japanese professed to admire Tanaka, if not for his ethics then at least for his determination and savvy. *Steal the Wisdom of Kakuei Tanaka: Why Do People Follow Him?* was the title of a 1984 book, which urged businessmen to study Tanaka's "good points." A book of sixty-one poems written by Osaka elementary school students included one entitled "I Like Kakuei Tanaka."

"I like Kakuei Tanaka," the eleven-year-old poet wrote.

He has courage.
I like his commanding way of walking.
And his characteristic way of raising a hand is also cool.
I think I'll walk in a commanding way like him when I grow up.

Whenever Tanaka made a public appearance, he was treated like a rock star. At a September 1984 speech in northern Japan, 160 buses jammed the parking lot and 12,000 people filled the auditorium, the balconies, and the halls, where television monitors were set up to transmit the talk to those who couldn't get seats; in near-100-degree heat, the crowd sat raptly through his nearly two-hour oration. "People have given up hope of cleaning up politics," an office worker who read a special new collection of Tanaka cartoons told a newspaper, attempting to explain this new national obsession. Instead, people "prefer to get some fun out of it."

Those who still attempted to take politics seriously, though, were outraged. "The situation is worse than it was a year ago," an *Asahi* editorial lamented on the first anniversary of Tanaka's conviction. "In the postwar years, no one else has wielded so [much] . . . power, not even Shigeru Yoshida," a columnist marveled, comparing the shadow shogun to the father of Japan's postwar conservative political line.

As Nakasone's term as prime minister neared expiration at the end of 1984, the *gundan* rewarded his obedience by throwing its full weight behind his reelection. The victorious Nakasone then once again dutifully awarded a dominant one fourth of his cabinet posts to the *gundan,* though Tanaka was now saying openly that his men should have gotten about half. Indeed, Tanaka was becoming increasingly outspoken, arrogant even, about his powers and his plans. He talked vividly and in great detail of far-reaching policy visions, from expanding the national railway system and reconstructing the nation's finances to bolstering U.S.-Japanese relations. "Although I won't expose my name publicly, I am preparing a concrete plan for administrative reform," he told one visitor. He was tanned, trim, relaxed. Since the verdict, his favored term for his souvenir calligraphy samples had been *"fudoshin,"* or "unshakable mind."

Tanaka sometimes spoke of stepping out of the shadows and making himself the nation's official leader. "In two years, the Lockheed incident will be cleared away. Nakasone is easy to use, so until then we'll put him up," he told a friendly MP at the end of 1984. And then "I'll be prime minister once again." Whether or not he really believed his own prediction, he did intend, in some form or another, to be in control for a long time to come. "I am turning sixty-six years old this year, and while I have often thought that I would continue in politics only until I turned sixty-five, I just cannot retire now," he told his assembled *gundan* in a September 1984 speech. "I cannot quit, even if I wanted to, until the Lockheed case is closed. I will take responsibility until I turn seventy-five, the average life expectancy. The heavens will not allow a peaceful life. I have convinced myself that this is what the gods want."

PART THREE

THE SECOND GENERATION: THE "BUBBLE POLITICS" OF SHIN KANEMARU, NOBORU TAKESHITA, AND ICHIRO OZAWA, 1985–1992

But Tanaka would prove to be mortal, prey to the overweening ambitions of his disciples. His downfall was finally engineered not by the hapless crowd of opponents, intellectuals, and reformers but by his closest followers, the ones famed for their ironlike unity in devotion to their boss. These pols were not driven by any repulsion to the machine or any desire to break it. On the contrary, they were enchanted by its enduring strength and desired ultimately to have it for themselves.

Despite its appearance of invincibility, Tanaka's power had actually rested on a fatal contradiction: his *gundan* was so effective because he recruited Japan's most capable, driven politicians and schooled them in his cutthroat ways; yet it relied on his keeping a lid on their ambitions. While helping his followers win elections and cabinet posts, he rejected all suggestions that he share control—real control—of the *gundan* with them. He tapped a series of elderly, easily manipulable, and disposable sycophants to be the titular heads of the group. He refused to designate a successor or even to acknowledge that he needed one, knowing full well that a worthy second in command would threaten his own clout. He forbade his followers from running for prime minister, since that would have scotched his own fantasies of returning to the post someday; informal power was the only type that Tanaka personally, as a felon, could wield until such time as he could be rehabilitated.

To justify relegating his faction members to underling status, he portrayed them as noble laborers who did the hard work while shirking glory. "Our people seem to be used to working subordinately . . . just like 'Miss Maids' or 'Miss Assistants,' working silently when told. I like it this way," he once said. "We are like snow that's trodden upon by wooden sandals," he liked to explain.

"Nobody wants to be trodden upon. But we must grin and bear it no matter how bitterly we resent it at times."

Even for Tanaka's men, however, endurance had its limits; the putsch came half a year later at the hands of Tanaka's most able lieutenants: Shin Kanemaru, Noboru Takeshita, and Ichiro Ozawa. The three were related to one another through a network of marriages—ties woven in part by Tanaka to foster greater unity among them. They came from two different generations of politicians and thus had different relations with their chief. Kanemaru and Takeshita had entered politics in the late 1950s and had already been fairly well established when the machine had been created. To Tanaka's Caesar, they had together played the role of Cassius—useful, yet, despite constant pledges of fealty, unsettling because of their "lean and hungry look." Ozawa joined Parliament in the late 1960s under Tanaka's tutelage. Always the boss's favorite, he became, in Tanaka's eyes, a kind of Brutus.

CHAPTER FOURTEEN

THE ODD COUPLE

SHIN KANEMARU (pronounced "KAH-neh-mah-roo") and Noboru Takeshita (pronounced "Tah-KEHSH-tah") had long been known as the odd couple of Nagatacho: Kanemaru, with crew cut and stolid, bulldog face atop his broad, athletic 198-pound frame, came across as menacing; the short, lithe Takeshita, with his apologetic, pained grin, appeared meek. Kanemaru was blunt, Takeshita polite and self-deprecating to a fault. Kanemaru was *"about-o"*—a Japanized English word connoting an imprecise, casual style—and, by his own admission, a politician who relied less on intellect than on his own infallible "animal instincts"; Takeshita was wily and meticulous. As Kanemaru put it, "I am a hatchet, Takeshita is a sashimi knife." After winning seats in Parliament in the same 1958 election, they virtually merged their ambitions, each helping the other as they climbed the ladder together. Kanemaru, ten years older, became the behind-the-scenes fixer, the "guardian" of the junior Takeshita, who played the front man. "Those two are one in body and spirit," Tanaka said of the pair, "like head and tail."

The partners came from similar roots, each the eldest son of a moderately wealthy, rural sake-brewing family. Kanemaru was born in 1914, in Yamanashi Prefecture, a landlocked valley at the foot of magnificent Mount Fuji, just sixty miles from Tokyo. The region sustained a rich and varied agriculture from grains to tobacco, and the young Kanemaru enjoyed sneaking into fields with his buddies to eat grapes and watermelons. Takeshita was born in 1924, in remote, mountainous Shimane (pronounced "Shi-MAH-neh") Prefecture, a rickety eighteen-hour train and bus ride from the nation's capital. Though located, like Tanaka's impoverished home of Niigata, in *ura Nippon* along the Japan Sea coast, Takeshita's western hamlet was at least blessed with a more temperate, fertile climate. The region was also rich with tradition, home to Japan's most ancient shrines, and famous for its verdant beauty.

Takeshita came from a long-established family; he was the twelfth-generation head of his clan, whose combined Chinese characters, *take* (pronounced "TAH-keh") and *shita,* literally mean "below the bamboo trees," a reference to the location of the 300-year-old family farm. In the 1860s, the Takeshitas opened a brewery. Before the war, sake production was a common source of prestige in small Japanese communities, since the producer necessarily had access to the valuable rice crop and the land on which the liquor's main ingredient grew. The fathers of both Kanemaru and Takeshita used their positions as springboards into local politics, each winning seats in their regional legislatures; the sons also used the family affluence to win friends, becoming known in their schools for distributing candies and other favors.

By their mothers, both boys were instructed to use power judiciously, to be sensitive to the needs of the less fortunate. Takeshita's mother, who was influenced by a famed local Marxist, abolished the near-feudal apprentice system in the brewery and changed the sake brand name from "Hinode," or "Sunrise," to "Taishu," or "The Masses." Kanemaru's mother was a Christian with an egalitarian streak who insisted that the brewery workers share the family's dinner. In response to tenant farmers' complaints of oppressive poverty in the 1930s, the Kanemarus gave the tenants parcels of land. And when, after the war, the American Occupation ordered just such reforms nationwide to restructure Japanese society, the twenty-two-year-old Takeshita served as a landlord representative in his community's land-reform council; he claims to have gone even further than the Americans, urging a transfer not just of the rice paddies but also of the mountains and forests, so that peasants could gather straw and firewood.

In their youths, both men displayed the traits that would later become their hallmarks as politicians. Kanemaru was a proud rogue, dedicated mainly to drinking, fighting, womanizing, and other moral and legal indiscretions—tales recounted with great glee, and perhaps some embellishment, in his two bawdy autobiographies. As children, he and his younger brother were enlisted to sneak illicit contributions to their father's campaigns. His mother would take the payoffs at home, stuff them into a lunch box, and send the innocent-looking boys to deliver the cash to the election office. "Good boy," the unsuspecting policeman stationed outside to watch out for bribes would say. "You brought lunch for your father."

Throughout his schooling, Shin was a poor student, constantly being suspended for mischief; he described his experience at the second-rate Tokyo Agricultural University as "walking through the entrance and walking out through the exit—but I did graduate." Books interested him less than brawling. A shy child until the second grade, he became outgoing and confident when he knocked out the school bully. He went on to gain some fame as a black-belt judo champion but also continued his extracurricular bouts. When a cop tried to arrest a college buddy for starting a barroom scrap, Shin jumped the officer; as he was dragged to the police station against his will, he knocked down motorbikes and fences. Kanemaru's boisterous streak continued during questioning, as he kicked the desks, and on into his jail cell, where he picked a fight with some local gangsters. He ended the night asleep in his underwear on the concrete floor. Alcohol helped fuel his temper; he would often fund his binges by pawning his possessions, including his bed.

Graduation was hardly a mellowing influence. He managed to get a job teaching biology and judo at a junior high school in Yamanashi, where he stunned the faculty gathered in the lounge by putting a hostile vice principal into a neck hold. In 1937, he spent just eight months in the Imperial Army, doing a brief stint in Manchuria before being discharged with pleurisy. Upon returning to Japan, he took over the family brewery, where wartime sales—and profits—were booming. He joked about selling sake so diluted that goldfish could swim in it. Kanemaru's own personal stash was certainly strong enough: "I bought a small Harley," he wrote of those days, and "because of my business I often drove in a state of being dipped in alcohol. It is probably more accurate to say I was bumping and crashing than driving." Kanemaru married in 1941, but that didn't stop him from indulging in the pleasures of the local geisha quarters, a district first introduced to him by his father. When his main mistress fell ill and died, he started tongues wagging by serving as chief mourner at the funeral, a grand public event attended by 150 geisha. Kanemaru tried to persuade his wife that he would reform; he slipped, however, when he told her he had visited the Ise shrine on a business trip but wrapped the relic he had bought her—actually purchased by a messenger—in a newspaper from Kyoto, where he had been carousing instead. Kanemaru's sons mainly remember him as being either silly—dancing naked, drawing pictures on his belly—or absent.

But it would be misleading to suggest that Kanemaru was merely a frivolous, selfish cad. While openly flouting social conventions, he portrayed himself as a man bound by his own strict code of honor who struggled to balance duty and feeling. He was said to embody the traits revered in traditional Japanese culture: *giri,* a deep allegiance bound by obligations, and *ninjo,* or "human feeling." He was a brutal realist who understood that performing good deeds might mean committing sordid acts, and he talked often of "wearing mud" and of *sutemi,* a word meaning "self-sacrifice," or literally "throwing away one's life." One of his early, famous acts of *sutemi* came during the war, when the government wanted to halve alcohol output and use the breweries for oxygen production and other military purposes; Kanemaru persuaded fellow Yamanashi brewers to comply by first closing his own operations.

To his many followers, Kanemaru's main flaws were not his improprieties but his stark honesty about his actions, his fidelity to friends less chivalrous than he, and his susceptibility to a sob story. "I once told him that he can't keep helping everybody with every problem," a supporter said. "His reaction was that he could not discriminate among people." Those traits, together with his boyish charm, won him unlikely friends and admirers. The showy funeral for his mistress, for example, drew the respect of a leading local banker, who became central to expanding Kanemaru's business: "Any other guy would have run away from such trouble," the banker said. "I'm glad I know you." "There are a lot of people here who were beat up by Kanemaru when he was a kid, but now all of us are his supporters," said a longtime hometown fan more than half a century later. "He gave these people sweets after he walloped them and, in this way, evened things out. He has been fair since he was a child."

One incident in particular, recounted in his autobiography, captures the subtle complexities behind his crass exterior. As a prominent community businessman, Kanemaru got involved in a parliamentary campaign in 1953. His role: to buy votes for his candidate, a crime the local authorities stumbled across on election eve. Tipped off that he was under investigation, Kanemaru was urged to skip town, but instead he headed straight to the town's geisha quarters for a final night of pleasure before entering the pen. The police finally tracked him down after midnight and summoned the suspect to a detective's house for questioning.

"Give me the names of the people you bribed," the inspector demanded. Kanemaru stoically refused to volunteer anything. Flustered, the policeman walked out of the room, leaving crucial evidence —the business cards of the payola recipients—on the table. Kanemaru thought fast: "I ripped up the cards and put them into my mouth," he wrote. "As you know, business cards are not easy to swallow." Fortunately there was sake on hand; when Kanemaru had first arrived that night, the detective's wife had offered him tea, and he had persuaded her to fill the kettle with liquor. "I drank the sake from the teapot, then swallowed the business cards. When I finished, I was very drunk." The detective, returning to the room, turned pale. "You can search me all over," Kanemaru taunted, "but if you don't have any evidence, I'm not guilty. So let me go." In the morning, the humiliated officer handed his troublesome suspect over to the prosecutors. As they interrogated other witnesses, Kanemaru fell asleep after his long night, interrupting the questioning with loud snores. "I've never seen anybody like you!" the exasperated prosecutor exclaimed. "I don't know if you're clever or stupid!" The answer, as was often the case with Kanemaru, was: much cannier than he might have seemed. Rather than becoming a black mark on his record, the brush with the law helped pave the way for Kanemaru's new career in public service.

The evidence-eating episode left Kanemaru intrigued, in his own way, with Japan's new democracy: he was ultimately spared prison, thanks to his candidate-employer's intervention, and "after that incident I felt . . . strongly the power of political influence." More important, Kanemaru's candidate, Hisatada Hirose, a member of a prominent Yamanashi business and political family, was extremely moved by the loyalty and *sutemi* ethic of his campaign volunteer. Five years later, Hirose urged Kanemaru himself to run for Parliament and offered his considerable clout to assist the campaign. (As further testimony to Kanemaru's political agility, even the outsmarted cop forgave the caper and later asked Kanemaru to head the wedding party at his daughter's wedding.)

Another inspiration for Kanemaru's entry into politics was his experience as an affluent executive. Like many a businessman who would, in later years, seek the help of the Tanaka political machine, Kanemaru had felt the irritations of Japan's meddlesome bureaucracy. The head of the Yamanashi tax office was constantly haranguing him, "convinced that all sake shops were cheats," Kanemaru wrote. "I became aware of political barriers." A career in government, he felt, could help himself and others like him. "I have literally experienced the trials and tribulations of small enterprises," he wrote in his campaign leaflets, promising to be their advocate, as well as that of the farmers and the underprivileged.

On the stump, the pudgy, sweating Kanemaru was awkward but enthusiastic. During the campaign, he also skirted the tight restrictions on political advertising by commissioning a confectionery company to make a candy named after himself, "Little Shin Sweets." He topped the list of candidates to become, at age forty-four, a member of Japan's national Parliament.

LIKE KANEMARU, the young Takeshita was an avid judo fighter, reaching the rank of black belt. But his technique was completely different. He became known as "Master of the Draw" for his tendency to avoid claiming victory over weaker opponents while averting defeat by larger foes. It was telling that, even in an organized fight, Takeshita could find a way to compromise, to mollify. The skinny, pale schoolboy with the nickname "Forehead" won a following for his skills as a mediator. In his boarding school dorm room, he talked the older boys out of torturing underclassmen with red-hot metal. When a teacher caught Noboru and his fifth-grade friends breaking school rules by visiting a noodle shop without their parents, he negotiated with the teacher to avoid punishment for the group.

Takeshita was an above-average student, and, though he failed twice to gain admission to his preferred college, he eventually went off to prestigious Waseda University in Tokyo. His studies were interrupted by the war, but he managed to stay in Japan, dispatched to a western region, where he gained the rank of second lieutenant as a special pilot instructor. While Takeshita was enlisted in the military, his wife, whom he had married just a year earlier, committed suicide. The tragedy—still clouded in dark rumors about the circumstances that had driven her to such despair—was said to be the last time that Takeshita, then twenty-one years old, displayed any strong emotion. He became obsessed with composure and self-control, boasting that he would never, under any circumstances, show anger. After the war, Takeshita remarried, this time a distant relative, completed his studies, and became a substitute English teacher, though he could barely speak the language. (Years later, he delivered a speech in English from a prepared text at an international conference; afterward, an audience member marveled, "I didn't realize Japanese was so similar to English.")

Takeshita's real passion was politics. He would come to say that he had been inspired to enter public service by the destruction he had seen in his homeland at the end of the war. And he did join his local Youth Association, part of an idealistic movement that sprouted across the country to help rebuild the devastated nation. Takeshita and his fellows hauled logs down from the mountains, extracted salt from ocean water, and scooped pebbles from rivers to rebuild the local kindergarten.

But it quickly became clear that Takeshita was obsessed with the process, as much as the purpose, of politics. He staged mock parliamentary sessions in his hometown, dividing friends into ruling and opposition parties and presiding over the sessions. He angled to become head of the Youth Association for all of Shimane Prefecture and used the group as his personal campaign organization to win a seat in the prefectural assembly in 1951, at age twenty-seven. During his two terms and seven years in the assembly, he spoke only three times during deliberations. He preferred not to make any enemies through public questioning, focusing instead on building up his personal network.

The most important political connection Takeshita sealed during his early career was with the Tanabe family, a household that for centuries had enjoyed near-monopoly control over Shimane's natural resources and thereby dominated the local economy, politics, and culture. The Tanabes were known as the "kings of the mountains and forests" and at their peak owned land exceeding the area of Tokyo. While the Tanabes' holdings were sharply reduced by the postwar Occupation reforms, their local clout was not; the head of the family presided as governor of the prefecture for twelve years. It was only with the "permission" of the Tanabe clan that Takeshita's ancestors had become sake brewers; the Takeshitas were considered all but Tanabe vassals. As a boy, Noboru's father took him often to pay obeisance to the Tanabes, and the magnate, according to one account, treated Noboru for a time "as if he were his own son."

Takeshita at first irked the Tanabes with his run for the prefectural assembly—the family was backing a rival candidate—but he regained their favor by, among other things, lobbying hard to run government-funded roads through the Tanabe-owned mountains.

In 1958, with the full backing of the local barons and his Youth Association machine, Takeshita declared his candidacy for the national Parliament. His platform consisted of two vague planks: to "send a new wind" to politics, and to "become a bridge" between the national and local governments. It was not a smooth campaign: ninety-seven of his supporters were arrested for campaign finance violations. Nevertheless, the thirty-four-year-old Takeshita led the field.

THAT ELECTION was the first contested for the powerful lower house of Parliament by the Liberal Democratic Party, an alliance of probusiness conservative forces created to counter the surging popularity of the Left. Kanemaru and Takeshita were among the many bright new prospects recruited by the party during that campaign. In Tokyo both newcomers were introduced, through their respective local patrons, to Eisaku Sato, then a rising star in the LDP, who would serve as prime minister from 1964 to 1972, until Tanaka's ascent. Kanemaru and Takeshita became fast friends as the junior members of Sato's faction. Takeshita impressed his elder with his ability to imbibe; asked three decades later about his first impression of Takeshita, Kanemaru replied in part, "We drank most of the time. Takeshita has a high tolerance for alcohol, and between the two of us we could empty a bottle of Suntory Old whiskey."

The two also had in common newfound financial troubles: the high cost of national politics had stretched both of their family fortunes. Takeshita was forced to live in a tiny flat in a dreary dormitory for MPs; at one point Kanemaru couldn't pay his bills at the legislature's restaurant, which cut him off. Kanemaru, as Takeshita put it, "was rich enough to own a car but not rich enough to hire a driver"; Takeshita could not afford his own car, so he would often hitch rides with Kanemaru. Early on, they went together in Kanemaru's Austin-Healy to receive money from Sato, their new political boss. Sato handed each of them a bundle of 10,000-yen notes, compact enough to fit in their pockets. "It's so small," Kanemaru blurted out. Sato's eyes widened as he sneered, "Shall I change them to hundred-yen bills?" Back in the car, Kanemaru showed

Takeshita the suitcase he had brought along in the hope of filling it. Takeshita pulled out his large cloth sack. The two shared a disappointed laugh.

Throughout the 1960s, the two men developed their political skills and reputations. Takeshita ingratiated himself with Sato and became the leader's favored disciple. He was permitted to stand in the back of the room during high-level meetings and was given a series of assignments designed to apprentice him in the nuts and bolts of politics, from election strategy to working with the bureaucracy to navigating legislation through Parliament. In time, Takeshita evolved from student to skilled practitioner, becoming known as the prime minister's "handyman."

Kanemaru, meanwhile, reverted to the talent that had won him his reputation as a youth: brawling. Those were the violent days in Japan's legislature, when the fate of bills sometimes hinged less on debates and votes than on blockades and scuffles. In his first term in Parliament, Kanemaru broke through one opposition barricade by leaping from the gallery into a committee room. He gained brief national, and international, fame for his role in ensuring ratification of the landmark U.S.-Japan security treaty in 1960. Moved by thousands of demonstrators protesting against the pact outside the Parliament building, Socialist legislators inside tried to stop the treaty from coming to a vote by surrounding the speaker of the lower house and occupying his podium. Kanemaru penetrated the opposition's defenses, reaching the diminutive speaker. He then lifted the elderly chairman over his head and carried him through the angry mob, administering judo kicks along the way, until he could gently lower the speaker to the microphone. The speaker's leg was sprained, but he was able to officially declare the session open, and the controversial treaty was adopted. In America, *Life* magazine featured the scene on its cover. Kanemaru put the incident to good use four years later, when, as a parliamentary vice minister for telecommunications, he traveled to Washington to take part in difficult negotiations over satellite broadcasting. After other Japanese officials failed to win the desired concessions, Kanemaru told the American official of his appearance in *Life*. "I put my life at stake," Kanemaru told him. "You're a hero," the American responded as he took Kanemaru's hand and relented.

In 1968, the friends became family when Kanemaru's eldest son married Takeshita's eldest daughter, further intermingling their fortunes. Three years later, Prime Minister Sato awarded Takeshita, his prize pupil, the plum assignment of chief cabinet secretary. Kanemaru, whose skills were less highly valued by party elders, was made the LDP's representative to the crucial Parliamentary Policy Committee. Kanemaru had been given his surprise promotion, he was told, because his son was married to Takeshita's daughter and the party elders thought that the two pols should have "matching posts."

The appointment turned out to be one of the most important stepping-stones in Kanemaru's career. The committee was an official body for ruling and opposition parties to try to smooth out their differences or, at the very least, to agree to allow peaceable deliberations on controversial bills; it became the main venue for the Tanaka-built machine's cynical co-option of the opposition parties. In characteristic style, Kanemaru—who had made a name for himself in the 1950s and early 1960s by literally clobbering Socialists—used the post to become the best buddy leftist MPs had in the conservative camp. Kanemaru went on to hold the post for four terms and developed close friendships with opposition leaders: he took them to dinner, hosted them at New Year's, played (and lost at) mah-jongg, bathed with them at hot-spring resorts, even went with them on European vacations. Kanemaru took care to befriend not just the politicians but their families as well. "He knows not only the opposition MPs' birthdays but also their wives' birthdays," Kanemaru's son said. "He sent better presents to the wives." To those who initially thought Kanemaru's extreme fraternizing with the parliamentary enemy odd, he invoked his code of the primacy of "human relations." Speaking of his ties with a leading Socialist, he explained, "I am a very flexible person, and he too has a flexibility rare in a Socialist lawmaker. . . . I understand his feelings, and he does mine. I think this is democracy." The personal trust and loyalty the opposition developed for Kanemaru became a source of power for him, as the LDP and the bureaucracy often pleaded for his help in handling tough legislative matters. "There must be at least ten top opposition party officials who would be willing to comply with my requests on the strength of a single phone call," he once boasted.

Near the end of the Sato administration, Kanemaru and Takeshita began to set their sights on one day making Takeshita himself premier. (Kanemaru, because he had entered politics relatively late, and because of his coarse manner, wasn't considered a serious contender. "I dislike formalities. All those guards and police cars that follow make me just want to lie across the backseat," he told an interviewer. "As long as I support someone who contributes to the nation, it's the same as if I were he.") Takeshita, glad to aim for the highest post, had no reservations about stating his goals explicitly, which he did, among other ways, in a drinking ditty he sang for an increasingly wide circle of friends. *"Toko zundoko, zundoko"* went the nonsense refrain; the lyrics reviewed the accomplishments of recent prime ministers and then prophesied, "In ten years, it will be time for Takeshita-san."

CHAPTER FIFTEEN

"ICHIRO . . . MY LOST SON"

In 1972, the logical move for any politician with higher aspirations was to jump onto Kakuei Tanaka's populist bandwagon. That's just what Takeshita and Kanemaru did, becoming early members of the *gundan* and backing Tanaka's dramatic bid for prime minister that summer. They were joined in the crusade by a much younger man, brimming with ambition and hypnotized by the new leader's magnetism: Ichiro Ozawa, not yet thirty years old. As the "baby" of the new fraternity, Ozawa was chosen to make the first toast of the *gundan*'s first meeting; he leaped to his feet and roared, "To a Tanaka administration!" For Ozawa, Tanaka was more than just a steppingstone; he was his political father.

Ozawa's real father, Saeki, was an MP who had died in 1968 at the age of seventy after a rags-to-riches life much like Tanaka's. He was born in the far-northern region of Iwate (pronounced "EE-wah-teh"), known as "the Tibet of Japan," where his father—Ichiro's grandfather—had squandered a decent family fortune in drink and was unable to pay for his son's education. When the dissolute elder tried to force Saeki into apprenticeship as a carpenter, the twelve-year-old boy fled to Tokyo to find a better life. With no friends or family, he slept nights in a public park until he was given housing by an army officer who found him there, and he took odd jobs—as ricksha puller, as custodian—to fund going to night school. Saeki's hardships, Ichiro would later insist, made both father and son "anti-establishment," a trait that eventually drew the son into the populist Tanaka's fold.

Saeki became a lawyer and then a leader in Tokyo city politics in the 1930s. He was repelled by Japan's turn to militarism and, during the war, retreated to his native Iwate to farm and open a country law practice. In 1946, he seized the opportunity presented by the new American-sponsored democracy, when many establishment politicians were being purged, to win a seat in the national Parliament. Over the next two decades—through four cabinet posts and numerous key parliamentary positions—he served as what his official biography calls a "main supporting actor" in establishing Japan's probusiness, conservative political order. As posts and telecommunications minister in the late 1940s, he worked to break the new militant labor unions. A stint as construction minister in the mid-1950s gave him early exposure to pork-barrel politics; the dams, trains, and flood prevention projects he brought to northern Japan became "the first foundation of Ozawa politics" in his district, according to a local journalist. In 1960, Saeki chaired the committee that railroaded the passage of the 1960 U.S.-Japan security treaty through Parliament. His passion was election strategy and the obscure but controversial issue of manipulating electoral rules to marginalize the Left's legislative role. Like the younger Kanemaru, Saeki was a leading parliamentary pugilist—he was called the "Fighting Bull of Iwate," and a framed cartoon hangs in the family home depicting the bespectacled Saeki wearing boxing gloves. In one famed melee, Saeki suffered a punctured eardrum; in another, he was tossed out of the committee room still clinging to his chair.

Saeki was a revered but distant figure to his only son, Ichiro, who was born in 1942, when Saeki was well over forty years old. Saeki left his son and two daughters back amid the rice fields of Iwate while he spent most of his time in Tokyo, tending to national policies and his many mistresses. Meanwhile, little Ichiro's life was shaped by the aura of his famous father. He was given police protection at the age of seven, when Saeki's union busting made the family a potential target of left-wing militancy. He cried on a school outing to the movies when a newsreel showed Saeki, blood streaming from his head, trying to chair a hearing that had turned into a fistfight. At the time, MPs were like local emperors, and Ichiro was treated by his classmates with a mixture of teasing and respect as the "minister's son." But Ichiro has almost no personal childhood memories of his father. He was raised mainly by his mother, Michi, whose "influence on my personality," he would later say, "was enormous."

Michi Ozawa came, as her son describes her, "from a landowner class, and was given a royalist and patriotic education." She instilled in Ichiro a fierce pride in her aristocratic samurai heritage—to this day, he refuses to visit Miyajima, one of Japan's most revered shrines, because it was built to honor a clan that fought a twelfth-century battle against his ancestors. His mother also trained him in a strict samurai code of discipline, teaching him *gaman,* or extreme endurance. In the winter, he was made to wash his face in freezing cold water, and he was given few luxuries despite the family's wealth. (Michi herself lived frugally; she wore plain clothes and traveled the district by bus.) He was told never to cry—a schoolteacher says Ichiro tried to hide burns he suffered on a field trip until somebody noticed the welts and took him to the hospital—to ignore insults, and never to fight, "even if somebody says black is white." "Behave impeccably, so that you don't give others cause to mock you as an MP's child," Michi directed. "She taught me responsibility," the grown Ichiro would say, "and gave me an autonomous spirit."

Michi was a driven woman, said to be more ambitious than her husband. According to local legend, she spent her wedding day carrying around a bucket of paste to stick up posters for Saeki's Tokyo city assembly campaign. Years later, she excoriated him for giving up a cabinet post to a friend: "I cannot go back and face our supporters who expected you to have a minister's post!" she shouted at him. "I cannot live with a man like you anymore! I'll leave home tomorrow!"

Despite her highbrow upbringing near Tokyo, she thrived in the new, raucous rural democracy of her adopted home of Iwate. Saeki rarely came back to his constituency, leaving management of the district office and campaigning almost entirely to her. When Ichiro came home from school, he often found his mother busy with a room full of petitioners seeking favors; so many came that a next-door neighbor sometimes had to house the overflow. The people of Mizusawa, the Ozawa hometown, took their elections very seriously—the candy stores and fish sellers were divided into pro-Ozawa and anti-Ozawa camps, and loyalists rarely shopped across party lines. And nobody worked the district better than Michi. "She remembered faces of people from the villages, saying 'Oh, Mr. So-and-so,' and smiled," recalls a family employee. "When Saeki would say 'Such-and-such a person is a pest,' she would scold, 'Don't say that! He can deliver thirty votes.' Elections were all she thought about." Saeki himself was an awkward figure as a campaigner; he suffered from a facial nerve disorder that made him look demonic whenever he tried to grin, but "people used to love to visit Michi just because of her warm and smiling welcome," said the employee.

Nurtured in such a remarkably political household, young Ichiro was surprisingly apolitical and unremarkable. He is remembered by schoolmates and teachers, and has been portrayed in numerous published accounts, as taciturn, shy, and deliberate. "He was such a quiet kid," recalls the family maid. "He was always upstairs by himself studying." "Unlike other children who aggressively raised their hands to answer questions, he always contemplated for a long time, slowly raising his hand," says an early teacher. "He never said anything unnecessary." Ichiro's parents wanted to send him to school in Tokyo; he failed an attempt to get into a prestigious junior high there but was later sent to the capital, at age fourteen, to attend high school.

In the big city, the other students laughed at Ichiro's strong north-country accent and he had few close friends. He dreamed of entering the elite Tokyo University, even memorizing its dormitory songs. But he was a mediocre student and, despite two tries, flunked the tough entrance exam. At his backup choice, Keio University in Tokyo, some remember Ichiro as a loner. "He never spoke out, unless we repeatedly asked him something," according to one classmate. His serious manner, accentuated by his stiff posture, inspired the moniker "Dad." Others saw him as frivolous, quick to laugh, quick to drink, dismissive of serious subjects. But nobody remembers him as a notable scholar. (Ozawa now bristles at the popular portrayal of an unexceptional adolescence: "I was a strong fighter. I was good at any sport, and I was very good at studying too," he told a friendly journalist years later. "Recent books say I was a very ordinary boy, but I wonder . . .")

Living in Tokyo with Saeki, Ichiro got some firsthand exposure to the excitement of national politics. At seventeen, he was forced to evacuate the family home by menacing protesters opposed to the U.S.-Japan security treaty, which Saeki was helping enact. "I had not felt close to my father before then," Ozawa later said, "but I was moved by his political creed and I was proud of him." In college, Ichiro became Saeki's chauffeur, driving him to high-level meetings. Yet politics was not considered Ichiro's destiny. He barely campaigned for his father and never visited Parliament when Saeki was alive. Saeki never encouraged his son to follow him; instead, he constantly lectured Ichiro: "Carve out your career by yourself. I built up my career by myself. I had nothing to rely on. Go your own way." "I don't want him to be a politician," Michi said of her son. "I'm fed up with the pains suffered by the family of a politician." Ichiro flirted with joining the military. "Japan's business world and political world have become corrupted," he told a friend. "I want to become an officer because I am longing for a pure world." He ultimately decided to seek a career in law, entering his father's alma mater of Nihon University; upon completion of his studies, he failed yet another exam, this time for the bar.

While Ichiro was busy studying to attempt the bar again, Saeki entered the hospital in the spring of 1968 with severe stomach pains. His health had been failing since a stroke shortly after the security treaty battle; he had long since given up cavorting with geisha and instead spent many evenings drinking alone, or with his son, at home. At the time, Saeki was chairman of a special committee on election laws; three weeks into his hospital stay, he told his son, "I will attend the committee meeting tomorrow." The next day, May 8, 1968, he died of acute heart failure.

By then, Michi, who had politics in her blood, had changed her mind about her son's future. A few weeks later, a mourner tried to console her, making the observation that she need not worry about elections any longer. "Well," she said, "I am thinking of pushing Ichiro as a successor." Ichiro reluctantly decided to give up pursuing a law career and run for his father's seat in Parliament. The problem was convincing Saeki's Iwate machine: some members had their own ambitions; others were simply unimpressed with Ichiro or miffed that he had never taken the time to get to know the group. In addition, the son was an unknown quantity, too green and too quiet. "I only rode in the car with him once," said one leader at a meeting of the group, raising an objection, "and I was left thinking I couldn't figure him out." "What can that greenhorn do?" the mayor of Mizusawa reportedly snapped at Michi, who sought his backing. "He needs at least two or three years of holding the bags for" a respected elder politician from the area.

But Michi continued to beg and cajole on behalf of her son. And there was the strong pull of inertia working in Ichiro's favor. In Iwate, as in many electoral districts around Japan, an MP's "support group" is as important as the MP himself. It is a finely calibrated confederation of interests that reaps favors only if the organization keeps sending a representative to Parliament. Succession always poses a problem for these groups, since a new candidate may not gain the same backing from all members; yet dissolution of the group would leave members with the onerous and uncertain task of building a new coalition. Choosing an MP's son is often considered the least disruptive course. That logic has been a major force in postwar Japanese politics; by the 1980s, more than 40 percent of all conservative MPs were so-called second-generation politicians who had inherited support organizations and seats. (Indeed, by the late 1970s, Ozawa was one of three second-generation LDP MPs sent from the Iwate Second District to Tokyo.) Such candidates are also desirable to the national parties because they don't require the expenditure of major resources to build new local bases.

So when a general election was called for December 27, 1969, Ichiro Ozawa was a candidate, backed squarely by his late father's organization—and his mother, Michi's, electoral wizardry. At strategy sessions, Ichiro sometimes stood silently by his mother's side while she did the talking. On one occasion, one of his father's secretaries took the new candidate to meet supporters, each of whom plied him with a welcoming drink; when Ichiro got sick, his mother bawled out the handler. Michi even gave a joint interview with Ichiro to the *Asahi* newspaper shortly before the election:

> MOTHER: You are so quiet, but somehow you often manage to get your own way.
>
> SON: Yes, I do show respect to my elders and make efforts to coordinate their views with mine gradually.

Ichiro did add some of his own color to the campaign: he formed a new Youth Action Team of former elementary school classmates, and he was persuaded by a professional campaign manager—over Michi's objections—to abandon the family preference for plain, cheap clothing and don expensive suits and ties.

On election day, Ichiro led the pack with 71,000 votes, 20,000 more than Saeki had won in his last contest. When Ichiro made his first appearance in Parliament, he created a minor stir by taking Michi with him, apparently in gratitude for her invaluable nurturing. "An MP coming to the legislature with his mother may be an unprecedented occurrence," one account reported.

Another important influence in Ozawa's election was the endorsement he received from Kakuei Tanaka, then still an exciting comer in the Liberal Democratic Party.

It took months for the candidate just to get an audience with the rough-hewn Tanaka, who was apparently suspicious of a law school student trying to ride his daddy's coattails into Parliament. At their first meeting at the Mejiro mansion, Tanaka gave Ichiro his usual sermon: don't just rest on your father's laurels; visit thirty thousand households and make fifty thousand speeches. Only then can you get elected. "He had tremendous force" was how Ozawa recalled the session. The neophyte, in contrast, "was so stiff and serious, standing with both hands stuck to his sides, that I almost broke out laughing" was a Tanaka aide's impression. After the senior pol's speech, the newcomer simply barked, "Yes!"

But Tanaka sensed that the younger Ozawa—who had his father's base and his own obvious determination—could win. Tanaka invited Michi, and then Ozawa's Iwate support group, to Mejiro; a caravan of five buses carrying two hundred Ozawa supporters made the overnight trek. A table laden with beer, sake, and food was waiting for them. Tanaka called Ichiro to stand next to him and, in an hour-long oration, promised, "I will take care of Ichiro as a successor to his father." Tanaka then dispatched an assistant to Iwate to help Michi with the campaign. The emissary visited local bigwigs, presented Tanaka's name card, and said, "My boss . . . will take responsibility for Ichiro. . . . We promise to make him into a professional politician."

In that 1969 election, Tanaka gave similar support to many aspiring pols as he actively cultivated followers for his impending push for prime minister. Those who entered Parliament under his guidance became a close-knit fraternity, developing friendships in a select club that would dominate their careers—and shape Japanese politics—for years to come. They drank together and traveled together. Ozawa and another colleague in the clique shared the same birthday, May 24, and the date became the occasion for an annual party for them all. The main bond uniting the group was their enthusiastic devotion to the man who had given them their start and their political education, the leader who was going to revolutionize their country. They prowled the Parliament buildings, lining up support for the Tanaka administration. "If you do not support Tanaka, I will consider you to be an enemy," one of them would say. "I will cut your legs off with a saw." They were given various nicknames: "Tanaka's bodyguards," the "seven magistrates," the "boys' detective unit."

Within this group, Ozawa did not, at first, stand out. He struck some members of the hardened parliamentary press corps as rather dim; when asked about issues, he would often simply respond, "Hmmmm." He was treated at first like a kid brother by his colleagues, who called him "Principal" with affectionate mocking since he was given many small administrative tasks. (Some press accounts describe colleagues doing the indolent Ozawa's laundry for him.) "Since Ozawa was young," one member of the "bodyguards" later wrote in his memoirs, "he did not like coming to the front. He was not interested in posts or being on TV."

But a special bond quickly formed between Tanaka and his youngest acolyte. Ozawa, who had lost the father he had never really grown close to, started calling Tanaka *"oyaji,"* a tender equivalent of "My Old Man." Tanaka had a son born in 1942—the same year as Ozawa—who had died at the age of three. He often claimed to see a resemblance between the two, as if Ichiro were the grown son he had never had. "Ichiro's hands are soft and warm. I hope he will grow up and become a successful man without losing the flexibility of ideas and the warmth of mind," Tanaka wrote in a support letter for Ozawa during the 1972 election—a time when Tanaka was prime minister and at the peak of his national popularity. "I have watched him these last three years and felt as if I've brought back my lost son. . . . For the future of Japan, I desire to have young Ichiro's brain and warm heart. He needs your warm consideration." While Tanaka felt he could mold Ozawa as he would a son, he also, perhaps, saw a bit of himself in his young follower. Though they had been raised in different classes, both Tanaka and Ozawa had grown up as country boys. And despite his quiet, deferential public image, Ozawa was in private cocky and strong-willed, insistent on standing his ground in debates with his elders, including Tanaka. The senior pol enjoyed the cheeky challenges. Above all, Tanaka sensed that Ozawa would be loyal; "He knew that I wouldn't be unfaithful," Ozawa said. Tanaka handpicked Ozawa's staff, and Ozawa became a kind of Tanaka mascot, spending more time hanging around his office than any other politician did. Sometimes Tanaka would call out, "Ichiro, let's play *shogi,*" and they'd play the Japanese chess game for hours, until the boss would say, "That's it."

"I wasn't simply a member of the Tanaka faction," Ozawa fondly reminisced in later years. "*Oyaji* guided me in both public and private life. He taught me about politics from the basics, and he looked after me as if he were my father, even in private matters." A classic blend of Tanaka's personal and political guidance was Ozawa's marriage in 1973. As a father figure, Tanaka was worried that Ichiro —then thirty-one and enjoying the playboy lifestyle of a big-shot bachelor—had not yet settled down. One day he summoned Ozawa and told him he had found him a wife and that the wedding date was set for three months hence. Ozawa was crestfallen but obedient. The choice of a mate was a masterful political gambit: Kazuko Fukuda, the eldest daughter of Tadashi Fukuda, chairman of Fukuda-gumi, the largest construction company in Tanaka's Niigata. In one stroke, Tanaka had literally married Ozawa to the construction industry, the chief sponsor of Tanaka's growing electoral and financial empire. (Tanaka later arranged the marriage of Ozawa's wife's sister to Takeshita's half brother, making Ozawa and Takeshita—and, by extension, Ozawa and Kanemaru—family.) More than a thousand guests, including the nation's top business and political leaders, attended the lavish Ozawa-Fukuda ceremony, held in Tokyo's swank New Otani hotel. One of Ozawa's fellow MP "bodyguards" was the master of ceremonies; another hosted the reception counter. Tanaka stood in as Ozawa's father.

THE INTERNAL DYNAMICS of the Tanaka apparatus changed subtly from 1974 to 1976, when its leader—hit in short order by the conflict-of-interest scandal and then his arrest in the Lockheed affair—was transformed in the public mind from a populist to a crook. Not that anybody in Tanaka's circle was planning to abandon him or was particularly disturbed by the allegations. "You can't conduct politics without money," Kanemaru said matter-of-factly in a public speech shortly after Tanaka's arrest. "Why is it wrong to accept monetary support? If Tanaka is guilty, so am I."

But Tanaka did begin to pose a problem for his brood, at least to those of Kanemaru and Takeshita's rank. According to the conventions of Japanese politics, a senior leader should become prime minister, then retreat to the sidelines, turning power over to the next generation; since the LDP's founding, nobody had ever returned to the highest post after relinquishing it. That was certainly the assumption Kanemaru and Takeshita had held when they had helped push Tanaka to the premiership. But Tanaka, forced to resign prematurely, felt he hadn't been given his full chance, and he wasn't ready to retire; he was becoming a "shadow shogun," a post for which there was no term limit. That created an uneasy balance from the mid-1970s through the mid-1980s—the three men all needed one another to keep their power but were increasingly rivals for future control.

Kanemaru and Takeshita were constantly testing Tanaka's resolve and support. "Now that the big boss has come to this plight," Kanemaru told *gundan* members after Tanaka's 1976 arrest, "we should rally around Takeshita as the new chairman." That bid failed, but four years later Kanemaru tried again by giving a much-publicized speech about the need for a "generational change"; he urged the leaders of all the LDP factions—including his own—to retire. Tanaka grew increasingly wary of, and testy with, the pair. When Takeshita sang his song, "It will be time for Noboru Takeshita," Tanaka barked, "Stop it! How stupid!" "I will make Takeshita scrub the floor for some time!" Tanaka would bellow, and periodically he would make sure that the conniving partners were temporarily denied important party and cabinet posts.

One reason Takeshita and Kanemaru failed to make headway was the unswerving loyalty of the "boys' detective unit." The third generation of politicians in the Tanaka machine still had much to gain from their mentor, and he made sure to be attentive to them. Tanaka carefully taught Ozawa, in particular, the skills of a well-rounded politician through hours of informal lectures, exposure to secret high-level meetings, and a series of low-profile but important appointments. Between 1974 and 1980, Ozawa served three terms as director of the lower-house Construction Committee and one as parliamentary vice minister of construction, strengthening his ties to that crucial industry. In 1983, Ozawa was the LDP's chief administrator and, with Tanaka's help, oversaw three major elections that year. He learned firsthand the intricacies of the nation's electoral map and "accumulated considerable basic knowledge . . . taking care of various persons and giving counsel," Ozawa later said. "Only I know how to give out money," he would boast after the experience. "*Oyaji* and I discussed how to handle it, how to look after everything."

Tanaka also instructed his charge in the ways of hardball. At one point, Ozawa was responsible for recruiting new faction members, and he was famous, according to one press account, "for telling them point-blank, 'If you join the Tanaka faction, you will receive funding and organizational backup. If you don't join, our faction will back a strong opponent in the district.' Ozawa has shown himself willing to live up to the threats, which has made him a very formidable figure in the party." Tanaka also hammered in the importance of funds: "In order to become prime minister," he would stress, "you have to have money, you have to act as the party's bank."

Ozawa, meanwhile, stood by Tanaka during his troubles more publicly than any other faction member did. He was the only politician to attend all 191 court hearings of the Lockheed trial, stretching from 1977 through 1983. "Ichiro came again today," Tanaka would say to his aide sitting next to him in the dock. As each hearing ended, Ozawa would rise and stand immobile, watching only the defendant; when the two men's eyes met, Ozawa would bow deeply. "I could not bear seeing him, once a man of power, sitting alone on the court bench with no one beside him," Ozawa later explained. "I felt I would never abandon him, to whom I was obliged."

When Tanaka was finally convicted in October 1983, Ozawa continued to support him. In the elections that shortly followed the verdict, the disciple kept a photo of himself shaking hands with the now-felon hanging prominently on his district home wall. His attitude, however, and that of the other members of his generation, was changing. It wasn't that they loved Tanaka less but that they loved their careers, and his machine, more. And the compatibility between the two appeared to be diverging.

By many measures, the Tanaka organization in late 1983 and 1984 was as powerful as ever, perhaps more so. It still controlled the largest bloc in the ruling party and was the pillar supporting the Nakasone administration. But to an astute insider, the group was straining at the seams. The main problem was Tanaka's refusal to designate a successor, even if the transfer were officially to be delayed a few years. "The change of generations," Tanaka told a gathering, "means that the father dies." The longer he put off the matter, the more impatient the senior faction members became. Even Tanaka's most trustworthy lackey—the seventy-five-year-old Susumu "My hobby is Kakuei Tanaka" Nikaido—made a defiant last-ditch bid to run for premier in late 1984, though Tanaka crushed him easily. Takeshita, too, was restive. Around then, the other major LDP factions were peacefully transferring leadership to men Takeshita's age, stoking his fears that he would fall behind his rivals. And if Tanaka were truly to control the group a decade longer, as he declared in 1984 that he would, Takeshita would be seventy years old before he got his chance.

Meanwhile, Takeshita and Kanemaru had continued to accumulate clout, now wielding far more influence than they had during their earlier, abortive attempts to ease Tanaka out. And they were using their power generously to win support from junior members. Tanaka's Lockheed conviction made it harder for him to perform public functions, forcing him to turn more responsibilities over to his aides. Takeshita, in particular, picked up the fund-raising slack. In 1984, according to official records, he personally collected more money than the rest of the faction combined, and he donated most of it to grateful faction members. Kanemaru worked diligently to befriend Ozawa, and Ozawa began to consider Kanemaru, more than Tanaka, his guarantor. When Ozawa was given a post to help manage Parliament in 1983, opposition leaders complained that he was too young; Kanemaru called his friends in the other parties and told them, "What Ozawa says is what I say; I will personally take responsibility for his actions."

At the same time, Tanaka's no-longer-so-youthful "bodyguards," the *gundan* members of Ozawa's generation, were becoming more sympathetic to Takeshita's gripes of stymied aspirations. They were starting to set their sights on cabinet assignments but were often disappointed. As part of Tanaka's campaign to build up a huge faction to preserve his shadow power, he was luring veteran pols—some from other factions, others who had no factional affiliation—by promising them juicy appointments. Those often came at the expense of the *gundan*'s stalwarts. "You are still young," Tanaka told one disgruntled follower who had yet to become a minister. "Even though you call us young, I will [soon] reach the age you were when you were already Prime Minister," the MP shot back.

Tanaka was usually astute at sensing trouble and swiftly diffusing it, but now he seemed blind and deaf. Ozawa tried repeatedly to warn Tanaka of the volatility within the *gundan* and to urge him to make some concessions. But the boss wouldn't listen. Ozawa began to sense that Tanaka's political judgment was being clouded by hubris and a crazed obsession with the Lockheed case. At the time, Ozawa was Tanaka's representative on a parliamentary ethics committee created to deal with the scandal's fallout. Ozawa had managed to defang all the proposals to oust Tanaka from Parliament but felt that some mild anticorruption legislation was inevitable. Whenever he tried to discuss the matter, Tanaka flew into a rage. "He was displeased just hearing the phrase 'political ethics,' " Ozawa observed.

Even if Ozawa were to stay faithful himself, it was not clear how long the rest of the *gundan* would. Maybe they could remain united behind Tanaka for a year or so longer. But not forever. Ozawa faced a choice: he could fight a rearguard defense out of blind loyalty, or he could be at the forefront of an inevitable generational change. He brought to the decision a brutal pragmatism worthy of a prize Tanaka student. "I believe that we should never let political decisions go by emotions," Ozawa would later say. "In this sense, I am cold."

CHAPTER SIXTEEN

THE COUP

THE CONSPIRATORS began active plotting at the end of 1984 in the greatest of secrecy. Despite the sense among Ozawa and others that the boss might be vulnerable, Tanaka was still extremely powerful. "It was like the vendetta of the Akoh samurai," Kanemaru later said of the planning, alluding to a famous eighteenth-century murder scheme that had been carried out with elaborate planning and secrecy. It started in mid-December with just 7 of the *gundan*'s 119 members, including Kanemaru, Takeshita, and Ozawa; over the next month, they carefully expanded the group to two dozen in a series of clandestine nighttime meetings at the private, high-priced Japanese restaurants, or *ryotei,* where political plots are often hatched. To avoid leaks, only pols known for their discretion were tapped; they were invited to the sessions without advance explanation and instructed to arrive by taxi so as not to leave a gaggle of black limousines outside—a telltale sign of news to roaming reporters. "I want you to take a blood oath," Kanemaru said to open one meeting. "If we fail, we will be decapitated." A nervous Takeshita made an uncharacteristically bold pledge: "I will burn myself to ashes."

Tanaka seemed completely oblivious to the rumblings beneath his feet. At his 1985 Mejiro New Year's Day bash, he worked the crowd as usual, tipping sake into visitors' cups. After his welcoming toast, the host invited Takeshita to make some remarks. The underling impishly began by describing a New Year's reception he had attended earlier that day at the Imperial Palace, where, he said, a fellow pol had greeted him with a poem about wanting to be the next prime minister. Tension briefly filled the room—the topic of such a leader arising from the *gundan* was, of course, taboo—until Takeshita, after a pause, added; "I composed my own poem . . . saying: 'The candidacy would be postponed as soon as we make public such a sentiment.' " Relieved laughter and applause restored the party's jovial mood. Later in January, at another *gundan* gala, when members took turns singing, Takeshita said he would revive a tune from ten years earlier, then belted out, "In ten years, it will be time for Noboru Takeshita. *Toko zundoko, zundoko.*" The unsuspecting again responded with mirth.

Finally, the plotters decided to go public with their uprising in order to expand their numbers. They did so, with wonderfully Japanese understatement, by forming a "study group." Takeshita, they said, would chair a new organization called the "Soseikai," or "Creative Politics Circle," to "quietly study policy within the framework of the Tanaka faction." It was so subtle, in fact, that even Tanaka seemed to miss the gauntlet meekly dropped at his feet. Takeshita called on his boss one Sunday evening to reveal the plan, and Tanaka advised him, "Fine, it's natural to study things if you think of your country. . . . Make this study as wide as possible." By the next evening, claiming Mejiro's blessing, the "study group" had rushed to sign up seventy "students," or more than half the *gundan*'s membership.

Tanaka soon wised up. What Takeshita hadn't mentioned that Sunday night was that, even before seeking approval, he had already lined up his troops, including some of Tanaka's closest disciples, and had set up supporting chapters in thirty-five of Japan's forty-seven prefectures. The actual "policies" to be "studied" weren't made clear; at the first public meeting, Takeshita promised mainly to foster "a pure, fresh study group . . . to study problems relating to a free-market economy and to promote friendship among members." But spies noted in ominous reports back to Mejiro that "friendship" was being promoted with concrete free-market incentives: semiannual stipends. Some recruiters openly stated the new group's purpose—to make Takeshita prime minister—and claimed that Tanaka had finally designated Takeshita as his successor. The press trumped up the maneuverings, the *Yomiuri* newspaper blaring that Takeshita, "by saying he would like to hold study meetings . . . [had] made a declaration of war." TANAKA'S LOYAL MEN, one concise headline observed, START LOOKING OUT FOR NO. 1.

Tanaka became livid. "It's still ten years too early for Takeshita!" he bellowed to visitors. "I will never let the Creative Politics Circle go beyond policy studies. I will never let them seek power." "Does Takeshita intend to buy with just 100 million yen the men I nurtured?" Tanaka groused to one backer. It wasn't clear whether it was the payment itself or the relatively low amount that irked Tanaka. "Takeshita is a traitor!" he snapped to another senior *gundan* member, offering him funds to form a rival group to undercut the rebels. At a memorial ceremony for a late business entrepreneur, Tanaka delivered the main address: "Everybody knows that it's hard to start a business; it's easy to take over a business that somebody else has started," he said, praising the deceased while issuing a veiled snipe. "Founders should be respected." In mid-February, two weeks after his initial visit to Mejiro, Takeshita stumbled back to the Tanaka manse, this time offering an apology for the commotion.

Tanaka had always been one to relish a good political scrap, but this one was different. Suddenly, his rivals were not the elitist bureaucrat-politicians, the intellectuals, or the Socialists. These were *his* men, the ones he had personally succored. After a week of intense counterpressure, Tanaka and his aides had managed to cut the renegade group's pledged membership to forty, or about half its peak number. But the most stubborn holdouts were his old "boys' detective unit," led by Ozawa. Ozawa had wept all night before the study group was formed, but when even Takeshita and Kanemaru had started to get cold feet, he had been the one to stiffen their resolve. Ozawa stopped Kanemaru from visiting Mejiro to discuss a compromise: "In a fight," he scolded, "if the weaker visits the stronger, that means surrender."

About a month after the rival group was formed, Ozawa and two of his cohorts went to Mejiro to explain their actions. Tanaka greeted them with a broad smile. "You people are so hasty," he chided gently. Ozawa explained that the group was not trying to force Tanaka's retirement but to "save" him from internal problems. Tanaka saw them out, shaking their hands. "Those are the ones I can't cut down," he said wistfully to a veteran *gundan* member standing by his side. "I love them, but they have already been taken away." His face was red from drink.

Tanaka's doctors had advised him to cut down his alcohol intake, and he had boasted just a few months earlier that he was imbibing less and playing golf more to keep fit for the latest rounds of intraparty battles. But throughout February 1985, he drank more and more; he greeted the usual flock of morning petitioners at his mansion with swollen eyes and some days didn't show up for his appointments at all. In his public remarks, he was turning reflective. On the night of February 25, about a month after the rebels announced their plot, Tanaka attended a fund-raising party for a young faction member and was summoned to the microphone. "Some say it is time to give way to the younger generation or to make Kakuei Tanaka resign," he said. "But you don't have to worry about that. I will be taken away anyway when the gods call me." The next evening, at a gathering of older politicians, he declared, "A fool speaks, a wise man listens. From now on, I will be wise and listen to all of you."

The next day, Tanaka canceled his evening engagements. Chest pains came on around noon, and he lay down on the floor. He got up to go to the bathroom and found he couldn't move his right arm or leg. He was checked into the Tokyo Teishin Hospital at 8:30 P.M. The diagnosis: a month of stress, heartbreak, and heavy drinking had given Tanaka a stroke.

Had Kakuei Tanaka's health held up, perhaps he could ultimately have crushed the insurrection. But this was a knockout blow. He had suffered a cerebral infarction, which had paralyzed his right side—including the right hand he so often raised in his famous wave—and reduced his speech to incomprehensible squeals and slurred mumbles for the remaining nine years of his life. While he seemed to understand normal conversation, it wasn't entirely clear whether he was completely conscious.

Yet so awesome was the aura of Tanaka's indestructibility that Takeshita and his partners still took more than two years to wrest control conclusively. In his nearly sixty-seven years, Tanaka had overcome so many obstacles that would have hobbled a lesser man that it was hard for politicians to accept that mere illness could stop him. And so, even as an invalid, Tanaka was able to wage—or, to be more precise, his family and their lackeys were able to use him to wage—a sustained, macabre power struggle worthy of a Kremlin plot.

When word about Tanaka's condition spread, the interest in the political world was immediate and intense. Despite the turmoil within his machine, Tanaka was still Japan's paramount strongman, and his health had potentially major implications for Japan's political system as well as its short-term policies; numerous matters, ranging from the new executive lineup at the giant telephone monopoly to the conservative party's candidate slate for an upcoming election, were reportedly bogged down for weeks. "The interest of politics is now focused on Tanaka's condition," one press report said. "Politicians overwhelmed by the former prime minister's sudden hospitalization seem to be at a loss to decide what they should do."

The morning after Tanaka's collapse, as an icy rain fell outside, his doctors met the army of reporters gathered at the scene and issued a surprisingly upbeat prognosis. They said he had suffered only a "mild stroke" and that he would take just "three to four weeks" to recover fully. Tanaka's trusty aide Hayasaka chimed in that his boss would certainly be returning to politics "soon." A week later, the doctors amended their statement to say that while Tanaka was on the mend, his return to work might actually take two to three months. On a regular basis, doctors, aides, and family members fed updates to the press at the hospital on the "shadow shogun's" treatments and progress, what he was saying, and how he was enjoying looking at the cherry blossoms from the roof of the hospital.

Doubts were first cast on the official accounts when one newspaper reported that—despite the doctor's detailed depictions, the Secret Service detail on the ninth floor of the hospital, the flowers sent to the ward by Prime Minister Nakasone, the visit by a cabinet minister to "inquire after" the patient's health—Tanaka had actually left the hospital and returned to Mejiro days earlier. A surreal series of denials and contradictory statements by the hospital, the Tanaka staff, and the Tanaka family followed: the report was false, they maintained; or yes, the patient had left the hospital briefly but then returned; or rather, he had stayed home from April 28 through May 3; or again, he was still at home on May 4 to celebrate his birthday. MYSTERY SURROUNDS TANAKA'S HEALTH AND WHEREABOUTS, ran a typically perplexed headline from those days. The press now divided its Tanaka watch into two contingents, one outside the hospital, another outside Mejiro. On May 9, a supporter from Niigata visited the Tanaka compound and told the waiting reporters that he had definitely seen his MP there. Two days later, Hayasaka and the hospital confirmed that Tanaka had indeed been released.

With Tanaka back home, his family strictly controlled access both to him and to information about him. They found a new set of doctors to treat him in his own quarters. They fired and banished most of his political staff, including Hayasaka. Tanaka rarely left the compound. Visitors were carefully chosen and apparently instructed on what they could disclose to outsiders. (Occasionally, there were slips. After a gravel merchant from Tanaka's district visited Tanaka, he told reporters, "He couldn't speak and he seemed pale. . . . Not just the right half of his body but also the left leg seemed disabled." But the visitor quickly retracted the statement after a chiding from an aide.)

Rumors spread that Tanaka was actually dead. From time to time, the *Monthly Etsuzan,* the official organ of Tanaka's Etsuzankai support group, would publish the most favorable photos possible of the group's idol with accompanying articles declaring him "hale and hearty," though in fact his face was gaunt and expressionless, his right hand limp. The mass media, too, printed the pictures on their front pages, along with detailed assessments from medical experts on what they seemed to convey. After a while, the press was let in to watch Tanaka—from ten yards away—confer with his closest political friends. "My father will never retire," his daughter, Makiko, would say. He ran for reelection in Niigata in July 1986 and, though he never made a campaign appearance, led the field of seven candidates with 179,000 votes—more than twice as many as his nearest rival.

Of course, the longer Tanaka stayed out of public view, the less credible the notion of a comeback became. But as long as even the remotest possibility remained—as long as nobody could definitively confirm that he was finished—any rational Japanese politician had to try to assess what Tanaka's intentions and preferences were and act accordingly. Tanaka himself couldn't articulate his goals. The most positive accounts of his condition had him uttering no more than a full sentence; the press, which continued to devote considerable resources to divining Tanaka's true state, had doubts even about that. The *Asahi* newspaper once published a roundtable discussion by its top political journalists. The discussion veered from a sophisticated analysis of ongoing parliamentary jockeying to an intricate dissection of Tanaka's diction. It read, in part:

> MODERATOR: I suppose the words that Kaku-san utters don't flow, probably three at the most . . .
> JOURNALIST A: *"Yoshi, yoshi"* [a variation on Tanaka's trademark *"Yossha, yossha,"* or "Okay, okay"] he said, didn't he?
> MODERATOR: Is it true he said *"Yo-o"* at the New Year?

Journalist C: I heard *"Yo-o."* Actually, it sounded like *"Yu-u,"* rather than *"Yo-o."*

Journalist B: I don't think he can speak at all. . . .

Back to Journalist C: It could be *"Yo-o."* Or it could be *"yo."* Well, it sounded like a moan, so it's not clear whether it was a word or not.

The intense interest in Tanaka's every utterance gave his daughter, Makiko, her husband, MP Naoki Tanaka, and a handful of elder pols fiercely loyal to the boss the opportunity to become his "spokesmen," "interpreting" and "conveying" his desires, like psychics, to the public and to top officials. According to them, an overriding wish of the fallen leader was to stop Takeshita; or if not to stop him, to delay his rise to power; and if not to delay him, at least to rattle and humiliate the man they blamed for Tanaka's plight.

For the first few weeks after Tanaka collapsed, Takeshita put his coup-by-study-group on hold. Any further meetings would have been unseemly—and in any case, the group had to gauge how seriously Tanaka was hurt. Takeshita resumed his activities a few months after the stroke, slowly but steadily picking up more and more support within the *gundan.* His cause was helped by the fact that he was able to make regular payments to supporters, while Tanaka could no longer do so. He then won appointment as secretary-general of the Liberal Democratic Party, a post considered a prerequisite to becoming prime minister and one that Tanaka had made sure that Takeshita had never gotten. In December 1985, Naoki demanded that Prime Minister Nakasone oust Takeshita from the cabinet in accordance with "the intention of the former prime minister." His demand was rejected. Still, with Makiko and Naoki publicly declaring Tanaka's ongoing opposition, many *gundan* members were reluctant to cast their lot with Takeshita.

A chill passed through the Takeshita camp at the end of 1986, when it was reported that Tanaka was resuming his year-end contribution to faction members, distributing, through intermediaries, a million yen to each. On January 1, 1987, Tanaka opened Mejiro and once again made a public appearance at his annual New Year's fête, which he had skipped the prior year. The chorus of carpenters arrived in the morning to serenade guests with their chant, just as they had in better years. Tanaka, sporting a dark blue suit and tie, sat in a rattan chair next to his wife, visible to but distant from the guests.

A select few were led to shake hands with him. Many top politicians came. Shortly after noon, Takeshita's limousine pulled up to the gate. With a lively crowd of MPs obviously inside and a line of television cameras standing by to record the moment, one of Tanaka's aides greeted the traitor: "This year the *sensei* is not seeing you; please just leave your name card." "I understand," Takeshita responded without getting out of the car. "Please send him my best." As his car did a U-turn and pulled away from the public humiliation, Takeshita strained to keep his cool, muttering, "Patience, patience. Forever patience."

That proved to be Tanaka's last hurrah. His appearance showed conclusively that he was in bad shape, unlikely ever to exert much energy again. In the following months, the rats abandoned the sinking ship in droves; even some of those who had long been most critical of Takeshita were claiming always to have been secretly supportive. In July 1987, Takeshita, Kanemaru, and Ozawa formally resigned from the Thursday Club, the official name of the Tanaka faction of the LDP, and created their own faction, the Keiseikai, a grandiose name taken from an old Chinese proverb meaning "Wise government, relieving the people's suffering." The *gundan*'s famous ironlike unity remained largely intact as 113 members joined the "new" faction.

More than a decade after he had first taken over the ruling conservative party, Tanaka's dominance over Japanese politics had officially come to an end.

CHAPTER SEVENTEEN

THE AGE OF LANGUOR

ALTHOUGH TANAKA was gone from the political scene, his machine survived, passed on to a new generation. Takeshita, in whose name the coup had been launched, started out as the leader; he eventually became one corner of a power triangle shared with Kanemaru and Ozawa. This council had been stitched together with the intricacy of a European royal family. The three men were distantly related through a series of marriages: Kanemaru's son was married to Takeshita's daughter, Takeshita's half brother to the younger sister of Ozawa's wife. While the connections may seem tenuous to an outsider, the three often talked of themselves as kin. "In Kanemaru's words, he, Takeshita and Ozawa became *uchikiri,* which in Yamanashi dialect means 'an exclusive family,'' said Takeshita's half brother. "Kanemaru believes in *uchikiri.*" "Mr. Kanemaru, Mr. Takeshita and me can't be separated from each other," Ozawa said in 1991. "If we quarrel among ourselves . . . we all lose." "Mejiro" was replaced as the media's shorthand for "national political power" by the pun "Kon-Chiku-Sho": the word was put together with alternative readings of the first Chinese characters of the name of each member of the triumvirate (the "Kane" in "Kanemaru" could also be read "Kon," the "Take" in "Takeshita" as "Chiku," the "O" in

"Ozawa" as "Sho"); the phrase was also an expletive meaning something like "Damn it!"

The "Kon-Chiku-Sho" reign lasted from 1987 to 1992. During the first half, Takeshita, as prime minister, was Japan's official ruler; subsequently, the three reigned together from behind the scenes, as a committee of "shadow shoguns." It was an era of contradictions, mirroring the personalities of the new potentates and the mood of the times. The Tanaka-built organization remained the hub of Japanese politics and, using the same tactics and distortions, seemed more dominant over the national government than ever. But the underlying conditions of Japan's political economy that had made Tanaka-style politics possible were changing, forcing the machine bosses into an increasingly untenable situation. As the nation's de facto rulers, they were responsible for mobilizing the government to respond to the issues of the day, which they adeptly did. But as Japan and the world around it changed, each response ended up altering the country's finely tuned political balance, shaking the very authority the machine had to make those decisions.

THE "KON-CHIKU-SHO" period opened auspiciously, with Japan entering what seemed to be a new gilded age. By the mid-1980s, the Asian powerhouse had already won the admiration and fear of the West with its miraculous postwar economic performance. Most experts predicted that the country had at last reached maturity and would henceforth face the moderate growth, and the consequent difficult trade-offs, that were saddling all the other industrialized nations. They were wrong. In the late 1980s, Japan enjoyed a stunning new affluence, with annual GNP growth rates of 4 percent to 6 percent, or twice what Americans, even in good times, could expect. Combined with a sharp rise in the value of the yen versus the dollar, Japan's wealth, compared with that of the rest of the world, exploded.

This expansion, though, had a different feel from earlier periods of prosperity. The nation's success in the 1960s and 1970s had been considered a triumph of hard work and efficiency, of staid, blue-chip manufacturing. The growth spurt of the late 1980s was an asset boom, clear and simple. The fuel was easy money generated by the central bank's low interest rates, and the stars of the late 1980s were moneymakers: bankers, stockbrokers, real estate agents. Fortunes were made overnight as the Nikkei stock index tripled in value within three years; in late 1989, the Tokyo Stock Exchange was worth 40 percent of all other world stock markets combined. Land prices reached dizzying heights: the mid-Tokyo plot under the Imperial Palace was estimated to surpass all of Florida in value; in the Ginza shopping district, a 10,000-yen note (worth about $80 at the time), if dropped wadded up as tightly as possible, could not purchase the ground it covered.

When Japan had first thrived in the early decades after the war, many Japanese couldn't quite believe their good fortune. Their poverty had been too extreme and too recent to be wiped out of the national consciousness. The nagging apprehension had been prolonged by the oil crises of the 1970s, which had appeared to expose the fragility of a nation that had built its affluence without indigenous natural resources; history, of course, had proved those fears unfounded. In the 1980s, perception and reality were transposed. By any rational analysis, the new cornucopia *wasn't* genuine: wealth was begetting wealth, grounded in nothing more solid than wisps of perception. With real estate and stock prices rising, banks eagerly lent to investors, and the loans in turn helped fuel rising prices, the cycle repeating itself over and over. For anybody looking, there were disconcerting signs. The stock market's price-to-earnings ratio—the usual reality check for investors—was well above the international norm. And the characters driving the expansion were hardly the sober industrialists of the past; they were land sharks, speculators, and eccentrics. Nui Onoue became a face defining the new Japanese economy: the Osaka red-light-district restaurateur became one of the richest people in the world through stocks chosen at her all-night seances.

Yet by the late 1980s, hardly anybody was willing to doubt Japan's growth. Analysts began to declare the economy, which had overcome so many fears and challenges, to be invulnerable. This time, success bred incredible arrogance: if Japan appeared to defy the laws of economic gravity, well, perhaps those laws didn't apply anymore. This was a time of extravagance and decadence: rather than stash away their windfall for a rainy day, many Japanese companies, and individuals, struggled to find new ways to spend it. Restaurants sprinkled food with gold flakes. Investors combed the world to buy golf courses and châteaux. Ryoei Saito, a paper mill magnate, stunned the art world by dropping $160 million in three days to buy *Au Moulin de La Galette* by Renoir and *Portrait of Dr. Gachet* by van Gogh; he caused another stir by declaring he wanted them cremated with him when he died.

The earlier sense of struggle in Japan's economy had dissipated. During those years, Japanese politics, too, took on a similar feel of unreal complacency.

For Tanaka, politics had always been a bitter struggle: his machine had been forged in angry defiance of his enemies; until the day he collapsed, his very endurance had been a hard-fought personal victory over those who claimed he had no right to rule. But by the late 1980s, the political and bureaucratic worlds had largely accepted the predominance of the Tanaka-built organization. They had come to rely on the predictability and efficiency it had imposed on Japan's government—especially once the founder's polarizing personality had been removed.

So the "Kon-Chiku-Sho" mission was different from Tanaka's: not to create but to maintain, not to challenge or to inspire, simply to lull everyone into continued cooperation. The new, languorous mood was evident even among those pols who had fought at great risk to bring about the change. "More than 90 percent of the members of the Tanaka faction say they belonged because they loved Tanaka," one journalist observed at the time. "Now they never say they love their boss." Ozawa, when asked in 1987 why he had rallied behind Takeshita, could only muster this response: "It's the logic of relative comparison; if there was such a person with a little more sting . . . then it might have been him. . . . However, among the members of our group, we all felt that Takeshita was the only person, and there was no further reason."

On becoming prime minister in late 1987, Takeshita talked of "a new kind of leadership." It was "no longer an age when you can tell others to 'just follow me,' " he would say, calling himself instead a politician "who would watch the situation and try to seek harmony." Takeshita was not an advocate; "In order to hear the opinions of everyone," he once demurred, "it is best for me not to say what I think." His greatest skill was, in his own term, as an "adjuster," a concept he elevated to a philosophy. "What sort of ideology will guide the Takeshita administration?" a reporter for the *Mainichi* newspaper asked shortly after he became premier. "I have always been one to take time and make sure a consensus is reached" was the answer. He could take an issue, any issue, listen to all parties, and magically find the middle ground that would satisfy the greatest number possible. Consensus took precedence over urgency; Takeshita always made time to let opponents save face. To criticism that he was indecisive, the premier's supporters said he was following the "ripe persimmon" approach to governance; rather than making a decision, he would quietly create the right atmosphere, wait patiently for the situation to "mature," then let the resolution just come, as if it were falling naturally from a tree.

That didn't mean Takeshita shirked the difficulties facing Japan during his administration. He used his mastery of the governmental process to settle a number of tough issues that had vexed his predecessors. But the high premium he placed on stability meant that his primary concern in any situation was to sidestep public controversy or even debate. The prime minister "seems to believe that politics consists of depoliticizing everything," a prominent commentator wrote a year into the Takeshita administration. Takeshita was uncomfortable with questions of right or wrong in which compromise was not possible. When one of his cabinet ministers caused a stir by defending Japan's militarism during the 1930s and 1940s, a matter that still deeply divided the country, Takeshita, under intense questioning in Parliament, awkwardly tried to straddle: "It is a fact that there is serious international criticism that Japan's wartime actions constituted an invasion," he noted, adding that the question of whether Japan was guilty of aggression "should be left to future historians to judge." When asked on a separate occasion to justify his membership in the Japan–South Africa Parliamentary League at a time when apartheid remained strong, Takeshita responded only, "I belong to all parliamentary leagues without exception."

Under Takeshita, Japan's politics reached their most machinelike state, in that the passion and argument of democracy were subdued and political discourse was reduced to mechanics, to matters of procedure and personnel. Takeshita's autobiography is filled with detailed descriptions of such questions as how cabinet seating arrangements were determined. He kept scrolls, both at his home and office, listing every cabinet formed since the war; he meticulously updated each by hand, and he could recite from memory the number of days certain politicians had served as ministers. "My tenure as finance minister came to five terms, or 1,586 days altogether," he would note. "That's the fifth longest in Japanese history, the third longest since the war." He once wrote that he and his hero, former prime minister Eisaku Sato, were "tied with a mysterious fate" because both men had been given certain appointments at the same age and because "both the Sato cabinet and the Takeshita cabinet were formed in the month of November," twenty-three years apart. After his first parliamentary interpellation as prime minister, he boasted that it had ended right on schedule, as if, one newspaper editorial cracked, "the quality of a [legislative] session is judged by how punctually it ends." His interaction with the press, pols, and bureaucrats often consisted of simply recalling the facts and figures he had memorized.

Takeshita's style, or lack of it, worked perfectly in soothing the myriad egos of the Nagatacho "Capitol Hill" district but had little appeal to the general public. It was a sign of how distant the machine had grown from its roots in Tanaka's fiery populism and how much political power—like the contemporaneous ascent of the Nikkei stock index—had taken on a self-perpetuating momentum with only a tenuous grounding. The machine had so effectively co-opted all the major factions and parties that the electorate had no practical alternatives. The lack of competition heightened the sense of inbred arrogance among the national leadership, making politics and the people appear less and less relevant to each other. In order to become prime minister in 1972, Tanaka had had to win a close, open vote in his party, a contest swayed by his surging national popularity. Takeshita and his two rivals in the 1987 contest tried to reach a settlement through amicable negotiations; they made a gentleman's agreement that each man would get "his turn" in the job. When they couldn't reach consensus on the order, they chose not to settle the matter through a ballot, instead leaving the official decision to the outgoing premier, Yasuhiro Nakasone.

As a national leader, Takeshita never connected with the country at large. His public persona was often described as *mu,* or a kind of "nothingness." He could not articulate why he wanted to be prime minister, saying before his nomination only, "The force of circumstances has pushed me to my present position." "Frankly speaking, I have the feeling that it is a surprise that I have come this far," he said after taking office. "However, someone has to assume [the prime minister's] office, and I came to include myself as one among them." Backers said his words reflected his modesty, but they were also part of a broader inability or unwillingness to make a coherent public political statement. He himself acknowledged a preference for clear diction and obscure meaning; Japanese joked that they needed an interpreter to understand him. His own spokesman said he "is not very straightforward and direct," making it hard for those outside Nagatacho to understand him.

"He's the type that cartoonists despair [of]," one noted satirist griped. "He's not the type to be a leading actor." Six months into

Takeshita's term, the cartoonist could portray the premier from the back or from the side but had yet to draw a full face. A popular rock group wrote a song dedicated to the new leader. "Although I've made my way through painful days on end, I don't understand what you say sometimes," the lyrics began. "We wanted to bring alive the words of the prime minister," a member of the group's production staff said, recounting how they had worked all night transcribing a Takeshita speech from a video. "We aimed at writing a driving song but . . . what we wound up with was a mildly folk-type song."

Takeshita's one direct appeal to the people during his administration was his proposal to revitalize the *furusato,* an evocative phrase equivalent to "my good old country hometown." It was vintage Takeshita, long on vague, inarguable homilies. "Until now, politics has had material affluence as its yardstick, and it has reached the point that we regret not taking spiritual affluence into account," Takeshita said to unveil the plan. This would be "an effort to create a land in which all Japanese can lead happier, more comfortable, more rewarding lives." Where Prime Minister Ikeda, in 1960, had announced his "income-doubling" plan, Takeshita envisioned a "happiness-doubling" plan. Where Tanaka, in 1972, had proposed to "remodel the Japanese archipelago" with roads and bridges, Takeshita waxed eloquent about renovating the national soul so that "the entire Japanese archipelago will be one vast, varied, and bountiful *furusato* for us all." After meeting a Japanese astronaut, Takeshita said he was inspired to expand his philosophy into a "worldwide *furusato* movement." "We are obligated," he wrote, "to make the earth, the common *furusato* of all mankind, a better place." That, he explained, would eventually lead "to arms cuts and peace."

When the gooey rhetoric was translated into concrete policy, however, the *furusato* plan seemed less concerned with restoring traditional Japanese values than with getting into sync with modern times—with a Japan enjoying extreme wealth and worried mostly about how to fritter it away. Under the "hometown creation plan" provisions of the fiscal 1988 and 1989 national budgets, nearly every city, town, and village in Japan—more than five thousand in all—regardless of size, was given 100 million yen each, or $770,000 at the exchange rate of the time, for a total cost of about 300 billion yen, or $2.3 billion. There were no strings attached, though central government officials urged local officials *not* to use the funds for something useful, such as roads or sewers, but rather to think of something creative.

Some communities, literally befuddled as to how to squander their windfall, held contests among their citizens, offering prize money from the fund. One village got seven proposals; all were rejected, so the money was instead used to take the contestants to a hot spring. The projects ranged from the playful to the frivolous to the bizarre. In Takeshita's home prefecture of Shimane, one coastal town built a sand clock, another a giant maze. The bigger the project, many towns felt, the better—the origami-thon, for example, that used a 310-square-foot piece of paper, or the 30-square-meter lavatory in northern Hokkaido housing "a toilet suitable for the concept of *furusato* creation." A textile town on the Japan Sea created a UFO museum shaped like a flying saucer; its bid to become "Japan's UFO mecca" faced competition, though, from another town up the coast, which used its funds to build public restrooms in the shape of spaceships, and by yet another that built a town hall in the shape of a flying saucer. Some communities displayed a subtle pragmatism, like the snow-country village that arranged a special tour that would "allow city people to experience clearing snow from roofs."

A common theme, befitting the zeitgeist, was gaudiness; gold, in particular, was a popular acquisition. A hamlet on Sado Island, once the bleak refuge of political exiles, created a golden mountain to lure tourists who wanted to go panning in the sand. One town bought a golden statue of a bonito fish, another commissioned one golden and one silver *kokeshi* doll—a local folk art turned spectacle—and housed them in the town hall, accompanied by a sign bearing a daily gold market quote to let the villagers know how much they were making. The small farming town of Tsuna, near Osaka, was the most straightforward of all: it simply bought a hunk of gold—32 centimeters wide, 10 centimeters long, weighing 62.7 kilograms—and stuck it in the public park. "People wanted to see what 100 million yen looked like," a town elder explained.

When he first became premier, Takeshita enjoyed a tepid honeymoon with the public. His support rate once reached 43 percent, although in answer to the question "What do you find good about the Takeshita cabinet?" more than half the respondents said "Nothing in particular." Only a few months later, his popularity had fallen to 22 percent; many people said it was because Takeshita's "style of politics" was "hard to understand." By April 1989, eighteen months after becoming prime minister, Takeshita's public approval had nearly evaporated—it had plummeted to 3.9 percent, an all-time low for a Japanese leader and perhaps for the leader of any major democracy. At the time, he was embroiled in a campaign contribution scandal, and that month he was forced to tender his resignation.

In announcing his plans to withdraw from high public office, Takeshita chose to quote the statement issued fifteen years earlier by Kakuei Tanaka when he had been forced to relinquish the premiership under similar circumstances. The younger Takeshita had read the statement to the press in 1974 in his then-capacity as government spokesman. "I remember reading aloud the words of one of my superiors before he resigned," Takeshita told the nation in 1989. "They went: 'One day, at a certain time, I listened carefully to the downpour of heavy rain on the earth and left my post, wishing to bring stability to the government.' " Takeshita said he had chosen the passage because "I believe politicians should retire in that spirit."

It was also an appropriate selection because Takeshita, like Tanaka before him, had no intention of releasing the reins of government just because he had given up the title of prime minister. If anything, his influence, and that of his two main accomplices, Kanemaru and Ozawa, grew.

CHAPTER EIGHTEEN
THE DON

FROM 1989 TO 1992, the "Kon-Chiku-Sho" leaders employed—and dramatically expanded—one of the most significant, warped legacies of Tanaka's rule, the so-called dual structure of government.

To obtain the formal trappings of power, a politician still had to forsake the substance; to acquire real clout, he still had to renounce the titles. The "Kon-Chiku-Sho" methodology was exactly the same as Tanaka's: the Tanaka-turned-Takeshita faction remained the largest in the ruling party—in 1989, 105 MPs, 25 more than its nearest rival; and after Takeshita's resignation, as after Tanaka's several years earlier, the group refused to nominate a candidate for prime minister from within its ranks. Thus the bloc held the swing vote in all contests for the nation's leader, a valuable commodity that commanded a high price. Like Tanaka, the Takeshita faction always received a large degree of informal authority, as well as a large number of high-ranking cabinet and party posts for its followers.

The gap between de facto and de jure power widened considerably during the "Kon-Chiku-Sho" era, because the ruling conservative party had by then been thoroughly emasculated. The LDP had once been divided between the so-called mainstream and antimainstream (which, from 1972 on, were synonymous with "pro-Tanaka" and "anti-Tanaka," respectively) tensions that had been reflected in the heated biannual leadership contests. By 1989, however, the whole party had become one big "mainstream" under "Kon-Chiku-Sho" dominance. To some observers, it seemed absurd that a bloc with just one fourth of the ruling party's MPs could dangle the government on a string. But the only way to break its hold was for the rest of the party to unite—and that was impossible as long as the other party barons were obsessed with trying to outgenuflect one another for the favor of the "shadow shoguns." As a respected party elder observed, "Everybody thinks 'I will become next' [*sic*], and so they cannot join hands" with one another. Criticism of "Kon-Chiku-Sho" power is "funny," sneered Ozawa. "Many people say such a thing while they also ask for the Takeshita faction's support."

The bloc's bargaining power was further enhanced by a rapid turnover of prime ministers and cabinets, increasing the frequency of these bidding contests. "Use and discard," Takeshita liked to joke. "Singers one year, party presidents two." In fact, a tenure of two years became a mark of unusual endurance. In the two and a half years after Takeshita resigned, he and his cohorts appointed three successive prime ministers: Sosuke Uno, Toshiki Kaifu, and Kiichi Miyazawa. The first two were unusually beholden to their "Kon-Chiku-Sho" sponsors because they had been plucked from near obscurity. At least the pols whom Tanaka had backed for prime minister —Masayoshi Ohira, Zenko Suzuki, and Yasuhiro Nakasone—had all served in a number of top party and government posts, headed their own intraparty factions, and been considered potential national leaders. But neither Uno nor Kaifu met any of those qualifications. Uno's highest office had been that of foreign minister; Kaifu's, education minister. With little high-level experience and no independent power base, they had to rely exclusively on their patrons. Kaifu aides described Takeshita as the premier's "private tutor."

In the weeks after Takeshita issued his resignation, the LDP left the matter of finding a successor entirely to him. He formally tapped Uno in June 1989, whereupon the new premier-to-be was instructed to provide Ozawa a roster for his proposed cabinet. The aspiring premier knew enough to leave blank all but two of the twenty available slots; he had the temerity to fill only the relatively minor posts of defense and agriculture, leaving the others for Ozawa and his faction to fill. His docility notwithstanding, Uno proved altogether expendable when a minor scandal broke just weeks into his administration. Within days of Uno's surprise promotion, a former geisha came forth to say publicly that she had been his mistress, and to provide sordid stories of sex on straw-mat restaurant floors and in hotel suites. It wasn't just the married Uno's infidelity that was considered outrageous, but his stingy handling of the affair. Uno allegedly paid his mistress only 300,000 yen a month, apparently a pittance by normal standards, then cut the relationship off suddenly without so much as a farewell gift.

Uno's humiliation, combined with an LDP setback at the polls in July, forced him to resign just sixty-eight days after taking office. Seemingly unfazed, the Takeshita-faction leaders convened one night at Kanemaru's Tokyo town house to dig up, hopefully to better effect, a successor. Someone floated Kaifu's name. Kanemaru asked the gathered gang whether he, like Uno, had any "relations with women." No, was the jeering response, Kaifu was too afraid of his wife to be prone to scandal. Satisfied with this mark of eligibility, Takeshita informed Kaifu of his appointment and assured him, "We will make all the necessary arrangements." Under Kaifu, Ozawa was made LDP secretary-general, and in that post he became the government's chief administrator of day-to-day affairs.

Under Uno and Kaifu, the dual structure of power became so blatant that there was little pretense—either in Tokyo or abroad—that the Japanese prime minister was more than a ceremonial figure. Even as Takeshita was leaving office, American President George Bush reportedly sent him a letter asking for his continued support. Indeed, Takeshita was a regular visitor to the White House over the next two years, as he, Ozawa, and Kanemaru took it upon themselves to handle directly the most delicate negotiations with the United States and other countries.

On issues of policy and personnel, Kaifu consulted first with the "Kon-Chiku-Sho" trio. He was apparently unable to so much as schedule a speech before Parliament without their permission. Sometimes he tried to strike out on his own, but on such occasions he was apt to declare publicly his position on an issue—the timing of an election, Japan's response to the Persian Gulf War, an answer to American trade demands—only to be forced later to retract his statements when he found that his "Kon-Chiku-Sho" handlers disagreed. Meanwhile, they would take action freely without even informing Kaifu, leaving him to find out from other pols or press reports what was happening under his administration. "What?" a flustered premier once blurted to reporters when told that one of his policies had been overturned. "Where was that decided?" "Isn't it true," a reporter asked Ozawa after two years of open toying with Kaifu, "that the Takeshita faction made Mr. Kaifu the party president and prime minister . . . because he is easy to manipulate by remote control?" "I don't deny that was part of the motivation," Ozawa responded. "But Mr. Kaifu played a useful role in the circumstances that prevailed at the time."

Kaifu was useful, among other reasons, because he proved surprisingly popular, his support ratings in public opinion polls often surpassing 50 percent. "The prime minister has a . . . special personality which titillates one's maternal instincts," a party senior offered as an explanation. "The people . . . feel sorry for him, as if he seems to be bullied somewhat and they have the feeling of supporting him. Such a point is his natural virtue."

Just as the "shadow shoguns" were tightening their grip over the LDP, they took their subversion of the opposition parties to new extremes. When the Socialists were voting on a new chairman in 1991, they chose Makoto Tanabe, a veteran politician whose main claim to fame was his close friendship with Kanemaru. Kanemaru did his bit to help Tanabe's campaign, implying in speeches that there would be better cooperation between parties if his buddy won. When some Socialists were critical of Tanabe, Kanemaru invited them to an extravagant dinner to ask that they support their new leader fully. "He listened to a great deal of what I had to say and authorized it, even though he met strong opposition in the LDP," Tanabe said of the relationship. "And I persuaded my members about his ideas even though there was opposition in our party." Tanabe was also on good terms with Ozawa. The year before, the two men and their wives—along with executives of two other opposition parties—had traveled through Europe together to "study electoral systems."

During the latter "Kon-Chiku-Sho" years, the focus of anybody trying to divine the course of Japan's politics narrowed sharply. Public opinion, Parliament, and the interactions among parties or among factions in the ruling party became secondary. Astute observers concentrated on the "Triangle Zone of Power," the three-block triangle down the hill from Parliament, where Kanemaru, Takeshita, and Ozawa had offices in neighboring buildings. "Kon-Chiku-Sho" relations were the subject of endless speculation, with constant rumors of rifts and subtly shifting preferences among the three. "Takeshita's rising influence was illustrated recently when a ranking member of his faction—who is considered an Ozawa confidant—started frequently visiting Takeshita's home and office" was considered a sufficiently important development for one newspaper to carry. Talk of marital discord between Takeshita's daughter and Kanemaru's son became grist for serious discussion; daughter Ichiko laughingly dismissed the hearsay in an exclusive interview with the *Sunday Mainichi* magazine and gave assurances of political stability by confirming that her father and father-in-law had recently gone out for a meal together with their mutual grandchildren. The magazine's headline: "COLD WAR" BETWEEN TAKESHITA, KANEMARU TURNS OUT TO BE A SHAM.

Out of that murky swamp, whose every emanating fume was analyzed for its significance, there gradually emerged an incredible assumption—equally humorous and disconcerting—about the true power structure of Japan. The more it was repeated, the more it was believed, and the more it was believed, the more it became a fact: that the real political boss of the world's second largest economy was Shin Kanemaru.

Even during his better days, Kanemaru had never been considered by his associates, or even by himself, as somebody who would lead his nation. He was a rough-edged man whose first legislative accomplishment had literally been busting heads. He had risen in national politics mainly as a useful fixer, handling the dirty work for more openly ambitious men like Tanaka and Takeshita. And the late 1980s weren't his best days. He was just shy of his seventy-fifth birthday when the Kaifu administration began. He had recently had two thirds of his stomach removed for what he himself said openly might have been cancer. He suffered from chronic diabetes, which affected his eyesight, and his faltering legs slowed his gait to a shuffle. "There's no end to rumors about Kanemaru, that 'He cannot see, and he shook hands with the wrong person,' " one magazine reported. Once, when a staffer served him coffee, she returned to find him sipping from his cup with a pile of sugar on the table next to the saucer. Some said he had only two good working hours a day. In his old age, Kanemaru's face had settled into an imposing, impassive, impenetrable mask, his eyes seemingly sealed into barely open slits. "We can't ever tell if he's smiling or asleep," said a friend.

"Even we don't know why he had power," Kanemaru's eldest son, Yasunobu, marveled a few years later as he reflected back on his father's rise. The best explanation anybody can offer is that, by the inverted logic that shaped Japanese politics at the time, Kanemaru's flaws made him the perfect chief. Takeshita was widely suspected, as

Tanaka had been, of wanting to become prime minister again, and Ozawa, still only forty-seven, would certainly be a candidate some day; but it was clear to everybody that Kanemaru could never seek the post. ("If I became prime minister," he once told a friend, "it would be an embarrassment to Japan.") And so, amid all the calculating egos in Nagatacho, only Kanemaru was truly credible as a selfless mediator, without any suspicion that he was really promoting himself. "When asked who is the most influential politician now," the *Asahi* newspaper reported in 1990, "most would respond that it is Shin Kanemaru." As such, he was the target of assassination attempts. Rightists threw Molotov cocktails at his house; at a Kanemaru speech, a gunman charged the stage and took three shots, barely missing Kanemaru's shoulder. He was thus given the kind of tight security detail usually accorded a top leader. Kanemaru had held numerous government posts in the 1970s and 1980s, his highest rank being deputy prime minister under Nakasone. But as he ascended to new heights in the 1990s, he had no formal government title; his only official position was "acting chairman" of the Takeshita faction. (Takeshita, after his resignation from the prime ministership, had also formally relinquished the chairmanship.) Kanemaru called himself the *gundan*'s "hired madam." The press labeled him "the Don."

In his Oz-like position behind the curtain, Kanemaru wielded influence by acting as a veritable oracle. His public utterances were subjected to intimate scrutiny and somehow caused rumors, as one analysis put it, "to become accomplished facts." Because he had no government post, no future, and no concern for his public reputation, Kanemaru could say bluntly what many politicians believed but were unable to express and could then retract anything that generated too much controversy. When businesses complained about an overly tight monetary policy, he suggested an interest rate cut, "even by beheading the Bank of Japan governor." Because he was believed to be powerful, his statements had an impact in shaping debate and policy. And because he had an impact, everything he said took on import. "Political stories in the 1980s and early 1990s depended to a large extent on Kanemaru's statements," a top journalist wrote.

Reading Kanemaru thus became a crucial art, yet a difficult one, since he did not always speak with clarity. He liked to use analogies that insinuated significance but were uncertain in intent. On the possibility of extending a session of Parliament, he once said, "It is not good that such a situation will come about where 'if you run after two hares, you will catch neither.' " On whether an election was imminent, he opined, "This situation is like a midwife when she touches the belly of a pregnant woman"; it was reported as a sign that the campaign would soon start. Sometimes he seemed to contradict himself in his various statements, even those made on the same day. And it became a challenge simply to parse Kanemaru's actual words since he could not, or would not, speak audibly; his voice would sink to a deep growl, and he took to mumbling. "Those listening to him have never been quite sure what to make of these comments," one columnist wrote. "We always wondered, 'Is this a test balloon, some form of manipulation, or merely chest pounding?' " Some suggested that Kanemaru himself wasn't aware of the weight his words would carry and that he was merely being used by other pols who were manipulating him.

For his first thirty years in politics, Kanemaru had been considered mainly a domestic pol, more concerned about the rough-and-tumble of factional balance than the geopolitical balance of power. In the twilight of his career, however, the Don decided to become a fixer on a global scale, guided not by the niceties of diplomacy but his own sense of *giri* ("duty") and *ninjo* ("feeling"). His supporters say he was, to the end, driven by his innate compassion and a desire to use his power to ever-broader good ends. Others speculate that in his hubris even Kanemaru became suffused with visions, however unlikely, of going down in history as a statesman. In the spring of 1990, as then–Soviet leader Mikhail Gorbachev was actively seeking peace with the West, Kanemaru took it upon himself to try to solve a territorial dispute that had chilled Japanese-Russian relations for four decades. With Japan now wealthy and the Soviets desperate for hard currency, Kanemaru pragmatically urged setting aside petty principles over the sovereignty of the islands in question, the southern Kuriles: "I have an idea to purchase them." Japan's horrified diplomats squelched the idea. Unabashed, Kanemaru decided to pay a visit to Beijing in late August 1990: "I have to talk with Deng [Xiaoping] in person to improve relations between China and Taiwan" was his rationale. China's aging paramount leader snubbed Japan's, and Sino-Taiwanese tensions remained. But Kanemaru did meet virtually every other top-level Chinese leader and vowed to send a Japanese cabinet minister to Beijing—despite Japan's prior pledge to the United States that it would avoid high-level contact so soon after the June 1989 Tiananmen Square massacre. "If Kanemaru says he wants [Education Minister Kosuke] Hori to visit, I guess it will happen," Ozawa said, and the trip took place within a few weeks of Kanemaru's trip.

Despite his failing health, Kanemaru took on a rigorous travel schedule. Three weeks after visiting Beijing, Kanemaru personally took his "shadow shogun" diplomacy to the isolated Stalinist regime of North Korea. He said he had initially been motivated by an emotional appeal he had received from the wife of a Japanese seaman whose fishing boat had been captured by the Communists and who had been held prisoner for seven years. But his five-day trip turned into a major foreign policy initiative. The two countries did not have formal relations with each other, and Kanemaru's entourage—which included ten senior bureaucrats from the Foreign, Trade, and Telecommunications Ministries—was the most important Japanese delegation ever to visit Pyongyang. He was treated like a head of state, honored with a mass calisthenics display featuring fifty thousand performers, and accorded three face-to-face meetings with dictator Kim Il Sung. Kanemaru used the meetings to try to foster broader bilateral ties. Ignoring official Japanese policy, he promised reparations payments to North Korea—not just for the period when Japan had occupied the peninsula from 1910 to 1945 but for the years since World War II as well. Kanemaru's promise caused chaos in Japan's diplomatic circles, as well as consternation in South Korea—Japan's ally and a foe of the North—and in Washington. "It was unprecedented for the Japanese to undertake such a wide-ranging initiative in Korea without consulting the countries that bore the principal responsibilities for maintaining peace and stability on the peninsula," Michael H. Armacost, the American ambassador to Tokyo at the time, later wrote. Asked whether Kanemaru was speaking for his country, an official Japanese government spokesman could only say, "That's a very difficult question." Kanemaru later had to retract his offer of reparations, and he flew to South Korea to apologize personally to the Seoul government. Still, he did win a promise that the fishing crew would be released, and Ozawa was dispatched to North Korea to make the pickup.

While Kanemaru's influence outside Japan proved mixed at best, his sway over Nagatacho was greater than ever, as demonstrated by the 1991 contest for prime minister. Kaifu's two-year term was expiring, and he indicated he would like another stint. But in early October, Kanemaru summarily withdrew his backing, forcing the premier to announce his resignation suddenly. The matter of choosing a successor became a show of brute force by the "Kon-Chiku-Sho" trio. In this race, it was no longer enough for a prospective premier to agree to cede authority; he had to publicly humiliate himself before the group as well.

Immediately after Kaifu's demise, Kanemaru engaged in a heavy-handed public drama with Ozawa in which he pleaded with his reluctant underling to take the job. "Can I have your husband's body," Kanemaru supposedly said in a phone call to Ozawa's wife, attempting to enlist her support. When Ozawa conclusively demurred, he, in turn, openly begged Kanemaru to take the title. Apparently, neither Ozawa nor Kanemaru was serious. Their feints were merely the opening gambits of a cruelly brilliant strategy—to show that the job of prime minister wasn't good enough for them and to invoke fear and desperation among those craven enough to want it. The field then narrowed down to three LDP faction leaders: Kiichi Miyazawa, Hiroshi Mitsuzuka, and Michio Watanabe.

Each appeared at Ozawa's office for an "interview," which would, in turn, be "reported" to Kanemaru. It was a particularly demeaning requirement since the three were all more than a decade older than Ozawa. During the sessions, Ozawa did nothing to ease the feeling of degradation. As Mitsuzuka presented his views on foreign affairs and political reform, Ozawa listened with closed eyes, and when the petitioner was done, he said simply, "I heard. See you." When Mitsuzuka asked if Ozawa had any questions, he was told "No." (Stung by criticism that he had been disrespectful toward his elders, Ozawa later issued a rebuttal, insisting, "I am observing proprieties toward senior members.")

During the "interviews," and during the days when the decision was under consideration, the candidates apparently competed to abase themselves to the "Kon-Chiku-Sho" trio in return for the keys to the premier's residence. Miyazawa made a point of visiting Ozawa's electoral district just before his appointment: in Iwate, he made a speech, saying "Ozawa is the most qualified person" to be prime minister; greeting Ozawa in Tokyo the next day, he gushed, "Yesterday, I went to our great leader's constituency." Of Kanemaru, Miyazawa said, "His skills in politics are in the domain of an art." Watanabe spent much of his time scurrying among the homes and offices of the three bosses, like a child caught in the middle of a particularly pitiless schoolyard game of "keep-away." After his session with Ozawa, he rushed to Takeshita's house to say that he would happily give up control of his cabinet appointments. Takeshita deflected the offer, saying that Ozawa was in charge of such matters. As Watanabe was leaving, Takeshita's dog walked up to the guest and relieved himself on him. "Sorry, the dog *never* does that," the host reportedly said. Then he punned, "Well, maybe you've got *un*" —a Japanese word that both means "luck" and is shorthand for "shit"—"on you." Watanabe met with Ozawa to reiterate his subservience and was told, "Kanemaru-san makes the final decision."

With the nation's titular leadership at stake, Kanemaru's remarks in those days came under especially intense examination. He made the front pages with a speech saying that Japan needed "a man who can conduct foreign policy with decisiveness"; he mentioned no names, but experts interpreted the words to mean a tacit endorsement of Miyazawa, who was considered an internationalist. Upon hearing the remarks, Watanabe immediately cut short an out-of-town meeting and rushed back to Tokyo to intensify his pleading.

The final decision was set for October 11. The night before, senior *gundan* members gathered at what had become the official site for selecting Japanese prime ministers—Kanemaru's Tokyo town house. By one A.M., with no resolution, Kanemaru was left alone to contemplate the matter. "I couldn't sleep a wink, wondering whom I should choose," he said the next morning. At midday, he was at the faction office, still heard to be muttering, "I simply don't know what to do. I'm utterly at a loss."

By evening, something coalesced inside Kanemaru's head, and he summoned the whole *gundan* to a meeting. He thanked them for coming despite the rain and for waiting so long for the caucus to start. He reviewed the prior few days, and finally, as if presiding over an Oscar awards ceremony, got to the point. "I was forced to think over how I should decide," he said. "I thought of this and that, and the conclusion is, I would like to have your support for Kiichi Miyazawa." A few people applauded. "I'm sorry, but I would like you to agree unanimously," the Don growled. The applause grew louder. Miyazawa himself was not informed until one of his aides, hearing a report of the meeting, scurried to find his chief to tell him the good news.

Why Miyazawa became prime minister was never made clear. Kanemaru said in a speech later that week that the new leader was "appropriate." "What really happened during the month of October 1991," one journal later said, reflecting on the whole process of how Kaifu had fallen and Miyazawa had risen, "remains puzzling not only to foreign observers but to Japanese."

For all his genuflecting, Miyazawa, seventy-two, was not as obviously pliant as his two predecessors, Uno and Kaifu. He was the elite of Japan's elite—a third-generation parliamentarian and a relative, by marriage, to several prominent business clans. He had already had an impressive career, spanning much of Japan's recent political history. A Tokyo University graduate, he had entered the Finance Ministry, where, like many bright young mandarins, he had won the favor of the elite bureaucrat-politicians who shaped Japan's early postwar conservative order. He was fluent in English and served as a translator at the 1951 signing of the U.S.-Japan peace treaty, when his country regained independence. By the time he became prime minister, Miyazawa had been an MP for four decades and had held thirteen cabinet posts, from finance to foreign affairs. He was one of Japan's most respected politicians abroad, once proudly inviting Henry Kissinger to attend one of his faction meetings, where the two men held a ninety-minute debate.

As a bureaucrat turned pol and a well-educated intellectual, Miyazawa was an exemplar of the class that Kakuei Tanaka disliked, and the two men did not get along. "He's not the type who could manage people" was Tanaka's assessment of Miyazawa. "As a secretary, he was good. But that's all. He's not a politician." Miyazawa referred to Tanaka as "uneducated" and "a parvenu." The tension continued with Tanaka's successors. Of Kanemaru, the tart-tongued Miyazawa once said to reporters, "A person like him should be rolled up in a bamboo blind and dumped into the water. . . . I hear there is a deep river in [Kanemaru's home region of] Yamanashi." "Mr. Kanemaru says he does not like Mr. Miyazawa," Ozawa had blithely said in a newspaper interview shortly before Miyazawa's selection. "And I may say I feel the same way."

In 1991, however, Miyazawa had done his best to persuade the old Tanaka clan that he was worthy of its consecration, and he paid a high price. He prostrated himself before men he disdained. He agreed to turn over control of nearly all his cabinet appointments; an aide explained to the press that the new prime minister didn't want to "interfere" with personnel matters. He reversed his long-held positions on key issues. Still, once he took office, the "Kon-Chiku-Sho" cabal did not consider him obsequious enough. Miyazawa had the audacity to hint at some small differences over the party executive lineup and did not actively pursue Ozawa's pet policies. Besides, "Those around Kanemaru say that since being elected . . . Miyazawa has failed to make as many visits to Kanemaru as expected to show his appreciation," a columnist wrote. "Although such matters do not have much direct bearing on national politics, they are serious enough to Kanemaru to make him feel that Miyazawa does not treat him with due courtesy." And that was serious enough for Miyazawa's administration to run into trouble quickly. Within two months of the Miyazawa inauguration, even routine legislation became stalled in Parliament, as the opposition parties started haranguing him over an old scandal he thought had been laid to rest. Rumors spread that Kanemaru and Ozawa were actually encouraging their friends in the other parties to tear down the prime minister they themselves had installed; at the least, they weren't doing much to help him. Commentators began predicting his administration's collapse just months after its establishment. Kanemaru branded the government "a boat of mud."

In January 1992, a chastened Miyazawa went crawling to Kanemaru. He offered the Don the formal title of LDP vice president and the informal role of co–prime minister. Kanemaru was put in charge of pushing legislation through Parliament, and suddenly the opposition became cooperative. Miyazawa made a point of introducing Kanemaru to President George Bush, who was visiting Tokyo for a summit at the time. Kanemaru was soon invited to the White House, where the president personally served his guest coffee and his wife, Barbara, presented him with a copy of her best-seller, *Millie's Book*, about the Bushes' dog. In Washington, Kanemaru won plaudits for offering new policies to reduce Japan's trade surplus. And back in Tokyo, he was again clearly pulling strings. "LDP Vice President Kanemaru met Noboru Takeshita . . . and reached accord" on the timing of a cabinet reshuffle, one newspaper later reported. "Prime Minister Miyazawa," the report continued, "was informed to that effect over the telephone."

Kanemaru and Miyazawa sealed their mutual cooperation pact at a remarkable ceremony in early February, held at a posh restaurant with a coterie of LDP heavyweights in attendance. Kanemaru, who did most of the talking, began the evening with a long, rambling soliloquy as he downed glass after glass of Chivas Regal with water: "Shin Kanemaru is a man. Even if my legs fail me, I will support the Miyazawa government. As long as you don't double-cross me, I'll keep my promise."

"Having you as [LDP] vice president, I have become confident," Miyazawa replied in his remarks. "I will not do anything that differs from the intentions of Mr. Kanemaru. I will consult you on everything."

The speeches ended, and the drunken revelry began. "Miyazawa," Kanemaru interrupted the proceedings with a bark, according to one published account. "You're next. Sing." The prime minister of Japan immediately obliged, performing for Kanemaru a traditional ballad to the melodic accompaniment of a samisen banjo.

CHAPTER NINETEEN
"ONE BIG SAFE"

When Kanemaru, Takeshita, and Ozawa first joined forces to topple Kakuei Tanaka in 1985, there was some talk that they might represent a new wave of political reform. For more than a decade, the press had pilloried Tanaka for his raw "money-power politics," making him the personification of corruption. His abrupt removal seemed to harbinger a cleansing of the nation's government, as if the body politic had amputated a putrefied limb. "It is to be hoped that the decision taken by Takeshita and his colleagues will weaken the grip of former Prime Minister Kakuei Tanaka on the political world, which has become distorted as a result [of Tanaka's power]," the *Asahi* newspaper, a longtime Tanaka foe, cautiously cheered. "We can hope . . . that [Takeshita's] 'Creative Politics Circle' would become a pioneer for the rejuvenation of the closed conservative politics," the *Mainichi* newspaper assented in an editorial. Takeshita and Company, suggested the English-language *Japan Times,* could "inject more reason and cleanliness into the process of selecting the nation's top leader."

Such hopes were quickly dashed. All the basic attributes that had made Japan's political climate susceptible to Tanaka-style hustling remained. Elections still cost a lot of money, more than could be raised by legitimate means. Businesses were still willing to foot the bill, since they needed as much help as ever in accessing the government budgets controlled by Tokyo's mighty and capricious bureaucracy and navigating the rules set by it. The lack of political competition—either between the LDP and the opposition or among the factions within the LDP—as well as the "dual structure" of government diminished both the accountability and the transparency of power. Besides, Tanaka's successors had learned his corrupt methods well, and they were not about to forsake them.

THE MAIN BENEFACTOR of the "Kon-Chiku-Sho" regime, as for Tanaka, was the construction industry—a large, profitable sector of the economy highly dependent on, and heavily controlled by, the central government.

Separately and together, the three pols had spent much of their careers creating ties with Japan's builders and with the bureaucracy that directed construction enterprises. Construction companies "are perfect for election campaigns," Ozawa would say, explaining the value of builders to politicians. "There are eight million people" working in the industry who are easily mobilized by their companies. "They campaign as hard as they can."

Ozawa's father had once served as construction minister, and he had bequeathed valuable national and local connections to his son. (Shortly after entering Parliament in 1969, Ozawa paid a call to the Construction Ministry, seeking help for the expansion of a road. "You are the son of Mr. Saeki," the attendant mandarin said with admiration. "Mr. Saeki was great.") Tanaka, as Ozawa's political father, had cultivated more such links for his disciple: not only had he brokered Ozawa's marriage to the daughter of Tadashi Fukuda, a leading contractor, but he had made sure the pol was, while in his thirties, appointed to key legislative posts overseeing the sector. Such positions gave Ozawa the knowledge and prestige to head his own league of construction-related MPs formed to lobby for pork-barrel funds; officially it was christened the National Land Construction Research Group, but it was more widely known as "the Ozawa school."

Like Tanaka, Kanemaru had business relations with construction companies. He was appointed minister of construction by Tanaka in 1972, an especially fortuitous time to hold the post because the new premier was launching his lavish plan to "remodel the

Japanese archipelago." "It was a lot of fun being construction minister at the time, because we had a huge budget," Kanemaru wrote nostalgically in his autobiography. "There is construction remaining in every city, town, and village in the country that I had a hand in. . . . I got to feel like the *Hanasaka Jiisan,*" a Japanese fairy-tale figure who magically made flowers bloom wherever he went.

Kanemaru held the ministerial post for only a year, but he later kept a close watch over ongoing projects as the longtime chairman of the LDP's Road Research Committee and as head of several leading industry-related associations, including the euphemistically named National River Conservation Society and the National Association of Disaster Prevention.

Takeshita took his turn as minister of construction in 1976 and was serving in the post at the time of Tanaka's arrest. The construction position was so important that the rivalry between the two men is said to have begun then, when Takeshita had the chance to solicit donations for himself from builders. "Don't try to steal water from a well others have dug!" Tanaka snapped. Marital alliances with the construction industry were a critical part of Takeshita's networking strategy: after his first daughter married Kanemaru's first son, his third daughter was betrothed to a scion of the Takenaka family, owners of Japan's fourth largest contractor; Takeshita's half brother had also married the second daughter of the owner of the Fukuda-gumi contractor, the man who was also Ozawa's father-in-law. Takeshita also had a financial stake in the industry, owning sixteen thousand shares in a leading builder.

For all three politicians, construction companies and related concerns formed the core of their electoral support. While their respective home districts were not as impoverished as Tanaka's Niigata, each came from a relatively poor, agricultural, unindustrialized region. Hence, the local economies—and local business profits—were highly dependent on public works funds from Tokyo. Like Tanaka, Kanemaru, Takeshita, and Ozawa, in varying degrees, based their appeal to constituents on their ability to bring home the pork—and they seemed to have great influence not just over what projects came to their districts but also over which contractors got the work.

Takeshita's first campaign promise in his first campaign, for example, had been to serve as a "bridge" from the national government to his Shimane Prefecture, and he diligently kept his word as the tax monies flowing to his district grew apace with his political influence. By the 1980s, Shimane had surpassed Niigata as the largest recipient, per citizen, of national funds; by the early 1990s, two thirds of all construction in Shimane was paid for by the government. The prefecture was second per capita in the number of its museums and art galleries, and, with a nation-leading three airports, "You are always within half an hour" of a plane ride, boasted a local representative. "There were times when the amounts were too much for us to handle," a former head of the Shimane prefectural Public Works Department was quoted as saying. "We sometimes gave money back to Tokyo."

In return, the local construction industries worked hard to ensure the continued reelection of their sponsors. Construction companies organized at least four separate Ozawa "support groups" in the Iwate Second District, including the "Ichi-Ken" association—the name is a blend of "Ichiro" and *kensetsu,* or "construction"—for local firms and another for the Iwate branches of national builders. The secretary-general of Ozawa's main hometown campaign group ran a timber company; his father had worked for Saeki Ozawa's election campaigns. Several local politicians close to Ozawa were construction company executives. And there was a high correlation between those firms backing Ozawa and those building the government-sponsored dam, tunnel, highway, waste-processing facility, racetrack, and school that he was credited with getting for Iwate; the Japan Communist Party's investigative newspaper asserted that Ozawa-friendly firms had been the top seven recipients of Iwate public works contracts. "Friends told me," says a contractor who recently moved to the district, "that I couldn't get any jobs unless I became an Ozawa supporter."

Of the triumvirate, Kanemaru, with his Yamanashi machine, most closely replicated the old Tanaka Etsuzankai model—and in some ways built a more sophisticated operation. More than Takeshita and Ozawa, he sought the Tanaka-style trophy projects for his district and took splashy credit for them. Near the Kanemaru family home was a project widely known as *"Shin-chan Bashi,"* or "Good Ol' Shin's Bridge." "There are no other bridges on any other prefectural roads that are as wide as this one. This is the only one in Japan. Isn't this bridge impressive?" he would boast with delight even late in his life. With highways and train lines, he vowed to open the world to his landlocked constituents, much as Tanaka had spoken of bulldozing the mountains between his Niigata and Tokyo. "Now we can all eat fresh fish from the sea," he wrote in a promise that must have resonated with people who for centuries had subsisted on fruits and mountain vegetables. In the two decades after Kanemaru served as construction minister, Yamanashi's ranking in per capita income jumped from thirty-seventh among Japan's forty-seven prefectures to twenty-seventh—a spurt fueled, at least in part, by a tenfold increase in nationally funded public works in the region. A 1990 national Economic Planning Agency survey ranked Kanemaru's district tops in living standards.

The crowning glory of Kanemaru's long career of hometown pork-barreling was the magnetically levitated linear motorcar test project, which was awarded to Yamanashi in 1989. The "mag-lev," which hovered ten centimeters above its tracks, was to be the bullet train of the twenty-first century, capable of whizzing along at 500 kilometers (312 miles) per hour, twice as fast as Japan's then-speediest-running train. Yamanashi was not a natural choice for the project: the mountainous terrain meant that 85 percent of the twenty-seven-mile test track would have to be run through costly tunnels; besides, planners had originally talked of using the 200-billion-yen ($2 billion) budget to help one of Japan's more impoverished regions. Nor was Kanemaru an expert on the technology—he kept calling it "Libya motor car" instead of "linear motor car." But he certainly knew how to capture a boondoggle. In addition to the government funds, the project created a boom in land prices in Yamanashi; in some places, the spurt started before the site selection was officially announced, indicating that Kanemaru's speculator friends had had advance knowledge of the decision.

Kanemaru was perhaps the most brazen of Japan's major machine bosses in doling out jobs to backers while punishing foes. Beginning in the late 1970s, his heavy-handed tactics created a kind of two-party system in Yamanashi Prefecture, pitting pro- and anti-Kanemaru contractors against each other. Many local elections were openly fought over how the spoils should be divided. From 1979 to 1991, when a friendly governor ran Yamanashi, some of Kanemaru's favorite builders saw their revenues spike up more than tenfold, while their competitors watched business drop by as much as two thirds. In 1991, when the Don's candidate faced a tough election fight, the national LDP dispatched a lineup of stars, including Prime Minister Kaifu, to the region's hustings.

"I never sought donations from construction companies," Kanemaru once said. Still, "they would come to me [with money], saying, 'Please use this' . . . to show gratitude." Alas, he added, "it became a habit." And what may have begun as a spontaneous gesture of appreciation evolved into a highly sophisticated, systematized habit at that. More than five hundred Yamanashi contractors organized the "Ken-Shin Association"—the "Ken" for *kensetsu*, or "construction," the "Shin" for Kanemaru's first name. One of its main functions was to funnel back to the region's most powerful pol some portion of the bounty he had brought to them. Each member was rated by size and assessed a proportionate semiannual membership fee, as well as a special levy each time Kanemaru faced reelection. More payments were expected when public works contracts were actually awarded: the winner contributed a "coffee fee" and, if it was a new project, also gave some *manju*, not the real sort—a bun filled with sweet bean paste—but, in Ken-Shin parlance, code for a 1-million-yen kickback. The number of *manju* offered depended on the size of the contract. According to one estimate, the Yamanashi construction industry generated 5 billion yen for Kanemaru over the course of a decade.

And Yamanashi was just a microcosm, albeit an extreme one, of similar activity on a national scale.

In the late 1980s and early 1990s, the Japanese government went on a new national public works spending spree, prompting a former Tanaka aide to crow, "The 'archipelago-remodeling plan' is now being revived." And there was no greater champion of the effort than Kanemaru. As head of the "MP's Public Investment Promotion Association," he prescribed pork as the cure for every economic downturn. In 1986, he became head of a special government commission that was designed to enhance "private-sector vitality" by subsidizing large-scale construction projects. The endeavors under Kanemaru's purview included colossal ventures worthy of a self-assured nation seeking monuments to flaunt its new wealth. Two projects alone cost a bell-ringing $11 billion plus each: Japan's first twenty-four-hour airport, built on a man-made island off Osaka, and a highway traversing Tokyo Bay that would require the widest undersea tunnels in the world.

While some Japanese were beginning to question the wisdom of the "public works state," Kanemaru stood ready to fend them off. The tightfisted Finance Ministry, for one, was constantly trying to tone down the binges, but "You can't keep everyone happy," Kanemaru said in a 1988 speech, "unless you're prepared to lay your life on the line and go about overturning the desk of the [ministry's] Director General of the Budget Bureau!" Environmentalists worried that the headlong rush to pave, bulldoze, and erect would cause irreparable damage to Japan's natural beauty and ecosystems; for twenty years, their objections had helped hold up efforts to dam the Nagara, one of the country's last remaining free-flowing rivers. In 1988, with Kanemaru's blessing, the $1.8 billion project finally began. Two years later, when the minister in charge of the Environment Agency questioned the plan, Kanemaru insisted, in numerous phone conversations, that he keep quiet. When the minister refused, he was shuffled out of the job—and he lost his parliamentary seat in the next general election as a Kanemaru-backed candidate drew votes away. While promoting and protecting construction spending, Kanemaru also inherited Tanaka's mantle as a chief national *dango* ("bid-rigging") mediator, helping determine which companies got which jobs. Eyebrows were raised when a certain national contractor got a major portion of the Tokyo Bay project even though the company's shaky financial condition should, by official guidelines, have disqualified it. "I asked Kanemaru-san," the company chairman told reporters inquiring about the reversal of fortune.

Like Yamanashi's builders, the big national contractors paid their advocate handsomely. Twice each year, Kanemaru reportedly got cash payments of up to 10 million yen from each of Japan's biggest builders, totaling about a billion yen annually by some estimates. And while Takeshita and Ozawa were not as openly active in the field as Kanemaru, they were also treated well. During the "Kon-Chiku-Sho" era, Shimizu Corporation, Japan's largest contractor, compiled a list ranking fifty-seven leading politicians by perceived influence in order to help the company determine how much money to give each, according to a newspaper report. Only two received an "A-plus" grade, qualifying them for the largest annual stipend of 20 million yen a year: Kanemaru and Takeshita. Ozawa was one of six to receive an "A," worth half as much money; that placed him in a category with the prime minister at the time, Miyazawa, and former prime minister Nakasone. Another puppet premier of the period, Kaifu, was given only a "B," while the third, Uno, did not make the list.

WHILE PRESERVING TIES with stalwart Tanaka patrons such as the construction industry, the "Kon-Chiku-Sho" regime also worked diligently to modernize the "general hospital," the wide-ranging services the Tanaka faction had offered constituents through its influence with the various ministries.

As the country changed in the 1980s, so did the chances for profiteering. Foreign aid was one burgeoning sector; with its new economic might, Japan had surpassed the United States as the world's largest donor to developing countries, and Japanese politicians saw fresh opportunities to swing government contracts for their patrons. Critics saw fund-raising as a not-so-hidden motive behind Kanemaru's controversial freelance diplomacy with North Korea; in the months after his visit, various Kanemaru aides flew back to Pyongyang, with chummy Japanese executives in tow, to scope out possible development projects. Even a mid-1980s campaign for deregulation and privatization—a drive aimed at reducing the government's extensive role in the economy, the foundation of the machine's moneymaking skills—became an occasion to seek donations; the proposals, a skeptical journalist wrote, "were twisted and turned to suit the needs of the large industries." Another great change in Japan's economy during the 1980s was the phenomenal expansion of the financial sector. Takeshita's four-plus years as finance minister had given him an unrivaled influence over the bureaucracy that regulated the nation's highly profitable banks, securities companies, and insurance underwriters—even after he left the post. The leaders of those firms were prominent members of, and contributors to, his various support groups.

The nature of political fund-raising was different for all MPs in the "Kon-Chiku-Sho" era, compared to Tanaka's time, partly as a result of the fallout from Tanaka's scandals. It wasn't that the flow of contributions diminished but that politicians and companies devised more elaborate channels for taking monies and returning favors, in order to better circumvent legal controls.

The whole "dual structure of power," for example, showed how well the politicians had learned the lessons of the Lockheed affair. Tanaka was convicted of bribery because he had taken money in exchange for a decision he had made while he was prime minister, a position of formal government authority. Japan's bribery laws applied only to people who held official responsibility at the time when a suspicious exchange occurred; they did not apply to "shadow shoguns" or "dons." As Tanaka and his perceptive disciples soon came to understand, his mistake wasn't that he had taken money or done a favor; it was that he had done so while holding the government title.

Although straight cash payments to politicians were, of course, still welcome in the late 1980s, so were complex new transactions, made possible by the thriving stock and land markets, which helped obscure the flow of funds. Brokerage houses amassed their resources to ramp up the value of certain stocks held by MPs. Real estate developers gave as gifts golf course memberships—a perquisite that, in the midst of the land boom, had nothing to do with participating in the sport but became a valuable, tradable commodity worth thousands of dollars. Art dealers became middlemen between businessmen and pols, masking payoffs in bogus "sales" of masterpieces. In one case extensively covered in the Japanese press, a bank executive publicly accused Takeshita of skimming as much as 300 million yen from the proceeds of a bank merger that the politician had helped engineer. The contribution had supposedly been laundered through the purchase of an antique Japanese gold-paper folding screen decorated with a painted procession of feudal-era aristocrats; according to the accusing businessman, one of the banks involved in the deal had paid an art dealer an inflated price for the screen, and the dealer, in turn, had passed on some of the markup to Takeshita. (Takeshita repeatedly denied the accusations, and he was never formally charged with any wrongdoing.)

The "money-power politics" of the 1980s was also shaped by the Political Funds Control Law, which had been passed in the mid-1970s in the wake of Tanaka's troubles. The regulations were ostensibly aimed at diminishing the influence of corporations on politics. But the law was full of loopholes, and Takeshita, by the time he became prime minister in 1987, was the acknowledged master of finding and exploiting them. The new rules set a strict ceiling, for example, on the total amount of money a single company could contribute to an individual politician. Rather than relying on a few large contributors, therefore, Takeshita developed what his aides called the "wide and shallow" strategy, which depended on a sophisticated nationwide network of donors who gave annually up to the legal cap. So systematized was his fund-raising that, in some prefectures, companies received each January an envelope accompanied by a note titled "Notice for Payment of Annual Membership Dues." Again, the laws limited how much money a company could give to a "political organization" but did not stipulate how many organizations an MP could establish. Takeshita unabashedly set up one national support group after another, for a total of five, as well as forty regional organizations, and it was perfectly legal for any company to donate money to all of them.

Most significantly, the regulations contained a surprisingly narrow definition of what exactly constituted a "contribution." One perplexing exception was the purchase of tickets to "encouragement parties." As a result, politicians started scrambling to host galas, selling large blocks of tickets to companies. The most successful such event ever was the Evening to Encourage Noboru Takeshita, held in the Phoenix Room of the Tokyo Prince Hotel on May 21, 1987. It was, in a sense, a coming-out party for the new machine leader, just as he was conclusively wresting control from Tanaka. More than thirteen thousand people crammed the event, so many that a number of guests became sick from the overcrowding. Those in attendance included leaders of the three main opposition parties. More impressive than the party itself, and more important from the standpoint of Takeshita's coffers, wasn't how many people came but how many had bought tickets. A total of sixty thousand—more than four times as many as the actual number of guests—had been sold, most in bulk to corporations; construction companies in particular had been major purchasers. At 30,000 yen a pop, the tickets raised about 2 billion yen, or $14.7 million, for Takeshita in one night, an all-time record in Japan. (By way of comparison, no single American political fund-raising event drew $12 million until 1995, and that was not for an individual candidate but for the Republican National Committee as a whole.)

WHERE DID ALL the money go?

To hear Japanese politicians tell it, the funds were necessary to cover the escalating costs of gaining and holding office, which by the late 1980s were even greater than when Tanaka had first assembled his machine in the early 1970s. The price of winning a seat in Parliament was now estimated at 500 million yen (about $4 million); having succeeded, an incumbent MP's annual expenses in a nonelection year ran about 100 million yen, while the MP earned an official salary of only 19 million yen. One survey said that an average Japanese MP spent twice as much per constituent as a typical U.S. congressman on a campaign. The gap was all the more surprising because the tight Japanese campaign regulations prevented the use of television, the major expense of American elections. Japanese legislators complained incessantly about the demands placed upon them by constituents, who still regularly expected their representatives to pay them. The remuneration was very rarely cast as a direct payoff for a vote. Rather, constituents expected their MP, as a leader of the community, to attend important events in their lives and to leave the customary gift. According to a 1989 survey of one hundred MPs, their monthly duties included attending an average of 6.6 weddings and 26.5 funerals, costing each politician a total of 550,000 yen a month in congratulatory or condolence gifts. During the New Year's season, an MP would be expected to keep up the breathless pace of attending thirty parties a day, shelling out 800,000 yen a month. And no sector of society was above demanding help with emergencies. As one LDP MP noted wryly in 1989, "A [Buddhist] temple representative visited an officer of my support group and asked him to donate 300,000 yen to fix a temple building."

If politics was expensive for even the lowliest pols, it was still more so for those aspiring to leadership positions in their parties. As in Tanaka's time, a prerequisite for winning followers was the ability to alleviate the crushing financial burdens of one's flock. "It is not *only* money," Ozawa insisted somewhat defensively to an interviewer in late 1989. "Money *follows* [on] human relations. . . . Unless the [recipient feels] that 'this man is alright [*sic*] to be my boss' . . . he never takes the money." Still, Ozawa acknowledged, "money is a means." Kanemaru, too, instinctively understood the importance of bankrolling for preserving his clout with junior pols. Imprecise in many matters, he never forgot whom he had paid; if the gift weren't acknowledged properly, he would make sure to ask, "What happened to that?" The annual cost of maintaining the Takeshita faction of LDP members was estimated to be about 2 billion yen in a nonelection year. And that was just part of the funds needed for Takeshita and his partners to maintain their political influence. Takeshita was known for underwriting politicians who had lost elections and were seeking to regain their seats, as well as friendly members of the opposition and helpful bureaucrats.

Yet for a politician to imply—as many did—that the unseemly piles of corporate contributions were necessary to carry out professional obligations was disingenuous. During the late 1980s, few Japanese MPs struggled to make ends meet. Many lived lavishly, with no visible means of support outside their ostensibly modest salaries.

Just as the fallout from Tanaka's bribery scandal did little to curb business payoffs to politicians, the heated attacks on Tanaka's rich living did little to dissuade pols from using public profit for personal gain. Technically, it was improper for an MP to treat political contributions as private income, but the laws governing the spending of those funds—like the regulations monitoring their raising—remained vague and ineffectual. On rare occasions, a politician might face some minor penalty for crossing the line: in 1979, for example, Takeshita was forced to revise his income tax return after he was found to have used political funds to build a house; the following year, Kanemaru similarly received a minor wrist slap for failing to report 32 million yen in income. But for the most part, the increasingly opulent lifestyles of Japan's leaders passed unquestioned. A top LDP boss, a rival to Takeshita, once had a personal tailor come to his office to take his measurements for a suit. With a journalist sitting in the room, he said to a group of visiting MPs, "Why don't you guys have your measurements taken, too? It's my treat." "Overjoyed, all of them had the tailor take their measurements," the reporter later wrote. "It was a scene unthinkable by the standard of the average citizen."

Few elected officeholders outstripped the living standards of the average citizen in the late 1980s and early 1990s more than Kanemaru. On paper, he was a man of only moderate wealth: in 1986, he reported a net worth of 127 million yen (about $900,000) in land, buildings, and securities. "We have lived in an era when thrift was regarded as a virtue," a Kanemaru aide said upon releasing the information. "Given fifty years of hard work, this may be just about the right amount of fortune."

Still, Kanemaru somehow managed to live like a king—or, rather, a kingmaker. In 1991, in his hometown of Yamanashi, he held a dedication ceremony for a $3 million addition to his family estate. His second wife, Etsuko, meanwhile purchased two separate Hawaii vacation homes for a total of $1.3 million. In Tokyo, he lived in a town house in Moto Azabu, one of the city's priciest neighborhoods. Adorned with expensive Western furniture, this home had a rooftop garden, a golf putting green, a karaoke room, and a mah-jongg parlor equipped with special machinery to help the awkward Kanemaru stack the small ivory pieces used in the Chinese game. A mynah bird would shriek, from time to time, "Good morning!" or "Shin Kanemaru!" He was chauffeured in the mornings in his black Bentley to a Nagatacho building aptly named "Palais Royal." There, where the rent was 2.5 million yen a month, his main office in Suite 605 was decorated with two oil paintings done by a famous Japanese painter, one of a European woman, the other of Kanemaru himself. In his second office, five floors above, guests were greeted by a stuffed tiger, mouth open in a growl. Kanemaru spent most days from two P.M. to six P.M. in the mah-jongg parlor located there. A main responsibility of his staff was rounding up enough MPs to join the high-stakes games.

Kanemaru appeared to have a careless, casual manner with his wealth. He had no formal record keeping for the money and gifts that poured into his office and went back out again, with political and personal funds all sloshing around together. Envelopes of cash sometimes sat around on tables. At the side of the main room of his office was a low sofa, perpetually piled sloppily with gifts he had received; secretaries never touched the loot, since Kanemaru, from time to time, would suddenly remember, "I put that gift from this person there. . . ." "The whole office," a close aide said, "was like one big safe."

PART FOUR

THE MACHINE COLLAPSES, 1992–1996

WHILE THE INTERNAL mechanics of the machine had never run so smoothly, the foundation it rested on was crumbling.

Some observers, witnessing the wire-pulling and plundering by "Kon-Chiku-Sho," asserted that Japan's government had devolved from a democracy to an oligarchy. That was hyperbole. The bosses could push around legislators and cabinets at will on day-to-day decisions, yet they ultimately drew their authority from a general social compact with the Japanese people. The machine style of government had been a natural consequence of postwar Japan's two main articles of faith: that the country would enjoy eternally escalating prosperity and that it could exist in blissful, peaceful isolation—courtesy of America's indulgent protection—from the stresses of global affairs. In that fantastic setting, Japanese politics was freed from the normal difficult choices and ideological divides of democracy. Leadership became a relatively easy matter of distributing the seemingly limitless wealth as widely as possible, of building an extensive, diverse coalition. There were few trade-offs, few pressing decisions. As long as enough constituencies were taken care of, as long as no sector or interest group was seriously angered or alienated, the majority of the electorate was willing to overlook some unsavory shenanigans, including the cynical separation of de facto and de jure authority, and a degree of overt political corruption that would probably be considered intolerable in other developed nations.

By the late 1980s, however, the bargain had begun to unravel. The demands facing Japan, both at home and abroad, were growing more complex, unsettling the delicate political balancing act. Policy responses to these new challenges often required acting quickly, taking sides, and asking for sacrifice, unpleasant tasks the machine hadn't been designed to perform. The sense deepened that, at a time when the system was funneling more and more to the pols, it was delivering less and less to the people it had been created to serve.

CHAPTER TWENTY

CRACKS IN THE FOUNDATION

In 1988, THE JAPANESE electorate's outrage over "money-power politics" erupted once again, reaching its highest pitch since the Lockheed scandal. The trigger this time was Recruit Company, a Tokyo-based enterprise that sought to accelerate its rapid commercial growth through heavy "investing" in politicians.

Recruit was a classic example of the type of business that Tanaka-style political brokerage had been designed to help, an aggressive outsider with no long-standing elite ties. Hiromasa Ezoe, a self-made entrepreneur from a lower-class family, had founded the company just after he had graduated from college in 1960. From its origins as a small job placement magazine issued out of a prefab rooftop office, Recruit had blossomed by 1988 into one of Japan's largest specialty publishers; its dozen magazines claimed more than 3 million readers, with annual revenues of 270 billion yen. Publishing was just the core of what had become the Recruit Group, headquartered in a gleaming tower near the upscale Ginza shopping district. The ten-thousand-employee conglomerate spanned about thirty subsidiaries covering sectors as disparate as driving schools, data transmission, resorts, and real estate.

Ezoe's business was often hailed as a model of private-sector innovation. But his success was inextricably linked to his ability to persuade, avert, or cajole Japan's intrusive bureaucracy. He actively sought good relations with the Education and Labor Ministries to keep his main business healthy—to provide access to crucial information such as student mailing lists, to ease regulations on employment recruiting that would hurt his magazines, and to closely enforce guidelines that would give him a boost. When the rules were not favorable to Recruit, the company sometimes bent them and then required assistance in averting the penalty. As Recruit diversified into new fields, Ezoe needed a wider range of bureaucrats who had the power to grant permission to buy land, waive height limits on buildings, and ensure access—low-priced, at that—to normally restricted supercomputers.

Ezoe regularly wined and dined the relevant bureaucrats and invited them, honorarium included, to speak at company seminars or write essays for his magazines. He also donated heavily to prominent politicians he thought could help plead one of his many causes. In addition to the conventional avenues of contributing funds, Ezoe, in an innovation appropriate to the 1980s, laundered many of his payoffs through a complex stock market scheme: when a new Recruit subsidiary was about to go public, the businessman offered select MPs the chance to buy shares in advance at a reduced "preflotation" price; when the firm's stock value soared after public trading opened—a near guarantee in the thriving market of the day—the pols could make a quick killing reselling their holdings. Ezoe transferred the shares through dummy companies aptly named, in English, "Big Way," "Do Best," and "Eternal Fortune." To politicians who did not want to take the risk of even a small initial investment, another Recruit affiliate, First Finance Company, lent the required capital.

Ezoe wisely made Takeshita one of his main beneficiaries. In the fall of 1985, shortly after Takeshita had challenged Tanaka, the magnate formed a business support group for the up-and-coming pol; at the end of 1987, Ezoe joined a group of young executives backing Takeshita as the new prime minister. During that period, Takeshita, his aides, and his relatives received a total of 200 million yen from Recruit in donations, loans, and cut-rate stock shares. At one rural Takeshita fund-raising party held in May 1987, Recruit bought 30 million yen in tickets, or 60 percent of all those sold; at the famous 2-billion-yen Takeshita party held in Tokyo the same month, Recruit and a subsidiary together sprang for about 50 million yen worth of tickets; the subsidiary bought 1,000, even though it had only 600 employees. Ozawa, too, received donations worth 2 million yen; Recruit even gave discount shares yielding more than 20 million yen in profits to a son of the Fukuda-gumi construction company president, an in-law of both Ozawa and Takeshita. An Ozawa aide was also paid a monthly retainer of 240,000 yen as an adviser to a Recruit affiliate. (Kanemaru's name, oddly, never surfaced on the public lists of Recruit funding recipients.) Ezoe also tried to curry favor well beyond the Takeshita camp. Takeshita's predecessor as prime minister, Nakasone, was a major recipient, as were Takeshita's two rivals in the 1987 premier's race, each of whom received 100 million yen during the contest. More than forty politicians—including nearly every ranking LDP member—received a total of 1.3 billion yen in Recruit monies, and MPs from two small opposition parties were also let in on the rising-stock-price gambit.

In its zeal, Recruit and many of its high-placed friends violated a number of laws. The scandal first broke as a two-bit municipal scam in the summer of 1988, when a newspaper reported that an official of Kawasaki, an industrial Tokyo suburb, had accepted Recruit stock before granting the necessary permits for a new "intelligent building" high-rise. As subsequent investigations suggested more extensive wrongdoing, the company launched a bungled cover-up campaign, which backfired when one antagonistic lawmaker invited a hidden camera crew to film a Recruit executive persistently pushing him to accept "favors" from the company; the footage was later broadcast on national television. When prosecutors concluded their investigation in May 1989, a total of seventeen people were indicted in the Recruit affair—for giving and taking bribes, violating securities laws, or breaking campaign contribution rules. The lineup included Ezoe, four of his employees, and three government bureaucrats.

Two politicians and four political aides were also nabbed in the dragnet. And while none was affiliated with the Takeshita faction, he and his gang were still hurt by the affair. The Recruit scandal, in the public's view, was about far more than illegalities. As details leaked out about the company's far-reaching payments, the electorate's outrage turned against the indecency of it all, even of what *was* legal, and against the deceitful greed that had become completely acceptable among politicians. Recruit seemed the perfect illustration of the way the country's elected leaders sought cash (eagerly), spent it (selfishly; one senior conservative had taken the profits from his Recruit shares to buy a house in a ritzy Tokyo neighborhood), and used the most flimsy, cynical methods to cover their tracks. Most had taken the money through aides. One veteran pol had received funds through his wife, who had been given a monthly retainer as a Recruit "consultant," while another had tried to hide his profits in his daughter's bank account. The public's revulsion was heightened when many MPs continued to take donations from Recruit well after the company was immersed in controversy.

The Recruit scandal thus came to symbolize an entire political establishment on the take, blind to appearances of impropriety. Any politician who accepted Recruit funds—whether proper or improper—was treated by the media as tainted. Three ministers in Takeshita's cabinet were forced to resign for such transgressions. A new justice minister, who pledged to satisfy public anger with a full investigation, was appointed in December 1988; he resigned three days later when it was disclosed that he too had received Recruit funds.

The opposition parties were limited in their ability to press the affair, since they were also implicated. But the public was aroused, and, as prime minister at the time, Takeshita was a chief target of the anti-Recruit campaign. At first he denied having taken any donations from the company. But then he was forced to admit, bit by bit, that his office had indeed received money. The man who had prided himself on meticulous attention to detail, on keeping cool under pressure, grew increasingly flustered during parliamentary interrogations. Under grilling by the Communist Party leader—one of the few ranking MPs untouched by the affair—Takeshita turned red and trembled. "I can tell you what I know, but I can't tell you what I don't remember," the premier responded to one question. In mid-April 1989, Takeshita promised that he had disclosed the full extent of his relationship with Recruit, with the contorted explanation of reversals and self-contradictions that "I do not remember details of my [earlier] statements, but I probably did not have a clear recollection." Two weeks later, the press reported that Takeshita's trusted aide of thirty years, Ihei Aoki, had received an unreported loan of 50 million yen. It was the final straw; on April 25, Takeshita announced his intention to resign as prime minister.

"Politics takes money," Aoki had said in an interview years earlier. "An aide has to collect money from various sources, and his first duty is to make sure that such activities will not cause trouble to the politician he serves. I believe that a secretary who divulges what he happens to know in his position is scum." The day after Takeshita announced his resignation, Aoki—in a gesture reminiscent of the Tanaka chauffeur who had asphyxiated himself during the Lockheed investigation—slashed his wrists, legs, and neck and, when that failed, hanged himself with a necktie from a curtain rod. The political world compared Aoki to the loyal samurai of old and honored his sacrifice. The Recruit scandal hardly seemed worthy of heroism on such a scale, but as Takeshita allowed, in a rare statement of self-reflection, "I did not think Recruit would lead to such a serious disenchantment with politics; my sense of money has too big a difference from that of the people."

And "the people" were especially sensitive to Takeshita's "sense of money" at that point, because at the same time as he, and the establishment he represented, were being exposed for reaping large personal profits from Recruit, the Takeshita administration was imposing a much-reviled new sales tax on the nation. The levy marked a symbolic reversal for a political machine that had been committed to a fiscal policy of magnanimity, in which budgets were for pork and taxes were for cutting. It was a signal that, if the bosses wanted to keep playing Santa Claus, they would also have to start acting like Scrooge.

The 3 percent tax on goods and services was considered necessary because, despite years of healthy economic growth, Japan's public coffers had run dry. The shortfall was a nasty legacy the "Kon-Chiku-Sho" trio had inherited from its mentor, the free-spending Kakuei Tanaka. As premier in the early 1970s, Tanaka had rejected Japan's earlier tendency toward fiscal rectitude, creating a precedent for profligacy that would infect national budgets for two decades. As part of his "archipelago-remodeling" vision, he had boosted public works spending by 33 percent in one year. During his short administration, he also declared the "first year of the Welfare Era," unveiling a package of new social security policies that included doubling national pensions in one shot and indexing subsequent payouts to inflation. Tanaka went further, hiking public employee salaries and promoting a sharp income tax cut. Many of the programs he launched remained embedded in subsequent budgets, and in his years as "shadow shogun," Tanaka continued to be a force for greater spending. But just as Japan's expenditures were accelerating, its revenues were declining; even though the country was still growing much faster than other industrialized nations, the pace had abated from its phenomenal 1960s rate. So Japan fell deeper and deeper into debt. For nearly thirty years after World War II, the Japanese government had essentially kept its books balanced; in

1975, the government had to borrow to cover one fourth of its spending; and by 1979, bonds were needed to raise 40 percent of its funds. By the mid-1980s, the national debt was close to half of the GNP, and the largest single government expense was interest on the deficit.

Experts grew increasingly worried about the impact of the massive deficits on the nation's long-term fiscal health. The trend was only projected to get worse since the population was aging rapidly, a demographic trend that would raise demand for welfare spending while reducing the tax base. "We are telling the people that money will not pour down from heaven," Takeshita said of Japan's fiscal state, "and they are going to be the ones to bear the burden" of chronic deficits. A consensus emerged among business and government leaders that the red ink would have to be stanched; the question remained how. In the early 1980s, the LDP embraced a platform of "fiscal reconstruction without tax increases," which meant several consecutive years of budget freezes or outright cuts. Over time, though, retrenchment proved unsatisfying, especially for pols who had won support—and donations—by promising ever-increasing access to government funds. In 1988, Takeshita, Kanemaru, and Ozawa used the full force of their wheeling-and-dealing skills to push the consumption tax through Parliament.

The new tax swiftly eroded public confidence in the political machine—more than any new policy since Tanaka had been premier. Polls showed that as many as two thirds of the electorate were opposed, and thousands of protesters attended antitax rallies around the country. The government argued that the legislation was part of a comprehensive attempt to make the tax system more equitable and that the revenue would ensure the viability of mass social spending for years to come. But most Japanese citizens saw the legislation differently—as an omen that, with resources becoming scarcer, the once-large circle of people nurtured by the government would shrink to a favored few. Media coverage of the tax reform focused on loopholes that benefited fat cats and special-interest groups; as part of a "streamlining" of levies, for example, the luxury tax on yachts and big cars fell from 20 to 30 percent to 3 percent. Land sales, securities transactions, and capital gains were all exempt from the new tax—an especially offensive exception when Takeshita and other pols were reaping the benefits of Recruit shares. The consumption tax and the Recruit scandal became intertwined, each stoking public anger over the other. It was just as the new tax went into effect and he was making new confessions about his Recruit ties that the premier's popularity sank to 3.9 percent, the lowest ever for a Japanese ruler —breaking Tanaka's mark of 12 percent—and probably a world record for democratic disenchantment.

Another jolt to the old machine formula during the "Kon-Chiku-Sho" era came from the United States. In many ways, Japan's domestic political culture was rooted in the nation's isolation from the rest of the world, an unnatural condition created by Washington's Cold War aims. The Cold War was ending, however, and with it American support for Tokyo's seclusion.

For nearly half a century, America's basic Japan strategy had been to create a reliable pawn in the global fight against communism. The United States had wrapped a diplomatic straitjacket around Japan, dictating its foreign policy, providing the national defense, and imposing a "peace Constitution" that barred the deployment of Japanese troops overseas. While Japan's conservatives had chafed at the restraints at first, they had soon adapted nicely to the cocoon. It had allowed them to define the national interest in the narrowest possible terms and to formulate policies slowly and deliberately, free from the urgencies of international crises. Absent the difficult issues of war and peace, philosophical divisions among the populace had become less relevant, which had helped Tanaka and his associates to unify an informal coalition that incorporated much of the ideological spectrum, a necessity for an effective national political machine. To help foster democratic and economic stability in Japan, Washington had also allowed the government to keep its markets largely closed to imports. That, too, had encouraged Tanaka-style politics. Major sectors of the Japanese economy had been insulated from the rigorous demands of global competition, which would have required more efficient practices, as well as clear, transparent business procedures. As a result, these industries were vulnerable to inefficient domestic political interference. Parliament, after all, was just like one big city council.

With the Soviet Union collapsing and Japan's economy soaring, the United States' attitude toward its chief Asian ally changed. Security concerns no longer required America's extreme coddling. By the time Japan accounted for 15 percent of world GNP in the late 1980s, Americans had come to expect Tokyo to shoulder more of the burden for the international peace and stability that made Japanese prosperity possible. U.S. companies and workers, meanwhile, were less tolerant of protectionism, since Japanese exporters had penetrated the

U.S. market so thoroughly; the unequal trade relationship contributed to a chronic imbalance of payments between the two nations that neared a record $60 billion in 1987. Indeed, trade friction in the late 1980s and early 1990s became the greatest threat to U.S.-Japanese relations in decades. American autoworkers smashed Toyotas, and legislators bludgeoned Toshiba radios on the Capitol steps. In 1987, President Reagan imposed punitive duties on Japanese imports. His successor, George Bush, was shriller yet in his ultimatums that Japan open its economy more to foreign companies; from 1989 to 1992, his administration forced thirteen separate market-opening agreements on Japan.

The demands posed an uncomfortable and unaccustomed dilemma for Japan's leaders. Resistance threatened to undermine the basis of Japanese security and diplomacy. Yet appeasement meant jeopardizing domestic political stability: U.S. trade negotiators were targeting Japan's most protected industries, which, by virtue of that government swaddling, had become the sectors most dependent on —and supportive of—the machine. American pressure forced Prime Minister Takeshita to ease tariffs and quotas on beef and citrus imports, infuriating the powerful farm bloc. U.S. officials then asked Japan's bosses to renounce one of the sacred vows of the postwar conservative catechism, the total ban on rice imports, and farmers became still more wary of their onetime protector's fidelity. Small shopkeepers, another constituency devoted to the LDP, also began to lose faith when the Bush administration, acting on behalf of Toys "Я" Us, pushed Japan's political leadership to ease its longtime restrictions on large-scale retailers. (Kanemaru best articulated the bind facing authorities, saying in a speech that a new, more permissive "large-scale retail store law must be introduced decisively—but not in Kofu," the capital city of his home prefecture.) While harassing traditional machine backers, the Americans also went after new sectors that the pols were just cultivating. The United States went to the brink of a trade war, for example, to force the entry of Motorola into Japan's rapidly growing telecommunications market.

Some of America's fiercest attacks were aimed at the machine's chief sponsor, the construction industry. Until the mid-1980s, U.S. firms had never really tried to penetrate Japan's lucrative public works market; when they did begin bidding in earnest in 1986, they encountered numerous obstacles, both formal and informal. At the time, Japanese firms were winning more than $100 million a year of U.S. government projects, and a furious Congress passed, nearly unanimously, resolutions barring Japanese companies from American public works jobs unless commensurate access was provided to U.S. companies in Japan. Japanese negotiators kept trying to pacify U.S. companies with affirmative action–type plans, guaranteeing token shares of certain designated projects. The Americans, however, insisted on far-reaching structural reforms of the industry, including an end to the rampant bid rigging, or *dango*. *Dango* was a trade barrier, the Americans argued, because the practice was used by established firms to carve up the market among themselves, thus keeping out newcomers. Yet *dango* was also a crucial element of the collusion between Japanese politicians and contractors—it allowed pols to help determine the contract winner and the winner to charge an inflated price, part of which got channeled back to the politician—and was thus impossible for any leading conservative to stop. Emboldened by American complaints, Japan's antitrust watchdog, the Fair Trade Commission, attempted an anti-*dango* crackdown in 1991, launching investigations and trying to raise the fines for violations. That was too much for Kanemaru and his henchmen, who squelched the moves. "The FTC is absurd," one leading member of the "Kon-Chiku-Sho" faction yelled at a heated meeting with the regulators. "There is no way," another MP chimed in. "You take [the proposal to boost fines] back today."

When U.S. negotiators failed to reach agreement with Japanese leaders, they took their case to the people: *dango*, they asserted, as much as tripled the cost of public works to Japanese taxpayers.

In 1989, the two countries began a set of talks dubbed the "Structural Impediments Initiative." The effort was designed to move beyond the incessant bickering over specific sectors and to address the underlying causes of the bilateral trade imbalance. In the talks, America, in effect, blasted Japan's whole machine style of politics: the cozy government-industry ties and the lack of transparency in official decisions, it argued, worked to shut out imports and raise prices to Japanese consumers. In one newspaper poll, most Japanese citizens said the government should accept at least some U.S. demands specifically because they felt such action would be "for the Japanese people's own benefit and for the improvement of quality of life." The press quipped that President Bush was the most effective political opposition leader in Japan. American companies did not always succeed in getting what they wanted, but their attempts were consequential just the same. The Japanese political machine's appeal to many of its domestic clients had always been the guarantee of ongoing government benefits; the U.S. pressure shook the credibility of any such promise.

THE TRADE TIFFS were symptomatic of a more general international resentment mounting against Japan's abdication of responsibility for world affairs. The shell of easy isolationism shattered conclusively on August 2, 1990, the day Iraq invaded Kuwait.

Tokyo had good reason to care about Saddam Hussein's aggression. With two thirds of its oil coming from the Persian Gulf, Japan was more dependent on the region than any other industrialized nation was. If Iraq's conquest were to proceed unchallenged, supplies were likely to become more costly and less secure. Yet, much to the consternation of the West and its Middle Eastern allies, the Japanese government treated the event as if it were, in a popular phrase, a "fire on the other side of the river."

The contrast between the responses of Tokyo and the rest of the world—in both substance and alacrity—was stark. Within hours of the invasion, the United States froze Iraqi assets in the country, the Soviet Union suspended arms sales to Iraq, and the United Nations passed a resolution condemning the act. By the end of August, more than 100,000 American troops had gathered in the Gulf, and by November the total neared a quarter million. In mid-January 1991, a remarkable consortium of twenty-eight nations launched "Operation Desert Storm" with massive air strikes against Iraq. By the end of February, Kuwait had been liberated and hostilities were winding down.

Given Japan's "peace constitution," Washington did not seriously expect its ally to send combat troops. But the anti-Iraq alliance did expect fulsome support in other forms. Instead, Japan acted sluggishly and only under duress. It took about a month after the invasion for Toshiki Kaifu, the prime minister at the time, to announce that Japan's role would be a vaguely defined package of aid to pro-Western Arab states; the government quantified the amount only when pressed, and the total—$1 billion—was derided overseas as a pittance, barely equaling the Pentagon's monthly expenses for the effort. Japanese officials repeatedly tried to come up with some sort of nonmonetary participation and repeatedly failed. They offered to send ships to run supplies but couldn't resolve the logistical issues until the need had passed. They proposed airlifting refugees but couldn't get the necessary legislative approval. Kaifu vowed to send a hundred doctors to the region but could scare up only two dozen volunteers, all of whom returned home before the shooting started. At the least, Washington thought it could count on help in transporting American troops and supplies from U.S. military bases to Saudi Arabia. But the proposal foundered after days of haggling. Japan would not make any military aircraft available, instead offering the services of a commercial airline. And the company insisted that it would need seven days to make the trip, with repeated transfers and cargo inspections. Ultimately, in desperation, an American company was contracted and in one day secured eighty direct flights for the job. While Japan did get around to sending four minesweepers and two other ships to help with the postwar cleanup, its effort was mainly limited to money. In fact, Japan's financial role was ultimately greater than that of any nation outside the Gulf, totaling $13 billion. Yet the bulk of the funding was held up as the war neared its conclusion, and it didn't clear Parliament until March, a month after the battle was over.

Japan's inertia reflected a political culture that, for nearly half a century, had been in the world but not of it. Because such matters had previously been left entirely to the United States, the Japanese government had no procedure in place to respond rapidly to international emergencies; politicians had no way of explaining to the people why they should worry about a conflict half a world away. (The public did care intently, however, about the Japanese caught among the hundreds of foreign hostages held in Baghdad; Western leaders were concerned about signs that Tokyo would sabotage allied solidarity by trying to cut a separate deal to free its own citizens.) The string of broken pledges of extramonetary efforts was, in effect, the paroxysms of a ruling class that encompassed an impossibly vast range of contradictory views on the appropriate world role for Japan. Some MPs strongly urged Japan to shoulder a greater burden, while others argued that the country had no reason to participate in the anti-Iraq alliance at all. The LDP—as well as the broader, informal LDP-opposition alliance—incorporated a wide range of ideologies, from rabid hawks to extreme doves. When Japan had been in seclusion, such distinctions had been unimportant. But as the Gulf War showed, any moves to alter the nation's detachment risked bringing latent divisions to the fore and splitting the old machine coalition.

At the same time, the Gulf conflict made it clear that Japan could maintain its isolation only at great cost to its world standing. "Checkbook diplomacy," pursued at a time when other nations were risking their own citizens' lives, meant that Japan was excluded from many victory celebrations, as well as Kuwait's public letter of gratitude to its saviors. The American people were disdainful of Japan's behavior: one poll showed that Japan was lumped together with Iran, Jordan, and Iraq as a nation that had lost U.S. respect; in another survey, more than two thirds of the respondents said Japan hadn't carried its fair share of the world's burden and that the U.S. government should step up its trade pressures as a result. Both the House and Senate passed anti-Japanese resolutions, one threatening to reduce America's military protection for Japan, the other issuing a general warning of a deterioration in the U.S.-Japanese alliance. "While the consequences of a lame response were difficult to calculate," Michael H. Armacost, the U.S. ambassador to Japan at the time, wrote, "Tokyo could not rule out profound changes in U.S. attitudes and policies toward Japan, including our future readiness to maintain the alliance."

The nation's unsettling doubts about the rudimentary assumptions that had long buttressed the political establishment spread in the months following the Gulf War, when it became clear that the great economic boom of the early "Kon-Chiku-Sho" era had collapsed. Rather than heralding a glorious age of boundless wealth, the heady growth had in fact been an empty, speculative bubble, which deflated as quickly as it had swelled. By the summer of 1992, the Nikkei stock index had tumbled toward 14,000, a 65 percent drop from its late 1989 peak near 40,000, while land prices had also plunged. By one estimate, more than a trillion dollars of wealth disappeared in three years. Brand-new office towers stood empty while half-completed luxury golf courses and other oases for the nouveau riche marked the landscape. Some Japanese, who just a few years earlier had ranked among the world's richest investors, were now the world's greatest debtors; one property developer had racked up half a billion dollars in debts. Boosters at first suggested that the damage would be contained to a handful of flashy, reckless investors, while the real economy remained strong. But the real economy, which had expanded by more than 4 percent in 1990 and 1991, grew by only 1 percent in 1992, beginning what would become Japan's longest recession since the war. In 1992, capital investment declined—an extremely rare occurrence in the industrial boom of postwar Japan. The official unemployment rate soon reached a postwar high of 3.4 percent; measured by the American formula, it was closer to 7 percent, according to economists. Japan's banks, the underwriters of the great asset boom, were saddled after the bust with nearly $400 billion in bad debts, roughly the equivalent of the U.S. savings and loan debacle of the late 1980s.

The dour statistics did not mean that Japan's economy had disintegrated. But the ebullient outlook was gone. Gold-laced sushi was out; cheap noodle dishes were in. Tiffany's was out; discount stores were in. In the public's mind, the miracle had finally ended. The country now faced a future of steady but moderate growth. And that would require a sharp adjustment for a political structure designed to distribute abundance.

At a time when average Japanese citizens were beginning to feel the economic pinch, they were given fresh reminders of just how well, in contrast, their politicians were faring. At the end of the summer of 1992, the government was hit by a sensational new wave of scandals that persisted through the following spring. Even for a populace already hardened by repeated displays of extreme political depravity, the latest exposés were shocking.

First came the Sagawa Kyubin Company affair, which broke in late August as prosecutors delved into financial irregularities at a parcel delivery firm. It was, in many ways, resonant of the Recruit incident that had rocked the political world just four years earlier. Like Recruit's Ezoe, Sagawa's founder, Kiyoshi Sagawa, had built an impressive nationwide business empire from scratch. He had started with no employees in 1957, personally hauling fifty kilograms of packages a day—on his back—seven days a week. By 1992, Sagawa ran the second largest private mailing service in Japan, with 20,000 workers, 10,000 trucks, and annual sales of 800 billion yen. Like Recruit, Sagawa Kyubin was heavily affected by government regulations and was constantly under suspicion for violating one rule or another. In particular, the delivery firm was frequently accused of breaking labor laws; the company was famous for pushing its workers nearly as hard as the founder himself had toiled in its early days. Also like Recruit, Sagawa Kyubin made generous donations to politicians in both the ruling and opposition camps to help cut through red tape.

The difference between Sagawa Kyubin and Recruit, as depicted by the extensive Japanese media coverage in 1992, was scale and style. Sagawa Kyubin's outlays to politicians were rumored to have totaled anywhere from 2 billion yen (roughly twice Recruit's expenditures) to fifty times that amount, disseminated over twenty years to more than two hundred MPs. And the delivery company hadn't even bothered trying to camouflage the payoffs through fancy stock deals or comparable devices: in the 1990 transaction that became a main focus of the scandal, an executive met a Kanemaru aide in a parking lot and turned over 500 million yen in cash—an amount far exceeding the 1.5-million yen annual legal limit on corporate donations to an individual politician. The aide loaded the cash on a trolley and wheeled it to Kanemaru's Palais Royal office.

Sagawa Kyubin didn't offer only money, however. In another uniquely disturbing aspect of the scandal, a company executive admitted that Kanemaru had used him to gain access to the Mob. Sagawa Kyubin had developed an unofficial side business in the 1980s as a kind of underworld bank, offering loans to *yakuza* gangsters seeking a slice of Japan's stock and real estate boom. The company had then asked its indebted clients to perform a variety of dirty little tasks for Kanemaru, mainly silencing fringe right-wing protesters who occasionally harassed him and Takeshita. Seemingly lacking any doubts about the wisdom of seeking favors from such quarters, Kanemaru went so far as to ask the parcel company to arrange a tête-à-tête with the head of one of Japan's most notorious organized crime families so that he could express his gratitude in person. Kanemaru opened the dinner of the dons—according to public testimony given in late 1992 by Kanemaru himself—by insisting that his godfather counterpart take the seat of honor, usually given to the guest of highest distinction. The *yakuza* leader demurred, asserting that it was the political boss who ranked above him and therefore deserved the privilege. Kanemaru later said he had been "impressed" by the gangland chieftain.

While the Japanese press was giving Sagawa Kyubin's filthy linen an excruciatingly public airing, the prosecutors were moving on to a separate, wider probe into Kanemaru's finances, which proved a fertile field. Investigation soon revealed that Kanemaru had had a long history of concealing his income, apparently in order to dodge taxes. He had traded stocks under fictitious names and, starting in 1984, had regularly converted much of his assets into special bonds that allowed the purchaser to remain anonymous—and had never declared the holdings. The pol's clandestine investment activity was so heavy that one bank had appointed a special staff to handle his account; sometimes a Kanemaru aide delivered cardboard boxes of cash to one of the bank's branches, while on other occasions bank employees made trips to Kanemaru's office to conduct the necessary transactions.

When Kanemaru realized that his secret holdings were under scrutiny, he scrambled to cover his tracks, hurriedly cashing in hundreds of millions of yen worth of the special bonds and stashing the money, among other places, in the countryside home of a distant relative and in a hidden safe in a secret room in a condo rented by his son. He was too late. On March 6, 1993, investigators summoned Kanemaru and his top aide for questioning; that night, the two men were placed under arrest for tax evasion. While the Don sat alone in a spare, tiny prison cell, a horde of G-men raided his luxury town house, his Palais Royal suite, and numerous other homes and offices in Tokyo and Yamanashi. With television cameras rolling, they hauled out part of the cumulative spoils from three and a half decades of political plundering: more than 3 billion yen in anonymous bond certificates, tens of millions of yen in banknotes, and, in what became the symbol of the ancien régime's decadence, 100 kilograms of gold bars.

Kanemaru's hidden wealth was one scandal; the source of the fortune was another. New controversy erupted shortly after the tax evasion revelations. The prosecutors found in Kanemaru's possession, in addition to the loot, a different sort of "treasure mountain," the term they used for the countless files they carted away from his many domiciles. The evidence found in those documents was not surprising: that a good part of Kanemaru's riches had been supplied by construction companies seeking public works contracts. But the papers apparently provided investigators with their most tangible leads ever about the long-suspected illegalities in the industry, from bid rigging to bribery. Yet another corruption probe was launched, and within weeks of the machine boss's arrest, many of his organization's main financiers—top executives from seven of the country's largest contractors—were also behind bars.

The many shocks of the late "Kon-Chiku-Sho" era—the scandals, the American free-trade offensive, the Gulf War, the recession—combined to widen the gap between leaders and populace and to raise questions about the machine's long-term ability to perform as it once had. Still, the old order retained great electoral strength. Japan's cautious voters were growing disaffected but not so angry or bold as to throw the bums out. Besides, the machine had so thoroughly penetrated the political establishment, both the ruling and opposition parties, that there was no real alternative.

The three elections held during the "Kon-Chiku-Sho" reign reflected this ambivalence. Popular indignation flared up in the summer of 1989, when the Recruit scandal was fresh, the sales tax recently implemented, and the beef and citrus markets just opened to imports. In July elections for the upper house of Parliament, the LDP suffered its worst drubbing ever, capturing only 36 of the 126 seats at stake and losing control of that half of the legislature for the first time since the party's founding. While the Liberal Democrats still held the more important lower chamber and thus the reins of government, there was much excitement in Japan about a potential political transformation by way of an anti-LDP coalition uniting to seize power for the first time in three decades.

Such talk proved ephemeral—not because the LDP was beloved but because the opposition remained feckless. The lack of competition in Japan's Parliament that had been so crucial to Tanaka-style politics endured into the late 1980s and early 1990s. Fresh from their 1989 victory, the opposition parties quickly fell to bickering among themselves; the Socialists, despite their briefly soaring popularity, could not field enough candidates in the next contest even to make the pretense of seeking a majority. In a February 1990 vote for the lower house of Parliament, the LDP retained its solid majority, mainly by default, winning 275 of 512 seats. In the upper-house campaign of July 1992, there were new rumblings of discontent. The turnout rate fell to a record-low 50 percent—down from 65 percent three years earlier—and surveys showed that only a third of the voters wanted the LDP to maintain its longtime predominance. Speaking to the growing desire for change, however undefined, a dynamic prefectural governor named Morihiro Hosokawa created a new "reform" party to vie in the 1992 election and did moderately well, taking four seats. His spiel: "Everyone knows that we have a structural conspiracy in this country among politicians, bureaucrats and businessmen." The political system, his Japan New Party platform said, had "grown moribund and out of touch with the realities of the world." Hosokawa, however, was more gadfly than menace. Despite his presence, the ruling conservative party fared well enough, winning 54 percent of the seats contested.

It was just a month after that election that the Sagawa Kyubin affair exploded, followed in rapid order by the other Kanemaru-related scandals. The public outcry and the LDP leadership's dismissive response during the nine-and-a-half-month stretch from late August 1992 to mid-June 1993 provided an elegant display of just how entrenched and arrogant the machine had become and of how the machine's dominance had allowed national politics to become a self-contained system driven by its own logic—a logic far removed from the common sense of the people supposedly being served.

Each disclosure exacerbated the people's ire. Ordinary citizens launched petition drives and hunger strikes around the country to protest Kanemaru's myriad transgressions. Demonstrators carried Kanemaru dolls out onto the streets, offering passersby the chance to smack the effigies. More than a hundred local governments passed resolutions calling for a full accounting of the scandals. (One notable exception was Kanemaru's Yamanashi prefectural assembly, which rejected by a vote of 29 to 10 a vaguely worded resolution calling for "the establishment of political ethics.") When the prosecutors appeared, for a time, to be pursuing the boss with insufficient vigor, the law enforcement agencies became the targets of anger; in Tokyo the prosecutors' headquarters were splattered with yellow paint, while a chunk of concrete was tossed through a window of a regional office. Some advocated a more drastic response. An officer of the Japan Self-Defense Forces wrote a manifesto, published in a national circulation magazine, that called for a coup d'état. "It has become impossible," the author despaired, "to correct improprieties legally through elections."

Kanemaru's consorting with *yakuza* was especially disturbing given that the government over which he presided had formally declared a crackdown on the underworld. "Can't he understand the feelings of detectives who are laying their lives on the line from early morning until late at night, fighting to eliminate gangsters?" a police chief exclaimed as he addressed a mass rally. And the juxtaposition of Kanemaru's outlandish stash with the news reports of deepening recession—slashed bonuses and anticipated layoffs—was infuriating; he was arrested less than a month after Nissan Motor Company announced plans for Japan's first auto factory closing since the war and Nippon Telegraph and Telephone Corporation, the country's largest company, said it would cut thirty thousand employees from its payroll.

Yet hardly anybody within the political establishment expressed contrition about what Kanemaru had done or concern about how his acts appeared to the voting public. Kanemaru himself was flip. Upon admitting receipt of the cartload of cash, he offered a brief apology, stating, "I deeply regret accepting the money because it contradicts ethics." And he tried to assuage the nation with the vow (issued just after his seventy-eighth birthday) "never to allow a thing like this to happen again in my life." He did not, however, offer much reassurance of holding to that pledge, especially since he qualified his public penance by adding, "However, I still greatly thank my friend [the Sagawa Kyubin executive who donated the money and introduced him to the Mob] for his goodwill." In response to the torrent of criticism against his too-close association with the *yakuza,* Kanemaru defended his strong "sense of obligation." "My political philosophy," he declared, "is to have some appreciation for a person who saves a drowning child in a river, even if that person happens to belong to a crime syndicate."

When the prosecutors wanted to ask Kanemaru a bit more about the illegal donations, he blithely refused to submit to questioning, insisting that he couldn't leave his house because of the large contingent of media camped outside his door; he eventually deigned to give a written statement, delivered by his attorney, and paid a 200,000-yen fine—a sum worth less than four days' interest on the ill-gotten contribution and the equivalent of a parking ticket in overcrowded Tokyo. When Parliament called him to testify for its own investigation, Kanemaru suddenly decided he needed eye surgery to counteract the effects of his long-standing diabetes. The legislative committee tracked Kanemaru down in his hospital room, but the bedside interrogation was hardly edifying; "I was drunk and don't remember" was his response to questions about his role in key events.

Nobody from within the *gundan* saw fit to criticize Kanemaru's acts or to distance themselves from him. To the contrary, the group was beset by a bitter debate about how best to "protect" their boss from facing any charges. On September 17, 1992, more than two weeks after the Sagawa Kyubin scandal surfaced, faction members flocked to Kanemaru's Moto Azabu town house to celebrate his birthday. The house was filled with gifts of orchids costing 10,000 yen per stalk, and the guests dined on fine delicacies. As they got drunk on Ballantine scotch, the pols sang a melancholy old military ballad that likened brave soldiers to dying cherry blossoms fluttering to the ground. "Let's all fall down for the state," they crooned, as if public opinion were an ignoble enemy unjustly challenging the honorable machine. Miyazawa, the premier then being propped up by Kanemaru, did not attend the gala but offered his allegiance in the form of a gift bottle of sake; he, too, refused to make any criticism of

Kanemaru's acts. While surveys showed that 80 percent of the people felt that Kanemaru should be forced out of Parliament, a Miyazawa spokesman said the tainted pol "has been the main pillar supporting the government, and the prime minister wants him to stay." (The LDP leadership instead directed its indignation at a judge who was vigorously pursuing the Sagawa Kyubin case, threatening him with impeachment, and at a young LDP member urging a housecleaning, who was stripped of a choice committee post.) Even the opposition parties' criticism was muted. The head of the Socialists at the time, Makoto Tanabe, was one of Kanemaru's best friends; while insisting that "as a public figure I will take a resolute stand," he admitted that he found his buddy's travails "personally unbearable."

Public furor over the Sagawa Kyubin affair did eventually force Kanemaru to quit Parliament in October 1992, and his subsequent arrest for alleged tax evasion finished off his political career conclusively. Unlike Tanaka, who rose to his greatest heights after scandal, the Don's legal troubles did him in. Yet even after Kanemaru's fall, most of the political leadership refused to acknowledge the popular consensus that his behavior reflected a deeper systemic flaw that needed correction. "This is a case of Kanemaru alone," Prime Minister Miyazawa said of his onetime master's corruption. "It has nothing to do directly with politics." In the weeks after Kanemaru's incarceration in March, the LDP tried to becalm the nation's fury by endorsing "political reform," dusting off anticorruption proposals that had been languishing in some corner of the legislature since the time of the Recruit scandal. By mid-June 1993, however, as that year's parliamentary session came to an end, the longtime ruling party withdrew the bills, saying the time was not appropriate for change after all. Once again, admonitions from the people and the press ensued. But they had no advocate within Nagatacho and thus, the establishment felt, could safely be ignored.

There seemed, in short, to be no clear threat to the machine in 1993. But there was a golden opportunity, ripe for exploitation by any politician who was disillusioned with the status quo and who was driven enough and capable enough to challenge it. And the threat did come—from within the inner sanctum, from the very heart of the "Kon-Chiku-Sho" "Triangle Zone of Power." Even while presiding over the political world—wooed by yes-men and trailed by reporters and their camera lights—Ichiro Ozawa, like so many of his constituents, began to lose faith that the machine could satisfy him much longer.

CHAPTER TWENTY-ONE

OZAWA AND HIS DISCONTENTS

To many critics, the main problem with the "Kon-Chiku-Sho" apparatus was that it had too much influence over the Japanese government. To a man of Ichiro Ozawa's ambition, however, it had too little. During his tenure as co–"shadow shogun," he came to see that the machine embodied a paradox of power, its dominance resting on an implicit agreement to use authority sparingly. A machine boss was a manager, a Takeshita-type coordinator; he could not be a leader. "Leadership," Ozawa concluded, "was not in the least bit desired."

The devil's bargain emanated from the machine's charter strategy, Tanaka's "power of numbers." The organization's primary goal was to lure as much overt or covert support—or at least cooperative acquiescence—as possible from both the ruling LDP and the opposition parties. The point was to create an immunity from the pressures of open democratic competition and from the uncertainties attendant on constantly changing regimes. But that security came at a price, imposing serious constraints of form and substance on the rulers.

The head of such an organization, for example, had to flatter, to cajole, to appease, to beg if necessary. His goal was to maximize the number of his allies, or conversely to minimize the number of his adversaries, by allowing challengers to save face and by taking as long as possible to make a decision in order somehow to take care of everyone affected. "If you want to rise to the top, you've got to reduce the number of your enemies" was one of Tanaka's favorite precepts. "Relations with other people are more important than my own life," Kanemaru said. "Politicians can't exist if they forget *giri* ["duty"] and *ninjo* ["feeling"]." Takeshita literally suppressed his own persona in order to stroke others, making himself *mu*, or "nothing."

While Ozawa relished the supremacy the machine gave him, he did not appreciate the limits it tried to place on his disposition. He had the arrogance and total self-assurance of a man who had been handed power as if it were his birthright: his seat in Parliament from his father, his primary political education from Tanaka, his kingmaking from Takeshita and Kanemaru. "He has the same aggressiveness as former prime minister Kakuei Tanaka," one LDP elder observed, "but his character has not been tempered by the hardships Mr. Tanaka went through." As Ozawa himself said proudly, "I have never experienced failure in my life."

The higher Ozawa rose, the more he ignored—or made a point of trampling on—all of the little etiquettes that had developed in the culture of the political court. He had strong opinions, which he did not hesitate to state bluntly: "I'd like to be able to flatter [people] and make them like me," he'd say, "but I can't." Indeed, he often ridiculed rivals' ideas as "stupid," "childish," or "absurd." If his comments insulted somebody, so be it. "Even friends cannot stay together if their views are irreconcilable," he would say. (Ozawa's darts were directed at older, as well as younger, pols, amplifying the offense caused in a highly seniority-conscious society.) He didn't return calls from, or consent to meetings with, other pols whom he did not consider immediately relevant. When he did agree to talk, he cut through the usual blandishments, getting straight down to business: "I don't like chatting for long about things that have nothing to do with work," he would say, "and it takes about five to ten minutes to discuss work." Ozawa had supreme confidence in his own judgment and saw no need to make a pretense of consulting others in making decisions; he was famous for doing *kumogakure*, or "hiding in the clouds"—that is, becoming completely unreachable by aides and associates during critical junctures until he had patched together his own solution to the issue at hand. And when he did come to a conclusion, Ozawa expected colleagues to follow his lead without question or complaint. "He has a tendency to skip explanations once he has set a goal," sighed a faction comrade. If MPs didn't readily obey, "he would leave his seat and disappear," said one of Ozawa's best friends. Ozawa's obtrusive aura was accented by a stocky build and a full, hard, impassive face that lit up with enthusiasm and affection only for his closest associates. To the public, cracked one pol, he looked like "a toad who has just licked something terribly bitter."

Even in seeking donations—an inherently supplicatory task—Ozawa was imperious: "I don't want to drop my head to receive money," he once told an interviewer. As the LDP's chief fund-raiser for the 1990 elections, he shirked the usual backroom groveling before endless numbers of executives. Instead, he took the unprecedented step of going straight to the Keidanren, Japan's big business trade group, and demanded 30 billion yen, about $200 million, to underwrite the campaign; business, he insisted matter-of-factly, "ought to bear the costs of democracy." He wore down the association's resistance with public threats, including a vow to get the chairman fired and hints of a tax increase on cars and exports. The machine's most generous backers, too, were subjected to his brash approach: "I heard from a senior man in the construction industry," a prominent journalist said, "that although it is natural to bow when asking for money, [Ozawa] takes a big attitude and asks in a high-handed manner."

Ozawa's frustrations with the machine went beyond the restraints of style to the shackles on policy making. By placing themselves at the center of a seemingly permanent administration, Tanaka and his successors had gained stable control over the nuts and bolts of governance—which MP got a cabinet post, which district got a pork-barrel project, which construction company got a contract. But to preserve the broad coalition that provided such command, the shogunate had to give over the right to change course in any way that might offend any sector of society. To maintain its sway over the minutiae of politics, the machine had gradually agreed to disregard its substance. Or, as Ozawa would put it with undisguised disdain, politics "has been reduced to the task of apportioning the dividends of 'Japan Inc.' "

Of course, nobody could apportion the dividends better than Ozawa, who had always enjoyed the clever stratagems of Tanaka's setup. Even after he began expressing doubts about the system, he continued, for example, his dexterous cat-and-mouse games with prime ministers. Yet he had reached the peak of power as measured by the machine early. He had been not yet fifty years old when he had joined the "Kon-Chiku-Sho" team. And as he surveyed the kingdom at his feet, he could not but wonder what greater heights remained for him to scale.

It was an unexpected crash course in international diplomacy that clarified for Ozawa the confines of machine power, as well as the potential for a much grander type of political power. Before the "Kon-Chiku-Sho" era, foreign policy had never been part of Ozawa's fast-track training. Geopolitics, global trade, and the like had been considered peripheral to the workings of Japanese politics, and Ozawa's mentors had carefully steered him into more consequential fields such as election strategies, parliamentary manipulation, and public works budgeting. He had stumbled into world affairs by accident: in 1988, when the U.S. government had been threatening sanctions unless Tokyo opened its construction market to American firms, Ozawa had been sent to Washington to negotiate. He was chosen because of his intimate familiarity with the relevant Japanese companies and bureaucrats. Experts worried that his inexperience with the complexities of diplomacy would hamper the talks; instead, Ozawa found that he was good at the bargaining. Americans considered his no-nonsense manner a refreshing contrast to the conventional Japanese foot-dragging and indirectness. "He just got to the heart of the matter," said Mike Smith, Ozawa's U.S. government counterpart in the talks. "The negotiations had gone on for two years—he and I reached an agreement in eight hours." The day began with the two men puffing on cigars that Smith had brought as an icebreaking gesture. It ended, the American marveled, so quickly that "I was home for dinner." From construction, Ozawa became the unofficial point man in the late 1980s and early 1990s for solving major nettlesome international economic disputes; he brokered deals with the U.S. government ranging from beef imports to cellular phone frequencies to coproduction of the so-called FSX fighter jet.

The trade talks showed Ozawa that he could apply his fixer skills to a much bigger arena than he had ever imagined. The training also forced him to contemplate a whole new range of perspectives and issues—Japan's place in a wider world and the problems his country would face if it did not adapt better to that world. Issues ranging from the General Agreement on Tariffs and Trade (GATT) to the demise of the Soviet Union kept him immersed. Then, with sudden urgency, the Persian Gulf crisis struck in the summer of 1990. It compelled a response, and Ozawa took charge.

It was a heady time to step out onto the global stage. The Cold War was ending, and forceful leaders were mobilizing their nations swiftly—Bush in the United States, Thatcher in Britain, Gorbachev in the Soviet Union—to build, in Bush's words, "a New World Order." If Ozawa had had his way, he and Japan would have joined those exalted ranks.

The price of entry was steep. Becoming a full participant in global affairs, especially the Gulf War, required dispatching citizens to distant lands to help police world stability. For Tokyo, that would require shattering overnight a half-century-long taboo against even the discussion of joining military ventures abroad. Many Japanese believed that the only way for their country to avoid a repetition of the horrors of World War II was total abstinence from war—a proclivity reinforced by the "peace constitution" banning involvement in foreign combat. In short, anything military was the third rail of Japanese politics. Ozawa, with characteristic audacity, was not afraid to touch it; he did not feel constrained by history or deep-rooted national sensitivities. Shortly after Iraq invaded Kuwait in 1990, he became a vocal advocate of sending Japanese personnel to the Mideast—to airlift refugees, to transport American troops—and even of sending Japanese troops, though only for noncombat duties. He managed to strong-arm the reluctant Kaifu cabinet into endorsing these ideas. But then he learned the limits of his clout.

Ozawa's proposals ran into severe resistance, not only from the opposition parties but from his ostensible subordinates in the ruling party and the bureaucracy. A senior leader of Ozawa's own LDP took to citing an ancient Chinese proverb—"The dike crumbles from a single ant hole"—to warn that any Japanese role in the conflict could begin a disastrous return to militarism. An official government commission implied that Ozawa's plans were unconstitutional. The heated public debate sparked by Ozawa's views turned personal: the mere fact that such suggestions were coming from a man of Ozawa's generation—he had been only three years old when the emperor had surrendered—horrified many of his compatriots. It was an article of faith, especially among older Japanese, that those who had not witnessed the tragedy would be most likely to repeat it. Ozawa had been "only a baby when Japan lost," one senior opposition member protested. "He did not experience the hardships of war." Unbowed, Ozawa retorted, "I would never repeat that folly." Then he had the temerity to question the sincerity of his accuser: "What did you [ever] do to oppose or prevent the war?" To another hesitant elder MP, he reportedly snapped, "Those who won't be around in the twenty-first century should remain silent." As his efforts languished, Ozawa found himself trapped between the expectations of the world and the inertia of his country. He found himself pleading with a group of visiting Americans: "I want to say to Washington that Japan is trying to join the world . . . but it is not so easy. . . . I will try to put an end to the idiotic arguments that are happening here and push Japan faster."

Japan's ultimate contribution to the war effort—the $13 billion to the U.S.-led alliance that came belatedly and grudgingly—left Ozawa chafing at his inability to move the system. It showed that one of Japan's most powerful politicians could not respond urgently and comprehensively to a global crisis—that is, he could not do in his own country what the American president and British prime minister could do in theirs. That in turn meant that, in an international setting, a Japanese boss could not be the equal of his foreign counterparts; he was simply a big fish in a small pond. Ozawa's disenchantment turned to personal humiliation in March 1991, when he was forced to cancel, at the last minute, a planned trip to the Mideast after the hostilities had ended. The mission was supposed to define a new role for Japan in helping to rehabilitate the region. "When the leaders of every other nation in the world are going there and entering into talks," Ozawa explained, "our country should also hold talks as well." But talks with the Egyptian and Saudi presidents couldn't be arranged, as they were busy preparing for the far more important pending visit by American Secretary of State James Baker. Ozawa considered a trip to Kuwait, but civilian planes were not yet being allowed to enter the country, and the United States rejected a request to make an American military jet available. OZAWA DIPLOMACY CIRCLES IN THE SKY was one derisive Japanese newspaper headline. NO PLANES. NOBODY TO MEET.

Reflecting later upon the lessons of the Gulf War—or Japan's "defeat," as he put it—Ozawa concluded that the whole machine mentality was to blame. The LDP, despite its parliamentary majority, had long avoided controversial proposals. The political structure could do no more than provide concrete favors to specific constituents; in other words, the machine was purely the sum of its parts, with no capacity for grander purpose that might alienate some of its constituents. By focusing solely on special interests, the government was unable "to define the national interest," Ozawa wrote. "The only function our government is expected to perform is to enable private interests to pursue their profits."

As Ozawa's disillusion with his own power base mounted, his public image went through a remarkable transformation. At the start of the "Kon-Chiku-Sho" era, he had appeared to be a callow machine hack, albeit an unusually cocky one. His stated agenda early on was control, bereft of any affectation of policy proposals. He was a staunch defender of the status quo: "At this point, ninety-nine percent of the people do not want change," Ozawa said in a 1987 interview. "The main thing today is a firm groundwork . . . for long-term stability." He was a classic "shadow shogun" who preferred to cut his deals in the seclusion of *ryotei* restaurants and luxury hotel suites, far from the glare of the public spotlight. As late as February 1990, when he was the LDP's chief election strategist, Ozawa avoided making speeches, focusing instead on private fund-raising. But within two years—even as he remained a machine ringleader—Ozawa had turned himself into a visionary and an orator. He became a prophet, thundering about the urgency of political change.

The mutation seemed to begin during the Persian Gulf War, when Ozawa, impeded in his attempts to work the levers of government, made a desperate pitch to, of all people, the Japanese public. He traveled the country, trying to rally popular support for some sort of Japanese participation. In the conflict's aftermath, he formed a special panel, grandly designated the "Twenty-first-century Study Commission." In contrast to the Creative Politics Circle study group that he had formed with Takeshita six years earlier, which had in fact made little pretense of "studying," this council brought together top bureaucrats and academics with enthusiastic young conservative MPs and began holding sober discussions of the country's future.

The evolution of Ozawa's image accelerated in June 1991, when he had a heart attack at the age of forty-nine. He was forced to convalesce for forty-two days, and while he did not suffer any lasting damage, he emerged from the hospital a changed man. As a practical matter, the doctors' restrictions on smoking, drinking, and late-night carousing forced him to curb the very activities that constituted the occupational description of "boss." ("Have you resumed political activities on a full scale?" a reporter asked Ozawa shortly after he returned to work. "When you say 'full scale,' " Ozawa replied, "it involves drinking. I'll [have to] stay away from meetings at night [for a while].")

Beyond that, the premature near-death experience seemed to act on Ozawa as a revelation. His rhetoric—in speeches, in interviews, in the treatises he was penning with greater frequency—began to suggest a newfound religious zeal. More than any critic, more than any opposition politician, Ozawa began depicting the various changes in Japan and the world that were undercutting the machine's foundation—not only the Gulf War but the trade tensions, the economic recession, even the political scandals—as harbingers of doom. Rather than attempting to douse the embers outside the gate, Ozawa chose to fan them into flames that would only menace his own organization.

"I keenly feel a sense of crisis," he warned in an essay for the December 1991 issue of *Bungei Shunju,* a leading intellectual journal. The problem, he emphasized, was a political structure—the structure he himself had helped build and continued to run—that was antiquated and immobile, yet still somehow invulnerable. "The LDP does not dare talk about taboos. Opposition parties have no will to wrest power from the LDP," he complained in a newspaper interview. "This makes it impossible for Japan's politics to respond to dramatic changes." He called for a "surgery-like political reform at any cost" before, he said ominously, "it [is] too late." To skeptics who wondered why someone at the very core of a seemingly supreme organization would advocate shaking things up, Ozawa retorted with his new trademark hyperbole: "Even if the LDP's political reins are guaranteed permanently, Japan itself will fall before that. That will leave us nothing."

Prophets and political machines do not mix well. Machines are, by their nature, designed to protect a cozy status quo, to disdain ideas, to keep politics quiet and smooth. Ozawa's old insolence had already made him a bit hard for his colleagues to take; now, cloaked in his new oratory, he became all but unbearable to many fellow pols. While he called himself a "reformer," they branded him a "dictator" and an "authoritarian," "high-handed" and "haughty"—not to mention hypocritical, since he continued to use freely the powers accorded him by the organization while claiming to be against its ways. (Given his continuing clout, his antagonists' snipes were fired mainly through anonymous comments to the press.) Criticism from his peers did not lead him to self-reflection; as with any classic seer, it only fed Ozawa's self-righteousness. "It's only natural people try to prevent me from succeeding," he said of the denunciations. "My ideas are extremely dangerous." "I know some people describe me as arrogant, but I have no intention of changing to suit them," he would come to say. "It is my duty to keep sounding the bell."

THE TENSIONS between Ozawa and his fellow *gundan* members were aggravated by a more profane matter: the next power struggle looming for control of the organization. Ozawa was heir apparent to Kanemaru and Takeshita. But the succession wasn't happening quickly enough for the youngest member of the "Kon-Chiku-Sho" triumvirate. He complained that Takeshita, in particular, was clinging to power too long—attempting, in a sense, to do to Ozawa what Tanaka had done to Takeshita. "What is to be criticized most about leaders," Ozawa lamented, "is that they do not foster the next generation." Relations between the two men degenerated to the point where they barely spoke to each other, and where Ozawa openly expressed contempt for his elder. And whenever Takeshita did step aside, a smooth transfer of authority was still far from assured, even if Ozawa had been more willing to play by the genteel rules of the club. At least six other MPs of Ozawa's generation also considered themselves potential bosses and were anything but unified around his solo command—especially since he was the youngest among them. These were the "seven magistrates," "the boys' detective unit," the gang of pols who had entered Parliament together as friends in the 1960s, joined by their devotion to the dynamic Tanaka. As they had grown older, their fraternity had become rivalry; it was inevitable, perhaps, that a clan whose core members were bound together mainly by naked ambition would have difficulty agreeing peaceably on succession. Attention focused, in particular, on a likely duel between Ozawa and the popular, strong-willed Ryutaro Hashimoto. In popular parlance, their struggle was dubbed the "Ichi-Ryu War": by 1991, the respectable media treated it as a given. The tabloids kept score on countless alleged tussles between the two men; a comic-book author managed 222 pages of superhero-type tales titled "Drama—Ryutaro Hashimoto vs. Ichiro Ozawa: Record of a Fierce Fight." In 1992, press reports suggested that the "Takeshita faction" would soon become the "Ozawa faction" but hedged, reminding readers, as one dispatch in the *Nihon Keizai* newspaper did, that "There is no guarantee that the [bloc], which has been [so] proud of its 'monolithic unity,' will not split" under Ozawa's rule.

As the multifarious jealousies, suspicions, and grudges seethed just beneath the surface, the once-solid bloc was held together in the summer of 1992 by a single thread: Kanemaru. The Don was feared and revered enough by his subordinates to retain the absolute loyalty of the anti-Ozawa camp, even as he actively backed Ozawa. Kanemaru had developed an abiding affection for Ozawa, much as Tanaka had, contributing to Ozawa's reputation as a *"jiji goroshi,"* or "granddaddy killer." The tough Kanemaru was apparently taken by Ozawa's boldness, calling his junior "the apple of my eye." Kanemaru wanted Ozawa to take over the *gundan,* and his unwavering endorsement was the only reason Ozawa could continue to rely on the full might of the machine while at the same time offending the group's sensibilities—and Ozawa flaunted his shield. "It is thanks to Kanemaru's patronage . . . that I'm in the media so much these days . . . even if I'm often the target of criticism," he gloated in a magazine interview published in September 1992 under the headline CHAIRMAN SHIN KANEMARU, MY BENEFACTOR, AND I. "What I am today is thanks to Kanemaru," he said. What Ozawa really was, to one critic within the *gundan,* was "a small man acting arrogantly through borrowed authority."

That authority suddenly evaporated in October 1992, when Kanemaru's scandals forced him out of Parliament. In the following weeks, all the *gundan*'s long-suppressed resentments and rivalries came gushing out into the open. A series of emergency faction meetings, called to set a new executive lineup in the wake of Kanemaru's departure, turned into denunciation sessions against Ozawa. As the repeated parleys dragged on, sometimes into the early morning, there were cries for Ozawa to apologize for his "arbitrary decisions" and to refrain from politics for a time in order to do penance for his affronts. "You don't consult us at all!" one veteran sniped as consenting voices called out for more "democratic" leadership of the machine. "Until now you've been monopolizing. Compared to you, we've been just like old used rags," one competitor among the "seven magistrates" griped. "We've done our best as old used rags. . . . But not anymore." Ozawa, usually impassive and silent, sat listening to the harangues. But he refused to relinquish his control.

For a few weeks, the clique tried to paper over the differences through a new "collective leadership," an unwieldy committee of eight pols, including Ozawa. "Members reached a narrow consensus to strengthen unity," one newspaper account of the brawling reported. (Outside observers were both amused and appalled by the ugly mud fight within Parliament's de facto ruling faction, especially at a time when the organization might have been expected to be busy handling issues such as the recession, trade tensions, and scandals. "Enough Is Enough!" an *Asahi* newspaper editorial sputtered. "The country appears to be [reduced to] running itself," the paper observed, asserting that the *gundan*'s self-obsession "indicates a structural gangrene, in its most extreme stage.") By the end of October, the efforts to achieve consensus collapsed, forcing a direct showdown over the selection of a new chief. The contest pitted Ozawa's supporters against an anti-Ozawa camp masterminded by Takeshita and joined by Hashimoto. The Ozawa side was crushed, drawing just 36 of the *gundan*'s 109 MPs to its cause.

To most members of the machine, the difficult business of succession had been settled fair and square, and things should now get back to normal; better than normal, in fact, now that the impudent Ozawa had been knocked down a peg and would henceforth have to abide by the group's code of conduct. Shortly after noon on October 21, Kanemaru—retired from politics but still hoping to keep his old gang together—summoned Takeshita and Ozawa to his office for a final conference of the "Kon-Chiku-Sho" team. "You are brothers," he told them. "Don't get me into a fight between brothers." Takeshita, the guru of patience and appeasement, assumed the role of Ozawa's patron, acting as if he were sincerely interested in the progress of his partner turned antagonist's career. Takeshita kindly counseled Ozawa to accept failure, to show more humility, to defer to his elders for a time, and to wait quietly for the time he could make his comeback.

Ozawa would have none of it. "That," he sneered later, "is seeing the situation merely from the standpoint of who will win or lose, who will emerge as the boss in the battle on monkey mountain." The clash, in his mind, had a more lofty import: "To me, it is quite clear that the split . . . is between reformers and the old guard." And that conflict was only just beginning. Ozawa, schooled from his earliest days as a politician in Tanaka's "power of numbers" creed, now summoned a higher power, that of righteousness. Speaking to his small band of three dozen loyalists after their setback, Ozawa invoked a famous nineteenth-century military battle between the idealistic young samurai who would bring Japan into the modern world and the corrupt, anachronistic ruling shogunate of the time. "The three thousand troops of Satsuma-Choshu vanquished the fifteen thousand of the Edo government," he told his troops, "because the age needed them."

Ironically, Ozawa's defeat proved liberating: having been stripped of his control over the Establishment, he no longer had a stake in it and was free to become a full-fledged antimachine crusader. In December 1992, Ozawa and forty-two supporters quit the *gundan*—the first major cleavage of the group since its formation twenty years earlier—to start their own rival faction within the ruling Liberal Democratic Party. Unlike other conservative factions, whose sole stated objectives were to advance their members' careers, the Ozawa clique declared itself dedicated to "reform." "Politics will have to be transformed by its very roots," their chief would proclaim in the coming months. "The more thorough the destruction of the old structure, the better."

CHAPTER TWENTY-TWO

THE BOSS TURNED REFORMER

Ozawa unveiled his reform agenda in the spring of 1993 in a 258-page manifesto titled *Blueprint for a New Japan,* the first serious appeal to the masses by a leading MP since Tanaka's *Building a New Japan* had swept the nation two decades earlier. Ozawa's message was a clever marriage of the new challenges facing the country with his own gripes about the system. Only by overhauling basic diplomatic and economic precepts, he argued, could Japan maintain its peace and prosperity. He insisted that those radical changes could be made quickly enough only by encouraging active leadership. And leadership could come only, he said, when politicians were granted power on the scale Ozawa coveted. The "lack of real leadership is not only burdensome to our foreign counterparts, it is also dangerous for Japan itself," he wrote in the opening chapter of his *Blueprint.* "The fundamental aim of political reform must therefore be to . . . [give leaders] both the responsibility and the power to make the necessary political decisions."

Ozawa's prescription for strengthening Japan's rulers was, in essence, repair of the myriad distortions of democracy that had developed under the machine. Where the old guard had toiled to create a permanent administration run by unelected bosses who were insulated from the vicissitudes of public opinion, Ozawa now advocated an openly competitive politics that was more directly accountable to the electorate. "We must . . . ensur[e] that the government periodically changes hands," he urged; MPs "must submit themselves to the judgment of the people they serve." To many observers, Ozawa's eyebrow-raising conversion from "machine boss" to "champion of democracy" was, as one wag put it, a "transmogrification that rivaled Saul of Tarsus' experience on the road to Damascus." But his turnabout had not come about, Ozawa made clear, through some misty-eyed epiphany set off by midlife musings on the Federalist Papers, nor as the result of an eleventh-hour endeavor to repent his past. Rather, he had concluded from firsthand experience that the real way to make political power "strong" was to accept the "clear and appropriate limits" imposed by competition. Even at their peaks, Tanaka, Takeshita, and Kanemaru had never really defied this law of democratic gravity; they had managed to shirk the normal risks of democracy only by waiving many of the normal rewards of leadership. Ozawa now wanted the rewards and felt confident enough to take the risks.

With the supposition that true power was made possible by accountability and competition, the starting point of Ozawa's reform campaign was to shatter the basic premise that had made the machine and all of its perversions possible: that the LDP would be the "eternal ruling party" and its putative adversaries "eternal opposition parties." He defined "reform," in concrete terms, as rewriting the electoral rules so as to force a more vibrant clash between strong rival parties for control of government. "If we are to break down our sheltered, comfortable politics and build opposition parties that truly seek to rule Japan," he contended, "we must begin by abolishing the [current] . . . electoral system." So the new Ozawa faction of the LDP set off by giving conservative leaders an uncomfortable ultimatum. It demanded that the LDP legislate a new set of electoral rules that would necessarily, over time, corrode its own dominance. If the LDP failed to comply, the Ozawa group threatened to bolt, immediately depriving the party of its thirty-eight-year-old parliamentary majority. The deadline Ozawa's men set for a decision was the end of the legislative session in June 1993.

OZAWA HAD BEGUN his rebel career as an outcast. While "reform" was a popular cause in Japan in early 1993, he was hardly an obvious leader of the movement. His vision, for one thing, did not sit well with many of Japan's other self-proclaimed reformers. They shared his short-term goal of trying to oust the LDP and change the electoral rules, but they were uneasy with his reasons for wanting to do so.

Most "reformers" were idealists, utopians even, who sought a kind of purification of democracy. They viewed the LDP as a cauldron of depravities, of politicians who pursued self-interest instead of a higher national interest; their aim was to purge, along with the party, all of the LDP's squalid preoccupations and petty turf battles. Ozawa's language contrasted sharply with that of other reformers: the idealists talked of reforming the nature of politicians; Ozawa accepted office seekers for the grubby creatures they were. His hard-nosed reforms were designed to reconfigure the arena in which base political desires were pursued—in fact, to create a system that could take advantage of power struggles and make them more integral to the functioning of government. "I have learned a lot since I entered politics. Naturally, it is not a world in which you can get by on your purity," Ozawa observed sardonically. "There would be no problems if all politicians upheld noble ideals and high ethical standards. But we are not divine. We are mundane." Ozawa's unabashed obsession with the workings of ambition was, to many Japanese, precisely the sort of thinking that reform should try to deter. OZAWA: TO BE WELCOMED OR FEARED? was a headline in the *Yomiuri* newspaper. "One of the most worrying things about Ozawa," the accompanying article fretted, "is the way in which he quickly links everything with power." "Even Adolf Hitler," a wary labor leader sniped, "was a reformer."

To most idealists, the main evil plaguing the system was the endemic "money-power politics." "Political reform" therefore meant one thing: ending the scourge of scandals. On this point, in particular, Ozawa was suspect, both for his platform and for his background. While his agenda did include some suggestions for cleaning up corruption, he plainly regarded the question as trivial, compared with the larger policy matters at stake. "So I'm not arguing the usual simple-minded 'Let's have a politics that doesn't cost money' view," he wrote in a magazine essay. "It's that very line of reasoning that's blocking the progress of political reform." Nor did Ozawa join the loud chorus demanding a thorough accounting of political crimes and an ousting of the perpetrators from Parliament. Strict enforcement of anticorruption laws, he objected, would lead to "massive indictments" and "the collapse of the constitutional state."

Furthermore, as the favored disciple of Japan's two most notorious political crooks—convict Tanaka and accused felon Kanemaru—Ozawa was widely considered to be part of the problem of politics, not a solution. "You should repent your many sins and reform yourself," Takashi Tachibana, the journalist who had most doggedly pursued Tanaka's scandals, scolded in a newspaper essay. "Admit you destroyed democracy and corrupted many of our institutions." Ozawa did nothing to try to allay this perception of guilt by association. Rather than renounce his tutors, he continued to speak of a "sense of obligation" toward them and portrayed them as victims of political witch-hunts. "I personally am absolutely opposed to the kind of social climate created by the media and others that forced . . . Kanemaru to resign from Parliament," he insisted.

The awkward discrepancy between Ozawa's murky breeding and his progressive pose was cast in stark relief from late 1992 through early 1993 as he launched his reform drive at the very time Kanemaru was engulfed in scandal. Ozawa himself was never charged with any transgressions, but he often appeared intimately connected with the shady actions of the man he called his "benefactor." When the Sagawa Kyubin affair first came to light, it was Ozawa who determined Kanemaru's defense strategy; when he failed to "protect" his patron, the younger pol "apologized to me . . . putting his head to the ground, crying," Kanemaru told associates. In February 1993, Ozawa was summoned before Parliament to testify about his possible role in the affair. While no incriminating evidence was presented, his denials stretched credibility. Asked about his recollections of one meeting to which he had accompanied Takeshita and Kanemaru to meet a Sagawa Kyubin executive, Ozawa responded, "I was just there as an attendant, so I did things like changing the drinks and cleaning the ashtrays . . . I was not directly involved in the discussion." In the months after Kanemaru resigned from Parliament, members of Ozawa's "reform" faction kept close contact with the disgraced Don, and a small group offered consolation by vacationing with him in New Zealand. And after Kanemaru was incarcerated for tax evasion in March, he said that the suspicious funds had been earmarked for "a future political realignment"; the vague claim was interpreted by the press—though never confirmed—to mean that Kanemaru's illicit stash was for bankrolling his acolyte's new activities.

The prosecutors' subsequent probe into the construction industry, a major Ozawa supporter, cast another cloud over the aspiring reformer. "Ozawa's next!" street demonstrators proclaimed amid the wave of arrests; others hoisted banners with a large "X" over his face. Ozawa's potential allies in building a new political order distanced themselves farther and farther from him. "There is no question that were we to link up with the . . . Ozawa group, it would deal a great blow to us," Morihiro Hosokawa, the founder of the Japan New Party, wrote in May as his own anti-LDP efforts were growing in popularity. "Collaborat[ing] with this group . . . would be tantamount to suicide for us." "The possibility of our cooperating with Ozawa," a leading liberal activist said, "is zero."

Distrusted by the progressives, Ozawa was meanwhile belittled by his old machine colleagues. They doubted his courage—and his ability—to make good on his threats to them. It was this skepticism that convinced the LDP it could safely ignore the ultimatum of the Ozawa faction and drop the issue of political reform in June 1993.

When the ruling party announced that it would shelve the package of anticorruption measures and new electoral rules—not just for the time being but for at least two years—the opposition parties protested by submitting a motion of no confidence against the cabinet, a procedure used by MPs in parliamentary systems to try and bring a government down. In this case, it was considered an empty gesture. The measure could prevail only with substantial support from within the LDP. Betrayal on the necessary scale would be an unprecedented event in the party's history and, despite the rumblings from the Ozawa camp, seemed a highly unlikely development. The Tanaka-built machine had always survived calls for reform by controlling the distribution of political favors; incumbents who backed change inevitably risked losing those benefits and likely their professional lives. The ruling party, now run by the shrunken Takeshita-led *gundan,* turned its tried-and-true strategy on their prodigal son, wielding every possible carrot and stick in an attempt to strip his backers away from him. The other faction leaders in the LDP, who harbored their own grudges against the former junior boss, were happy to join in the harassment campaign; they talked of a partywide "encircling net" around him. Even if Ozawa were personally crazy enough to vote against his party's leaders, experts expected just a handful of his men to join him, certainly not enough to do serious damage. "Observers predict that a majority of Ozawa's supporters will desert him in consideration of future elections, cabinet posts, and funding," one newspaper reported. Because, as one

Ozawa pal turned foe liked to say, "A politician can't feed himself on reform."

THE ORNATE RITUALS of Japan's Parliament offer the potential for grand political theater. The legislature continues to shun the modern convenience of instantaneous electronic balloting. When a matter is brought to a vote, MPs walk one by one to the front of the dark-paneled chamber and hand a small rectangular wooden block to a Parliament official, who drops the block into a lacquer box. A white block means support for the issue under consideration. Green signifies opposition. The outcome of the tally gradually takes shape, literally, before viewers' eyes as the competing "aye" and "nay" stacks rise alongside each other. One of the many cynical legacies of the Tanaka machine was that it had, over the years, robbed this rite of its natural drama; by rigging all of the major political parties, the *gundan* had typically settled important legislative affairs in the back rooms beforehand, turning the actual vote into a predictable charade.

On June 18, however, as the roll call on the anti-LDP no-confidence motion proceeded, it became evident that, for once, the usual fix was not in. The white pile indicating support for the motion grew higher and higher, tension mounting along with it. The usually thorough bosses began to realize that they had miscalculated the level of support for the proposal. The old guard's collective horror was reflected in the visage of Prime Minister Miyazawa, who sat tight-lipped in front of the ballot box, tears welling in his eyes. When the stately procession finally ended, the no-confidence motion —ridiculed up to the last moment by nearly every pol and pundit— passed by a vote of 255 in favor, 220 opposed.

The reason for the surprise outcome was the unforeseen solidarity of the LDP's Ozawa faction against the party leadership. Every member cast his ballot in favor of the protest motion, ensuring its passage. Having mutinied, Ozawa and his gang quit the party within the week—the first serious split of the conservative camp since 1955 —and formed their own Japan Renewal Party. The reactionaries' mistake was not that they had misjudged the fervor of Ozawa's men for reform; rather, they had failed to understand his agility in employing the tactics of the machine in his campaign to destroy the machine. Asked later how he had managed to preserve the unity of his troops, Ozawa gave the answer of a ward heeler, not of a proselytizer: "Everybody was pretty worried. . . . They were always asking me, 'Are we going to leave the LDP? What's happening? What's happening?' " he recounted. "I said, 'I'll promise you guys two things.' " The first: "If we make a new party, you will all win reelection for sure." The second: the new party would "definitely take power. . . . I will definitely pull that off." That is, he didn't ask his followers to feed themselves on reform; rather, he promised to feed them in the usual ways if they backed his reforms. No active politician had gotten better training than Ozawa on how to deliver the goods, and his followers trusted him implicitly. After he gave his assurances, Ozawa recalled, "Everybody said, 'We got it. No complaints.' "

IN THE WAKE of the stunning passage of the no-confidence motion, Japanese politics suddenly came to life. The languorous cynicism—the sense that nothing could ever change no matter how upset the electorate became—crumbled. Ebullient commentators went so far as to compare the vote to the collapse of the Berlin Wall, as the people developed a renewed interest—and even a cautious hope—in their democracy. TV political talk shows became all the rage, and political books became instant best-sellers—half a million copies of Ozawa's *Blueprint* were snapped up in weeks. Even U.S. President Bill Clinton, visiting Tokyo in early July for a summit of the leading industrialized nations, got caught up in the enthusiasm: in a speech to Japanese university students, he urged them to embrace "change," the spiel he had used to win the American presidency a few months earlier.

The no-confidence vote having forced the LDP to dissolve Parliament, government was up for grabs and elections for the lower house were scheduled for July 18. A number of new "reform" parties entered the contest, and all did well. Among them was Ozawa's Japan Renewal Party. True to the promise he had given his men, every member won reelection despite—and perhaps because of—their defection from the LDP; the party even picked up nineteen seats. (In addition to riding the wave of popular sentiment for reform, Japan Renewal Party members still had many of the same campaign resources they had enjoyed under the LDP, including plenty of money from their boss as well as construction company support.) Hosokawa's Japan New Party scored a surprisingly big victory, winning thirty-five seats in the first lower-house election the group had ever contested.

But the various "reform" parties were too small and inexperienced to win a resounding victory. Even after the defections and the vote, the LDP still had 228 seats, by far the largest bloc in Parliament. A hectic scramble among the numerous political blocs ensued as leading politicians tried to put together a coalition big enough to take over the government. During that period, the purists came to a queasy conclusion: they had no choice but to let Ozawa into their tent. In the public mind, the first step toward "reform"—whatever the ultimate goal, whatever the background of the reformer—was ousting the LDP from power; to that end, there was no luxury for splits among the disparate anti-LDP camps. Besides, just as the reactionaries had misjudged Ozawa's ability to use the old machine tactics on behalf of reform, the idealists were now discovering that they had underestimated their need for—and susceptibility to—those all-too-political skills. Among the anti-LDP contingent, only Ozawa had the nitty-gritty experience of actually putting a cabinet together.

In the days after the election, while most of the political leaders made the rounds of the talk shows, debating potential scenarios and the ideal policies of a future government, Ozawa slipped out of view. "I'm disappearing," he said like a sorcerer the day after the vote, heading to the secrecy of a hotel suite to cut the deals necessary to form an administration. He easily sealed an alliance with his old friends in the smaller opposition parties, ties he had formed under Kanemaru's guidance in the old days when they had secretly been fixing parliamentary sessions. To win cooperation from the Socialists —long the most vociferous torchbearers of the notion that purity should take priority over power—he offered some of the juiciest forbidden fruits: the speakership of Parliament's lower house and six cabinet posts, including the lucrative construction minister's job.

The last piece of the puzzle was Hosokawa, the populist who, just two months earlier, had dismissed the prospect of a linkage with Ozawa as "suicide." Hosokawa's Japan New Party, combined with the other parties Ozawa had lined up, would add up to a total of 260 MPs, or four more than necessary to form a cabinet. Ozawa saved his trump card for this seduction, offering to make Hosokawa prime minister of the anti-LDP government. Some Hosokawa aides were against the idea. "I thought it was a trick," one ally later said; another argued that the group should instead stay out of government for a while "and spend more time studying and observing." But Hosokawa was enticed by the prospect, just as the string of LDP premiers propped up by Tanaka and the "Kon-Chiku-Sho" trio had been before him. "I will be willing to join hands with anybody, even with the devil, for the sole purpose of bringing the LDP's hold on power . . . to an end," he would say. (In announcing his decision to accept the offer, though, he called it "heaven's will.") The sticky question of Ozawa's role in the alliance was finessed, the way Tanaka's always had been: though Ozawa would have great influence over the administration, he would take no formal position. He would be the "shadow shogun" for reform.

On August 6, Parliament elected Hosokawa as prime minister of Japan, heading a remarkable eight-party coalition. The event heralded the nation's first transfer of power in nearly four decades, a historic development that no knowledgeable observer would have predicted just three months earlier. Hosokawa turned out to be the perfect face for this achievement, and he became the embodiment of all the changes the Japanese people hoped had come to their politics. He was everything the old guard was not. He was relatively youthful —at fifty-five years old, the youngest premier since Tanaka had won the post at age fifty-four. He was eloquent and candid. He was handsome and stylish, winning rave reviews at home and abroad for the natty scarf he donned for a summit meeting with President Clinton. He was a Nagatacho outsider, having spent eight years as governor of the southern prefecture of Kumamoto. He was a renaissance man with glamorous friends and diverse interests—from skiing to piano—beyond the narrow confines of the political world. He did not come across as ambitious or power-hungry; as the eighteenth-generation scion of feudal lords, power seemed to gravitate to him naturally, as a kind of noblesse oblige. And despite his blue blood, he had a hip, commoner's touch, once playing one of his own ancestors in a movie. Hosokawa also had an intuitive feel for the importance of imagery, a trait rarely on display in a Japanese pol; to give his cabinet a fresh feel, he appointed a record three women to posts, as well as two nonpoliticians.

Within a month of taking office, Hosokawa had an astronomical 71 percent approval rating, the adoring public and press desperately wanting to believe that he marked a sharp break with all of the ugly practices of the past. They were so eager, in fact, that they were willing to overlook, for a time, some blemishes. Hosokawa was not, for example, quite as politically chaste as he was often portrayed. Like Ozawa, he had gotten his start in politics under Kakuei Tanaka's wing, serving for a dozen years as a member of the Tanaka faction of the LDP in the national Parliament before quitting to run for governor. And there were vague reports that Hosokawa had never fully distanced himself from Tanaka-style "money-power politics."

The Japanese people also did not seem to mind at first that, for all the talk of change, the infamous "dual structure of power" that had developed under the machine continued into this new age. Hosokawa was not in charge of his administration. Matters of policy, personnel, and legislative strategy were plainly left to Ozawa, whose dominance was, in some ways, even more pronounced than it had been during the "Kon-Chiku-Sho" era, since the coalition was made up largely of longtime opposition parties and political neophytes; Hosokawa had no prior cabinet experience, nor had nineteen of his other twenty ministers. Ozawa constantly seemed to be dictating important decisions to Hosokawa just before he was to unveil them; the fumbling prime minister could sometimes barely explain the policy, making glaring errors before an incredulous press corps. The other coalition leaders were still more out of the loop, reduced to learning of their government's position just before—or during broadcast of—the announcement. In one newspaper poll, only 16.6 percent of those surveyed said they felt Hosokawa was "taking the substantive initiative in the Hosokawa cabinet"; 60.9 percent identified Ozawa and his old *gundan* cronies as being the ones doing so.

The driving mission of the Hosokawa coalition was "reform," defined specifically as tightening campaign finance rules and changing the electoral system in the manner that Ozawa had advocated. The combination of Hosokawa's popularity and Ozawa's tactical proficiency proved felicitous; less than six months after taking office, they succeeded in pushing the landmark changes through the legislature. By representing a transfer of political power and by changing the fundamental electoral rules, the Hosokawa administration thus augured a new era of Japanese politics. The comfortable old certainties of Nagatacho were gone, and the rough-and-tumble competition that Ozawa had envisioned was starting to take root.

THE MOST VIVID evidence of the success of Ozawa's reforms was the swift comeuppance of Ozawa himself. Even as he was engineering a wholesale restructuring of Japan's political order, Ozawa remained equivocal about the full implications of the changes he was implementing. As a polemicist, he could clearly articulate the trade-offs in a democracy between power and its constraints. As a politician—especially a pol who had spent his entire career steeped in a machine culture—he had a much better grasp of, and interest in, the authority than the limits. It wasn't necessarily that Ozawa was disingenuous, that he didn't believe in concepts such as competition and accountability. Rather, he seemed to think he was somehow impervious to them. In his first quarter century in politics, Ozawa had always been at the center of power; in that electrifying summer of 1993, he was able to stay there, despite discarding his two main props, the *gundan* and the LDP. By the beginning of 1994, Ozawa acted as if it were unfathomable to him, no matter what the rules, that he could ever be anywhere but in charge.

Had Ozawa been content merely to use his shadow authority to stay in control of the government, he probably could have done so for some time. But that was the old machine-style thinking he despised and had set out to destroy. As he had written in his *Blueprint,* the point of his reforms was to "liberate" power. Ozawa saw the Hosokawa administration as a vehicle for rapid, dramatic, controversial changes in policies from reforming the tax code to curbing the might of the bureaucracy to strengthening military cooperation with the United States. He was driven by an urgent sense that he had to seize the momentum for change before it faded. He was also, perhaps, egged on by expectations, both in Japan and in the United States, of continued miracles. The deep pessimism of a year earlier—that nothing would ever change in Japanese politics—had been replaced by a wild optimism that deep-seated practices could be transformed overnight.

But the reality was that the coalition government was shaky, with unity on a mandate for just one policy—political reform. After that was achieved, the alliance found itself divided on almost everything else, especially the economic and diplomatic proposals Ozawa put forth. On more than one occasion, Hosokawa publicly endorsed an Ozawa plan without notifying the other coalition parties, only to be forced to back down in the face of stiff resistance from his partners. "He [Ozawa] was often unreasonable and his ideas were opposed by public opinion," one of Ozawa's main foes within the coalition said. Ozawa did not make things easier with his blunt, haughty response to that resistance. He tried to get his critics fired from the cabinet and insulted uncooperative coalition partners. "I've been speaking regularly with people who used to be in the opposition, and what I tell them is that nobody pays serious attention to the fine-sounding talk they're so fond of," he told an interviewer in a national magazine. " 'You're part of the ruling coalition now,' I say, 'and it's time for you to wake up!' "

The public perception of the coalition was quickly transformed, the image of Hosokawa's wholesome face replaced by Ozawa's scowling, secretive mask. Ozawa aggravated this public relations problem by engaging in a ruinous war with the media. He attacked coverage that was critical of him in Nixonian terms, deriding "black journalism" and portraying himself "in a war against violence by the pen." Furious with continued press investigations into his "money-power politics," he contended that "Reformers . . . are always apt to be the target of criticism and slander." He tried to bar certain newspapers he considered irresponsible from his press conferences, and when the press corps protested, he stopped talking to Japanese journalists altogether. Ozawa claimed that he had no obligation to give press conferences, calling them a "service" to the media. But given his unofficial clout in the government, the decision conveyed the impression, as one critic noted, that "the process of government decision-making is being hidden from the public."

During the "Kon-Chiku-Sho" era, Ozawa had been able to get away with such behavior; public opinion hadn't mattered much, and MPs disgruntled with him had had no place to go, since the machine had monopolized all the routes to power. But this was the new age of competition that Ozawa himself had championed. For the first time in decades, Japan had an opposition party that, as he had encouraged in his book, was truly seeking to rule Japan—the LDP, which was every bit as capable and ruthless as he. From the day they lost power, the elders of the onetime ruling party were itching to get it back, a hunger whetted by the added desire for vengeance against the traitor who had humiliated them.

The first gambit in the LDP's counteroffensive was to smear the pristine stature of Ozawa's front man. Hosokawa had his roots in the LDP, the conservative party members reiterated in speeches and interviews, and thus he was just as dirty as they were. In particular, they seized on a suspicious loan he had received from the Sagawa Kyubin delivery company, the very firm that had dragged Kanemaru down. In the spring of 1994, Parliament was paralyzed for weeks as the opposition kept peppering the premier with questions about his finances. Hosokawa's forthrightness faded and he appeared every bit as dissembling and evasive as Takeshita had five years earlier during the Recruit scandal. On April 8, 1994, eight months after taking office and less than three months after the triumphant passage of the reform legislation, Hosokawa resigned in disgrace.

Ozawa countered by putting up as the new prime minister another popular coalition member, Tsutomu Hata, an affable, loquacious pol who had left the *gundan* with Ozawa. Under Takeshita's guidance, the LDP widened its attacks, actively trying to split the coalition apart. It wasn't hard. Many members of the government, fed up with both Ozawa's policies and his manners, were willing to abandon him. In June the eight-party anti-LDP alliance unraveled. Ozawa's Japan Renewal Party was dumped onto the back benches of the opposition, while the government was taken over by an outlandish partnership between the LDP and the Socialists, the parties that ostensibly had been bitter foes for thirty-eight years. The deal was sealed, in the classic pattern established by Tanaka in the LDP—and continued by Ozawa with his coalition—by making Socialist leader Tomiichi Murayama a puppet prime minister, to be directed by his conservative puppeteers. The union was widely treated with derision as an unprincipled, unholy alliance. But that wasn't quite right. A new dividing line, surpassing the fading passions of right versus left, ran down the middle of Japanese politics: anti-Ozawa versus Ozawa.

Once again, Japan had a real opposition, only now it was Ozawa. And he was not passive in defeat. He fully intended to try to recapture power as quickly as possible. The question remained how. To have to compete openly for power—and from the opposition—was a challenge he had never faced before. As a leader of a ruling party, he had been able to stay in the back room, quietly pushing all the buttons and pulling all the levers of government in order to maintain and expand his support. But in the opposition, there were no posts to promise, no pork to dole out; the back room was bare. He tried to replay the insider's Nagatacho chess game—to attempt to pry enough incumbent MPs loose from the LDP to give him another parliamentary majority, just as the LDP had done to his coalition. But his effort was doomed to failure: by mid-1994, Ozawa had antagonized too many veteran pols.

He had no choice but to go outside Nagatacho in order to remake the legislature; that is, to take his case to the Japanese people, to win a mandate for his policies and for himself—in other words, to become accountable. It was, in fact, the very first lesson Ozawa had been given at Mejiro, that day in 1969 when he had been a wide-eyed twenty-six-year-old running for his father's seat and Tanaka—not yet prime minister, not yet a felon—was still Japan's beloved man of the people. Visit thirty thousand households and make fifty thousand speeches, Tanaka had advised. "You have to visit voters one by one." Tanaka, after all, had won power as a populist first, only becoming a "shadow shogun" later to preserve his clout. And now Tanaka's political son, trained mainly as a "shadow shogun," would have to become a populist—not because he wanted to but because he was desperate, having no other way to achieve his ambitions.

Ozawa became the official leader of a new opposition party, the New Frontier Party, cobbled together from the remaining elements of his anti-LDP alliance. It was the first time he had formally chaired a political group, despite years of running them. The politician who had once managed a national election campaign without making speeches was seen passing out handbills and shaking hands outside Tokyo's busy Shinjuku station, his first street appearance in the capital in a decade. The man who had once been able to order bureaucrats and prime ministers to carry out his policies started trying to affect government decisions the old opposition way: by commanding sit-ins in the halls of Parliament and chanting slogans, a banner across his chest, at the head of street demonstrations.

One morning in December 1995, Ozawa found himself in, of all places, VELFARRE, one of Tokyo's largest and most fashionable discotheques. His famous haughtiness, his dislike for flatteries and explanations, would be contained that day as he fielded questions from the audience of three hundred teenagers and college students "which," one snide newspaper account reported, "he would be angry about if he were asked at a press conference." "Have you ever seen a porn video?" was one inquiry. "A few times," was the answer. "Is your smile real, or are you just putting it on?" "This is real." "What are you afraid of?" "My wife." "What sort of woman do you like?" "Someone with a good heart." To one youngster who expressed concern about finding a job in Japan's depressed economy, Ozawa earnestly promised that if his New Frontier Party won the next election, it would work to boost employment.

Ozawa's theatrical entrance at VELFARRE was a neat metaphor for his personal transformation from the symbol of one political age to the personification of another. The stage under the sparkling disco lights was empty. The electronic sign flashed "Ichiro and VELFARRE." The Ozawa Internet Web site filled a large screen, showing pages titled "My Policies" and "Ichiro Ozawa and His 31 Secrets."

Green laser lights started pulsing frenetically to the thump of a disco beat. Smoke filled the hall. And slowly a figure ascended from a platform hidden beneath the stage. It was Ichiro Ozawa, sporting his blue suit and MP's badge, literally rising out of the shadows and blinking awkwardly into the glare of the public spotlight.

CONCLUSION

How will the machine's demise affect Japan's course? This book has been mainly about process, not policy. It has told the story of a machine—which is, by definition, a story about the mechanics of politics, not ideology. The narrative of Japan's postmachine era, which is only just beginning, will be different. The Tanaka organization became vulnerable when Japan's postwar consensus frayed in the late 1980s and early 1990s and the country could no longer easily ignore difficult questions.

When he dragged down the machine, Ichiro Ozawa made a point not just of attacking the structures of power but of resuscitating many dormant debates. "We must reform our politics, our economy, our society, and our consciousness," he proclaimed. More specifically, he helped force a reassessment of the two main tenets of the postwar political order: a domestic policy of heavy bureaucratic interference in the economy and a foreign policy of isolationism.

For years, it had been an article of faith that the strong state was a crucial element of Japan's economic success. Since the deep recession of the 1990s, however, many leaders have come to conclude that national government interference in the economy can be more of a hindrance than a help to growth; "deregulation" and "decentralization" are now popular slogans. "Management of this kind became untenable as . . . the Japanese economy grew too big," Ozawa wrote in his best-selling *Blueprint for a New Japan*. Morihiro Hosokawa, who served as the first prime minister of the 1993–1994 anti-LDP government, made attacks on the central bureaucracy a staple of his crusading oratory. He generated public opposition to excessive red tape by recounting the numerous frustrations he had experienced as a regional governor in the 1980s, his favorite example being his inability to so much as move a local bus stop without approval from Tokyo. A number of bureaucratic scandals and bungles in recent years have continued to fuel public support for reining in the mandarins—a sentiment intensified in 1998 with the sensational arrest of ranking Finance Ministry officials, as well as the ministry's terrifying mishandling of the country's banking system. Even the traditionally probureaucracy Liberal Democratic Party has felt compelled to embrace the rhetoric of sweeping deregulation. Ryutaro Hashimoto—the one-time Ozawa rival in the Tanaka faction who stayed loyal to the LDP when Ozawa defected—became prime minister in 1996 in part by pledging a major overhaul of the ministries. When Hashimoto was forced to resign after an electoral defeat in the summer of 1998, his LDP successor, Keizo Obuchi—another Ozawa rival in the Tanaka group—was forced to move even further to clip the most powerful bureaucracies' wings.

On foreign policy, the most heated argument centers on whether Japan should become a "normal nation," a phrase popularized by Ozawa, who defines it to mean "a nation that willingly shoulders those responsibilities regarded as natural in the international community." Such responsibilities, Ozawa insists, would include sending troops to world trouble spots for peacekeeping operations—a new role that would violate the traditions of Japan's postwar pacifist isolationism but is encouraged by an American government fed up with Japanese freeloading. Ozawa, Hashimoto, and other leaders of their generation say they favor maintaining the close alliance with the United States. But they argue that Japan, as a "normal nation" with a fully engaged diplomacy, should also develop a clearer sense of its own national interests.

While Ozawa has set the terms of the new public debate in Japan, the discourse is still in its early phases, and little has yet changed in policy terms. Public opinion has reflected a general dissatisfaction with the status quo, but no consensus has materialized around specific new approaches. Regarding deregulation, entrenched interests—notably the bureaucrats who administer the rules—have so far adeptly blocked all but the most cosmetic modifications. In diplomacy, the Japanese government has, since the embarrassment of the 1990–1991 Persian Gulf War, taken some modest steps toward a more active world role. Japanese soldiers have performed limited, noncombat peacekeeping tasks in Cambodia, Mozambique, Rwanda, and the Mideast. A new security pact signed with the United States in mid-1997 commits Japan to play a more active role in supporting U.S. military actions. But public opinion remains a check on any sharp increase in foreign activity; fifty years after World War II, much of the Japanese populace, fearing a return to the militarism of the 1930s, continues to be wary of any expanded role for the armed forces. In explaining his vision of a "normal nation," Ozawa has been careful to avoid jingoistic rhetoric; he has insisted that Japan's military should operate abroad only under U.N. command. Even so, many Japanese consider his proposals dangerous, a form of closet militarism.

OBSERVERS are watching closely for signs of shifting policy. But the most important transformation in Japanese politics so far has been more about structure than substance—the infusion of the political competition that is the necessary prerequisite for redefining the nation's priorities, and that is so essential to a fully functioning democracy. That is a momentous change after nearly forty years of one-party rule and a generation of machine dominance.

From 1955 to 1993, Japan never experienced a transfer of power, as the Liberal Democratic Party faced no serious challenge to its hold over national government. The longer the excessive stability endured, the more it developed beyond a simple fact into a pervasive mind-set, among the people and the politicians, that turnover was inconceivable and perhaps even dangerous. The Tanaka machine, which emerged in the latter half of the LDP's reign, was a natural outgrowth of the torpor. The machine then reinforced the rigidity by actively seeking to co-opt all possible rivals within the LDP and among the opposition parties. And as its strength became obvious, the Tanaka machine became a magnet for the most ambitious, capable MPs, thereby tightening its grip.

The absence of competition can spawn various undesirable patterns, many of which appeared in Japan under the LDP–Tanaka reign. Leadership became complacent and arrogant. Because the people had no real choice, the politicians felt less and less need to be attentive to the people. The logic of Nagatacho, Japan's Capitol Hill, increasingly deviated from the common sense of the electorate. The separation of power between the elected prime minister and the unelected "shadow shoguns" was one example of this dissonance. So was the the flagrant corruption and the utter lack of shame about it. Policies were inflexible despite changing times, geared more to specific special-interest groups than broader popular demands.

With the fall of the machine, the main props of Japan's uncompetitive politics have disappeared. When the Tanaka faction of the LDP split at the end of 1992, Japan's most talented and cutthroat politicians no longer were in collusion with one another but rather were suddenly pitted against one another. When the defectors from the Tanaka faction, led by Ozawa, left the LDP in June 1993, they instantly shattered the conventional wisdom that the ruling party was invincible. The creation of the anti-LDP coalition government two months later showed that a transfer of power was possible. It also affirmed that a change of administration need not be frightening and that the basic functions of government could continue to operate smoothly without the LDP.

Equally momentous has been the mutation of the nature of the political opposition, from one that lacked any credibility as a possible alternative government to a group that has the experience and determination to try to take control. For years, the LDP's most serious opponent was the Japan Socialist Party. The Socialists never really sought power, an attitude displayed in the party's stubborn adherence to an untenable far-left platform. The Socialists' ambivalence about real-world politics acted as a damper on their will to compete. But in the upheaval of 1993, they were forced to wake up when they joined a governing coalition, and shortly thereafter saw their leader, Tomiichi Murayama, propped up as prime minister by his LDP handlers. In office, Murayama and his fellow Socialists did not impose their putative extremism on policies. Instead, the imperatives of responsibility forced them to abandon their unrealistic platform. And today, the Socialist Party has all but vanished. Japan no longer has an irrational, inexperienced opposition. By 1998, the anti-LDP forces were made up of a very different sort of politician than earlier generations of political opposition. For the first time in years, Japan's Parliament includes, outside the LDP, numerous seasoned veterans who have held government posts and are eager to return to power. The opposition's humiliation of the LDP in the September 1998 parliamentary debate over bank reform legislation marked a turning point in Japanese politics, a new era in which anti-LDP parties could also shape the policy agenda. Though the opposition parties were still fragmented, their new empowerment marked the early stages of a broader realignment.

Party realignment will likely accelerate in the coming years, spurred by new electoral rules that were enacted in January 1994 under the anti-LDP coalition. From 1957 to 1993, elections for Japan's lower house of Parliament—the chamber that effectively forms governments—were held under an unusual multiseat district system, in which any given legislative district might send as many as six representatives to Parliament. Now, voting for the three hundred of five hundred seats is held under a single-seat system so that each parliamentary district, like American congressional districts, elects only one representative. (The remaining two hundred are elected under a regional "proportional representation" system.) Under the old rules, the concept of competition was blurred, since numerous candidates could win. Under the new rules, the contest will be sharpened by the fact that only one victor will emerge from single-seat contests. Beyond the specific details of the changes, the mere fact of change—that long-complacent incumbents now find themselves running in new districts under new conditions—is likely to generate a healthy uncertainty.

Despite these developments, many pundits in Tokyo and abroad still doubt the long-term viability of open, democratic competition in Japan. They cite as impediments historical and cultural factors, such as the national predilection for consensus over confrontation and the preference for stability and clear hierarchy over the "confusion" resulting from transfers of power. Skeptics found indications of the resilience of one-party democracy in the LDP's resurrection after its 1993 setback. The longtime ruling party retook the premiership as part of a coalition government in 1996, then regained its majority in Parliament's powerful lower house in 1997. But the LDP's comeback appears to have been short-lived. In elections for the upper house in July 1998, the party suffered a crushing defeat at the hands of voters furious with its inability to fix the country's economic woes. Though the party still controlled the lower house of Parliament—and thus the prime ministership and the cabinet—its hold on power was greatly weakened.

The longer Japan's travails continue—and the more radical the prescribed solutions become—the stresses and strains on the LDP become greater. Indeed, there is strong evidence that, whatever the culture, certain common forces shape democracies. Japan did experience vigorous political competition both before and immediately after World War II. And even in a supposedly consensus-oriented society like Japan, it is difficult for one party or bloc to satisfy the ambitions of every proficient politician forever. The Tanaka machine did for a while, until it simply grew too big to contain all the egos it had cultivated.

If political competition takes root in Japan, it should lead to greater flexibility, greater responsiveness, and greater transparency. It should move power farther out of the shadows. If parties frequently traded control over government, bureaucrats would be forced to cater to a wider range of politicians, weakening the ability of one bloc to monopolize policy making. With more than one mainstream group competing for power, parties would have to try to differentiate themselves from one another in their appeals to voters. The dialogue on major issues would become more thorough, more open, more accessible, and more widely supported. And more issues would likely get an airing.

The changes will be a matter of degree. Competition will not be a cure-all. Japanese hoping, for example, for a purification of politics will likely be disappointed. The voters will have a better opportunity than before to throw out a government they consider excessively dishonest. Corruption, therefore, may diminish. Corruption may also be curbed by the new legislation regulating political funds that was adopted at the same time as the 1994 electoral reforms. But the bonds between money and politics are strong in all democracies. Politicians and donors seeking favors inevitably find ways of circumventing curbs.

Nor does competition mean that the old guard will necessarily be purged. Since the fall of the Tanaka machine, its disciples have remained central players in the political world. Through 1998, Tanaka-trained pols led the governing LDP. Both Hashimoto, who served as prime minister through July, and Obuchi, who succeeded him, grew up in the Tanaka faction, and both governed with Takeshita and other Tanaka men pulling the strings behind the scenes. Numerous Tanaka men played critical roles in the main opposition party, the Democratic Party. Ozawa's smaller Liberal Party—created after the 1997 dissolution of his New Frontier Party—often allied with the

Democrats in cornering the LDP. In late 1998, the desperate ruling party was forced to enter negotiations with Ozawa's Liberal Party to form a coalition in order to get any major legislation passed. In return, he demanded that the LDP embrace some of his more radical reform proposals. That *gundan* politicians are playing a leading role in post-*gundan* Japan is not surprising. For twenty years, Tanaka ran Japan's best school for politicians. His disciples are the best trained to thrive, whatever system is in place.

Similarly, competition does not guarantee that the self-proclaimed "reformers" from the Tanaka camp will prevail. Reformers themselves may fail the tests of the new, vigorous style of political battle—as Ozawa demonstrated for much of the first five years after he split from the LDP. One reason that the LDP has been able to enjoy some success in recent years has been Ozawa's continued unpopularity with Japanese voters and fellow politicians. While many agree with his ideas, they mistrust him for his past and dislike his haughty style. Even some of his closest allies, those whom he had led out of the LDP four years earlier, split with him. The tiny Liberal Party he led at the end of 1998 was about one-fifth the size of the LDP. To some critics, Ozawa's late 1998 flirtation with the LDP was tantamount to his rejoining the party and giving up on his campaign for political reform.

But neither Ozawa's demise nor a new linkup with the LDP would spell the end of political change in Japan. Ozawa did not create Japan's reform movement out of thin air. He accelerated, and gave voice to, changes that were already under way and that will be difficult for anybody to turn back.

Notes

Note: *Full citations for works cited in short form can be found in the Selected Bibliography.*

ABBREVIATIONS:
AEN = *Asahi Evening News; DY* = *Daily Yomiuri; JT* = *Japan Times; MDN* = *Mainichi Daily News.*

PART ONE

Kakuei Tanaka: Man of the People, Man of Means, 1918–1976

19 There were more than 6 million Japanese: Description of Japanese repatriation at the end of World War II from: Wayne C. McWilliams, *Homeward Bound: Repatriation of Japanese from Korea after World War II.*

19 Tanaka somehow was able to orchestrate: Description of Tanaka's return from Korea from: Shigezō Hayasaka, *Oyaji to watashi,* pp. 89–90; Takashi Tachibana, *Tanaka Kakuei kenkyū: zen kiroku,* vol. 1, pp. 181–91; *Niigata Nippō,* ed., *Za Etsuzankai,* pp. 25–6; Kakuei Tanaka, *Watashi no rirekisho,* pp. 99–102.

Chapter One: From Penury to Parliament

21 Most of what is known: Description of Tanaka's youth from: Tanaka, *Watashi no rirekisho.* Supplemental sources are: Kakuei Tanaka,

Watakushi no shōnen jidai; Tatsuhiko Sakamoto, "Ningen Tanaka Kakuei," pp. 48–59; *Shokun!,* "Supesharu da: Kakuei hitori butai," television interview, aired May 6 and 13, 1984.

22 One year he sold: Tanaka, *Watashi no rirekisho,* p. 12.

22 "My father used to drink": Sakamoto, "Ningen Tanaka Kakuei," p. 51.

23 A familiar image: Ryūzō Saki, *Etsuzan Tanaka Kakuei,* p. 116.

23 "Although my mother was": Tanaka, *Watashi no rirekisho,* p. 20.

23 one in five babies died: Kyūichi Yoshida, *Nihon hinkonshi,* vol. 2, p. 324.

24 "but we are the sculptors": Tanaka, *Watashi no rirekisho,* pp. 28–9.

24 "I've studied enough": Ibid., p. 29.

25 "if you are driven": Ibid., p. 34.

25 rural cash incomes: Edwin O. Rieschauer and Albert M. Craig, *Japan: Tradition and Transformation,* pp. 245–6.

25 more than doubling: Thomas Wilkinson, *The Globalization of Japanese Labor, 1868–1955,* p. 54.

25 "They constantly shift": Mikiso Hane, *Peasants, Rebels and Outcastes: The Underside of Modern Japan,* pp. 34–6.

26 "My master will not": Tanaka, *Watashi no rirekisho,* pp. 38–9.

26 "Immediately, I jumped": Ibid., p. 48.

27 "If a job was": Tachibana, *Tanaka Kakuei kenkyū,* vol. 1, p. 180.

27 "She's my kind of woman": Tanaka, *Watashi no rirekisho,* p. 86.

27 "I wasn't substantial enough": Ibid., p. 74.

28 "You've got a bad attitude": Ibid., p. 89.

28 the Riken Industrial Group: *Riken no kenkyū katsudō,* p. 21; Monica Braw, *The Atomic Bomb Suppressed,* p. 12.

29 "I was involved": Tanaka, *Watashi no rirekisho,* p. 83.

29 "kindly looked after me": Ibid., p. 97.

29 "When I got married": "The Man Who Broke the Mold," *Newsweek,* international edition, July 17, 1972, p. 18.

29 with the Sakamoto venture: Tachibana, "Kakuei Tanaka: His Money & His Men," part 7, November 4, 1974.

30 Tanaka Construction was quickly: Kakuei Tanaka, *Building a New Japan: A Plan for Remodeling the Japanese Archipelago,* p. 225.

30 With some liquor: *Niigata Nippō,* ed., *Za Etsuzankai,* pp. 25–6.

30 "It was the time": *Mainichi Daily News,* ed., *Fifty Years of Light and Dark: The Hirohito Era,* p. 212.

30 There, Japanese soldiers had told women: Ibid., p. 159.

31 "sever for all time": Jon Livingston, Joe Moore, and Felicia Oldfather, eds., *Postwar Japan: 1945 to the Present,* p. 18.

32 "blast from their entrenched positions": *Kōdansha Encyclopedia of Japan,* vol. 6, p. 52.

32 Such a purge: Junnosuke Masumi, *Postwar Politics in Japan, 1945–1955,* p. 94.

32 "Anyone could be a candidate": "Tanaka Kakuei dokuhaku-roku:

'Waga sengo hishi' " (Kakuei Tanaka monologue: My secret postwar history), *Gendai*, February 1994, p. 30.

32 "There was no sign": Tanaka, *Watashi no rirekisho*, p. 103.

33 "Do you mind contributing": Ibid.

33 "I had a haircut": Ibid., p. 104; *Niigata Nippō*, ed., *Za Etsuzankai*, pp. 34–6.

33 "I had not even read": "Tanaka Kakuei dokuhaku: 'Waga sengo hishi' " (Kakuei Tanaka monologue: My secret postwar history), *Gendai*, February 1994, p. 29.

33 the hometown Futada crowd: Saki, *Etsuzan Tanaka Kakuei*, p. 117; *Niigata Nippō*, ed., *Za Etsuzankai*, pp. 34–5.

33 "Just spend 150,000 yen": Tanaka, *Watashi no rirekisho*, pp. 103–4.

33 Some of his supporters: *Niigata Nippō*, ed., *Za Etsuzankai*, p. 33; Tanaka, *Watashi no rirekisho*, p. 105; Tachibana, "Kakuei Tanaka: His Money & His Men," part 7, November 4, 1974.

34 He set up branch offices: Tanaka, *Watashi no rirekisho*, p. 106.

34 He made over his image: Kichiya Kobayashi, *Kakuei ichidai: Rüda to soshiki—zen hassō*, p. 25.

34 "with young energy": *Niigata Nippō*, ed., *Za Etsuzankai*, p. 43.

34 "I was sleeping all day": Tanaka, *Watashi no rirekisho*, pp. 106–7.

34 "a gathering place for the tainted": Masumi, *Postwar Politics in Japan*, p. 94.

34 "Shout of the Young Blood": *Niigata Nippō*, ed., *Za Etsuzankai*, pp. 34–6; Tanaka, *Watashi no rirekisho*, p. 106.

34 "Hey, everybody, let's cut down": *Niigata Nippō*, ed., *Za Etsuzankai*, pp. 42–4; Shigezō Hayasaka, *Hayasaka Shigezō no "Tanaka Kakuei" kaisōroku*, pp. 33–4.

Chapter Two: Snow Country

37 "People used to get": Sakamoto, "Ningen Tanaka Kakuei," pp. 50–1.

37 "Getting sick in the winter": *Niigata Nippō*, ed., *Kakuei no fūdo*, pp. 16–7.

37 "Blizzards rage day after day": Bokushi Suzuki, *Snow Country Tales: Life in the Other Japan*, p. 198.

37 "Until cherry blossom season": Kobayashi, *Kakuei ichidai*, p. 17.

37 "To mention Echigo or Sado": Suzuki, *Snow Country Tales*, p. xxxi.

38 remained in *omote Nippon:* Tanaka, *Building a New Japan*, p. 21.

38 "We people who live": Yujiro Miya, "Harsh Snow-country Environment Proves Background for Political Strength," p. 22.

38 Even communities hit: Chalmers Johnson, "Tanaka Kakuei, Structural Corruption, and the Advent of Machine Politics in Japan," p. 8.

38 The men of Ojiya: *Niigata Nippō*, ed., *Kakuei no fūdo*, pp. 20–8; author interviews in Niigata.

38 Like an internal colony: Johnson, "Tanaka Kakuei," p. 3; *Niigata Nippō*, ed., *Shomin no ayunda Niigata-ken 50 nen shi*, p. 51.

38 Many joined an annual migration: *Niigata Nippō*, ed., *Kakuei no fūdo*, pp. 115–39; Kobayashi, *Kakuei ichidai*, pp. 86–92.

39 "Who has supported": *Niigata Nippō*, ed., *Kakuei no fūdo*, pp. 90–1.

39 The young girls of Niigata: *Niigata Nippō*, ed., *Shomin no ayunda Niigata-ken 50 nen shi*, pp. 42, 141–87.

39 Niigata's economic and social problems: *Niigata Nippō*, ed., *Shomin no ayunda Niigata-ken 50 nen shi*, pp. 41–70, 112.

40 its most popular politician was: *Niigata Nippō*, ed., *Kakuei no fūdo*, pp. 223–70.

41 Tanaka was considered: *Niigata Nippō*, ed., *Za Etsuzankai*, pp. 38–42; *Asahi Shimbun* Niigata Shikyoku, ed., *Tanaka Kakuei to Etsuzankai: shinsō no kōzu*, pp. 106–7.

41 "Young Tanaka was": Kobayashi, *Kakuei ichidai*, p. 53.

41 A newspaper account: *Asahi Shimbun*, January 18, 1949, cited in *Niigata Nippō*, ed., *Za Etsuzankai*, pp. 17–8.

41 "Our younger brothers and sisters": Tōru Hayano, "Mite kiite hanashita 'Kaku-san' no sugao," p. 15.

41 Kinjiro Hiraishi: *Niigata Nippō*, ed., *Za Etsuzankai*, pp. 95–6; *Asahi Shimbun* Niigata Shikyoku, ed., *Tanaka Kakuei to Etsuzankai*, pp. 47–8.

42 "Niigata has a large population": *Asahi Shimbun* Niigata Shikyoku, ed., *Tanaka Kakuei to Etsuzankai*, pp. 86–9.

42 In 1953, he formed: *Niigata Nippō*, ed., *Za Etsuzankai*, pp. 82–95.

42 To Tanaka, the contractor turned politician: *Asahi Shimbun* Niigata Shikyoku, ed., *Tanaka Kakuei to Etsuzankai*, pp. 92–119; *Niigata Nippō*, ed., *Za Etsuzankai*, pp. 80–1.

42 "Tanaka is so great": *Niigata Nippō*, ed., *Za Etsuzankai*, pp. 336–7.

43 When landowners in Shimoda Village: *Asahi Shimbun* Niigata Shikyoku, ed., *Tanka Kakuei to Etsuzankai*, pp. 124–5.

43 When another group: *Niigata Nippō*, ed., *Za Etsuzankai*, pp. 104–11.

43 "Hey, chief, this is my": Ibid., pp. 49–51.

43 Tanaka had a desk: *Niigata Nippō*, ed., *Kakuei no fūdo*, p. 80.

43 Another conservative MP, unable: Kobayashi, *Kakuei ichidai*, pp. 86–92.

43 Kashiwazaki City's chamber of commerce: *Niigata Nippō*, ed., *Za Etsuzankai*, pp. 211–13.

43 Tanaka, the pragmatist: *Niigata Nippō*, ed., *Kakuei no fūdo*, pp. 207–8.

44 Train lines were extended: Steven Hunziker and Ikuro Kamimura, *Kakuei Tanaka, A Political Biography of Modern Japan*, pp. 71–3, 85–6.

44 Tanaka persuaded them: Ibid., pp. 72–3; *Niigata Nippō*, ed., *Za Etsuzankai*, pp. 202–6.

44 The previously apolitical shopkeepers: *Niigata Nippō*, ed., *Za Etsuzankai*, pp. 217–19.

44 "We need to have": *Asahi Shimbun* Niigata Shikyoku, ed., *Tanaka Kakuei to Etsuzankai*, pp. 48–9.

Chapter Three: Kaku-san Versus the Elite

47 "had not even shared": Masumi, *Postwar Politics in Japan*, pp. 308–9; Nathaniel B. Thayer, *How the Conservatives Rule Japan*, pp. 11–2.

47 Three dozen top executives: Chitoshi Yanaga, *Big Business in Japanese Politics*, pp. 63–8.

48 hundreds of thousands of protesters: George R. Packard, *Protest in Tokyo: The Security Treaty Crisis of 1960*, p. 295.

48 "absence of diplomacy": Haruhiro Fukui, "LDP's Foreign Policy and Process of Making It," *Kokusai Mondai*, April 1972, trans. in *Summaries of Selected Japanese Magazines*, American Embassy, September 1972, p. 9.

48 "more a trading company": Donald C. Hellmann, "Japanese Politics and Foreign Policy: Elitist Democracy Within an American Greenhouse," p. 358.

49 "The 21st century is Japan's": Eisaku Sato, "Now I Can Talk: Turbulent Seven Years and Eight Months," *Bungei Shunjū*, January 1973, trans. in *Summaries of Selected Japanese Magazines*, American Embassy, February 1975, p. 5.

50 a Japanese leader had: John Welfield, *An Empire in Eclipse: Japan in the Postwar American Alliance System*, p. 169.

50 "I will be a Parliament member": *Niigata Nippō*, ed., *Kakuei no fūdo*, pp. 34–5.

52 "insolence typified the worst": Packard, *Protest in Tokyo*, p. 246.

52 He had been a willing: Kent E. Calder, *Crisis and Compensation: Public Policy and Political Stability in Japan, 1949–1986*, p. 95; p. 341 note 72.

52 As a young train stationmaster: Shinkichi Etō, *Nihon saishō retsuden: Satō Eisaku*, p. iv.

52 he preferred to spend: Takashi Oka, "As the Japanese Say: Premier Sato Would Tap His Way Across a Stone Bridge to Be Sure It Was Safe," p. 144.

52 When he did go drinking: *Mainichi Daily News*, ed., *Fifty Years of Light and Dark*, pp. 351–2.

53 "would tap his way:" Oka, "As the Japanese Say," p. 142.

53 "I am rather dull": "Eisaku Sato's Intentions," *Shūkan Asahi*, August 3, 1962, trans. in *Summaries of Selected Japanese Magazines*, American Embassy, August 13, 1962, p. 19.

53 "Everybody! Politics is life": Tanaka Kakuei o aisuru seiji kisha gurūpu, *Tanaka Kakuei saihyōka*, p. 56.

53 "It's you, not the prime minister": *Niigata Nippō*, ed., *Za Etsuzankai,* pp. 229–32.

53 At fancy hotel banquets: Hayasaka, *Oyaji to watashi,* p. 164.

54 "Japanese intellectuals disdained anything traditional": Author interview with Shigezō Hayasaka, April 4, 1994.

54 Tokyoites should send their children: Tanaka Kakuei gurūpu, *Tanaka Kakuei saihyōka,* p. 55.

54 Tanaka broke into *naniwabushi: Niigata Nippō,* ed., *Za Etsuzankai,* pp. 140–4; Shigezō Hayasaka, *Seijika Tanaka Kakuei,* p. 141; Hunziker and Kamimura, *Kakuei Tanaka,* p. 69.

54 Later, in 1962: Hayasaka, *Seijika Tanaka Kakuei,* pp. 166–7; *Niigata Nippō,* ed., *Za Etsuzankai,* p. 230.

54 Reporters could always get: "Why So Much Haste?," *MDN,* April 14, 1971; "The Man Who Broke the Mold," *Newsweek,* international edition, July 17, 1972, p. 18.

54 "I think my father": "Prime Minister Tanaka's 'Fight,' as Described by His Daughter Makiko," *Shūkan Asahi,* October 26, 1973, trans. in *Summaries of Selected Japanese Magazines,* American Embassy, December 1973, p. 8.

55 "Unless I have two glasses": Takashi Tachibana, *Kyoaku vs. genron: Tanaka Rokkiido kara jimintō bunretsu made,* pp. 141–2.

55 a large stable . . . daughter's name: "Prime Minister Tanaka's 'Fight,' as Described by His Daughter Makiko," *Shūkan Asahi,* November 2, 1973, trans. in *Summaries of Selected Japanese Magazines,* American Embassy, December 1973, p. 10.

55 "You think my speech": Hayano, "Mite kiite hanashita 'Kaku-san' no sugao," p. 14.

55 "the complete works of world literature": "*Pureibōi* intabyū: Tanaka Kakuei," *Pureibōi,* July 1983, p. 209.

55 He had huffily refused: Sakamoto, "Ningen Tanaka Kakuei," p. 57.

55 "A man who has": Hayano, "Mite kiite hanashita 'Kaku-san' no sugao," p. 14.

55 "Don't idle away the time": Takaya Kodama, "Sabishiki Etsuzankai no joō."

55 "I once refused": "Genroku Politics—Interview with Kakuei Tanaka," *Yomiuri Shimbun,* May 8, 1969, trans. in *Daily Summary of Japanese Press,* American Embassy, June 26, 1969, p. 8.

55 When Tanaka took up golf: Hayasaka, *Oyaji to watashi,* pp. 175–86.

56 only a few stations . . . Tanaka overruled: Hayasaka, *Seijika Tanaka Kakuei,* p. 135.

56 In 1965, fear spread: Kent E. Calder, "Kanryō vs. Shomin: Contrasting Dynamics of Conservative Leadership in Postwar Japan," p. 13.

56 In 1957, when leftists: Tetsuya Kataoka, *The Price of a Constitution: The Origin of Japan's Postwar Politics,* p. 182.

56 In 1969, when student radicals: Hayasaka, *"Tanaka Kakuei" kaisōroku,* pp. 139–42; Hayasaka, *Seijika Tanaka Kakuei,* pp. 216–23.

57 "dynamism and quick thinking": "New Minister Speaks: Will Boost China Trade," *MDN,* July 7, 1983.

57 "a man of the rickshaw class": "From the Japanese Magazines: Tanaka: Man of the Year," *MDN,* November 5, 1983.

57 Tanaka did prevail, but: "Shinkakuryō no yokogao" (Profiles of new cabinet ministers), *Asahi Shimbun,* July 18, 1962; "Ikeda kaizō naikaku e keizaikai no koe" (The economic world's voice toward the reshuffled Ikeda cabinet), *Asahi Shimbun,* July 19, 1962; "Watashi wa kō suru: Zōshō Tanaka Kakuei shi" (I will do this: Finance Minister Mr. Kakuei Tanaka), *Asahi Shimbun,* July 20, 1962.

57 "open and extroverted personality": "Tanaka Keeps Top LDP Post," *JT,* January 13, 1970.

57 "like a right hand to me": Hayasaka, *Seijika Tanaka Kakuei,* p. 195.

57 Tanaka should have posed: This section draws on the detailed comparison of Tanaka and Fukuda in Calder, "Kanryō vs. Shomin," pp. 1–28.

58 Years later, Fukuda still talked: *Niigata Nippō* Hōdōbu, ed., *Saishō Tanaka Kakuei no shinjitsu,* pp. 62–7.

58 such delicate "high arts": "Four Waiters in the Wings," *Newsweek,* international edition, December 9, 1974, p. 10.

58 "The nation's economic circles": Yosei Amano, "Tanaka Ushers in New Aspects," *MDN,* July 6, 1972.

Chapter Four:
Building a New Japan

59 "The super-express *Nippon*": "Why So Much Haste?," *MDN,* April 14, 1971.

59 "Japan has never enjoyed": *Mainichi Daily News,* ed., *Fifty Years of Light and Dark,* p. 376.

60 The postwar industrial boom: Reischauer and Craig, *Japan,* pp. 294–7; Calder, *Crisis and Compensation,* p. 349.

60 those left behind: Nobuo Danno, "The Changing Face of Agriculture," *Japan Quarterly,* July–September 1972, pp. 293–9; "Deserted Villages, Crammed Towns," *Japan Quarterly,* January–March 1972, p. 6.

61 "The technocrat . . . takes the most": Jun Ui, "The Singularities of Japanese Pollution," *Japan Quarterly,* July–September 1972, pp. 290–1.

61 Sato was reportedly playing golf: Eisaku Satō, "Now I Can Talk: Turbulent Seven Years and Eight Months," *Bungei Shunjū,* January 1973, trans. in *Summary of Selected Japanese Magazines,* American Embassy, February 1973, p. 6.

61 "I have done everything": Welfield, *An Empire in Eclipse,* p. 295.

62 The pervasive, unnerving sense: *Mainichi Daily News,* ed., *Fifty Years of Light and Dark,* pp. 389–420; Hans H. Baerwald, *Japan's Parliament: An Introduction,* p. 105.

62 The LDP's indifference: Calder, *Crisis and Compensation,* pp. 106, 344, 346, 371–2.

62 By the spring of 1972: *Mainichi Daily News,* ed., *Fifty Years of Light and Dark,* pp. 352–4.

63 "We are sick and tired": Vox Populi, Vox Dei, "Go to It, Kaku-san!," *AEN,* July 7, 1972.

63 "Sato's 'politics of waiting' ": "Appraisal of Sato Cabinet and Birth of Tanaka Cabinet," *Trends of Japanese Magazines* (August Issues, 1972), American Embassy, pp. 1–2.

63 "He's got enough guts": "Tanaka Preoccupied with 8-Point Plan," *JT,* August 16, 1971.

63 "Any troubles that occur": "Post-Sato Perspective. Kakuei Tanaka: Alliance with Ohira," *AEN,* February 2, 1972.

63 "various contradictions [that] have surfaced": Tanaka, *Building a New Japan,* p. 17.

63 "asphalt jungle": Ibid., p. 197.

63 "cherry blossoms are dying . . . three hours away": Ibid., pp. 37–51.

63 "the physically handicapped": Ibid., p. 162.

63 "There are better new towns": Ibid., p. 106.

64 "replace the pursuit of growth": Ibid., p. 68.

64 "boldly reverse this torrential": Ibid., p. iv.

64 "scrapping the existing industrial areas": Ibid., p. 87.

64 "at least 8 yards": Ibid., p. 198.

64 "a society where every home": Ibid., p. 220.

64 "Sato never advanced": Yoshirō Hoshino, "Remodeling the Archipelago," *Japan Quarterly,* January–March 1973, p. 40.

65 numerous Japanese business delegations: Welfield, *Empire in Eclipse,* p. 314.

65 "It is finally the year": "Post-Sato Perspective. Kakuei Tanaka: Alliance with Ohira," *AEN,* February 2, 1972.

65 "Beyond the party is the state": Welfield, *Empire in Eclipse,* p. 311.

65 "traitors who defy the wishes": "Disintegration of the Conservative Main-Current Sato Faction," *Sankei Shimbun,* June 21, 1972, trans. in *Daily Summary of Japanese Press,* American Embassy, June 23, 1972, pp. 14–5.

66 "vote for Fukuda": Masaya Itō, *Jimintō sengokushi,* vol. 1, pp. 52–4.

66 He sweated, and back home: *Niigata Nippō,* ed., *Za Etsuzankai,* pp. 284–6.

66 "There is a mountain": "Tanaka's Policy Speech," *AEN,* October 30, 1972.

66 The long-suffering people of Niigata: *Niigata Nippō,* ed., *Za Etsuzankai,* pp. 284–6.

66 Within ten days: "Premier Wins Respect of Masses: Creates 'Tanaka Boom,' " *JT,* August 16, 1972; "Dialogue with People," *JT,* August 16, 1972.

67 Within a month, he established: Hunziker and Kamimura, *Kakuei Tanaka,* p. 94.

67 "Everyday new ideas": "Tanaka Administration: Fresh Ideas, Directives Flow from New Gov't Making It Popular," *JT,* August 3, 1972.

67 The leaders of the main: Welfield, *Empire in Eclipse,* pp. 318–9.

67 His arrival in Beijing: "Tanaka Arrives in China, Hopes to Establish Ties," *The New York Times*, September 25, 1972; "Japan Anthem Played in China: Stirs Poignant Bitter Memories," *JT*, September 27, 1972.

67 During the six-day visit: Welfield, *Empire in Eclipse*, p. 320.

67 not with Western pens: "Japan, China Establish Relations," *JT*, September 30, 1972.

67 "has given me great confidence": "Remodeling Japan Discussed in China," *JT*, September 28, 1972.

67 a record-high 62 percent: *Trends of Japanese Magazines* (December Issues, 1972), American Embassy, p. 3.

67 *The New York Times* praised: "New Japanese Premier Urges Vast Changes in Nation's Ways," *The New York Times*, August 23, 1972.

68 "No American party leader has": Max Lerner, "Japan as Remodeler," *JT*, October 9, 1972.

68 "Very forceful, very direct": Ibid.

68 Japanese commentators saw significance: "Tanaka Administration: Fresh Ideas, Directives Flow from New Gov't Making It Popular," *JT*, August 3, 1972; "Remodeling Japan Discussed in China," *JT*, September 28, 1972.

68 reports of a "Tanaka shock": Reischauer and Craig, *Japan*, p. 322.

68 Tanaka's Beijing visit, crowed: "Press Comments: Premier's Visit to China," *JT*, September 23, 1972.

68 "the most powerful person": "Kaku-san to yobareru seiji o: Shomin no negai to kitai o uragiruna" (Practice Kaku-san politics: Don't betray the people's expectations), *Yomiuri Shimbun*, evening edition, July 5, 1972.

Chapter Five: The Politician as Entrepreneur

69 As he climbed steadily: Hunziker and Kamimura, *Kakuei Tanaka*, p. 85.

70 Beginning in the 1950s: Tachibana, "Kakuei Tanaka: His Money & His Men," part 4, October 31, 1974; "Details of Land Deals Said to Involve Tanaka," *AEN*, November 12, 1974; Robert Shaplen, "Annals of Crime: The Lockheed Incident," p. 48; Hunziker and Kamimura, *Kakuei Tanaka*, p. 95; Hiroshi Sasaki, "Tanaka moto sōri o meguru aijin rokunin shū no shōtai" (Six mistresses of ex–prime minister Tanaka identified), *Seikai Ōrai*, March 1983; Saki, *Etsuzan Tanaka Kakuei*, p. 188.

70 As the company's dynamic: *Niigata Nippō*, ed., *Za Etsuzankai*, pp. 56, 62–7; Hunziker and Kamimura, *Kakuei Tanaka*, p. 56; Tachibana, "Kakuei Tanaka: His Money & His Men," part 7, November 4, 1974.

71 Over the next decade: *Niigata Nippō*, ed., *Za Etsuzankai*, pp. 75–77, 154–68; Hunziker and Kamimura, *Kakuei Tanaka*, pp. 75–6; Tachibana, "Kakuei Tanaka: His Money & His Men," part 6, November 2, 1974.

71 As he assembled: *Niigata Nippō*, ed., *Kakuei no fūdo*, pp. 101–5; *Asahi Shimbun* Niigata Shikyoku, ed., *Tanaka Kakuei to Etsuzankai*, pp. 152–60.

71 Such men were called "well-fence politicians": Gerald L. Curtis, *The Japanese Way of Politics*, pp. 178–9.

71 erected a commemorative bust: *Niigata Nippō*, ed., *Kakuei no fūdo*, pp. 101–2; *Asahi Shimbun* Niigata Shikyoku, ed., *Tanaka Kakuei to Etsuzankai*, p. 158.

72 Tanaka tended to concentrate: *Niigata Nippō*, ed., *Za Etsuzankai*, pp. 104–19; *Asahi Shimbun* Niigata Shikyoku, ed., *Tanaka Kakuei to Etsuzankai*, p. 169; Takashi Tachibana, *Tanaka Kakuei shin kinmyaku kenkyū*, pp. 83–8; Hunziker and Kamimura, *Kakuei Tanaka*, pp. 62–3.

72 In the 1960s, "Tanaka Inc.": Tachibana, "Kakuei Tanaka: His Money & His Men," part 5, November 1, 1974, and part 8, November 5, 1974; *Niigata Nippō*, ed., *Za Etsuzankai*, pp. 169–89; Hunziker and Kamimura, *Kakuei Tanaka*, pp. 80–1; "AMA Head Promises Probe into Purchase of Land—By Tanaka Family Firm," *AEN*, May 24, 1975; "Probe of Tanaka's Klondike," *MDN*, September 14, 1975; "Attacks Against Tanaka Remain Unabated in Diet," *AEN*, November 27, 1974; "Scandal-plagued Company Given Free Hand with Land," *JT*, November 2, 1977.

72 "modern alchemy": "Bed of Shinano River," *AEN*, November 4, 1977.

73 The son of a tenant farmer: Eiji Ōshita, "Japan's Robber Baron," *Business Tokyo*, July 1987, pp. 44–7.

73 "This is the time": Tachibana, *Tanaka Kakuei kenkyū*, vol. 1, p. 213.

73 he had gone on to amass: "Japanese Mogul Kenji Osano Dies at 69," *Los Angeles Times*, October 31, 1986.

73 He cornered the Waikiki Beach hotel business: "The 'Monster' Man in Tanaka's Shadow," Associated Press, in *Stars and Stripes*, November 4, 1974.

73 When Osano died at age sixty-nine: Eiji Ōshita, "Japan's Robber Baron," *Business Tokyo*, July 1987, p. 44.

73 the tabloid sobriquet "Monster": "Osano—Monster Merchant of Japan," *MDN*, February 8, 1976.

73 "sworn friend": Tachibana, *Kyoaku vs. genron*, p. 142; *Niigata Nippō*, ed., *Za Etsuzankai*, pp. 145–7.

73 "We'd go drinking": "The 'Monster' Man in Tanaka's Shadow," Associated Press, in *Stars and Stripes*, November 4, 1974.

73 Osano was a frequent investor: Tachibana, "Kakuei Tanaka: His Money & His Men," part 9, November 6, 1974; Hunziker and Kamimura, *Kakuei Tanaka*, p. 82.

74 During his summit meeting: "High Court Gives Osano Suspended 10-Month Term," *DY*, April 24, 1984; "Osano's Influence Still Strongly Felt," *MDN*, April 18, 1976.

74 "Tanaka-Osano Trading House": Author interview with Takashi Tachibana, May 23, 1994.

74 "Tanaka is somebody who walks on the fence": Tachibana, *Kyoaku vs. genron*, p. 142.

74 "You can't be called a man": *Niigata Nippō*, ed., *Za Etsuzankai*, p. 111.

74 He had, in fact, landed there: Tachibana, "Kakuei Tanaka: His Money & His Men," part 7, November 4, 1974; Yujiro Miya, "Money Provides Power Source for Tanaka's Political Gains," p. 21; Yujiro Miya, "Party Politics Determine Success of Protagonists," p. 24; Kobayashi, *Kakuei ichidai,* pp. 61–3; *Niigata Nippō,* ed., *Za Etsuzankai,* pp. 10–6; "A Farm Boy's Rise to Fortune," *JT,* July 28, 1976.

74 Over the next twenty years: Hunziker and Kamimura, *Kakuei Tanaka,* pp. 86, 67, 71–3; Tachibana, "Kakuei Tanaka: His Money & His Men," part 7, November 4, 1974; *Niigata Nippō,* ed., *Za Etsuzankai,* pp. 56–75, 202–6, 219–26, 233–4, 239–41.

74 suspicion of wrongdoing trailed Tanaka: Takao Sekiguchi, *Oshoku no kōzōgaku,* p. 221; Seichō Matsumoto, *Gigoku 100 nen shi,* p. 260; *Niigata Nippō,* ed., *Za Etsuzankai,* pp. 233–4, 239–41; Hunziker and Kamimura, *Kakuei Tanaka,* pp. 82–3.

75 the opposition parties managed: Hunziker and Kamimura, *Kakuei Tanaka,* pp. 95–6.

75 a Communist MP alleged: "Tanaka the Irascible," *DY,* May 7, 1973.

75 instead of investigating: "Details of Land Deals Said to Involve Tanaka," *AEN,* November 12, 1974.

75 In 1973, business conditions: Chalmers Johnson, *MITI and the Japanese Miracle,* pp. 294–300.

76 The people wanted a "firm determination": "Premier Clings to His Style," *JT,* November 29, 1973.

76 By early 1974, Tanaka's grandiose: "Tanaka Promises Forcible Policies to Overcome Crucial National Problems," *DY,* January 22, 1974; Hunziker and Kamimura, *Kakuei Tanaka,* p. 95.

76 disgraced in Southeast Asia: "Tanaka's Troubled Trip," *Newsweek,* international edition, January 21, 1974, pp. 12–3; "The Ruined Visit," *Newsweek,* international edition, January 28, 1974, pp. 8–9.

76 A group of young right-wing politicians: "Blue Storm over Japan," *Time,* international edition, March 18, 1974.

77 "Some call him mini-Hitler": "Choice from the Weeklies: Some Call Him Mini-Hitler Now," *JT,* May 14, 1973, quoting *Shūkan Asahi,* May 18, 1973.

77 "His face shows": "Tanaka in Difficulties: Premier Fails to Meet People's Trust with 'Decision and Action,' " *JT,* January 31, 1974.

77 Major banks, automakers, and steel producers: "Big Business Pulling Strings in Poll," *JT,* June 16, 1974.

78 "The trend of money-based politics": " 'Tanaka-Fukuda' Vision Competition: Ranging from Political Posture to Operation of the Economy," *Nihon Keizai Shimbun,* May 13, 1974, trans. in *Daily Summary of Japanese Press,* American Embassy, May 16, 1974, p. 30.

78 "gold-studded background": Tachibana, "Kakuei Tanaka: His Money & His Men," part 4, October 31, 1974.

78 the authors typically cited: Ibid.

78 "Was there a connection": Ibid.

79 "It is regrettable": "Tanaka Shrugs Off His Detractors," *MDN,* October 23, 1974.

79 "to stay out of legal prosecution": "Premier's Integrity Questioned," *MDN,* October 24, 1974.

79 "He should have been critical": "'Almighty Money' Caused Tanaka's Fall," *DY,* November 27, 1974.

79 When Tanaka promised: "Will Honesty Pay?," *AEN,* January 23, 1974.

79 "Let's kill Tanaka's [$3,000] carp": "Japan: Up, Up and Away," *Newsweek,* January 7, 1974, p. 35.

80 During a state banquet: Tanaka Kakuei gurūpu, *Tanaka Kakuei saihyōka,* pp. 107–8.

80 "I am in a serene": "A Serene State of Mind," *MDN,* November 27, 1974.

80 "I have not rested": "Tanaka Statement," *DY,* November 27, 1974; "Full Text of Prime Minister Tanaka's Resignation Statement," *Nihon Keizai Shimbun,* evening edition, November 26, 1974, trans. in *Daily Summary of Japanese Press,* American Embassy, November 28–29, 1974, p. 8.

81 "I must have been possessed": Hayano, "Mite kiite hanashita 'Kaku-san' no sugao," pp. 14–5.

Chapter Six: Arrested

82 one suspicious land deal: "Probe of Tanaka's Klondike," *MDN,* September 14, 1975; "Tanaka Money Problem," *AEN,* September 15, 1975.

82 A criminal case, meanwhile: "2 of Tanaka's Henchmen Plead Guilty," *MDN,* October 30, 1975; "2 Tanaka Aides Found Guilty," *JT,* December 13, 1975.

82 the only penalty: "Tanaka Will Have to Pay 40 Million Yen in Tax Arrears," *JT,* March 10, 1975.

83 "He is still young": "Inside the Weeklies," *JT,* February 3, 1975, quoting Sunday *Mainichi.*

83 Then "Tanaka's money veins": Description of the Lockheed scandal from daily Japanese press accounts as the scandal was unfolding, and three lengthy English-language accounts: Larry Warren Fisher, *The Lockheed Affair: A Phenomenon of Japanese Politics;* A. Carl Kotchian, *Lockheed Sales Mission—70 Days in Tokyo;* Shaplen, "Annals of Crime: The Lockheed Incident," *The New Yorker,* January 23, 1978, pp. 48–74, and January 30, 1978, pp. 74–91.

83 nearly four hundred: Fisher, *The Lockheed Affair,* p. 109.

83 when Prime Minister Miki: Ibid., p. 103.

84 Now two representatives: "Tanaka Shokku: Black Mist at the Top," *Time,* international edition, August 9, 1976, p. 10; Shaplen, "Annals of Crime," January 30, 1978, pp. 74–5.

84 "We are very sorry": Shaplen, "Annals of Crime," January 30, 1978, p. 75.

84 "Please take care of yourself": "Ketchaku mizu ni itta munen" (Regrets that he died without resolution), *Aera,* December 27, 1993, p. 14.

84 "pig-box": Murray Sayle, "Big Boss to the Pig-box," *The Spectator,* October 13, 1983.

84 Hiro Hiyama . . . had come calling: Shaplen, "Annals of Crime," January 23, 1978, p. 48.

85 called the ANA president: Kotchian, *Lockheed Sales Mission,* pp. 216–7; Fisher, *The Lockheed Affair,* pp. 81–2; Shaplen, "Annals of Crime," January 30, 1978, p. 77.

85 in four installments: Details of the transaction from: Shaplen, "Annals of Crime," January 30, 1978, p. 77; Fisher, *The Lockhead Affair,* pp. 95–6.

85 One Japanese commentator scoffed: "Kakuei Tanaka Indicted for Taking Lockheed Bribes," *DY,* August 17, 1976.

85 "The nation was shocked": "Restore Faith in Democracy," *DY,* July 28, 1976.

86 Crowds gathered in a downtown park: Details of the public reaction come from: "Tanaka Arrest Takes Japan by Surprise," *DY,* July 31, 1976; " 'Tanaka, Commit Harakiri!,' " *MDN,* August 19, 1976; "Japan: Shame by Association," *Time,* March 22, 1976, p. 26.

86 The most bizarre response came: Fisher, *The Lockheed Affair,* p. 117.

86 "The Lockheed scandal has rocked": Shaplen, "Annals of Crime," January 30, 1978, p. 90.

87 The scandal's fallout even forced: Fisher, *The Lockheed Affair,* pp. 133, 136.

87 "establish a climate in which": Shaplen, "Annals of Crime," January 23, 1978, p. 54.

87 Kodama had apparently pulled off: Johnson, "Tanaka Kakuei," p. 14.

87 That a man such as Kodama: Details on Kodama come mainly from: Tachibana, *Kyoaku vs. genron,* pp. 366–407; Jim Hougan, "The Business of Buying Friends," pp. 58–9; Fisher, *The Lockheed Affair,* pp. 39–43.

88 The very night before: Fisher, *The Lockheed Affair,* p. 119.

88 his friends in the police: Shaplen, "Annals of Crimes," January 30, 1978, p. 85.

88 "The whole LDP and its traditional": "Scandal, 'Tanaka Factor,' and LDP," *JT,* July 31, 1976.

88 "All of the evils accumulated": "Tanaka Arrested," *MDN,* July 28, 1976.

88 "I think you should recognize": Shaplen, "Annals of Crime," January 23, 1978, p. 66.

88 "I thought [such] rampant": Fisher, *The Lockheed Affair,* p. 219.

88 "RAGS TO RICHES": "Rags to Riches to Jail," *JT,* August 1, 1976.

88 For twenty-one days: "Tanaka Shokku: Black Mist at the Top," *Time,* international edition, August 9, 1976, p. 13; "Jailed Tanaka's Spirits Reportedly Bearing Up," *JT,* July 29, 1976.

89 His longtime chauffeur, prodded: Hunziker and Kamimura, *Kakuei Tanaka,* p. 113.

89 The ritual public humiliation peaked: "Tanaka, Ex-Marubeni Executives on Trial: Former Prime Minister Denies Getting Bribes from Lockheed," *JT*, January 28, 1977; "Tanaka, on Stand, Denies Accepting Bribe by Lockheed," *The New York Times*, January 28, 1977; "Tanaka on Trial," *AEN*, January 29, 1977; Shaplen, "Annals of Crime," January 30, 1978, p. 82; Tachibana, *Kyoaku vs. genron*, pp. 56–61.

89 "The foundations of this establishment-oriented": Shaplen, "Annals of Crime," January 30, 1978, pp. 86, 91.

90 a "springboard": "Tanaka Arrested," *MDN*, July 28, 1976.

90 "This is an opportunity": "Sanin Rokkiido tokubetsui shōhō; sossen shite seiji fushin kaishō, shushō ga hyōmei" (Detailed report of Upper House Special Committee on Lockheed; PM vows to take lead in removing distrust of politics), *Mainichi Shimbun*, evening edition, July 28, 1976.

PART TWO

The "Shadow Shogun of Mejiro": Building a National Machine, 1976–1985

93 Every Wednesday morning: Description of the court scene from: Fumiaki Fukuda, *Tanaka Kakuei: Harikomi satsuei nisshi 1974–1993*, pp. 36–48; Tachibana, *Kyoaku vs. genron*, p. 179.

93 "seriously damaged popular trust": "The Prosecution's Demands," *AEN*, January 28, 1983.

93 But for the rest: Description of Tanaka's Mejiro routine from: Kōichi Yamamoto, *Tanaka Kakuei zen kiroku: mitchaku ni nen han, ni man katto kara no hōkoku*, chap. 7; "Tanaka," *Pureibōi*, pp. 51, 53, 58, 65; "Tanaka hikoku no iken chinjitsu"; (Statement by defendant Tanaka), *Asahi Shimbun*, January 28, 1977; E. S. Browning, "Shadow Shogun: Japan's Kakuei Tanaka Retains Great Power Although in Disgrace; The Former Prime Minister Controls Party Machinery, Bestows Favors on Friends; Holding Court for Supplicants," *The Wall Street Journal*, December 20, 1984; "Tanaka Wields Political Power Years After Resignation," *Asian Wall Street Journal*, May 5, 1981; "Interview: Kakuei Tanaka. 'The Seventh Fleet Will Protect Us,' " *Newsweek*, international edition, May 4, 1981, p. 52; "Yomiuri sunpyō" (Yomiuri comment), *Yomiuri Shimbun*, July 5, 1972; *Niigata Nippō*, ed., *Za Etsuzankai*, pp. 97–8.

94 "Visiting Tanaka at his home": Author interview with Kōzō Watanabe, June 9, 1984.

94 Tanaka boasted to one visitor: *Nihon Keizai Shimbunsha*, ed., *Jimintō seichōkai*, p. 64.

94 "Some people are": Sakamoto, "Ningen Tanaka Kakuei," p. 51.

95 "conveyor belt": "Tanaka hikoku no iken chinjutsu" (Statement by defendant Tanaka), *Asahi Shimbun*, January 28, 1977.

Chapter Seven:
Back to the Snow Country

97 "the stern judgment of the public": "Tanaka Hints in Article He May Seek Reelection," *JT,* October 20, 1976.

97 "The battle of the century": "Tanaka and Election—Etsuzankai: Kakuei's Party, Not the LDP's," *AEN,* November 13, 1976.

97 It had been thirteen years: This account of Tanaka's 1976 campaign comes from: Kobayashi, *Kakuei ichidai,* pp. 160–4; *Niigata Nippō,* ed., *Kakuei no fūdo,* pp. 9–11, 165; "Tanaka and the 'Lockheed Election,' " *The Washington Post,* December 5, 1976; Akio Igarashi, "Daigishi kōenkai no seishinteki soshikiteki kōzō," p. 79.

98 "I do not think it appropriate": *Niigata Nippō,* ed., *Za Etsuzankai,* pp. 292–4.

98 Local schoolteachers had been mortified: "It's Business as Usual in Tanaka's Home District," Kyodo News Service, in *JT,* September 3, 1976.

98 The sharpest harangues: "Tanaka Makes Wrong Move," *DY,* October 21, 1976; "Tanaka's Candidacy," *MDN,* October 23, 1976; "As I See It," *AEN,* November 19, 1976.

98 "He must stop": Kobayashi, *Kakuei ichidai,* p. 165.

99 The Etsuzankai's campaign leaflets: "Tanaka and Election: Campaign Manager and Publisher of 'Etsuzan,' " *AEN,* November 12, 1976.

99 "People over there have never": Saki, *Etsuzan Tanaka Kakuei,* pp. 19–21.

99 "I will apologize": Kobayashi, *Kakuei ichidai,* p. 163.

99 "Tanaka *sensei,* banzai!": " 'Ro-jiken yori jisseki': Etsuzankai kansei" (Putting actual achievements above Lockheed: Etsuzankai's shouts of joy), *Asahi Shimbun,* December 6, 1976.

99 these results "purified" him: Kobayashi, *Kakuei ichidai,* p. 166.

99 One poll taken: Michael Blaker, "Conservatives in Crisis," p. 18.

100 Tanaka's standard 1976 stump speech: Tanaka's discussion of the Lockheed case during the 1976 campaign comes from: *Niigata Nippō,* ed., *Kakuei no fūdo,* pp. 9–11; "Tanaka and the 'Lockheed Election,' " *The Washington Post,* December 5, 1976; "Tanaka Hints in Article He May Seek Reelection," *JT,* October 20, 1976.

100 "By your help twenty years ago": "Tanaka and the 'Lockheed Election,' " *The Washington Post,* December 5, 1976.

100 if the parent had not: "Niigata Psyche: Behind Tanaka's Overwhelming Victory," *AEN,* December 16, 1976.

100 His best applause lines: *Niigata Nippō,* ed., *Kakuei no fūdo,* p. 163; Tetsuya Chikushi, *Nipponjin haiken,* p. 40.

100 "Our voters are told": Eiichi Katō, "Toshi no fukushū," p. 22.

100 Tanaka bestowed favors: Description of Etsuzankai operations from: "Tanaka and Election—Etsuzankai: Kakuei's Party, Not the LDP's," *AEN,* November 13, 1976; *Niigata Nippō,* ed., *Za Etsuzankai,* pp. 91–3; *Asahi Shimbun* Niigata Shikyoku, ed., *Tanaka Kakuei to Etsuzankai,* pp. 22–3; Junnosuke Masumi, *Contemporary Politics in Japan,* p. 243.

101 "assisting people to make": Tachibana, *Kyoaku vs. genron,* pp. 284–6.

101 "I learned from the Boy Scouts": *Niigata Nippō,* ed., *Za Etsuzankai,* p. 97.

101 Tanaka called the top-ranking: Browning, "Shadow Shogun"; author inteviews in Niigata.

101 Tanaka was a pragmatic politician: "Tanaka and Election—Etsuzankai: Kakuei's Party, Not the LDP's," *AEN,* November 13, 1976; Kobayashi, *Kakuei ichidai,* pp. 28–31.

102 It was the Etsuzankai: Masumi, *Contemporary Politics in Japan,* p. 242; "It's Business as Usual in Tanaka's Home District," Kyodo News Service, in *JT,* September 3, 1976.

102 The people in: *Niigata Nippō,* ed., *Kakuei no fūdo,* pp. 48–9; author interviews in Niigata; *Niigata Nippō,* ed., *Za Etsuzankai,* pp. 192–3; Kobayashi, *Kakuei ichidai,* pp. 40–4.

102 communities often competed: *Niigata Nippō,* ed., *Za Etsuzankai,* pp. 189–90; "Tanaka and Election—Etsuzankai: Kakuei's Party, Not the LDP's" *AEN,* November 13, 1976.

102 "we have somehow accomplished sixty percent": "Tanaka," *Pureibōi,* p. 58.

103 "there will be a flow": Saki, *Etsuzan Tanaka Kakuei,* pp. 19–21.

103 "This is the last thing": *Asahi Shimbun* Niigata Shikyoku, ed., *Tanaka Kakuei to Etsuzankai,* p. 131.

103 By 1983: Johnson, "Tanaka Kakuei," p. 8; "Why Is Tanaka Still Popular?," *JT,* September 29, 1983; Calder, *Crisis and Compensation,* p. 28.

103 by the early 1980s: Johnson, "Tanaka Kakuei," p. 9; Calder, *Crisis and Compensation,* p. 281; Hunziker and Kamimura, *Kakuei Tanaka,* pp. 85–6, 102; *Niigata Nippō,* ed., *Za Etsuzankai,* pp. 310–12.

103 The supplicants of Ojiya: *Niigata Nippō,* ed., *Kakuei no fūdo,* pp. 53–7; "Why Is Tanaka Still Popular?," *JT,* September 29, 1983.

104 "Let's do bullet trains": Ochiai and Hino, "Tanaka Kakuei to seiji shinkansen," pp. 76–87; *Niigata Nippō,* ed., *Za Etsuzankai,* pp. 278–9.

104 The Niigata bullet-train line: "Tanaka's Express," *AEN,* November 19, 1982; Hunziker and Kamimura, *Kakuei Tanaka,* pp. 90–1; Miya, "Harsh Snow-country Environment," p. 23.

104 "The length of the platform": "In the Bullet's Path—A Town in the 'Snow Country' Catches the Train," *The Boston Globe,* February 12, 1985.

104 The Etsuzankai—founded in the 1950s: Description of the evolution and spread of the Etsuzankai from: Masayuki Fukuoka, "Naze tsuyoi Kakuei seiji," pp. 33–9; *Niigata Nippō,* ed., *Za Etsuzankai,* pp. 77–86; *Asahi Shimbun* Niigata Shikyoku, ed., *Tanaka Kakuei to Etsuzankai,* pp. 22–3; Terry MacDougall, "The Lockheed Scandal and the High Cost of Politics in Japan," p. 218; "Tanaka and Election—Etsuzankai: Kakuei's Party, Not the LDP's," *AEN,* November 13, 1976; Johnson, "Tanaka Kakuei," p. 5; Masumi, *Contemporary Politics in Japan,* pp. 242–3; author interviews in Niigata.

105 "virtually controls": "Tanaka and Election—Etsuzankai: Kakuei's Party, Not the LDP's," *AEN*, November 13, 1976.

105 The law enforcement agencies: Akiko Satō, *Watashi no Tanaka Kakuei nikki*, p. 159.

105 "Those who do not join": *Niigata Nippō*, ed., *Za Etsuzankai*, pp. 195–9.

105 "Tanaka *sensei* is the politician": "Tanaka Certain to Enter Election," *MDN*, September 16, 1976; Kobayashi, *Kakuei ichidai*, p. 161.

106 according to a poll, 75 percent: "Why is Tanaka Still Popular?," *JT*, September 29, 1983.

106 "It is the destiny of someone: Hayano, "Mite kiite hanashita 'Kaku-san' no sugao," p. 14.

Chapter Eight: Bags of Money

108 "Politics is power": *Niigata Nippō*, ed., *Za Etsuzankai*, p. 330.

108 The government salary for MPs: Curtis, *The Japanese Way of Politics*, pp. 175–83; Fisher, *The Lockheed Affair*, pp. 191–2.

109 Tight campaign restrictions: Curtis, *The Japanese Way of Politics*, pp. 170–2; Fisher, *The Lockheed Affair*, p. v; Thayer, *How the Conservatives Rule Japan*, pp. 122–3.

109 a "bullet": Tachibana, "Kakuei Tanaka: His Money & His Men," part 2, October 29, 1974; Johnson, "Tanaka Kakuei," p. 11.

109 "The reason we lost": Thayer, *How the Conservatives Rule Japan*, p. 173.

109 "You can't put the septic": Takashi Tachibana, "My Nine Years With Kakuei Tanaka; Greeting Money Veins-Lockheed Trial and 'Tanaka Verdict,' " p. 37.

110 Eisaku Sato willingly shared: Itō, *Jimintō sengokushi*, vol. 1, p. 29; Miya, "Money Provides Power Source," p. 18; Shirō Matsumoto, "Tanaka-ha wa ijō bōchō buttai de aru: Shijō saikyō no gundan ga busō kaijo sareru toki," pp. 114–15.

110 "by money": *Niigata Nippō*, ed., *Za Etsuzankai*, pp. 138–40.

110 maintained personal control: Shirō Matsumoto, "Tanaka-ha," pp. 114–5.

110 That was also one way: "Tanaka Election, Nanoka Kai Watchwords: 'Giri,' and 'Ninjo,' " *AEN*, November 11, 1976; "Focus on Japanese Politics," *AEN*, September 21, 1976.

110 "I am called the governor": Hayasaka, *"Tanaka Kakuei" kaisōroku*, p. 312.

110 all factions provided members: Tachibana, *Tanaka Kakuei kenkyū*, p. 111; Tachibana, *Kyoaku vs. genron*, p. 183; Kenji Utsumi, *Soredemo Tanaka Kakuei wa fumetsu de aru*, pp. 202, 238; "Inside the Weeklies," *JT*, February 3, 1975; "Tanaka and Money," *AEN*, August 19, 1976.

110 "Perhaps you need this": "Kinken, yaburareta seiyaku: Zushitto omoi kanshoku" (Money-oriented, broken promises: The heavy touch),

Mainichi Shimbun, July 26, 1983; "Kinken, yaburareta seiyaku: 'Kimi wa uchi da' " (Money-oriented, broken promises: "You are with us"), *Mainichi Shimbun,* July 27, 1983; "Kinken, yaburareta seiyaku: Makaritōru gorioshi" (Money-oriented, broken promises: Pushing his way through), *Mainichi Shimbun,* July 28, 1983.

110 "When I said I hadn't": Tachibana, *Kyoaku vs. genron,* p. 183.

111 Tanaka had paid 700 million yen: Ibid., p. 98; Itō, *Jimintō Sengokushi,* vol. 3, p. 166.

111 Another LDP elder: Tachibana, *Kyoaku vs. genron,* p. 77.

111 "There were rumors": T. Fukuda, *Kaiko kyūjū nen,* p. 202.

111 Tanaka was said: Tachibana, "Kakuei Tanaka: His Money & His Men," part 1, October 28, 1974; "Tanaka's Rise to Riches Stirs Controversy in Japan," *The Washington Post,* October 19, 1974; "Tanaka Shokku: Black Mist at the Top," *Time,* August 9, 1976, p. 12.

111 As premier, Tanaka continued: "Oct. 12—Day of Judgment for Money Politics: Philosophy of Settling Things with Money," *MDN,* October 11, 1983; Fisher, *The Lockheed Affair,* p. 204; Tachibana, *Kyoaku vs. genron,* p. 211.

111 "the money flows by [Tanaka]": Kichiya Kobayashi, *Ningen Tanaka Kakuei,* pp. 185–7.

111 "It's not that Tanaka made": Author interview with Kiichi Miyazawa, May 31, 1994.

111 "Distribute this at once": Tachibana, "My Nine Years with Kakuei Tanaka," p. 29.

112 When the wife: Tachibana, *Kyoaku vs. genron,* p. 251.

112 Attempting to persuade: Keiji Shima, *Shimageji fūunroku: hōsō to kenryoku, 40 nen,* pp. 159–60.

112 "to the level where we": Author interview with Hayasaka, April 4, 1994.

112 "The most difficult thing": Hayasaka, *"Tanaka Kakuei" kaisōroku,* pp. 89–90.

112 Tanaka understood that any reluctance: Tachibana, *Kyoaku vs. genron,* p. 252; "Tanaka Election, Nanoka Kai Watchwords: 'Giri,' and 'Ninjo,' " *AEN,* November 11, 1976.

112 "When are you coming back?": Author interview with Kiichi Miyazawa.

112 "I was expecting that Kaku-san": Hayasaka, *"Tanaka Kakuei" kaisōroku,* p. 91.

113 Another MP: Shirō Matsumoto, "Tanaka-ha," p. 118; Kobayashi, *Ningen Tanaka Kakuei,* pp. 188–9.

Chapter Nine: "Politics Is Power, Power Is Numbers"

114 "The Tanaka *gundan*'s speedy response": Yamamoto, *Tanaka Kakuei zen kiroku,* chap. 9.

115 "Even a new guy": Author interview with Fumio Ikeuchi, *Asahi Shimbun,* June 14, 1994.

115 When Iwao Matsuda: Author interview with Iwao Matsuda, June 9, 1994.

115 Hajime Funada came: Author interview with Hajime Funada, July 15, 1994.

115 The other significant benefit: Account of Tanaka faction activity in elections from: "Tanaka and the Lockheed Trial: Money Reigns Supreme over the Political World," *DY,* October 3, 1983; author interview with Ikeuchi; "Tanaka Still Shows Strong Influence," *JT,* May 19, 1983; "Charisma Ups Tanaka Power Despite Scar," *JT,* January 23, 1983; Browning, "Shadow Shogun"; "Tanaka," *Pureibōi,* p. 51.

115 "Sixty percent of my life": "Tanaka," *Pureibōi,* p. 49.

116 "I am sure": *Niigata Nippō* Hōdōbu, ed., *Tanaka no shinjitsu,* p. 104.

116 Kishiro Nakamura worked: " 'Tanaka gata seiji' ga teiryū ni" (Tanaka-style politics is the undercurrent), *Asahi Shimbun,* April 1, 1994.

116 Every summer in the resort town: Yamamoto, *Tanaka Kakuei zen kiroku,* chap. 9.

116 When Yukio Hatoyama decided: Author interview with Yukio Hatoyama, June 7, 1994.

116 "We do not have": *Niigata Nippō* Hōdōbu, ed., *Tanaka no shinjitsu,* p. 107.

117 "My biggest sales point": Author interview with Kazuo Aichi, May 19, 1994.

117 "When I campaign for someone,": "Interview with Kakuei Tanaka (Part 2)—Expansion of Tanaka Faction," *Sankei Shimbun,* August 10, 1981, trans. in *Daily Summary of Japanese Press,* American Embassy, August 21, 1981, p. 16; "Tanaka," *Pureibōi,* p. 52.

117 In several districts: "Tanaka gundan: Medatsu fushin" (The Tanaka *gundan:* distinct depression), *Asahi Shimbun,* July 12, 1977.

117 "The Tanaka *gundan* . . . is in": Ibid.

118 "I felt some doubt": Author interview with Funada.

118 "A man of immediate use": "Pork Barrel for Votes: The Politics of Benefits Gaining Momentum," *AEN,* October 11, 1983.

118 "I decided to become": "I Am the Attraction-drawing Panda"; Defiant Tanaka Says at His First Public Appearance in Odawara," *Mainichi Shimbun,* May 28, 1980, trans. in *Daily Summary of Japanese Press,* American Embassy, May 31–June 2, 1980, p. 13.

118 A campaign rally: "Why Is Tanaka Still Popular?," *JT,* September 29, 1983.

118 One recruit left: "Tanaka Group's Growth: Continues to Put It at the Center of Politics," *AEN,* October 7, 1983.

119 "Even if a politician": Shirō Matsumoto, "Tanaka-ha," pp. 120, 124.

119 Eiichi Nishimura, a longtime Tanaka ally: Tachibana, *Kyoaku vs. genron,* pp. 102–3.

119 only two people quit voluntarily: Shirō Matsumoto, "Tanaka-ha," p. 120.

119 When young *gundan* member Ryutaro Hashimoto: Satō, *Watashi no Tanaka Kakuei nikki,* p. 156.

119 Keisuke Nakanishi, another follower: Author interview with Keisuke Nakanishi, June 22, 1994.

120 "My hobby is Kakuei Tanaka": Yamamoto, *Tanaka Kakuei zen kiroku,* chap. 5; Utsumi, *Soredemo Tanaka Kakuei wa fumetsu de aru,* p. 40.

120 "Tanaka was very sensitive": Author interview with Akira Asaka, July 20, 1994.

120 "Even if [members] say 'no' ": Yamamoto, *Tanaka Kakuei zen kiroku,* chap. 9; "Tanaka," *Pureibōi,* pp. 54–5.

120 "Our faction will turn right": "Political Scene: Tanaka Retains 'Kingmaking Power,' " *Japan Economic Journal,* May 22, 1984.

120 "If all these members": "Tanaka Still Shows Strong Influence," *JT,* May 19, 1983.

120 "The power structure of the LDP": Minoru Shimizu, "Why Tanaka Still Has Political Influence," *JT,* July 10, 1980.

120 "The might of the Tanaka *gundan*": "Tanaka-Fukuda War to Continue in '83," *JT,* December 2, 1982.

121 "immediately ask, 'what does Mejiro think?' ": Takeo Miki, "Do Not Be Arrogant, Mr. Kakuei Tanaka; I Make Bold to Speak Out Candidly in Order to Defend Japan's Democracy and the Liberal Democratic Party," *Bungei Shunjū,* August 1982, trans. in *Summaries of Selected Japanese Magazines,* American Embassy, September 1982, p. 6.

121 except, in a cheeky gesture: Johnson, "Tanaka Kakuei," p. 16.

121 That did not mean: Description of Tanaka's relationship with prime ministers from: "Illness of Japan's Kingmaker Roils Politics and Weakens Prime Minister Nakasone," *The Wall Street Journal,* May 29, 1985; "Tanaka's Position 5 Years After Scandal," *JT,* July 24, 1981; Masashi Kitakado, *Tanaka Kakuei dai gundan 101 nin,* p. 68; "Former Prime Minister Tanaka Is Dominating the Party; Miki Criticizes Suzuki Cabinet's Posture," *Nihon Keizai Shimbun,* evening edition, June 19, 1982, trans. in *Daily Summary of Japanese Press,* American Embassy, June 24, 1982, p. 13.

122 "He is acting": "Inside Nagatacho," *AEN,* August 24, 1979.

122 "just a hat": "Tanaka Refuses to Quit," *AEN,* October 31, 1983.

122 Tanaka compared himself: Browning, "Shadow Shogun."

122 he was akin: "Interview with Kakuei Tanaka (Part 2)—Expansion of Tanaka Faction," *Sankei Shimbun,* August 10, 1981, trans. in *Daily Summary of Japanese Press,* American Embassy, August 21, 1981, p. 16; "Interview with Kakuei Tanaka," *Yomiuri Shimbun,* June 21, 1981, trans. in *Daily Summary of Japanese Press,* American Embassy, June 27–29, 1981, p. 16.

122 After Suzuki made a serious: "Interview with Kakuei Tanaka," *Yomiuri Shimbun,* June 21, 1981, trans. in *Daily Summary of Japanese Press,* American Embassy, June 27–29, 1981, p. 9.

122 Nakasone, he complained: "Tanaka," *Pureibōi,* p. 62.

122 "Nakasone may be": "Ailing, Hurt by Scandal, Japan's Tanaka Faces a New Struggle in Party," *Los Angeles Times,* May 18, 1985.

122 They called themselves: Masumi, *Contemporary Politics in Japan,* p. 196.

123 "How would you answer": "Fundamental Question," *AEN,* November 4, 1982.

123 "Politicians are now faced": Ibid.

123 "I want to be": Utsumi, *Soredemo Tanaka Kakuei,* p. 91.

123 "with Tanaka we always win": "From the Japanese Magazines: Tanaka: 'Man of the Year,' " *MDN,* November 5, 1983.

124 "I am fully aware": "Tanaka Casts Shadow over Ohira Regime?," *JT,* December 14, 1978.

124 "It is only the newspapers": "Former Prime Minister Tanaka Is Dominating the Party; Miki Criticizes Suzuki Cabinet's Posture," *Nihon Keizai Shimbun,* evening edition, June 19, 1982, trans. in *Daily Summary of Japanese Press,* American Embassy, June 24, 1982, p. 13.

124 Nakasone claimed: "Nakasone Reveals His Intention to Up Nation's Defense Capability," *JT,* November 28, 1982.

124 "Reign of Kakueiism": Vox Populi, Vox Dei, "Reign of Kakueiism," *AEN,* December 6, 1982.

124 Tanaka's disposable bathroom tissue: TV anchor Tetsuya Chikushi, quoted in Tachibana, *Kyoaku vs. genron,* p. 202.

124 "We concluded we must see him": "Tanaka," *Pureibōi,* p. 47.

124 Deng Xiaoping, made sure to take: "Teng's Courtesy Call: Almost a Great Day for Tanaka," *MDN,* October 25, 1978.

124 On January 1, 1981: Description of New Year's party from: "Gantan wa senkyakubanrai!!" (Flood of guests on New Year's day!!), *Shūkan Yomiuri,* January 18, 1981, pp. 27–8; "Aa! Koko ga futatabi Nihon o ugokasunoka!" (Oh dear! This place is going to move Japan again!), *Sandē Mainichi,* January 18, 1981, pp. 16–22; "Why Does Tanaka Still Maintain Power?," *JT,* January 8, 1981.

124 Two weeks later, when Tanaka collapsed: Description of Tanaka's collapse and others' reaction come from: "Sōryoku Shuzai! 'Tanaka Kakuei taoru' no shōgeki!" (All-out coverage! The shock of 'Kakuei Tanaka's collapse'!), *Shūkan Gendai,* January 29, 1981, pp. 32–5; "Kinkyū tokuhō: 'Kakuei taoru!' de seikai o hashiraseta yami shōgun no iryoku" (Emergency special report: The influence of the shadow shogun who made the political world scramble with the news 'Kakuei's collapse'!), *Shūkan Asahi,* January 23, 1981, pp. 159–61; "Tanaka moto shushō taoreru; jitaku de ichiji kokyū konnan" (Ex–prime minister Tanaka collapses; momentarily had difficulty breathing at his home), *Asahi Shimbun,* evening edition, January 12, 1981; "Kaku-san shokku rankōge, igaini tsumetai zaikai hannō mo" (Kaku-san shock violent fluctuation, unexpectedly cool reaction from business world), *Yomiuri Shimbun,* January 13, 1981.

125 "If Tanaka has health problems": " 'Yami shōgun' no chikara mazamaza" (The influence of "shadow shogun" was clearly seen), *Yomiuri Shimbun,* January 13, 1981.

Chapter Ten: The Loyal Opposition

126 "We have heard": "Tanaka," *Pureibōi,* p. 53.

127 "A farmer's viewpoint will change": *Niigata Nippō,* ed., *Kakuei no fūdo,* pp. 252–61.

127 "We must manage the party": Curtis, *The Japanese Way of Politics,* p. 132.

127 "political coach": Description of Tanaka's relations with Komeito from: Hirotatsu Fujiwara, *Tanaka Kakuei: Godfather of Japan,* pp. 66–8; Junya Yano, "Seikai shikakenin gokuhi memo zen kōkai" (Full revelations of top-secret memos of political world fixer), *Bungei Shunjū,* October 1993, p. 104; Satō, *Watashi no Tanaka Kakuei nikki,* p. 75.

128 "looked after these parties": Author interview with Hayasaka.

128 "At the end of each year": Hideo Yamahana, former vice chairman of Socialist Party Central Committee, "Gyōkai kenkin kotowaru kibishisa o" (Getting strict on refusing contributions from industrial world), *Asahi Shimbun,* July 28, 1976.

128 As an LDP executive: Description of Tanaka's relations with the opposition parties comes from: "Kesareta gijiroku: Kokkai no yamaba ni shūchū" (Deleted minutes of proceedings: Concentrating on the climax of parliament session), *Mainichi Shimbun,* August 10, 1983; "Kesareta gijiroku: Hōkandan no hiyō mo?" (Deleted minutes of proceedings: The expenses of delegates to South Korea, too?), *Mainichi Shimbun,* August 11, 1983; "Kesareta gijiroku: Shushō ga 'te wa utta' " (Deleted minutes of proceedings: The prime minister said, "I've worked on that"), *Mainichi Shimbun,* August 12, 1983; "Nagatachō no urakanshū: Kokutai rūru no mājan" (Nagatacho's behind-the-scene customs: Mah-jongg played under Parliament's steering committee rules), *Mainichi Shimbun,* August 25, 1983; "Nagatachō no ura kanshū: Nichijō teki ni kane o maku" (Nagatacho's behind-the-scene customs: Spending money on a daily basis), *Mainichi Shimbun,* August 26, 1983; "Nagatachō no ura kanshū: Bakuro jiken irai, inshitsu ni" (Nagatacho's behind-the-scene customs: Becoming secretive since exposure), *Mainichi Shimbun,* August 31, 1983; Tachibana, "My Nine Years with Kakuei Tanaka," pp. 29–30.

128 "The days of Tanaka's cabinet": "Fuhai no rūtsu: Kyūzō yahari, ano jidai" (The roots of corruption: It surged since that era, as one can imagine), *Mainichi Shimbun,* September 16, 1983.

128 "nobody could deny": Author interview with Hajime Tamura, June 7, 1994; Hajime Tamura, *Seijika no shōtai,* p. 219.

128 "I have criticized": "Nagatachō no ura kanshū: Kojin teki kōsai no waku koe" (Nagatacho's behind-the-scene customs: Beyond the framework of private friendship), *Mainichi Shimbun,* August 27, 1983.

128 "felt indebted": Junya Yano, "Seikai shikakenin gokuhi memo zen kōkai" (Full revelations of top-secret memos of political world fixer), *Bungei Shunjū,* October 1993, p. 104; Satō, *Watashi no Tanaka Kakuei nikki,* p. 75.

129 The 1969 Parliament showed: Ellis S. Krauss, "Conflict in the Diet: Toward Conflict Management in Parliamentary Politics," pp. 249–50; Hayasaka, *Seijika Tanaka Kakuei,* p. 227.

129 "widespread and justifiable concern": Krauss, "Conflict in the Diet," p. 429.

129 By the late 1970s: Seizaburo Sato and Tetsuhisa Matsuzaki, "The Liberal Democrats' Conciliatory Reign," *Economic Eye,* December 1985, pp. 29–30.

129 "It will be difficult": "People in the Spotlight: Tanaka Kakuei," *Japan Quarterly,* April–June 1979, p. 203.

130 "Let's decide the script": Tamura, *Seijika no shōtai,* p. 136.

130 "It's normal," Shigezō Hayasaka, *Saishō no utsuwa,* pp. 110–1.

Chapter Eleven: General Hospital

131 "Tanaka served": Tachibana, *Kyoaku vs. genron,* p. 235.

132 "Exalt the Officials": John Creighton Campbell, "Democracy and Bureaucracy in Japan," p. 114.

132 Japan experienced: Daniel I. Okimoto, *Between MITI and the Market, Japanese Industrial Policy for High Technology,* pp. 216–25.

133 "I am more afraid": *Niigata Nippō,* ed., *Za Etsuzankai,* p. 128.

133 "So far I have been reading": *Niigata Nippō* Hōdōbu, ed., *Tanaka no shinjitsu,* p. 167.

133 Unusual among politicians, Tanaka: Description of Tanaka's early career as a legislator comes from: Chalmers Johnson, "MITI, MPT, and the Telecom Wars: How Japan Makes Policy for High Technology," p. 204; Hayasaka, *Oyaji to watashi,* p. 109; Kobayashi, *Kakuei ichidai,* pp. 70–1; *Nihon Keizai Shimbunsha,* ed., *Jimintō seichōkai,* p. 64.

133 "When a person is addressed": Shirō Matsumoto, "Tanaka-ha," p. 121.

133 At ribbon-cutting ceremonies: *Niigata Nippō,* ed., *Za Etsuzankai,* pp. 270–1.

134 "I know I don't have": Tachibana, *Kyoaku vs. genron,* p. 45.

134 "I am [merely] a graduate": Hayasaka, *Seijika Tanaka Kakuei,* pp. 115, 162.

134 "The trouble with bureaucrats": Katō, "Toshi no fukushū," pp. 20–1.

134 When frugal finance officials: *Asahi Shimbun* Niigata Shikyoku, ed., *Tanaka Kakuei to Etsuzankai,* pp. 202–3.

134 He worked to raise: Calder, "Kanryō vs. Shomin," pp. 10–11.

134 In the summer 1983 parliamentary elections: Tachibana, *Kyoaku vs. genron,* p. 228.

135 At one dedication ceremony: *Niigata Nippō,* ed., *Za Etsuzankai,* pp. 269–70; *Asahi Shimbun* Niigata Shikyoku, ed., *Tanaka Kakuei to Etsuzankai,* pp. 165–6; Kobayashi, *Kakuei ichidai,* p. 90.

135 bringing in boxed meals: Tachibana, *Kyoaku vs. genron,* p. 249.

135 "he paid all our expenses": Shigemasa Chamoto, "Denpa gysōei:

'Tanaka seiji' no kongen" (Broadcast administration: The root of "Tanaka politics"), *Sekai,* March 1983, p. 91.

135 a high-class British clothier: *Nihon Keizai Shimbunsha,* ed., *Kanryō: kishimu kyodai kenryoku,* p. 77.

135 by a factor of ten: Tachibana, *Kyoaku vs. genron,* p. 250.

135 honorary member of their *doki-kai:* Calder, "Kanryo vs. Shomin," p. 11; *Nihon Keizai Shimbunsha,* ed., *Kanryō,* pp. 78–9.

135 "I'm sorry, this one": *Niigata Nippō,* ed., *Za Etsuzankai,* pp. 274–5.

136 "just walk into": Kobayashi, *Kakuei ichidai,* p. 56.

136 His activist term: Description of Tanaka's role in enhancing political influence over the bureaucracy comes from the following sources in general and, in particular, from the specific page numbers cited: *Nihon Keizai Shimbunsha,* ed., *Jimintō seichōkai,* pp. 1–3, 19–20, 101, 123–4, 156–9, 195, 207; Johnson, "MITI, MPT, and the Telecom Wars," pp. 177–240; Takashi Inoguchi and Tomoaki Iwai, *Zoku giin no kenkyū,* pp. 150, 295–304; Utsumi, *Soredemo Tanaka Kakuei wa fumetsu de aru,* pp. 137, 147; Haruhiro Fukui, "The Policy Research Council of Japan's Liberal Democratic Party: Policy Making Role and Practice," pp. 3–30.

136 "High Party, Low Bureaucracy": Inoguchi and Iwai, *Zoku giin no kenkyū,* p. i.

136 " 'LDP-bureaucracy compound' ": Seizaburo Sato and Tetsuhisa Matsuzaki, "Policy Leadership by the Liberal Democrats," *Economic Eye,* December 1984, p. 26.

136 more than half the LDP's: Inoguchi and Iwai, *Zoku giin no kenkyū.*

137 "It's hard to maintain": Hayasaka, *"Tanaka Kakuei" kaisōroku,* pp. 319–20; "Tanaka," *Pureibōi,* p. 53.

137 "the all-expenses-paid geisha": Johnson, "MITI, MPT, and the Telecom Wars," p. 206.

137 assume the mammoth company's presidency: "Executive Refuses Key Job at NTT: Cites Intervention by Japanese 'Political Circles,' " *Los Angeles Times,* March 21, 1985.

137 "I am," Tanaka brazenly pronounced: Sakamoto, "Ningen Tanaka Kakuei," p. 54.

137 "If one is reticent": Masataka Kosaka, "Tanaka jidai no owari ga hajimatta" (The ending of the Tanaka era has begun), *Shokun!,* May 1985, pp. 56–7, cited in Johnson, "Tanaka Kakuei," p. 25.

Chapter Twelve: The Public Works State

138 "Though Mejiro has not": Katō, "Toshi no fukushū," pp. 20–3.

139 "Companies are founded": Raizō Matsuno, *Hosokawa-Ozawa seiken: in-yō no baransu ga kuzureru toki,* pp. 216–7.

139 he once proposed: Tachibana, "Kakuei Tanaka: His Money & His Men," part 2, October 29, 1974.

139 perhaps a procurement order: "Tanaka Forcible 'Donation' Getter," *DY*, July 28, 1976.

139 There was gold, he perceived: Katō, "Toshi no fukushū," pp. 22–3.

140 "I don't want a bribe": "Tanaka Forcible 'Donation' Getter," *DY*, July 28, 1976.

140 he concentrated his men: Inoguchi and Iwai, *Zoku giin no kenkyū*, p. 150.

140 He put his greatest effort: The main published sources for the description of the relationship among the construction industry, Tanaka, the Tanaka faction, and politicians in general are: Brian Woodall, *Japan Under Construction: Corruption, Politics, and Public Works;* Inoguchi and Iwai, *Zoku giin no kenkyū; Nihon Keizai Shimbunsha,* ed., *Jimintō seichōkai;* Gavan McCormack, *The Emptiness of Japanese Affluence*, pp. 25–77; Karel van Wolferen, *The Enigma of Japanese Power*, pp. 114–20; "Bidding for Influence," Kyodo News Service, fourteen-part series, in *JT*, January 28–February 16, 1994; Tatsuya Suwa, *Dangō o ura de ayatsuru yakunin no teguchi;* Kōji Tatesawa, *Kensetsu gyōkai: dangō rettō Nippon.*

141 Beginning in the early 1960s: Woodall, *Japan Under Construction*, p. 29.

141 as a percentage of GNP: Curtis, *The Japanese Way of Politics*, p. 264 note 26; Calder, *Crisis and Compensation*, p. 240.

141 Japan's government spent more: McCormack, *Emptiness of Japanese Affluence*, p. 33.

141 "Asphalt blanketing the mountains": Woodall, *Japan Under Construction*, p. 65.

141 PLEASE BRING PETITIONS IN THE AFTERNOON: *Nihon Keizai Shimbunsha,* ed., *Jimintō seichōkai*, p. 140; van Wolferen, *The Enigma of Japanese Power*, p. 115.

142 collusive bid rigging, or *dangō:* Description of *dangō* and the connection with politicians and political contributions from: Woodall, *Japan Under Construction*, pp. 11, 36–48, 95; Suwa, *Dangō*, pp. 14–61; *Nihon Keizai Shimbunsha,* ed., *Jimintō seichōkai*, pp. 128–9; van Wolferen, *The Enigma of Japanese Power*, pp. 117–9.

142 inflated the cost to taxpayers: Woodall, *Japan Under Construction*, p. 48; p. 166 note 11.

142 The awesome electoral force: Ibid., p. 76; van Wolferen, *The Enigma of Japanese Power*, p. 117.

142 "favored-contractor policy": Woodall, *Japan Under Construction*, p. 114.

143 "He wined, dined": Tachibana, "Kakuei Tanaka: His Money & His Men," part 6, November 2, 1974.

143 Ueki-gumi, which had backed Tanaka: *Niigata Nippō*, ed., *Za Etsuzankai*, pp. 247–52.

143 In Tokyo during those same years: Description of Tanaka's political role supporting construction from: *Nihon Keizai Shimbunsha,* ed., *Jimintō seichōkai*, pp. 64–5, 195–201; Shigezō Hayasaka, "Tanaka Kakuei mumei no jū nen," pp. 372–94; Hayasaka, *Seijika Tanaka Kakuei*, pp. 29–30; Calder, *Crisis and Compensation*, p. 191 note 60.

144 the blueprint called: McCormack, *Emptiness of Japanese Affluence,* p. 54; Woodall, *Japan Under Construction,* p. 110.

144 "For the first category": *Nihon Keizai Shimbunsha,* ed., *Jimintō seichōkai,* p. 196.

144 "I'm always thinking": Sakamoto, "Ningen Tanaka Kakuei," pp. 53–4.

144 Tanaka's cronies in the industry: Description of the role of construction companies in elections from: Tachibana, *Kyoaku vs. genron,* pp. 284–6; *Niigata Nippō,* ed., *Za Etsuzankai,* 244–6; *Nihon Keizai Shimbunsha,* ed., *Jimintō seichōkai,* p. 77; Woodall, *Japan Under Construction,* pp. 76–7, 91–4.

144 "would talk to the construction industry": Author interview with Ikeuchi.

144 Nearly every conservative politician: Description of Tanaka-faction dominance over the construction tribe from: Woodall, *Japan Under Construction,* pp. 76, 110, 112–3; pp. 169–70 note 11; Calder, "Kanryō vs. Shomin," p. 10; *Nihon Keizai Shimbunsha,* ed., *Jimintō seichōkai,* pp. 74–8, 165–8.

145 "A lot of LDP members": "Bidding for Influence," Kyodo News Service, part 5, "LDP Pressure Cowed the Watchdog," February 2, 1994.

145 "Tanaka had his own ideas": Author interview with Noboru Horii, retired Tobishima Construction executive, September 4, 1994.

145 winning contractor delivered a payment: "Bidding for Influence," Kyodo News Service, part 4, "Bid-rigging Became Systematic: Tanaka's Margin Notes Thought to Indicate Kickbacks," February 1, 1994; Suwa, *Dangō,* p. 45; Johnson, "Tanaka Kakuei," p. 25; McCormack, *Emptiness of Japanese Affluence,* p. 38.

145 "Tanaka-san is running": Tachibana, "Kakuei Tanaka: His Money & His Men," part 6, November 2, 1974.

Chapter Thirteen: Court Justice, Political Logic

146 "Tanaka is at once": Susumu Nishibe, "Tanaka Kakuei no shakai teki hiyō," pp. 62–8.

147 "an enormous burden weighing": Hayasaka, *Oyaji to watashi,* p. 189.

147 "fine if I were": Satō, *Watashi no Tanaka Kakuei nikki,* pp. 160–1, 182.

147 "against humanity": Hunziker and Kamimura, *Kakuei Tanaka,* p. 115.

147 "relief from the strained political": "Tanaka the Kingmaker," *Newsweek,* international edition, July 7, 1980.

147 A turning point came: Takashi Tachibana, *Rokkiido saiban to sono jidai,* vol. 2, pp. 287–8; "Zenmen hinin no Tanaka o tsūgeki, Hiyama kyōjutsu, 5 oku en 'misshitsu no yakusoku' ukibori" (Tanaka, who denies everything, hit hard, Hiyama testimony delineates "promise behind closed door"), *Asahi Shimbun,* October 25, 1979.

148 It was late December 1982: Description of Tanaka interrogation from Haruyuki Kawashima, "Sōryoku tokushū dotanba no Kakuei, shuki: 'Sabakareru shushō no hanzai' o egakitsuzukete 6 nen Tanaka Kakuei ga hōtei de miseta igai na 'sugao' " (Six years that I have been continuing to sketch "the crime by prime minister trial": Unexpected "real face" that Kakuei Tanaka showed at trial), *Shūkan Bunshun,* February 3, 1983, pp. 30–3; Kiichirō Kamiya and Takashi Tachibana, "Hōtei de mita 'Mejiro no yami shōgun' taidan" ("Shadow shogun of Mejiro" whom we saw in court), *Shokun!,* March 1983, pp. 42–55.

149 One newspaper poll showed: "'Muzai shucho shinjinu' 8 wari," *Asahi Shimbun,* September 12, 1983.

149 "My eyes stuck out": Hayano, "Mite kiite hanashita 'Kaku-san' no sugao," p. 15.

149 Shortly after entering the courtroom: F. Fukuda, *Tanaka Kakuei: harikomi satsuei nisshi,* p. 68; "Shogun Under a Shadow," *Time,* international edition, October 24, 1983, pp. 8–9.

150 "I won't forgive this": Hayasaka, *"Tanaka Kakuei" kaisōroku,* p. 340.

150 When Tanaka arrived: "Undaunted Tanaka Set to 'Win or Die,' " *DY,* October 13, 1983; Tachibana, *Kyoaku vs. genron,* pp. 254–7; "Shogun Under a Shadow," *Time,* international edition, October 24, 1983, pp. 8–9.

150 Nakasone first sent: Satō, *Watashi no Tanaka Kakuei nikki,* p. 184.

151 The conversation: " 'I'm innocent': Tanaka," *AEN,* November 5, 1983.

151 "indirectly advised": "Nakasone 'Urged' Tanaka to Resign, LDP Panel Told," *DY,* November 2, 1983.

151 "The proposition is utterly outrageous": "Tanaka Refuses to Quit," *AEN,* October 31, 1983.

151 Now it was the voters' chance: Description of 1983 election from: Johnson, "Tanaka Kakuei," pp. 17–8; daily press accounts of the time.

152 Among the *gundan*'s new MPs: "Kingmaker's Son-in-Law Vulnerable on Ethics," *JT,* December 16, 1983.

152 "is still in the people's subconscious": Sakamoto, "Ningen Tanaka Kakuei," p. 52.

152 "a peasant rebellion": Hayano, "Mite kiite hanashita 'Kaku-san' no sugao," p. 15; "Tanaka Scores Massive Win in Niigata," Kyodo News Service, in *DY,* December 20, 1983.

152 "eliminate Kakuei Tanaka's so-called": Browning, "Shadow Shogun."

153 Ozawa huffily rebutted: "Tagawa's Statement," *AEN,* September 20, 1984.

153 Soichiro Honda, the maverick founder: Yamamoto, *Tanaka Kakuei zen kiroku,* chap. 2.

154 *Steal the Wisdom of Kakuei Tanaka:* "New Book Flatters Tanaka," *Japan Times Weekly,* October 13, 1984.

154 "I like Kakuei Tanaka": "Schoolboy Publishes Poem Praising Kakuei Tanaka," Kyodo News Service, in *JT,* October 6, 1984.

154 At a September 1984 speech: Yamamoto, *Tanaka Kakuei zen kiroku,* chap. 4.

154 "People have given up": "Bulldozing Through the Book World," *DY,* December 20, 1983.

154 "The situation is worse": "Tanaka's Influence," *AEN,* October 13, 1984.

154 "In the postwar years": Masumi Ishikawa, "Abnormal Situation: Gov't Here Totally Under Tanaka's Thumb," *AEN,* October 11, 1984.

154 becoming increasingly outspoken: Description of Tanaka at the end of 1984 from: Utsumi, *Soredemo Tanaka Kakuei,* pp. 242–3; Sakamoto, "Ningen Tanaka Kakuei," p. 54; Yamamoto, *Tanaka Kakuei zen kiroku,* chaps. 1, 7; Satō, *Watashi no Tanaka Kakuei nikki,* p. 217.

154 "Although I won't expose": Sakamoto, "Ningen Tanaka Kakuei," p. 55.

155 "In two years, the Lockheed incident": Junya Yano, "Seikai shikakenin gokuhi memo zen kōkai" (Full revelations of top-secret memos of political world fixer), *Bungei Shunjū,* October 1993, p. 101.

155 "I am turning sixty-six": Yamamoto, *Tanaka Kakuei zen kiroku,* chap. 9.

PART THREE
The Second Generation: The "Bubble Politics" of Shin Kanemaru, Noboru Takeshita, and Ichiro Ozawa, 1985–1992

159 "Our people seem to be": "Tanaka Kakuei maboroshi no dokuhaku tēpu dokusen kōkai" (Exclusive disclosure of secret tape of Kakuei Tanaka monologue), *Shūkan Bunshun,* February 24, 1994, p. 176.

159 "We are like snow": "Suzuki an Engineer of the Power Struggle," *AEN,* February 6, 1985.

Chapter Fourteen:
The Odd Couple

161 "I am a hatchet" *Asahi Shimbun* Seijibu, ed., *Tanaka shihai to sono hōkai,* p. 86.

161 "Those two are one": *Asahi Shimbun* Seijibu, ed., *Takeshita ha shihai,* p. 56.

162 the young Kanemaru enjoyed sneaking: Shin Kanemaru, *Hito wa shiro; hito wa ishigaki; hito wa hori,* p. 12.

162 the sons also used: Hyōden Kanemaru Shin Hensankai, ed., *Kanemaru Shin: Saigo no Nihonteki seijika hyōden,* p. 43; author interviews in Shimane.

162 Takeshita's mother, who was influenced: "Japan's Power Broker," *Tokyo Business Today,* December 1987, pp. 17–8; Rei Shiratori, "Takeshita Cautiously Showing Political Colors," *MDN,* October 17, 1988.

162 Kanemaru's mother was a Christian: Shin Kanemaru, *Tachiwaza newaza,* pp. 16–8.

162 In response to tenant farmers': Mamoru Naka, *Kanemaru Shin: newazashi no kenkyū,* pp. 58–9.

162 the twenty-one-year-old Takeshita served: Noboru Takeshita, *The Furusato Concept: Toward a Humanistic and Prosperous Japan,* p. 94.

163 "Good boy": Naka, *Kanemaru Shin,* pp. 54–5.

163 "walking through the entrance": Hyōden Kanemaru Shin Hensankai, ed., *Kanemaru Shin: Saigo no Nihonteki seijika hyōden,* p. 49.

163 A shy child: Kanemaru, *Hito wa shiro,* pp. 20–1.

163 He went on to gain: Hyōden Kanemaru Shin Hensankai, ed., *Kanemaru Shin: Saigo no Nihonteki seijika hyōden,* pp. 45–6.

163 When a cop tried: Kanemaru, *Hito wa shiro,* pp. 38–44.

163 he would often fund his binges: Hyōden Kanemaru Shin Hensankai, ed., *Kanemaru Shin: Saigo no Nihonteki seijika hyōden,* p. 49.

163 a job teaching biology: Ibid., p. 50; Andrew Marshall with Michiko Toyama, "The Man Who Would Be Kingmaker," p. 35.

163 He joked about selling sake: Kanemaru, *Tachiwaza newaza,* p. 44; Jeff Shear, "The Shadow Shogun: In Japan, Shin Kanemaru, a Black Belt in Political Judo, Is the Maker of Kings."

163 "I bought a small Harley": Kanemaru, *Tachiwaza newaza,* p. 51.

163 a district first introduced: Kanemaru, *Hito wa shiro,* p. 27.

164 serving as chief mourner: Ibid., p. 46; Hyōden Kanemaru Shin Hensankai, ed., *Kanemaru Shin: Saigo no Nihonteki seijika hyōden,* pp. 54–5; Marshall, "The Man Who Would be Kingmaker," p. 35; Kanemaru, *Tachiwaza newaza,* p. 46.

164 he slipped, however: Hyōden Kanemaru Shin Hensankai, ed., *Kanemaru Shin: Saigo no Nihonteki seijika hyōden,* pp. 54–5; Marshall, "The Man Who Would Be Kingmaker," p. 35.

164 Kanemaru's sons mainly remember him: Author interviews with Yasunobu Kanemaru, July 12, 1994, and Shingo Kanemaru, September 1, 1994.

164 One of his early, famous acts: Hyōden Kanemaru Shin Hensankai, ed., *Kanemaru Shin: Saigo no Nihonteki seijika hyōden,* p. 55.

164 "I once told him": Author interviews in Yamanashi.

164 "Any other guy": Kanemaru, *Tachiwaza newaza,* p. 46.

164 "There are a lot": Author interviews in Yamanashi.

164 One incident in particular: Kanemaru, *Hito wa shiro,* pp. 57–63; Marshall, "The Man Who Would Be Kingmaker," pp. 32–4.

165 "after that incident I felt": Kanemaru, *Tachiwaza newaza,* p. 59.

165 Hirose urged Kanemaru himself to run: Hyōden Kanemaru Shin Hensankai, ed., *Kanemaru Shin: Saigo no Nihonteki seijika hyōden,* pp. 58–60; Naka, *Kanemaru Shin,* pp. 70–1.

165 As further testimony to Kanemaru's: Author interviews in Yamanashi; Marshall, "The Man Who Would Be Kingmaker," p. 36.

166 "convinced that all sake shops": Marshall, "The Man Who Would Be Kingmaker," p. 35.

166 "I have literally experienced": "Kanemaru: for my Constituency's Sake," *AEN,* March 10, 1993; Kanemaru, *Hito wa shiro,* pp. 69–70.

166 On the stump, the pudgy: Marshall, "The Man Who Would Be Kingmaker," pp. 35–6.

166 "Master of the Draw": Takeshita, *The Furusato Concept,* p. 93; Shigezō Hayasaka, *The Making of a Japanese Prime Minister: How to Become No. 1 in Japan,* p. 36.

166 the nickname "Forehead": "Year of Competition; Character Sketches of New Leaders," *Yomiuri Shimbun,* January 3, 1987, trans. in *Daily Summary of Japanese Press,* American Embassy, January 21, 1987, p. 12.

166 In his boarding school dorm: Damon Darlin, "Japan's Front-Runner Stresses Consensus."

166 When a teacher caught Noboru: Author interviews in Shimane.

166 While Takeshita was enlisted: Hisashi Kikuchi, *Shin Takeshita giwaku no keifu,* pp. 169–95; "Japan's Power Broker," *Tokyo Business Today,* December 1987, p. 18; "Modesty, Consensus-building Are Basic Traits of Japan's New Prime Minister," *Business Japan,* May 1988, p. 25.

167 Takeshita and his fellows: Author interviews in Shimane.

167 He staged mock: "The Compromise Prime Minister," *Japan Quarterly,* January–March 1988, p. 40.

167 During his two terms: Jiji Tsūshinsha Seijibu, ed., *Takeshita sōri zen dēta,* pp. 174–5.

167 The most important political connection: Yasunori Tateishi, "Takeshita Noboru o sōri no za ni oshiageta 'Shimane no sanrinō' " ("King of the mountains and forests," who pushed Noboru Takeshita up to the position of prime minister), *Purejidento,* December 1990.

168 His platform consisted: Noboru Takeshita, *Shōgen hoshu seiken,* p. 11.

168 "We drank most of the time": Jiji Tsūshinsha Seijibu, ed., *Takeshita sōri zen dēta,* pp. 51–2.

168 Kanemaru couldn't pay: Marshall, "The Man Who Would Be Kingmaker," p. 36.

168 "was rich enough": Takeshita, *Shōgen hoshu seiken,* p. 16.

168 Sato handed each of them: Ibid., p. 17; Kanemaru , *Hito wa shiro,* p. 72; Takeshita, *Shōgen hoshu seiken,* p. 17; Marshall, "The Man Who Would Be Kingmaker," p. 36.

169 prime minister's "handyman": Iida, *Takeshita-san ni manabu,* pp. 67–8.

169 Kanemaru, meanwhile, reverted: Kanemaru, *Hito wa shiro,* pp. 86–90; Marshall, "The Man Who Would Be Kingmaker," p. 36.

170 "matching posts": Kanemaru, *Hito wa shiro,* p. 93.

170 The appointment turned out: Author interview with Yasunobu Kanemaru; *Asahi Shimbun* Seijibu, ed., *Takeshita ha shihai,* p. 162.

170 "He knows not only": Author interview with Shingo Kanemaru.

170 "I am a very flexible": Kanemaru, *Tachiwaza newaza,* p. 92.

170 "There must be at least": "Kingmaker's Background Reign," Associated Press, in *DY,* December 3, 1990.

170 "I dislike formalities": Jiji Tsūshinsha Seijibu, ed., *Takeshita sōri zen dēta,* p. 52.

171 a drinking ditty: "Takeshita's Soul-Searching," *AEN,* February 11, 1985; Darlin, "Japan's Front-Runner Stresses Consensus."

Chapter Fifteen: "Ichiro . . . My Lost Son"

172 "To a Tanaka administration!": Eiji Ōshita, *Ichi o motte tsuranuku: ningen Ozawa Ichirō,* p. 139; Christopher Redl, "Curse of the Kingmakers," p. 38.

172 his father—Ichiro's grandfather—had squandered: "Chokugeki Ozawa Ichirō ga kataru: Nihon no koto seiji no koto" (Direct hit Ichiro Ozawa talks: About Japan, about politics), *Sandē Mainichi,* January 2–9, 1994, p. 32; Ichiro Ozawa, "Wareware wa naze kaikaku o mezasu ka," p. 10.

172 When the dissolute elder tried: "Power Behind the Throne: LDP Secretary General Ichiro Ozawa," *Tokyo Business Today,* July 1990, p. 12.

173 made both father and son: "Chokugeki Ozawa Ichirō ga kataru: Nihon no koto, seiji no koto" (Direct hit Ichiro Ozawa talks: About Japan, about politics), *Sandē Mainichi,* January 2–9, 1994, p. 32; Edward W. Desmond, "Ichiro Ozawa: Reformer at Bay," p. 123.

173 "main supporting actor": Ozawa Ichirō Kōenkai-Rikuzankai, ed., *Ningen Ozawa Saeki,* p. 5.

173 As posts and telecommunications minister: Redl, "Curse of the Kingmakers," p. 36.

173 A stint as construction minister: "Power Behind the Throne: LDP Secretary General Ichiro Ozawa," *Tokyo Business Today,* July 1990, p. 12; author interviews in Iwate; Ozawa Ichirō Kōenkai-Rikuzankai, ed., *Ningen Ozawa Saeki,* pp. 362–3.

173 "Fighting Bull of Iwate": Ibid., p. 6; Shūji Okuno, *Ozawa Ichirō: hasha no rirekisho,* p. 11.

173 In one famed melee: Kensuke Watanabe, *Ano hito: hitotsu no Ozawa Ichirō ron,* p. 91; "Power Behind the Throne: LDP Secretary General Ichiro Ozawa," *Tokyo Business Today,* July 1990, p. 12.

173 Saeki left his son: Redl, "Curse of the Kingmakers," p. 37.

173 He cried on a school outing: Teru Gamō, *Ozawa Ichirō shinjitsu no sakebi,* pp. 147–8.

174 almost no personal childhood memories: *Asahi Shimbun* Seijibu, ed., *Ozawa Ichirō tanken,* p. 145.

174 "influence on my personality": Ichirō Ozawa with Taiichirō Kobayashi, *Kataru,* p. 142.

174 "from a landowner class, and was": "Chokugeki Ozawa Ichirō ga kataru: Nihon no koto, seiji no koto" (Direct hit Ichiro Ozawa talks: About Japan, about politics), *Sandē Mainichi,* January 2–9, 1994, p. 32.

174 Michi herself lived frugally: Kensuke Watanabe, *Ano hito,* p. 100.

174 He was told never to cry: Author interviews in Iwate.

174 "Behave impeccably": Kensuke Watanabe, *Ano hito,* p. 101.

174 "She taught me": Author interview with Ichirō Ozawa, September 2, 1994.

174 According to local legend: Okuno, *Ozawa Ichirō*, p. 181.

174 "I cannot go back": Ōshita, *Ichi o motte tsuranuku*, p. 57; Kensuke Watanabe, *Ano hito*, p. 104.

174 Despite her highbrow upbringing: Author interviews in Iwate.

175 Nurtured in such a remarkably: Description of Ozawa's youth through his early years in Parliament from: Ōshita, *Ichi o motte tsuranuku*, pp. 40–146; Kensuke Watanabe, *Ano hito*, pp. 75–8, 85–128; *Asahi Shimbun* Seijibu, ed., *Ozawa Ichirō tanken*, pp. 142–52; Okuno, *Ozawa Ichirō*, pp. 122–86; Redl, "Curse of the Kingmakers," pp. 36–7; Hajime Oda, *Ozawa Ichirō zen jinzō*, pp. 18–33; author interviews in Iwate.

175 "He never spoke out": *Asahi Shimbun* Seijibu, ed., *Ozawa Ichirō tanken*, p. 155.

175 "I was a strong fighter": Ozawa, *Kataru*, p. 143.

175 "I had not felt close": Kensuke Watanabe, *Ano hito*, p. 108.

176 "Carve out your career": Ōshita, *Ichi o motte tsuranuku*, pp. 43–5.

176 "I want to become": Ibid., p. 52.

176 "I will attend the committee": Ibid., p. 75.

176 "I am thinking": Ibid., p. 79.

176 "I only rode": Okuno, *Ozawa Ichirō*, pp. 170, 183.

177 more than 40 percent: Curtis, *The Japanese Way of Politics*, p. 95.

177 Mother: You are so quiet: "Ozawa Ichirō 'kaizō keikaku' " ("Reform" plan for Ichiro Ozawa), *Views*, March 23, 1994, p. 106; *Asahi Shimbun* Seijibu, ed., *Ozawa Ichirō tanken*, pp. 145, 150–1.

177 Ichiro did add: Ōshita, *Ichi o motte tsuranuku*, pp. 88–9.

177 When Ichiro made: Okuno, *Ozawa Ichirō*, p. 184; "TEMPO: mazā conpurekkusu datta 'Ozawa Ichirō' " (TEMPO: "Ichiro Ozawa" had a mother complex), *Shūkan Shinchō*, March 9, 1995, p. 20; "Hajimete kakareta Ozawa Ichirō 'hadaka no rirekisho' " ("Naked personal history" of Ichiro Ozawa that has been written for the first time), *Shūkan Gendai*, January 8, 1994, p. 30.

178 "He had tremendous force": Ushio Shiota, "We Are the 'Takeshita Boy-Detectives Group'; Who Is the Most Likely Candidate in the Successor Race, Which Has Already Started?," p. 22.

178 "was so stiff and serious": Redl, "Curse of the Kingmakers," p. 37; *Asahi Shimbun* Seijibu, ed., *Ozawa Ichirō tanken*, p. 46.

178 "I will take care": Ōshita, *Ichi o motte tsuranuku*, p. 102.

178 "My boss . . . will take responsibility": Redl, "Curse of the Kingmakers," p. 37.

178 Ozawa and another colleague: Kōzō Watanabe, *Seijika ni tsukeru kusuri*, p. 133.

179 "If you do not": Ōshita, *Ichi o motte tsuranuku*, p. 141.

179 Some press accounts describe colleagues: Akifumi Ise, *Ozawa Ichirō no wanryoku pointo yomi*, p. 122; "Ozawa Ichirō 'kaizō keikaku,' " p. 105.

179 "Since Ozawa was young": Kōzō Watanabe, *Seijika ni tsukeru kusuri,* pp. 129–30.

179 He often claimed: Hayasaka, *The Making of a Japanese Prime Minister,* p. 67.

179 "Ichiro's hands are soft": Kensuke Watanabe, *Ano hito,* p. 136.

179 "He knew that I wouldn't": Author interview with Ozawa.

179 "Ichiro, let's play": Ise, *Ozawa Ichirō no wanryoku pointo,* pp. 94–7.

180 "I wasn't simply a member": "Ozawa Ichirō oyaji Kakuei o kataru; Tanaka Kakuei moto shushō shisu" (Ichiro Ozawa talks about *oyaji* Kakuei; Ex–prime minister Kakuei Tanaka died), *Sandē Mainichi,* January 2–9, 1994, p. 26.

180 "Why is it wrong": "Kanemaru's True Nature Hidden Behind Rhetoric," *AEN,* May 9, 1993.

181 "Now that the big boss": Shiota, "We Are the 'Takeshita Boy-Detectives Group,' " pp. 13–4.

181 "Stop it! How stupid!": Shigezō Hayasaka, *Kago ni noru hito, katsugu hito: Jimintō rimenshi ni manabu,* pp. 11–2.

181 "I will make Takeshita scrub": Shiota, "We Are the 'Takeshita Boy-Detectives Group,' " p. 25.

181 "accumulated considerable basic": "Interview with Secretary General Ichirō Ozawa: How Do You Feel About Your Being Called 'Mini-Kakuei?,' " *Bungei Shunjū,* December 1989, trans. in *Summaries of Selected Japanese Magazines,* American Embassy, December 1989, p. 35.

181 "Only I know how": Seiji Ōie, *Keiseikai shitō no nanajū nichi,* p. 169.

182 " 'If you join' ": "Power Behind the Throne: LDP Secretary General Ichiro Ozawa," *Tokyo Business Today,* July 1990, p. 14.

182 "In order to become": Author interviews in Iwate.

182 "Ichiro came again": Redl, "Curse of the Kingmakers," p. 37.

182 "I could not bear": Kensuke Watanabe, *Ano hito,* p. 159.

182 In the elections: Ōshita, *Ichi o motte tsuranuku,* p. 190.

182 "The change of generations": Ibid., p. 164.

183 he personally collected more money: Curtis, *The Japanese Way of Politics,* p. 182.

183 "What Ozawa says": Ōshita, *Ichi o motte tsuranuku,* p. 199; Ise, *Ozawa Ichirō no wanryoku pointo yomi,* pp. 100–1.

183 "You are still young": Shiota, "We Are the 'Takeshita Boy-Detectives Group,' " p. 20; Kōzō Watanabe, *Seijika ni tsukeru kusuri,* pp. 66–7.

184 "He was displeased just hearing": Kensuke Watanabe, *Ano hito,* p. 190.

184 "I believe that we": Ibid., p. 163.

Chapter Sixteen:
The Coup

185 The conspirators began active: Description of the coup plot through Tanaka's stroke from daily press accounts of the time and: *Asahi*

Shimbun Seijibu, ed., *Tanaka shihai to sono hōkai,* pp. 274–301, 358; Kenji Gotō, *Obuchi Keizō zen jinzō,* pp. 109–45; Ōie, *Keiseikai shitō no nanajū nichi,* p. 133.

185 "It was like the vendetta": Jiji Tsūshinsha Seijibu, ed., *Takeshita sōri zen dēta,* pp. 49–50.

185 "I want you to take a blood oath": Gotō, *Obuchi Keizō zen jinzō,* pp. 119–22.

185 "I will burn myself": Takeshita, *Shōgen hoshu seiken,* p. 162.

186 "I composed my own poem": "3 'New Leaders' Consolidating Positions: Finance Minister Noboru Takeshita," *MDN,* February 1, 1985.

186 "quietly study policy": "History Repeats Itself?," *JT,* February 7, 1985.

186 "Fine, it's natural to study": Hayano, "Mite kiite hanashita 'Kaku-san' no sugao," p. 15; "Tanaka's Loyal Men Start Looking Out for No. 1," *DY,* February 8, 1985.

186 "a pure, fresh study group": *Asahi Shimbun* Seijibu, ed., *Tanaka shihai to sono hōkai,* p. 282; "Tanaka's Loyal Men Start Looking Out for No. 1," *DY,* February 8, 1985.

187 "by saying he would like to hold": "Challenge to Tanaka," *DY,* February 1, 1985.

187 TANAKA'S LOYAL MEN: "Tanaka's Loyal Men Start Looking Out for No. 1," *DY,* February 8, 1985.

187 "It's still ten years": *Asahi Shimbun* Seijibu, ed., *Tanaka shihai to sono hōkai,* p. 279.

187 "Does Takeshita intend to buy": "Tanaka's Hospitalization," *AEN,* March 11, 1985.

187 "Takeshita is a traitor!": "Ozawa Ichirō yo, kimi wa taijin janai, hisuterii onna da!" (You, Ichiro Ozawa, you are not a great man but a hysteric woman!), *Shūkan Hoseki,* July 20, 1995, p. 50.

187 "it's hard to start": Gotō, *Obuchi Keizō zen jinzō,* p. 141.

187 Ozawa had wept: Ōie, *Keiseikai shitō no nanjū nichi,* p. 94.

187 "In a fight": Ōshita, *Ichi o motte tsuranuku,* p. 217.

187 "You people are so": Shiota, "We Are the 'Takeshita Boy-Detectives Group,' " p. 28; "Yamashita Ganri ga akasu bannen no hiwa" (Ganri Yamashita reveals secret stories of Tanaka's late years), *Sandē Mainichi,* January 2–9, 1994, p. 30; Oda, *Ozawa zen jinzō,* p. 107.

188 "Some say it is time": Hayano, "Mite kiite hanashita 'Kaku-san' no sugao," p. 15.

188 "A fool speaks": Gotō, *Obuchi Keizō zen jinzō,* p. 143.

188 even as an invalid, Tanaka: Description of the power struggle from February 1985 to July 1987 from daily press accounts of the time and: *Asahi Shimbun* Seijibu, ed., *Tanaka shihai to sono hōkai,* pp. 294–314; Gotō, *Obuchi Keizō zen jinzō,* pp. 143–59.

189 numerous matters: "Who Replaces Tanaka as Master Coordinator?," *Japan Economic Journal,* May 21, 1985.

189 "The interest of politics": "Tanaka's Hospitalization," *AEN,* March 11, 1985.

189 MYSTERY SURROUNDS: "Mystery Surrounds Tanaka's Health and Whereabouts," *Japan Economic Journal,* May 14, 1985.

190 "He couldn't speak": "Illness of Japan's Kingmaker Roils Politics and Weakens Prime Minister Nakasone," *The Wall Street Journal,* May 29, 1985.

190 "My father will never retire": "Kakuei oyako no 'yōki' o ukagau seijika tachi" (Politicians carefully watch "unusual mood" of Kakuei and his daughter), *Shūkan Posuto,* July 5, 1985, p. 54.

190 Moderator: I suppose the words: *Asahi Shimbun* Seijibu, ed., *Tanaka shihai to sono hōkai,* pp. 329–30.

191 In December 1985, Naoki: "Tanaka's Oracle," *MDN,* February 2, 1985.

192 "This year the *sensei* is": *Asahi Shimbun* Seijibu, ed., *Tanaka shihai to sono hōkai,* p. 313.

192 "Patience, patience": Jiji Tsūshinsha Seijibu, ed., *Takeshita sōri zen dēta,* p. 182.

Chapter Seventeen: The Age of Languor

193 "In Kanemaru's words": Author interview with Wataru Takeshita, July 27, 1994.

193 "Mr. Kanemaru, Mr. Takeshita and me": "Ozawa's Views of LDP Race," *AEN,* September 5, 1991.

195 in the Ginza shopping district: Edward Seidensticker, *Tokyo Rising: The City Since the Great Earthquake,* p. 337.

195 Nui Onoue became a face: Richard McGregor, *Japan Swings: Politics, Culture and Sex in the New Japan,* pp. 21–3.

196 "More than 90 percent": *Asahi Shimbun* Seijibu, ed., *Tanaka shihai to sono hōkai,* p. 344.

196 "It's the logic": Jiji Tsūshinsha Seijibu, ed., *Takeshita sōri zen dēta,* p. 66.

196 "a new kind of leadership": "Overall Comparison of the 'Personal and Monetary Connections' of Abe, Takeshita, and Miyazawa, with Approach of Party Presidential Race," *Sunday Mainichi,* June 1, 1986, trans. in *Summaries of Selected Japanese Magazines,* American Embassy, August 1986, p. 25; Takeshita, *Shōgen hoshu seiken,* p. 174.

196 "In order to hear the opinions": "Patient Takeshita," *AEN,* May 28, 1987.

196 "What sort of ideology": "Takeshita: Consensus as My Guide," *MDN,* November 2, 1987.

196 the "ripe persimmon" approach: "Patient Takeshita," *AEN,* May 28, 1987.

197 "seems to believe": Kenzo Uchida, "Slow and Steady: The Takeshita Administration's First Year," *Japan Quarterly,* October–December 1988, p. 375.

197 "It is a fact": "Japan's Political Leaders Use Words to Cloud Issues," *AEN,* June 4, 1988; "A Japanese Taboo: History Lessons Ignore Realities of WWII," *AEN,* March 7, 1989.

197 "I belong to all": "Takeshita Politics: A No-Principle Flexibility," *AEN*, May 7, 1988.

197 Takeshita's autobiography is filled with: Takeshita, *Shōgen hoshu seiken*, pp. 101, 112.

197 "My tenure as finance minister": Takeshita, *The Furusato Concept*, p. 147.

197 "tied with a mysterious fate": *Shōgen hoshu seiken*, p. 180.

198 "the quality of a [legislative] session": "P.M. All Defense, No Substance," *AEN*, December 3, 1987.

198 "The force of circumstances": "Noboru Takeshita: Pragmatic Stance," *MDN*, October 2, 1987.

198 "Frankly speaking, I have": "Why I Was Designated: Interview with Noboru Takeshita by Soichiro Tawara, *Bungei Shunjū*, December 1987, trans. in *Summaries of Selected Japanese Magazines*, American Embassy, April 1988, p. 1.

198 His own spokesman said: "Takeshita Not Indecisive, Cabinet Spokesman Says," *JT*, November 12, 1987.

198 "He's the type that cartoonists": Quotes from cartoonist and rock group from: "Takeshita Politics: Support for Doing Nothing," *AEN*, May 6, 1988.

199 "Until now, politics has had": "Takeshita Vows to Open Markets, Let People Enrich Themselves, Associated Press, in *Los Angeles Times*, November 27, 1987.

199 "happiness-doubling" plan: Takeshita quotes on *furusato* plan from: Takeshita, *The Furusato Concept*, pp. 29–30, 45, 137, 144.

200 Some communities, literally befuddled: Description of how communities spent *furusato* funds from: *Kyū chiji ga kataru furusato sōsei*, pp. 184–92; Chihō Jichi Seisaku Kenkyūkai, *Zenkoku furusato sōsei ichioku en dēta bukku;* Takeshita, *Shōgen hoshu seiken*, pp. 218–27; "Japan Government Gives Away Riches to Towns and Cities: Museum Shaped Like a UFO, a 138-Pound Gold Lump Among Far-Fetched Ideas," *The Wall Street Journal*, April 11, 1989; "Noboru Takeshita's Legacy," *DY*, March 16, 1990.

200 "People wanted to see": "Japan Government Gives Away Riches to Towns and Cities: Museum Shaped Like a UFO, a 138-Pound Gold Lump Among Far-Fetched Ideas," *The Wall Street Journal*, April 11, 1989.

200 His support rate once reached: "Takeshita Politics: Support for Doing Nothing," *AEN*, May 6, 1988.

200 his popularity had fallen: "Public Support for Takeshita Gov't Slips to 22 Percent," *MDN*, September 8, 1988.

200 "I remember reading aloud": "Japan: Bowing Out," *Time*, international edition, May 8, 1989, p. 13.

Chapter Eighteen:
The Don

203 "Everybody thinks": Masayoshi Ito, "Frank Advice: Kanemaru's Diplomacy Ought to be Discontinued," *Bungei Shunjū*, January, 1991,

trans. in *Summaries of Selected Japanese Magazines,* American Embassy, March 1991, p. 14.

203 "Many people say": "Ozawa: Takeshita Faction to Keep Aloof," *DY,* September 21, 1991.

203 "Use and discard": "Power of Prime Minister: Why Is Prime Minister Miyazawa Being Obsequious?," *Kankai,* May 1992, trans. in *Summaries of Selected Japanese Magazines,* American Embassy, September 1992, p. 20.

203 Kaifu aides described Takeshita: *Asahi Shimbun* Seijibu, ed., *Takeshita ha shihai,* p. 48.

203 The aspiring premier knew enough: Gotō, *Obuchi Keizō zen jinzō,* p. 253.

203 Within days of Uno's surprise promotion: William J. Holstein, *The Japanese Power Game: What It Means for America,* pp. 124–6.

204 Seemingly unfazed, the Takeshita-faction leaders: "Thorough Dissecting of Takeshita Faction, 'Manager' of Prime Minister's Official Residence," *Kankai,* October 1991, trans. in *Summaries of Selected Japanese Magazines,* American Embassy, April 1992, p. 13.

204 "We will make all": Hayasaka, *The Making of a Japanese Prime Minister,* p. 46.

204 Even as Takeshita was leaving office: Ibid., p. 31.

204 On issues of policy and personnel: Examples of "Kon-Chiku-Sho" open control over Kaifu in: *Asahi Shimbun* Seijibu, ed., *Takeshita ha shihai,* pp. 17, 48–50; "A Talk with Takeshita: Japan's Former Leader Denies He's Still in Charge," *The New York Times,* January 17, 1990; Masayoshi Ito, "Frank Advice: Kanemaru's Diplomacy Ought to Be Discontinued," *Bungei Shunjū,* January 1991, trans. in *Summaries of Selected Japanese Magazines,* American Embassy, March 1991, p. 9; "Ozawa Makes Washington Fidget," *DY,* April 20, 1990.

204 "Where was that decided?": "Maneuvering Begins over a Successor to Kaifu," *Los Angeles Times,* October 5, 1991.

204 "Isn't it true": "Ozawa's Views of LDP Race," *AEN,* September 5, 1991.

205 "The prime minister has": Masayoshi Ito, "Frank Advice: Kanemaru's Diplomacy Ought to Be Discontinued," *Bungei Shunjū,* January 1991, trans. in *Summaries of Selected Japanese Magazines,* American Embassy, March 1991, p. 13.

205 When the Socialists were voting: "Kanemaru Speaks His Mind—Again," *DY,* June 22, 1991; "The Cabinetmaker: LDP Powerbroker Kanemaru Has Grand Plan for Complete Political Control," *AEN,* November 25, 1991.

205 "He listened to a great deal": Author interview with Makoto Tanabe, June 9, 1994.

205 The year before, the two men: *Asahi Shimbun* Seijibu, ed., *Takeshita ha shihai,* pp. 192–3.

205 "Triangle Zone of Power": Ōie, *Keiseikai shitō no nanajū nichi,* p. 160.

205 "Takeshita's rising influence was illustrated": "Takeshita Picks Up Clout as Main Rivals Wane," *Japan Economic Journal,* March 23, 1991.

206 "COLD WAR" BETWEEN TAKESHITA, KANEMARU: " 'Cold war' Between Takeshita, Kanemaru Turns Out to Be a Sham," trans. in *MDN*, July 23, 1990.

206 "There's no end to rumors": "Thorough Dissecting of Takeshita Faction, 'Manager' of Prime Minister's Official Residence,' *Kankai*, October 1991, trans. in *Summaries of Selected Japanese Magazines*, American Embassy, April 1992, p. 13.

206 "We can't ever tell": Author interviews in Yamanashi.

206 "Even we don't know": Author interview with Yasunobu Kanemaru.

207 "If I became prime minister": "Keeping Up with Kanemaru," *Time*, international edition, October 22, 1990, p. 15.

207 "When asked who is": "Dangling the Carrot: Kanemaru Plays Kingmaker by Divide and Tease," *AEN*, May 29, 1990.

207 the *gundan*'s "hired madam": *Asahi Shimbun* Seijibu, ed., *Takeshita ha shihai*, p. 57; Hayasaka, *The Making of a Japanese Prime Minister*, p. 156.

207 "the Don": See, e.g., "Don Shin Kanemaru Says 'Takeshita Won't Do It,' " *Shūkan Asahi*, May 31, 1991, trans. in *Summaries of Selected Japanese Magazines*, American Embassy, July 1991, p. 36.

207 "to become accomplished facts": "LDP Vice-President Distorted Design for Power," *Kankai*, September 1992, trans. in *Summaries of Selected Japanese Magazines*, November 1992, American Embassy, p. 36.

207 "even by beheading": "Kanemaru and BOJ," *MDN*, March 1, 1992.

207 "Political stories in the 1980s": Ōie, *Keiseikai, shitō no nanajū nichi*, pp. 75–6.

207 "It is not good": "Political Power Is Something Which Ought to Be Obtained Through Battle; Factions Create President; Tax System Reform; To Move Organ for Consultations into Gear, First of All," *Tokyo Shimbun*, May 12, 1987, trans. in *Daily Summary of Japanese Press*, American Embassy, May 19, 1987, p. 10.

208 "This situation is like a midwife": Shear, "The Shadow Shogun."

208 "Those listening to him": "Comic Books and Kanemaru," *AEN*, August 29, 1992.

208 "I have an idea": "Kanemaru Comments Make Splash: 'Northern Territories' Proposal Untimely with Talks in Prospect," *JT*, April 30, 1990.

208 "I have to talk with Deng": "Kanemaru's China Trip a Bust," *DY*, September 8, 1990.

208 "If Kanemaru says he wants": " 'Kuromaku' Kanemaru Dictates Govt Policy," *Los Angeles Times*, reprinted in *DY*, September 27, 1990.

209 "It was unprecedented": Michael H. Armacost, *Friends or Rivals? The Insider's Account of U.S.-Japan Relations*, p. 146.

209 "That's a very difficult question": "Pyongyang Surprise," *Newsweek*, international edition, October 8, 1990, p. 26.

210 Kanemaru engaged in: Hayasaka, *The Making of a Japanese Prime Minister*, p. 116.

210 Their feints were merely: Description of selection of the prime minister in October 1991 from daily press accounts and *Asahi Shimbun* Seijibu, ed., *Takeshita ha shihai*, pp. 87–123.

210 "I heard. See you": *Asahi Shimbun* Seijibu, ed., *Takeshita ha shihai,* p. 110.

210 "I am observing proprieties": Ichiro Ozawa, "Therefore, We Chose Miyazawa: Grade Book on Interviews with Candidates for LDP Presidency Decisive Factors Leading to Victory," *Bungei Shunjū,* December 1991, trans. in *Summaries of Selected Japanese Magazines,* American Embassy, May 1992, p. 6.

210 "Ozawa is the most qualified": *Asahi Shimbun* Seijibu, ed., *Takeshita ha shihai,* p. 107.

211 "Sorry, the dog *never* does": *Asahi Shimbun* Seijibu, ed., *Takeshita ha shihai,* p. 102.

211 "a man who can conduct": "Takeshita Faction Abandons Attempt to Field Candidate," *JT,* October 10, 1991.

211 "I couldn't sleep": "Kanemaru Wavered to the Last," *AEN,* October 24, 1991.

211 "I was forced to think": *Asahi Shimbun* Seijibu, ed., *Takeshita ha shihai,* pp. 118–21.

211 the new leader was "appropriate": "Kanemaru Reveals Process for Miyazawa Selection," *AEN,* October 16, 1991.

211 "What really happened": Michitoshi Takabatake, "Miyazawa Kiichi: A Statesman on Trial," *Japan Quarterly,* January–March 1992, p. 7.

212 once proudly inviting Henry Kissinger: Hayasaka, *The Making of a Japanese Prime Minister,* p. 122.

212 "He's not the type": Ibid., p. 121.

212 "uneducated" and "a parvenu": Kitakado, *Tanaka Kakuei dai gundan 101 nin,* p. 63.

212 "A person like him": Ōie, *Keiseikai shitō no nanajū nichi,* pp. 17–8.

212 "Mr. Kanemaru says": "Ozawa's View of LDP Race," *AEN,* September 5, 1991.

212 He agreed to turn over: *Asahi Shimbun* Seijibu, ed., *Takeshita ha shihai,* pp. 138, 149–51.

212 "Those around Kanemaru say": "On a Sea of Problems in a Boat of Mud," *AEN,* January 21, 1992.

213 Kanemaru was soon invited: Hyōden Kanemaru Shin Hensankai, ed., *Kanemaru Shin: Saigo no Nihonteki seijika hyōden,* pp. 15–6.

213 "LDP Vice President Kanemaru": "LDP Vice-President Distorted Design for Power," *Kankai,* September 1992, trans. in *Summaries of Selected Japanese Magazines,* American Embassy, November 1992, p. 31.

213 Kanemaru and Miyazawa sealed: Description of ceremony from: "Why the Party Never Ends for Politicans," *AEN,* February 28, 1992; "Kanemaru-shi, horoyoi de nagajōzetsu" (Tipsy Mr. Kanemaru rambles on), *Yomiuri Shimbun,* February 5, 1992.

Chapter Nineteen: "One Big Safe"

215 "It is to be hoped": "Turmoil in Tanaka Faction," *AEN,* February 7, 1985.

215 "We can hope": "LDP Rejuvenation Attempt," *MDN,* February 10, 1985.

215 "inject more reason and cleanliness": "Mr. Takeshita's Opportunity," *JT,* May 21, 1987.

216 "are perfect for election campaigns": Author interview with Ozawa, September 2, 1994.

216 "You are the son": Ōshita, *Ichi o motte tsuranuku,* p. 127.

216 Such positions gave Ozawa: *Mainichi Shimbun* Shakaibu, ed., *Seiji fuhai o utsu: "fushin" no meisaisho,* pp. 162–3; " 'Ozawa gakkō' hōkai no yoha" (Aftermath of "Ozawa school" collapse), *Asahi Shimbun,* November 14, 1992.

217 "It was a lot of fun": Kanemaru, *Tachiwaza newaza,* pp. 100–2.

217 "Don't try to steal water": Kikuchi, *Takeshita giwaku no keifu,* p. 74.

217 Takeshita also had: *Mainichi Shimbun* Shakaibu, ed., *Seiji fuhai o utsu,* p. 118.

218 By the 1980s, Shimane had: Description of public works boom in Shimane from: "Pork-Barrel Politics Benefited Home Prefectures of Kanemaru, Takeshita," *MDN,* May 3, 1993; "Yoshida vs. Takeshita," *AEN,* November 15, 1992; Calder, *Crisis and Compensation,* pp. 274–6; *Mainichi Shimbun* Shakaibu, ed., *Seiji fuhai o utsu,* p. 115; author interviews in Shimane.

218 "There were times when": "Pork-Barrel Politics Benefited Home Prefectures of Kanemaru, Takeshita," *MDN,* May 3, 1993.

218 Construction companies organized: Description of construction companies and their role in Iwate politics from: *Mainichi Shimbun* Shakaibu, ed., *Seiji fuhai o utsu,* pp. 280–6; Hajime Yokota, "Ozawa ōkoku: Iwate o aruku" (Walking around Iwate, the Ozawa empire), *Sekai,* February 1994; Masashi Takekawa, "Tōhoku zenekon no teiō, Ozawa Ichirō no shihai no kōzu o hagu!" (The emperor of Tohoku general contractors, Ichirō Ozawa's control structure revealed!), *Uwasa no shinsō,* December 1993; Okuno, *Ozawa Ichirō,* pp. 221–9; author interviews in Iwate.

218 "Friends told me": Author interviews in Iwate.

218 "There are no other bridges": Ōie, *Keiseikai shitō no nanajū nichi,* p. 16.

218 "Now we can all eat": "Pork-Barrel Politics Benefited Home Prefectures of Kanemaru, Takeshita," *MDN,* May 3, 1993.

219 a tenfold increase: Marshall, "The Man Who Would Be Kingmaker," p. 37.

219 The crowning glory: Description of linear motorcar project from: "Powerbroker Behind the Japanese Political Throne," *Financial Times,* August 3, 1989; "Kanemaru Gravy Train Wins Yamanashi Hearts," *The Economist,* reprinted in *DY,* June 23, 1990; "Faster Than a Speeding Bullet, It's Magnet-Train," *The New York Times,* November 8, 1990; Shear, "The Shadow Shogun"; *Mainichi Shimbun* Shakaibu, ed., *Seiji fuhai o utsu,* p. 41.

219 "Libya motor car": Ōie, *Keiseikai shitō no nanajū nichi,* p. 29.

219 his heavy-handed tactics: Description of Yamanashi local politics from: "Loyalty to Kanemaru Brought Lucrative Rewards for Firms," *MDN,*

March 19, 1993; "Reform Bid System for Public Works Projects," *AEN*, April 14, 1993; "Kanemaru Had Willing Help on the Other End," *MDN*, April 17, 1993.

219 "I never sought donations": "Kanemaru Comes Clean," *MDN*, July 28, 1993; "Kanemaru Trial Opens," *DY*, July 23, 1993.

220 And what may have begun: Description of Kanemaru's relations with Yamanashi construction companies from: "Yamanashi's Building Firms Said to Have Set Up Group to Supply Kanemaru Money," *AEN*, March 13, 1993; "Kanemaru's Arrest Illuminates Affair: Investigation Finds Wife, Haibara Were Key Assistants in Scandal," *DY*, March 14, 1993; "View of Kanemaru Machine Emerging: Industry Association Played Major Part in Raising Money," *MDN*, March 17, 1993; "Court Detains Kanemaru, Haibara for 10 More Days," *JT*, March 18, 1993; "Kanemaru Allegedly Received 50 Mil. Yen at Every Election: Money Collected from Construction Group," *AEN*, March 18, 1993; "Loyalty to Kanemaru Brought Lucrative Rewards for Firms," *MDN*, March 19, 1993; "Money Trail Leads to Construction Firms: Donations to Kanemaru Allegedly Used to Buy Favors," *Nikkei Weekly*, March 22, 1993; "Kanemaru Had Willing Help on the Other End," *MDN*, April 17, 1993.

220 "The 'archipelago-remodeling plan' ": Tsutomu Kuji, *Rikurūto jiken ni "shūketsu" wa nai*, pp. 48–9; Hayasaka, *Seijika Tanaka Kakuei*, p. 510.

220 "You can't keep everyone happy": Eisuke Sakakibara, "The Japanese Politico-Economic System and the Public Sector," p. 68.

221 In 1988, with Kanemaru's blessing: "Dam Nuisance: A Blot on the Nagara River Becomes a Rallying Point for Japanese Upset by the Way Their Country Has Sacrificed Its Environment to the Demands of Economics," *Asian Wall Street Journal*, April 18, 1994.

221 Kanemaru also inherited Tanaka's mantle: Yūzō Okabe, *Rinkaifukutoshin kaihatsu, dokyumento: zenekon yuchaku 10-chō en purojekuto*, pp. 86–93; "Underdog Got Part of Bay Project with Kanemaru's Help," *MDN*, May 1, 1993; "Takeshita Received 10 Mil. Yen Annually from Tobishima," *MDN*, December 9, 1993.

221 "I asked Kanemaru-san": *Mainichi Shimbun* Shakaibu, ed., *Seiji fuhai o utsu*, p. 123.

221 Like Yamanashi's builders, the big national: "Construction Industry Made Regular Donations to Kanemaru," *DY*, March 17, 1993; "Contractors Paid Kanemaru Regularly: Yearly Sum of 20 Million Yen Disclosed," *MDN*, March 23, 1993; "Prosecutors to Quiz Ex–Takeshita Faction Members," *MDN*, March 25, 1993; "Kanemaru's Legal Troubles Continue to Mount," *Nikkei Weekly*, March 29, 1993; "Kanemaru Case Seen as Tip of Graft Iceberg," *JT*, March 31, 1993.

221 And while Takeshita and Ozawa: "Kajima Allegedly Secretly Donated Funds to Takeshita," *JT*, October 30, 1993; "Takeshita Received 10 Mil. Yen Annually from Tobishima," *MDN*, December 9, 1993; "Kajima Gave 5 Mil. Yen to Ozawa Last Year, Paper Says," Kyodo News Service, November 5, 1993; "Tobishima Allegedly Gave Millions to Ozawa, Watanabe," Kyodo News Service, December 9, 1993; "Kajima, Ozawa-shi ni 500 man en sakunen jūnigatsu" (Kajima gave 5 million yen to Mr. Ozawa last

December), *Asahi Shimbun*, November 5, 1993; "Kajima, Takeshita moto shushō ni yami kenkin" (Kajima gave ex–prime minister Takeshita illegal donations), *Asahi Shimbun*, October 29, 1993.

221 During the "Kon-Chiku-Sho" era: *Mainichi Shimbun* Shakaibu, ed., *Seiji fuhai o utsu*, pp. 42–3.

222 Critics saw fund-raising: Ibid., pp. 52–5.

222 "were twisted and turned": Kuji, *Rikurūto jiken ni "shūketsu" wa nai*, p. 50.

222 Takeshita's four-plus years: "Japan's Power Broker," *Tokyo Business Today*, December 1987, p. 18; "Takeshita Power Ignites Business Ardor," *Japan Economic Journal*, December 26, 1987; "Prime Minister Takeshita's Businessmen Aides," *Tokyo Business Today*, August 1988, p. 39.

223 complex new transactions: *Mainichi Shimbun* Shakaibu, ed., *Seiji fuhai o utsu*, pp. 190–256.

223 In one case extensively covered: Description of bank merger case from: Ibid., pp. 61–6; "Black Mist Around Takeshita," *DY*, October 16, 1992; "Day of Reckoning for Takeshita," *DY*, October 23, 1992; "Takeshita on Memo for Overpriced Screen: Former Auditor Testifies on Bank Management Feud," *MDN*, February 17, 1993; "Takeshita's Name Linked to Art Deal: Ex–Heiwa Sogo Bank Auditor Testifies in Civil Court," *AEN*, February 17, 1993; "Auditor Testifies: 'Memo Ties Takeshita to Payout,' " *JT*, February 17, 1993.

223 But the law was full: Curtis, *The Japanese Way of Politics*, pp. 180–7.

223 Rather than relying: *Mainichi Shimbun* Shakaibu, ed., *Seiji fuhai o utsu*, pp. 102–7.

223 Takeshita unabashedly set up: Hayasaka, *The Making of a Japanese Prime Minister*, pp. 15–6; Jiji Tsūshinsha Seijibu, ed., *Takeshita sōri zen dēta*, pp. 151–3.

224 The most successful such event ever: Description of Takeshita fund-raiser from: *Asahi Shimbun* Seijibu, ed., *Tanaka shihai to sono hōkai*, pp. 79–88; Gotō, *Obuchi Keizō zen jinzō*, pp. 172–4; Darlin, "Japan's Front-Runner Stresses Consensus"; "Takeshita Should Declare Candidacy Shortly: Kanemaru," *JT*, May 23, 1987; "Strong Turnout at Party Raises Takeshita's Hopes," *JT*, May 22, 1987.

224 To hear Japanese politicians tell it: Description of expenses for Japanese politicians from: Kojiro Shiraishi, *The Recruit Scandal and "Money Politics" in Japan;* Holstein, *The Japanese Power Game*, pp. 74–5, 144–6; Curtis, *The Japanese Way of Politics*, pp. 176–80; "New Resignation Clouds Outlook for Takeshita," *Asian Wall Street Journal*, February 8, 1989; "When Will Takeshita Go?," *Newsweek*, international edition, April 24, 1989; "More Than Takeshita," *The Economist*, April 29, 1989; Ōie, *Keiseikai shitō no nanajū nichi*, pp. 169–70; "Takeshita: Luckiest LDP Faction Boss," *DY*, June 22, 1987; "Kane to enkirenu Nihon seiji" (Japanese politics cannot sever money), *Aera*, December 27, 1988, pp. 42–3; "Seiji katsudō ni nen 9400 man en, jimintō 100 nin ankēto" (94 million yen for one year of political activities, survey of 100 LDP MPs), *Asahi Shimbun*, April 4, 1989; "Seiji no daidokoro; jimintō daigishi 100 nin ankēto kara"

(The kitchen of politics: From survey of 100 LDP MPs), *Asahi Shimbun*, April 7–9, 1989.

225 "A [Buddhist] temple representative": Shiraishi, *The Recruit Scandal*, p. 39.

225 "It is not *only* money": "Interview with Secretary General Ichiro Ozawa: How Do You Feel About Your Being Called 'Mini-Kakuei'?," *Bungei Shunjū*, December 1989, trans. in *Summaries of Selected Japanese Magazines*, American Embassy, December 1989, p. 36.

225 "What happened to that?": Ōie, *Keiseikai shitō no nanajū nichi*, p. 29.

225 The annual cost of maintaining: "Vanity, Thy Name Is Kanemaru," *AEN*, October 27, 1992.

225 Takeshita was known for underwriting: "Tanaka's 'Ultimate Triumph,' " *AEN*, July 28, 1987; "Patient, Considerate Takeshita," *AEN*, October 22, 1987; *Ōkura Kanryō no shōtai*, p. 165.

226 On rare occasions, a politician: " 'Patience, Consideration' Take Takeshita to Top Post," *AEN*, October 20, 1987; "Powerbroker Behind the Japanese Political Throne," *Financial Times*, August 3, 1989.

226 "Why don't you guys have": "Slush Funds and Sleazeballs: Kanemaru's Fall Demonstrates What Many Already Knew," *AEN*, October 3, 1992.

226 "We have lived in an era": "End Pocket-lining Politics," *AEN*, March 9, 1993.

226 Still, Kanemaru somehow managed: Description of Kanemaru properties from: Shear, "The Shadow Shogun"; Ōie, *Keiseikai shitō no nanajū nichi*, pp. 77–8, 160–5; "Kanemaru Indicted," *MDN*, March 15, 1993; "Kenryoku no uragawa" (The dark side of power), *Asahi Shimbun*, March 16, 1993; "Hawaii fudōsan 4 oku 4 sen man en" (440 million yen real estate in Hawaii), *Yomiuri Shimbun*, March 20, 1993; "Sesse to chikuzai, Kanemaru ryū" (Diligently saving up in Kanemaru style), *Mainichi Shimbun*, March 8, 1993; "Omote to ura de shisan 100 oku en" (Public and hidden assets totaling 10 billion yen), *Asahi Shimbun*, March 14, 1993.

227 He had no formal: Description of Kanemaru's office finances from: Ōie, *Keiseikai shitō no nanajū nichi*, pp. 29–30, 160–2; "Kanemaru Comes Clean," *MDN*, July 28, 1993.

227 "The whole office": Ōie, *Keiseikai shitō no nanajū nichi*, p. 29.

PART FOUR
The Machine Collapses, 1992–1996

Chapter Twenty: Cracks in the Foundation

233 Recruit was a classic example: Description of Recruit's history and ties to bureaucrats and politicians from: Holstein, *The Japanese Power*

Game, pp. 92–107; Kuji, *Rikurūto jiken ni "shūketsu" wa nai,* pp. 32–108, 125–6, 160–3; Yasunori Okadome, *R no sōkatsu,* pp. 15–45, 139–64; "Recruit, the Zealous Outsider," *The Washington Post,* in *International Herald Tribune,* April 26, 1989; "A Moral Test for Mr. Takeshita," *JT,* August 3, 1988.

234 Ezoe wisely made Takeshita: Description of Recruit donations to Takeshita from: "PM Enumerates Full Extent of Donations from Recruit: Tells Panel the 151 M. Yen Not Bribes," *MDN,* April 12, 1989; Kuji, *Rikurūto jiken ni "shūketsu" wa nai,* pp. 10–3, 151–2; "Say What?," *AEN,* April 12, 1989.

235 Ozawa, too, received: " 'Rikurūto' kōenkai e kenkin, Ozawa kanbō fukuchōkan mo" ("Recruit" also made donations to support groups of deputy chief cabinet secretary Ozawa), *Asahi Shimbun,* October 1, 1988; "Ozawa shi hisho ga yakuin, Rikurūto kanren gaisha kansa yaku, sakunen matsu made" (Mr. Ozawa's secretary was a director of Recruit-related company as auditor until last December), *Asahi Shimbun,* evening edition, February 9, 1989; Masashi Takekawa, "Tōhoku zenekon no teiō, Ozawa Ichirō no shihai no kōzu o hagu!" (The emperor of Tohoku general contractors, Ichiro Ozawa's control structure revealed!), *Uwasa no shinsō,* December 1993, p. 85.

235 Ezoe also tried: Description of Recruit donations to other politicians and totals from: "Sagawa Kyubin Case vs. Recruit Scam," *AEN,* September 8, 1992; "A Talk with Takeshita: Japan's Former Leader Denies He's Still in Charge," *The New York Times,* January 17, 1990; "Takeshita Resigning, *AEN Extra,* April 25, 1989; "Using the Inchworm Method," *Time,* international edition, January 9, 1989; "Hunkered Down in the Diet," *Time,* international edition, April 17, 1989.

236 "I can tell you what": "It's Takeshita's Turn on Hot Seat," *MDN,* February 20, 1989.

236 "I do not remember details": "PM Enumerates Full Extent of Donations from Recruit: Tells Panel the 151 M. Yen Not Bribes," *MDN,* April 12, 1989.

236 "Politics takes money": "30 Years as Takeshita's Alter Ego," *AEN,* May 1, 1989.

236 The day after Takeshita announced his resignation: "Close Aide to Takeshita Commits Suicide at Home," *JT,* April 27, 1989; "Cash Is King: Aoki's Financial Wizardry Was Crucial," *Baltimore Sun,* in *DY,* April 30, 1989.

237 "I did not think Recruit": "Fatal Flaw That Felled Mr. Takeshita," *Financial Times,* April 26, 1989.

237 As premier in the early 1970s: Description of Tanaka's spending binge deficits from: Junko Kato, *The Problem of Bureaucratic Rationality: Tax Politics in Japan,* p. 115; John Creighton Campbell, *How Policies Change: The Japanese Government and the Aging Society,* pp. 154–5; Yukio Noguchi, "Public Finance," pp. 191, 205.

237 For nearly thirty years: Noguchi, "Public Finance," pp. 119–20; "Will Begin Moving from This Moment Toward Takeshita Administration: Finance Minister Takeshita vs. Political Critic Masaya Itō," *Chūō Kōron,*

September 1985, trans. in *Summaries of Selected Japanese Magazines,* American Embassy, November 1985, pp. 26–7.

238 "We are telling the people": "Will Begin Moving from This Moment Toward Takeshita Administration: Finance Minister Takeshita vs. Political Critic Masaya Itō," *Chūō Kōron,* September 1985, trans. in *Summaries of Selected Japanese Magazines,* American Embassy, November 1985, p. 26.

238 Polls showed that: "The Public Speaks on Taxes," *JT,* October 12, 1988.

238 Land sales, securities transactions: J. Kato, *The Problem of Bureaucratic Rationality,* pp. 193, 215.

240 forced thirteen separate market-opening agreements: Armacost, *Friends or Rivals?,* p. 44.

240 "large-scale retail store law": "Outcry from Country Doomed Kanemaru," *JT,* October 15, 1992.

240 Some of America's fiercest attacks: Woodall, *Japan Under Construction,* pp. 25–6; "Getting to Know 'Nobu,' " *Newsweek,* international edition, January 25, 1988, p. 15; "U.S., Japan Set Pact on Opening Building Market," *The Wall Street Journal,* June 3, 1991.

241 "You take": "LDP 'Tribe' Blocked FTC Efforts," Kyodo News Service, in *JT,* January 28, 1994.

241 nearly half of Japanese citizens: "Japanese Poll Indicates U.S. Pleas for Opening Market Are Sinking In," *The Wall Street Journal,* March 28, 1990.

242 Japanese officials repeatedly tried: Description of Japanese government efforts from: Armacost, *Friends or Rivals?,* pp. 98–127; Ichiro Ozawa, *Blueprint for a New Japan,* pp. 37–8; John B. Judis, "Burden Shirking: A Free Ride for the Japanese in the Gulf," *The New Republic,* March 4, 1991.

243 Japan's inertia reflected: Armacost, *Friends or Rivals?,* pp. 99–100, 112.

244 "While the consequences": Ibid., p. 125.

245 Like Recruit's Ezoe, Sagawa's founder: Description of Sagawa's background and political activities from: Hisahi Kikuchi, *Sagawa no kane kutta akutoku seijika,* pp. 74–106; "An Offer He Couldn't Refuse," *MDN,* September 13, 1992; "Takeshita Testifies Today: Lawmakers to Grill Him on Mob-Political Links," *DY,* November 26, 1992; Tachibana, *Kyoaku vs. genron,* pp. 624–37.

245 Sagawa Kyubin's outlays to politicians: "Takeshita's Career on Trial," *JT,* November 26, 1992; "Kanemaru Quits Post," *MDN,* August 28, 1992.

246 in the 1990 transaction: "Japan's Top Politician Quits Posts over Mob Scandal," *The New York Times,* October 15, 1992; "Three Bags Were Full; Haibara Tells How He Got Cash," *JT,* December 12, 1992.

246 In another uniquely disturbing aspect: "Top LDP Figures Singled Out in Ceasing Rightist Attacks," *AEN,* November 6, 1992; "Watanabe: Kanemaru Sought Influence of Syndicate Head to End Rightist Harassment," *AEN,* August 29, 1992.

246 Kanemaru went so far as to ask: "3 Testimonies Riddled with Contradictions," *MDN*, November 29, 1992; "Kanemaru zen jimintō fuku sōsai no rinshō jinmon; gaiyō" (Ex–LDP VP Kanemaru's hospital-bed testimony; summary), *Asahi Shimbun*, November 28, 1992.

246 under fictitious names: "Kanemaru Began Buying Debentures in 1984: Sources," *AEN*, March 8, 1993; "Bank Gave Kanemaru VIP Treatment," *DY*, March 10, 1993; "Kanemaru Indicted for Tax Evasion," *JT*, March 14, 1993; "Kanemaru's Arrest Illuminates Affair," *DY*, March 14, 1993.

247 When Kanemaru realized: "Probe of Kanemaru's Finances Widening," *Nikkei Weekly*, March 15, 1993; "Prosecutors to Quiz Ex–Takeshita Faction Members," *MDN*, March 25, 1993; "Kanemaru Pleads Innocent to Evasion," *JT*, July 23, 1993; "Not Guilty, Pleads Kanemaru," *MDN*, July 23, 1993.

247 they hauled out part: "Kanemaru Stashed Gold Bars," *DY*, March 10, 1993; "Take a Look Within First: Kanemaru Connection Hurts LDP Reformists," *AEN*, March 11, 1993; "Probe of Kanemaru's Finances Widening," *Nikkei Weekly*, March 15, 1993; "Money Trail Leads to Construction Firms," *Nikkei Weekly*, March 22, 1993.

248 "Everyone knows that we have": "Shoguns' Foe Takes a Page from Past (and Perot)," *The New York Times*, July 14, 1992.

249 One notable exception was Kanemaru's: "Yamanashi Prefectural Assembly Nixes Resolution Against Kanemaru," *AEN*, October 8, 1992.

249 "It has become impossible": "Coups Only Lead to Worse," *AEN*, November 14, 1992.

249 "Can't he understand the feelings": "Kanemaru's Gangster Ties," *AEN*, October 14, 1992.

249 "I deeply regret accepting": "Tainted Kanemaru Bows Out for Govt's Sake," *DY*, August 28, 1992.

250 "never to allow": "Kanemaru Back in Business: Kingpin, Ozawa to Retain Faction Posts," *MDN*, October 2, 1992.

250 "However, I still greatly thank": "Tainted Kanemaru Bows Out for Govt's Sake," *DY*, August 28, 1992.

250 "My political philosophy": "Scandal Drains Japan's Ruling Party," *The New York Times*, November 29, 1992; "Kanemaru zen jimintō fuku sōsai no rinshō jinmon; gaiyō" (Ex–LDP VP Kanemaru's hospital-bed testimony; summary), *Asahi Shimbun*, November 28, 1992.

250 "I was drunk and don't remember": "LDP Elders' Testimony Stirs Outrage," *Asian Wall Street Journal*, November 30, 1992.

250 On September 17, 1992: Ōie, *Keiseikai shitō no nanajū nichi*, pp. 76–8.

251 "has been the main pillar": "Departure Is a Setback for Miyazawa," *JT*, August 28, 1992.

251 "as a public figure": "Confusion Reigns in SDPJ," *JT*, October 20, 1992.

251 "This is a case of Kanemaru": "Cut to the Core of Politics," *AEN*, March 11, 1993.

Chapter Twenty-one: Ozawa and His Discontents

252 "Leadership," Ozawa concluded: Ozawa, *Blueprint for a New Japan*, p. 34.

253 "If you want to rise": Hayasaka, *The Making of a Japanese Prime Minister*, p. xv.

253 "Relations with other people": Marshall, "The Man Who Would Be Kingmaker," p. 34; Kanemaru, *Hito wa shiro*, p. 14.

253 "He has the same aggressiveness": *AEN*, November 12, 1991.

253 "I have never experienced failure": Ozawa, *Kataru*, p. 144.

253 "I'd like to be able": "Ozawa: 'The People Don't Want Me Now,' " *Nikkei Weekly*, March 28, 1992.

253 Indeed, he often ridiculed: "Ozawa Sees Need for Regrouping," *AEN*, June 18, 1991; Ichirō Ozawa, "My Commitment to Political Reform," p. 9.

253 "Even friends cannot stay together": "Ozawa's Strong Suit," *Political Reform*, Kyodo News Service, in *JT*, November 15, 1992.

253 "I don't like chatting for long": Ozawa, *Kataru*, p. 77.

254 "He has a tendency": Author interview with Hajime Funada, July 15, 1994.

254 "he would leave his seat": Author interview with Kōzō Watanabe, June 9, 1994.

254 "a toad who has just": Marshall, "The Man Who Would Be Kingmaker," p. 36.

254 "I don't want to drop": Kensuke Watanabe, *Ano hito*, p. 110.

254 "ought to bear the costs": Ozawa "My Commitment to Political Reform," p. 10.

254 "I heard from a senior": Takeshige Kunimasa and Takashi Tachibana, "Saigo no Tanaka ha Ozawa Ichirō" (The last Tanaka faction member Ichiro Ozawa), *Sekai*, February 1994, p. 30.

254 "has been reduced to the task of apportioning": Ozawa, *Blueprint for a New Japan*, p. 22.

256 "The dike crumbles": Armacost, *Friends or Rivals?*, p. 116.

256 "only a baby": "Ozawa-shi no kokka kan; ima no Nihon wa hannin mae" (Mr. Ozawa's view towards his state; current Japan is not independent), *Aera*, March 24, 1992, p. 15; "Blunt Strongman Deals Behind Scenes in Japan," *The New York Times*, March 29, 1992.

257 "Those who won't be around": Redl, "Curse of the Kingmakers," p. 36.

257 Ozawa's disenchantment turned: Description of Ozawa's canceled trip from: "Ozawa gaikō karamawari: Hikōki mo naku, aite mo nakute" (Ozawa diplomacy circles in the sky: No planes, nobody to meet), *Asahi Shimbun*, March 10, 1991.

257 Reflecting later upon the lessons: Ozawa's conclusions about the Gulf War and the political system's inability to address such issues from: Ozawa, *Blueprint for a New Japan*, pp. 27, 36–43.

258 "At this point, ninety-nine percent": Jiji Tsūshinsha Seijibu, ed., *Takeshita sōri zen dēta*, p. 67.

258 "Have you resumed political activities": "Ozawa's Views of LDP Race," *AEN*, September 5, 1991.

259 "I keenly feel a sense": Ozawa, "Therefore, We Chose Miyazawa," p. 5.

259 "The LDP does not dare": " 'The Japanese Must Try to Make Their Views Understood,' " *JT*, January 1, 1992.

259 "surgery-like political reform": Ozawa, "Therefore, We Chose Miyazawa," pp. 4–5.

259 "It's only natural": "The Next Wave in Japanese Politics: Three Top Contenders," *Tokyo Business Today*, July 1993, p. 42.

259 "I know some people": "The Art of a Political Warrior," *Financial Times*, May 4, 1993.

260 "What is to be criticized": "Chairman Shin Kanemaru, My Benefactor, and I: Former LDP Secretary General Ichiro Ozawa," *Seiron*, September 1992, trans. in *Summaries of Selected Japanese Magazines*, American Embassy, December 1992, p. 2.

260 a comic-book author managed: Takao Saitō, *Gekiga—Hashimoto Ryūtarō vs. Ozawa Ichirō: gekitōfu*.

260 "There is no guarantee": "Re-organization of Factions; Will Takeshita Faction Face Crisis of Split?; Creaking with Shift to 'Ozawa Faction'; Moves of Kajiyama and Others Also to Become Key," *Nihon Keizai Shimbun*, January 1, 1992, trans. in *Daily Summaries of Japanese Press*, American Embassy, January 11–13, 1992, p. 9.

261 "the apple of my eye": Ibid., p. 8.

261 "It is thanks to Kanemaru's patronage": "Onjin Kanemaru Shin kaichō to watashi" (Chairman Shin Kanemaru, my benefactor, and I), *Seiron*, September 1992, p. 83.

261 "a small man acting arrogantly": "Political World Divided About Ozawa: Some See Him as Rising Star, Others a 'Despot' Who Sows Confusion," *DY*, October 25, 1992.

261 "You don't consult us": Ōie, *Keiseikai shitō no nanajū nichi*, p. 115; "Sentiment Mounts Against Kanemaru," *JT*, October 9, 1992.

261 "Until now you've been monopolizing": Ōie, *Keiseikai shitō no nanajū nichi*, p. 166.

261 "Members reached a narrow consensus": "Ozawa Criticisms Weight Meeting: Sources Say Reelection May Fail," *DY*, October 17, 1992.

262 "Enough Is Enough!": "Enough Is Enough!," *AEN*, October 19, 1992.

262 "You are brothers": Ōie, *Keiseikai shitō no nanajū nichi*, pp. 192–201.

262 "is seeing the situation": "Ozawa's Strong Suit, Political Reform," Kyodo News Service, in *JT*, November 15, 1992.

262 "To me, it is quite clear": "Wareware wa naze kaikaku o mezasu ka" (Why we aim at reform), *Bungei Shunjū*, December 1992, p. 137.

262 "The three thousand troops": Ōie, *Keiseikai shitō no nanajū nichi*, p. 205.

263 "Politics will have to be": Ozawa, *Blueprint for a New Japan,* p. 63.

Chapter Twenty-two: The Boss Turned Reformer

264 "lack of real leadership": Ozawa, *Blueprint for a New Japan,* pp. 25–6.

265 "We must . . . ensur[e] that": Ibid., p. 29.

265 "must submit themselves": Ibid., p. 75.

265 "transmogrification that rivaled Saul": Robert Angel, quoted in Chalmers Johnson, *Japan: Who Governs? The Rise of the Developmental State,* p. 227.

265 "clear and appropriate limits": Ozawa, *Blueprint for a New Japan,* p. 28.

265 "If we are to break down": Ibid., p. 64.

266 "I have learned a lot": "Chokugeki Ozawa Ichirō ga kataru: Nihon no koto, seiji no koto" (Direct hit Ichiro Ozawa talks: About Japan, about politics), *Sandē Mainichi,* January 2–9, 1994, p. 33.

266 "There would be no problems": "Ozawa's Strong Suit, Political Reform," Kyodo News Service, in *JT,* November 15, 1992.

266 OZAWA: TO BE WELCOMED: "Ozawa: To Be Welcomed or Feared?," *DY,* December 8, 1992.

266 "Even Adolf Hitler": Akira Yamagishi, *"Renritsu" shikakenin,* pp. 21–2.

266 "So I'm not arguing": Ichirō Ozawa, "Dakara wareware wa Miyazawa o eranda: sōsai kōho mensetsu no saitenbo gōkaku made no kimete towa," *Bungei Shunjū,* December 1991, p. 113.

266 "the collapse of the constitutional state": "Creating a Blueprint for Political Reform," *Nikkei Weekly,* February 1, 1993.

267 "You should repent": Takashi Tachibana, "Tainted Wine from Old Bottles," *Asahi Shimbun,* June 24, 1993, trans. in *Japan Views,* August 1993.

267 "I personally am absolutely opposed": Ozawa, "My Commitment to Political Reform," p. 9.

267 when he failed to "protect": Ōie, *Keiseikai shitō no nanajū nichi,* p. 19.

267 a small group offered consolation: "Take a Look Within First: Kanemaru Connection Hurts LDP Reformists," *AEN,* March 11, 1993; "Kanemaru's Old Buddies Turn a Cold Shoulder on Their Ex-Don," *MDN,* March 16, 1993; "Fear and Loathing in Nagatacho," *MDN,* April 21, 1993.

267 earmarked for "a future political realignment": " 'Seikai saihen no shiken' shisan hoyū, bengodan, arasou kamae" (The assets were "funds for political realignment," lawyers take confrontational stance), *Asahi Shimbun,* March 28, 1993; " 'Kanemaru saiban' zenmen taiketsu ni" ("Kanemaru trial" will be all-out confrontation), *Nihon Keizai Shimbun,* July 23, 1993.

268 "Ozawa's next!": "Kanemaru Began Buying Debentures in 1984: Sources," *AEN,* March 8, 1993.

268 "There is no question that": Morihiro Hosokawa, " 'Seiken kōtai kisei dōmei' no teishō" (A proposal on the 'alliance towards a change of governments'), *Chūō Kōron,* June 1993, p. 68.

268 "The possibility of our cooperating": " 'Sagawa' and Politics; Tekkō Rōren (Japan Federation of Steel Workers' Union) Chairman Etsuya Washio: Urges Unifying of New Political Forces; To Hasten, with May of Next Year as Target," *Mainichi Shimbun,* November 10, 1992, trans. in *Daily Summary of Japanese Press,* American Embassy, November 17, 1992, p. 5.

268 "Observers predict that a majority": "Ozawa Never Had a Chance," *DY,* October 27, 1992.

269 "A politician can't feed himself": "LDP Feels Little Pain After Ex-Boss Nailed," *Nikkei Weekly,* March 15, 1993.

269 "Everybody was pretty worried": Ozawa, *Kataru,* pp. 81–2.

270 Renewal Party members still had: Okuno, *Ozawa Ichirō,* pp. 219–24; Takeshige Kunimasa and Takashi Tachibana, "Saigo no Tanaka ha Ozawa Ichirō" (The last Tanaka faction member Ichirō Ozawa), *Sekai,* February 1994, pp. 30–1; "The Eye of the Storm," *Newsweek,* international edition, January 18, 1993, p. 11.

271 "I'm disappearing": "Hosokawa pokeberu sōri wa joshikōsei reberu!?" (Hosokawa "Pocket Bell" PM is on high school girl's level!?), *Shūkan Taishū,* August 23–30, 1993, pp. 27–9; "Hosokawa shi yōritsu: 'ichidai kesshin o' 'saidaigen sasaeru,' Ozawa shi senkō, kudokiotosu" (Supporting Mr. Hosokawa: 'Make greater decision' 'I will support you to the maximum' Mr. Ozawa went underwater, persuaded him), *Mainichi Shimbun,* August 2, 1993.

271 "I thought it was a trick": "Takemura Masayoshi zen kanbōchōkan ga kataru: Ozawa san no kokoga kira . . ." (Ex–chief cabinet secretary Masayoshi Takemura talks: I do . . . like these things about Mr. Ozawa), *Shūkan Asahi,* May 27, 1994, p. 23; Shūsei Tanaka, *Sakigake to seiken kōtai,* p. 84.

272 "I will be willing": "Upstart Japan New Party Sets Bold Strategy to Break LDP's Hold," *JT,* May 24, 1993.

273 In one newspaper poll: "Tremendous Popularity; Somewhat Dissatisfied with Leadership; Requests of 'First of All, an Economic Upturn,' " *Sankei Shimbun,* August 13, 1993, trans. in *Daily Summary of Japanese Press,* American Embassy, August 21–3, 1993, p. 3.

274 to "liberate" power: Ozawa, *Blueprint for a New Japan,* p. 34.

274 "often unreasonable and his ideas": Author interview with Masayoshi Takemura, June 10, 1994.

274 "I've been speaking regularly": Ichirō Ozawa and Kazuya Fukuda, "Me o samase, Nihon seiji," *Voice,* October, 1993, trans. as "Turning Japan into a Self-Reliant Nation," in *Japan Echo,* vol. 20, no. 4, 1993, p. 24.

275 "black journalism": "Ozawa Says Media Treats Him Badly," *AEN,* May 17, 1994.

275 "Reformers . . . are always apt": "Socialists Drop Their Demand for Ozawa to Testify," *AEN,* November 12, 1993.

275 the decision conveyed the impression: "Ozawa's Silence Raising Concerns," *MDN,* December 6, 1993.

276 A new dividing line: "Political Line Is Drawn: Join or Topple Ozawa," *Nikkei Weekly,* June 20, 1994; "A New Kind of Battle," *AEN,* April 23, 1994.

277 "You have to visit voters": Kensuke Watanabe, *Ano hito,* p. 121.

277 One morning in December 1995: Description of Ozawa disco appearance from author interviews; "Ozawa shi disuko de furumai kōyaku" (Mr. Ozawa makes generous promises at a disco), *Sankei Supōtsu,* December 23, 1995.

Conclusion

280 "We must reform our politics": Ozawa, *Blueprint for a New Japan,* p. 11.

280 "Management of this kind became": Ibid., p. 199.

281 a "normal nation": Ibid., p. 94.

Selected Bibliography

The material for this book comes from more than one hundred author interviews with members of Japan's Parliament, political journalists, and academics in Tokyo, as well as from visits to the home districts of each of the four main characters: Tanaka's Niigata, Kanemaru's Yamanashi, Takeshita's Shimane, and Ozawa's Iwate. The book is also based on my experience as a reporter in the *Wall Street Journal*'s Tokyo bureau from 1989 through 1994.

In addition to original reporting, I relied on materials published or broadcast in English and in Japanese. The main works used are listed below. Other materials, such as daily press accounts, are cited in full in the endnotes.

English translations of Japanese documents were commissioned specifically for this book, unless otherwise noted.

Armacost, Michael H. *Friends or Rivals? The Insider's Account of U.S.-Japan Relations.* New York: Columbia University Press, 1996.

Asahi Shimbun Niigata Shikyoku, ed. *Tanaka Kakuei to Etsuzankai: shinsō no kōzu* (Kakuei Tanaka and the Etsuzankai: The deep underlying structure). Tokyo: Yamate Shobō, 1982.

Asahi Shimbun Seijibu, ed. *Ozawa Ichirō tanken* (An exploration of Ichiro Ozawa). Tokyo: Asahi Shimbunsha, 1991.

———. *Takeshita ha shihai* (Rule of the Takeshita faction). Tokyo: Asahi Shimbunsha, 1992.

———. *Tanaka shihai to sono hōkai* (Tanaka rule and its collapse). Tokyo: Asahi Shimbunsha, 1987.

Baerwald, Hans H. *Japan's Parliament: An Introduction.* London: Cambridge University Press, 1974.

Blaker, Michael. "Conservatives in Crisis." In *A Season of Voting: The Japanese Elections of 1976 and 1977,* Herb Passin, ed. Washington, D.C.: American Enterprise Institute for Public Policy Research, 1979.

Braw, Monica. *The Atomic Bomb Suppressed.* New York: M. C. Sharpe Inc., 1991.

Browning, E. S. "Shadow Shogun: Japan's Kakuei Tanaka Retains Great Power Although in Disgrace; The Former Prime Minister Controls Party Machinery, Bestows Favors on Friends; Holding Court for Supplicants." *The Wall Street Journal,* December 20, 1984.

Calder, Kent E. *Crisis and Compensation: Public Policy and Political Stability in Japan, 1949–1986.* Princeton: Princeton University Press, 1988.

———. "Kanryo vs. Shomin: Contrasting Dynamics of Conservative Leadership in Postwar Japan." In *Political Leadership in Contemporary Japan,* Terry Edward MacDougall, ed. Ann Arbor: Center for Japanese Studies, University of Michigan, 1982.

Campbell, John Creighton. "Democracy and Bureaucracy in Japan." In *Democracy in Japan,* Takeshi Ishida and Ellis S. Krauss, eds. Pittsburgh: University of Pittsburgh Press, 1989.

———. *How Policies Change: The Japanese Government and the Aging Society.* Princeton: Princeton University Press, 1992.

"Chairman Shin Kanemaru, My Benefactor, and I: Former LDP Secretary General Ichiro Ozawa." *Seiron,* September 1992. Translated in *Selected Summaries of Japanese Magazines,* American Embassy, December 1992.

Chihō Jichi Seisaku Kenkyūkai (Regional Autonomy Policy Research Council). *Zenkoku furusato sōsei ichioku-en dēta bukku* (National one billion yen hometown creation plan data-book). Tokyo: Daiichi Hōki, 1989.

Chikushi, Tetsuya. *Nipponjin haiken* (Taking a look at the Japanese). Tokyo: Asahi Shimbunsha, 1988.

Curtis, Gerald L. *The Japanese Way of Politics.* New York: Columbia University Press, 1988.

Darlin, Damon. "Japan's Front-Runner Stresses Consensus." *Asian Wall Street Journal,* October 9–10, 1987.

Desmond, Edward W. "Ichiro Ozawa: Reformer at Bay." *Foreign Affairs,* September–October 1995.

Etō, Shinkichi. *Nihon saishō retsuden: Satō Eisaku* (Biography series of Japanese prime ministers: Eisaku Sato). Tokyo: Jiji Tsūshinsha, 1987.

Fisher, Larry Warren. *The Lockheed Affair: A Phenomenon of Japanese Politics.* Ph.D. dissertation, University of Colorado, Boulder, 1980.

Fujiwara, Hirotatsu. *Tanaka Kakuei: Godfather of Japan.* Sapporo: Nihon Shoko Shinkokai, 1985.

Fukuda, Fumiaki. *Tanaka Kakuei: harikomi satsuei nisshi 1974–1993* (Kakuei Tanaka: A photographic diary of the stakeout 1974–1993). Fukuoka: Ashi shobō, 1994.

Fukuda, Takeo. *Kaiko kyūjū nen* (Looking back on ninety years). Tokyo: Iwanami Shoten, 1995.

Fukui, Haruhiro. "The Policy Research Council of Japan's Liberal Democratic Party: Policy Making Role and Practice." *Asian Thought & Society,* March 1987.

Fukuoka, Masayuki. "Naze tsuyoi Kakuei seiji." *Chūō Kōron,* January 1983. Translated as "Tanaka Kakuei's Grass Roots." *Japan Echo,* vol. 10, no. 1, 1983.

Gamō, Teru. *Ozawa Ichirō shinjitsu no sakebi* (Ichiro Ozawa: A shout of truth). Tokyo: Sanshindō Shuppansha, 1994.

Gotō, Kenji. *Obuchi Keizō zen jinzō* (Keizo Obuchi, the whole portrait). Tokyo: Gyōken, 1991.

Hanaoka, Nobuaki, and Shizuo Kobayashi. *Takeshita Noboru zen jinzō* (Noboru Takeshita, the full portrait). Tokyo: Gyōken, 1988.

Hane, Mikiso. *Peasants, Rebels and Outcastes: The Underside of Modern Japan.* New York: Pantheon, 1982.

Hayano, Tōru. "Mite kiite hanashita 'Kaku-san' no sugao" (The real face of "Kaku-san," whom I watched, listened, and talked to). *Aera,* December 27, 1993.

Hayasaka, Shigezō. *Hayasaka Shigezō no "Tanaka Kakuei" kaisōroku* (Shigezo Hayasaka's "Kakuei Tanaka" reminiscences). Tokyo: Shōgakukan, 1994.

———. *Kago ni noru hito, katsugu hito: jimintō rimenshi ni manabu* (People who ride a planquin, those who carry it: Learning from the behind-the-scenes history of the LDP). Tokyo: Shōdensha, 1988.

———. *The Making of a Japanese Prime Minister: How to Become No. 1 in Japan.* Translated by Atsushi Kobayashi. Tokyo: Sekai-no-Ugokisha, 1992.

———. *Oyaji to watashi* (Me and the old man). Tokyo: Shūeisha, 1993.

———. *Saishō no utsuwa* (The capacity of the prime minister). Tokyo: Kuresutosha, 1992.

———. *Seijika Tanaka Kakuei* (Kakuei Tanaka, the politician). Tokyo: Shūeisha, 1993.

———. "Tanaka Kakuei mumei no jū nen" (Kakuei Tanaka's ten years without fame). *Chūō Kōron,* November 1986.

Hellmann, Donald C. "Japanese Politics and Foreign Policy: Elitist Democracy Within an American Greenhouse." In *The Changing International Context,* vol. 2 of *The Political Economy of Japan,* Takashi Inoguchi and Daniel I. Okimoto, eds. Stanford: Stanford University Press, 1988.

Holstein, William J. *The Japanese Power Game: What It Means for America.* New York: Plume, 1991.

Hougan, Jim. "The Business of Buying Friends." *Harper's,* December 1976.

Hunziker, Steven, and Ikuro Kamimura. *Kakuei Tanaka: A Political Biography of Modern Japan.* Los Gatos, Calif.: Daruma International Press, 1994.

Hyōden Kanemaru Shin Hensankai (Shin Kanemaru Critical Biography Editorial Association), ed. *Kanemaru Shin: Saigo no Nihonteki seijika hyōden* (Shin Kanemaru: Critical biography of the last Japanese-style politician). Tokyo: Keizai Seisaku Konwakai, 1992.

Igarashi, Akio. "Daigishi kōenkai no seishinteki soshikiteki kōzō: moderu toshiteno Etsuzankai" (MPs' support groups: Etsuzankai as a model). *Shisō,* May 1989.

Iida, Kensuke. *Takeshita-san ni manabu . . . kikubari mekubari shussejutsu* (To learn from Mr. Takeshita . . . a thoughtful mind and watchful eyes, a strategy for moving up). Tokyo: Tokyo Shuppan, 1988.

Inoguchi, Takashi, and Tomoaki Iwai. *Zoku giin no kenkyū* (A study of tribal MPs). Tokyo: Nihon Keizai Shimbunsha, 1987.

Ise, Akifumi. *Ozawa Ichirō no wanryoku pointo yomi* (A point-by-point reading of Ichiro Ozawa's strength). Tokyo: Asuka Shuppansha, 1994.

Itō, Hirotoshi. *Kon-Chiku-Shō no kane to kenryoku* (Money and power of the Kon-Chiku-Sho trio). Tokyo: Nihon Shakaitō Kikanshi Kyoku, 1993.

Itō, Masaya. *Jimintō sengokushi* (History of the LDP's civil wars), vols. 1–3. Tokyo: Asahi Shimbunsha, 1985.

Jiji Tsūshinsha Seijibu, ed. *Takeshita sōri zen dēta* (The full data on Prime Minister Takeshita). Tokyo: Jiji Tsūshinsha, 1987.

Johnson, Chalmers. *Japan: Who Governs? The Rise of the Developmental State.* New York and London: W. W. Norton & Company, 1995.

———. *MITI and the Japanese Miracle: The Growth of Industrial Policy, 1925–1975.* Tokyo: Charles E. Tuttle Company, 1987.

———. "MITI, MPT, and the Telecom Wars: How Japan Makes Policy for High Technology." In *Politics and Productivity: The Real Story of Why Japan Works,* Chalmers Johnson, Laura D'Andrea Tyson, and John Zysman, eds. Cambridge, Mass.: Ballinger Publishing Company, 1989.

———. "Tanaka Kakuei, Structural Corruption, and the Advent of Machine Politics in Japan." *Journal of Japanese Studies,* Winter 1986.

Kanemaru, Shin. *Hito wa shiro; hito wa ishigaki; hito wa hori* (Man is a castle; man is a stone wall; man is a moat). Tokyo: Ēru Shuppansha, 1983.

———. *Tachiwaza newaza* (Tricks of the fight). Tokyo: Nihon Keizai Shimbunsha, 1988.

Kataoka, Tetsuya. *The Price of a Constitution: The Origin of Japan's Postwar Politics.* New York: Crane Russak, 1991.

Katō, Eiichi. "Toshi no fukushū." *Chūō Kōron*, June 1983. Translated as "Urban Discontent Under Tanaka's Machine." *Japan Echo*, vol. 10, no. 4, 1983.

Kato, Junko. *The Problem of Bureaucratic Rationality: Tax Politics in Japan*. Princeton: Princeton University Press, 1994.

Kikuchi, Hisashi. *Sagawa no kane kutta akutoku seijika* (Bad politicians who ate Sagawa's money). Tokyo: Yamate Shobō Shinsha, 1992.

———. *Shin Takeshita giwaku no keifu* (The new genealogy of suspicions about Takeshita). Tokyo: Poketto Bukkusha, 1994.

———. *Takeshita giwaku no keifu* (The genealogy of suspicions about Takeshita). Tokyo: Poketto Bukkusha, 1993.

Kitakado, Masashi. *Tanaka Kakuei dai gundan 101 nin* (Kakuei Tanaka's great army of 101 men). Tokyo: Yamate Shobō, 1981.

Kobayashi, Kichiya. *Kakuei ichidai: riidā to soshiki—zen hassō* (Kakuei the hero: The leader and organization—complete recollections). Tokyo: Nippon Eizō Shuppan, 1994.

———. *Ningen Tanaka Kakuei* (Kakuei Tanaka, the person). Tokyo: Kōbunsha, 1989.

Kodama, Takaya. "Sabishiki Etsuzankai no joō." *Bungei Shunjū*, November 1974. Translated as "Melancholic Queen of Etsuzankai." Three-part series in *Mainichi Daily News*, November 7–9, 1974.

Kōdansha Encyclopedia of Japan. Tokyo: Kōdansha Ltd., 1983.

Kotchian, A. Carl. *Lockheed Sales Mission—70 Days in Tokyo*. Unpublished English manuscript, 1976. Published in Japanese as *Rokkiido urikomi sakusen Tokyo no 70 nichi kan*. Tokyo: Asahi Shimbun, 1976.

Krauss, Ellis S. "Conflict in the Diet: Toward Conflict Management in Parliamentary Politics." In *Conflict in Japan*, Ellis S. Krauss, Thomas P. Rohlen, and Patricia G. Steinhoff, eds. Honolulu: University of Hawaii Press, 1984.

Kuji, Tsutomu. *Rikurūto jiken ni "shūketsu" wa nai* (There is no "resolution" to the Recruit case). Tokyo: Shinsensha, 1991.

Kyodo News Service. "Bidding for Influence." Fourteen-part series in *Japan Times*, January 28, 1994–February 16, 1994.

Kyū chiji ga kataru furusato sōsei (Nine governors talk about hometown creation). Tokyo: Gyōsei, 1989.

Livingston, Jon, Joe Moore, and Felicia Oldfather, eds. *Postwar Japan: 1945 to the Present*. New York: Pantheon, 1973.

MacDougall, Terry. "The Lockheed Scandal and the High Cost of Politics in Japan." In *The Politics of Scandal: Power and Process in Liberal Democracies*, Andrei Markovits and Mark Silverstein, eds. New York: Holmes & Meier, 1988.

Mainichi Daily News, ed. *Fifty Years of Light and Dark: The Hirohito Era*. Tokyo: The Mainichi Newspapers, 1975.

Mainichi Shimbun Shakaibu, ed. *Seiji fuhai o utsu: "fushin" no mei-*

saisho (Attacking political corruption: A specification of "distrust"). Tokyo: Mainichi Shimbunsha, 1993.

Marshall, Andrew, with Michiko Toyama. "The Man Who Would Be Kingmaker." *Tokyo Journal,* December 1992.

Masumi, Junnosuke. *Postwar Politics in Japan, 1945–1955.* Translated by Lonny E. Carlile. Berkeley: Institute of East Asian Studies, University of California, 1985.

———. *Contemporary Politics in Japan.* Translated by Lonny E. Carlile. Berkeley and Los Angeles: University of California Press, 1995.

Matsumoto, Seichō. *Gigoku 100 nen shi* (100-year history of corruption). Tokyo: Yomiuri Shimbunsha, 1977.

Matsumoto, Shirō. "Tanaka-ha wa ijō bōchō buttai de aru: Shijō saikyō no gundan ga busō kaijo sareru toki" (The Tanaka faction is overexpanded: When the strongest *gundan* in history will be disarmed), *Bungei Shunjū,* March 1983.

Matsuno, Raizō. *Hosokawa-Ozawa seiken: in-yō no baransu ga kuzureru toki* (Hosokawa-Ozawa government: When the yin-yang balance collapses). Tokyo: Nihon Terebi Hōsōmō, 1994.

McCormack, Gavan. *The Emptiness of Japanese Affluence.* Armonk, N.Y., and London: M. E. Sharpe, 1996.

McGregor, Richard. *Japan Swings: Politics, Culture and Sex in the New Japan.* Australia: Allen & Unwin Pty, 1996.

McWilliams, Wayne C. *Homeward Bound: Repatriation of Japanese from Korea After World War II.* Hong Kong: Asian Research Service, 1988.

Miya, Yujiro. "Harsh Snow-country Environment Proves Background for Political Strength." *Business Japan,* February 1994.

———. "Money Provides Power Source for Tanaka's Political Gains." *Business Japan,* June 1984.

———. "Party Politics Determine Success of Protagonists." *Business Japan,* November 1984.

Naka, Mamoru. *Kanemaru Shin: newazashi no kenkyū* (Shin Kanemaru: A study of fighting tricks). Tokyo: Tōyō Keizai Shinpōsha, 1990.

Nihon Keizai Shimbunsha, ed. *Jimintō seichōkai* (The LDP's Policy Affairs Research Council). Tokyo: Nihon Keizai Shimbunsha, 1983.

———. *Kanryō: kishimu kyodai kenryoku* (The bureaucracy: The gigantic power that creaks). Tokyo: Nihon Keizai Shimbunsha, 1994.

Niigata Nippō, ed. *Za Etsuzankai* (The Etsuzankai). Niigata: Niigata Nippō Jigyōsha, 1983.

———. *Kakuei no fūdo* (The natural features and spiritual climate of Kakuei's hometown). Niigata: Niigata Nippō Jigyōsha, 1983.

———. *Shomin no ayunda Niigata-ken 50 nen shi* (The people's path: Fifty-year history of Niigata Prefecture). Niigata: Niigata Nippō Jigyōsha, 1975.

Niigata Nippō Hōdōbu, ed. *Saishō Tanaka Kakuei no shinjitsu* (The truth about Prime Minister Kakuei Tanaka). Tokyo: Kōdansha, 1994.

Nishibe, Susumu. "Tanaka Kakuei no shakai teki hiyō." *Chūō Kōron,* March 1983. Translated as "Tanaka Kakuei, Product of Japanese Democracy." *Japan Echo,* vol. 10, no. 2, 1983.

Noguchi, Yukio. "Public Finance." In *The Domestic Transformation,* vol. 1 of *The Political Economy of Japan,* Kozo Yamamura and Yasukichi Yasuba, eds. Stanford: Stanford University Press, 1987.

Ochiai, Hiromitsu, and Masahiko Hino. "Tanaka Kakuei to seiji shinkansen" (Kakuei Tanaka and the political bullet train). *Sekai,* March 1983.

Oda, Hajime. *Ozawa Ichirō zen jinzō* (Ichiro Ozawa, the whole portrait). Tokyo: Gyōken, 1992.

Ōie, Seiji. *Keiseikai shitō no nanajū nichi* (The seventy days of the Keiseikai's desperate struggle). Tokyo: Kōdansha, 1995.

Oka, Takashi. "As the Japanese Say: Premier Sato Would Tap His Way Across a Stone Bridge to Be Sure It Was Safe." *The New York Times Magazine,* November 16, 1969.

Okabe, Yūzō. *Rinkaifukutoshin kaihatsu, dokyumento: zenekon yuchaku 10-chō en purojekuto* (Tokyo Bay development, document: 10 trillion yen project tied to general contractors). Tokyo: Akebi Shobō, 1993.

Okadome, Yasunori. *R no sōkatsu* (A roundup of Recruit). Tokyo: Mokuba Shokan, 1990.

Okimoto, Daniel I. *Between MITI and the Market: Japanese Industrial Policy for High Technology.* Stanford: Stanford University Press, 1989.

Okuno, Shūji. *Ozawa Ichirō: hasha no rirekisho* (Ichiro Ozawa: A ruler's personal history). Tokyo: Dētā Hausu, 1994.

Ōkura Kanryō no shōtai (The truth about finance ministry bureaucrats). Tokyo: Takarajimasha, 1995.

Ōshita, Eiji. *Ichi o motte tsuranuku: ningen Ozawa Ichirō* (Carrying through with one: Ichiro Ozawa, the person). Tokyo: Kōdansha, 1993.

Ozawa, Ichiro. *Blueprint for a New Japan.* Translated by Louisa Rubinfien. Tokyo, New York, and London: Kodansha International, 1994.

———. "Dakara wareware wa Miyazawa o eranda: Sōsai kōho mensetsu no saitenbo gōkaku made no kimete towa." *Bungei Shunjū,* December 1991. Translated as "Therefore, We Chose Miyazawa: Grade Book on Interviews with Candidates for LDP Presidency—Decisive Factors Leading to Victory." *Summaries of Selected Japanese Magazines,* American Embassy, May 1992.

———. "Wareware wa naze kaikaku o mezasu ka." *Bungei Shunjū,* December 1992. Translated as "My Commitment to Political Reform." *Japan Echo,* vol. 20, no. 1, 1993.

———, with Taiichirō Kobayashi. *Kataru* (Talk). Tokyo: Bungei Shunjū, 1996.

Ozawa Ichirō Kōenkai-Rikuzankai, ed. (Ichiro Ozawa Rikuzankai support group). *Ningen Ozawa Saeki* (Saeki Ozawa, the person). Tokyo: Fumaidō Shuppan, 1980.

Packard, George R. *Protest in Tokyo: The Security Treaty Crisis of 1960.* Princeton: Princeton University Press, 1966.

"Pureibōi intabyū: Tanaka Kakuei" (*Playboy* interview: Kakuei Tanaka). *Pureibōi,* July 1983.

Redl, Christopher. "Curse of the Kingmakers." *Tokyo Journal,* May 1993.

Reischauer, Edwin O., and Albert M. Craig. *Japan: Tradition and Transformation.* Boston: Houghton Mifflin Company, 1978.

Rikagaku kenkyūjo, ed. *Riken no kenkyū katsudō* (Riken's research activities). Wako: Rikagaku kenkyūjo, 1988.

Saitō, Takao. *Gekiga—Hashimoto Ryūtarō vs. Ozawa Ichirō: gekitōfu.* (Drama—Ryutaro Hashimoto versus Ichiro Ozawa: Record of a fierce fight). Tokyo: Nihon Furōraru Āto Shuppan Kyoku, 1991.

Sakakibara, Eisuke. "The Japanese Politico-Economic System and the Public Sector." In *Parallel Politics: Economic Policymaking in Japan and the United States,* Samuel Kernell, ed. Washington, D.C.: The Brookings Institution, 1991.

Sakamoto, Tatsuhiko. "Ningen Tanaka Kakuei" (Kakuei Tanaka, the person). *Gekkan Asahi,* March 1994.

Saki, Ryūzō. *Etsuzan Tanaka Kakuei* (Etsuzan Kakuei Tanaka). Tokyo: Asahi Shimbunsha, 1977.

Satō, Akiko. *Watashi no Tanaka Kakuei nikki* (My Kakuei Tanaka diaries). Tokyo: Shinchōsha, 1994.

Schlesinger, Joseph A. "Political Machines." In *The Encyclopedia of Democracy,* S. M. Lipset, ed. Washington, D.C.: Congressional Quarterly, 1995.

Seidensticker, Edward. *Tokyo Rising: The City Since the Great Earthquake.* New York: Alfred A. Knopf, 1990.

Sekiguchi, Takao. *Oshoku no kōzōgaku* (Study of the structure of corruption). Tokyo: Yūbunsha, 1980.

Shaplen, Robert. "Annals of Crime: The Lockheed Incident." Two-part series in *The New Yorker,* January 23–30, 1978.

Shear, Jeff. "The Shadow Shogun: In Japan, Shin Kanemaru, a Black Belt in Political Judo, Is the Maker of Kings." *Los Angeles Times,* August 9, 1992.

Shima, Keiji. *Shimageji fūunroku: hōsō to kenryoku, 40 nen* (Record of times of change: Broadcasting and power, forty years). Tokyo: Bungei Shunjū, 1995.

Shiota, Ushio. "We Are the 'Takeshita Boy-Detectives Group'; Who Is the Most Likely Candidate in the Successor Race, Which Has Already Started?" *Bungei Shunjū,* May 1988. Translated in *Summaries of Selected Japanese Magazines,* American Embassy, November 1988.

Shiraishi, Kojiro. *The Recruit Scandal and "Money Politics" in Japan.* Cambridge, Mass.: Program on U.S.-Japan Relations, Harvard University, 1990.

Shokun! "Supesharu da: Kakuei hitori butai" (Special: Kakuei one-man show). Television interview aired May 6 and 13, 1984.

Suwa, Tatsuya. *Dangō o ura de ayatsuru yakunin no teguchi* (The government officials' covert ways in manipulating *dango*). Tokyo: Ēru Shuppansha, 1994.

Suzuki, Bokushi. *Snow Country Tales: Life in the Other Japan.* Translated by Jeffrey Hunter with Rose Lesser. New York and Tokyo: Weatherhill, 1986.

Tachibana, Takashi. *Kyoaku vs. genron: Tanaka rokkiido kara jimintō bunretsu made* (Evil versus free speech: From the Tanaka Lockheed case to the breakup of the LDP). Tokyo: Bungei Shunjū, 1993.

———. "My Nine Years with Kakuei Tanaka; Greeting Money Veins-Lockheed Trial and 'Tanaka Verdict.'" *Bungei Shunjū,* November 1983. Translated in *Summaries of Selected Japanese Magazines,* American Embassy, March 1984.

———. *Rokkiido saiban to sono jidai: 1978 nen 5-gatsu–1980 nen 7 gatsu* (Lockheed trial and its age: May 1978–July 1980). Tokyo: Asahi Shimbun, 1983, 1984.

———. *Tanaka Kakuei kenkyū: zen kiroku* (Kakuei Tanaka: The complete research records). Tokyo: Kōdansha, 1991.

———. "Tanaka Kakuei kenkyū: sono kinmyaku to jinmyaku." *Bungei Shunjū,* November 1974. Translated as "Kakuei Tanaka: His Money & His Men." Nine-part series in *Mainichi Daily News,* October 28–November 6, 1974.

———. *Tanaka Kakuei shin kinmyaku kenkyū* (Kakuei Tanaka: New research on his money veins). Tokyo: Asahi Shimbunsha, 1985.

Takeshita, Noboru. *The Furusato Concept: Toward a Humanistic and Prosperous Japan.* Translated by Simul International. Unpublished.

———. *Shōgen hoshu seiken* (Testimony of a conservative administration). Tokyo: Yomiuri Shimbunsha, 1991.

Tamura, Hajime. *Seijika no shōtai* (The true identity of politicians). Tokyo: Kōdansha, 1994.

Tanaka, Kakuei. *Building a New Japan: A Plan for Remodeling the Japanese Archipelago.* Translated by Simul International. Tokyo: The Simul Press, 1972.

———. *Watashi no rirekisho* (My personal history). Tokyo: Nihon Keizai Shimbunsha, 1968.

———. *Watakushi no shōnen jidai* (My boyhood). Tokyo: Kōdansha, 1973.

Tanaka, Shūsei. *Sakigake to seiken kōtai* (Sakigake and the change of administrations). Tokyo: Tōyō Keizai Shinpōsha, 1994.

Tanaka Kakuei o aisuru seiji kisha gurūpu (The political journalists' group that loves Kakuei Tanaka). *Tanaka Kakuei saihyōka* (A reevaluation of Kakuei Tanaka). Tokyo: Sōyōsha, 1994.

Tatesawa, Kōji. *Kensetsu gyōkai: dangō rettō Nippon* (The construction industry: The Japanese *dango* archipelago). Tokyo: Paru Shuppan, 1993.

Thayer, Nathaniel B. *How the Conservatives Rule Japan.* Princeton: Princeton University Press, 1969.

Utsumi, Kenji. *Soredemo Tanaka Kakuei wa fumetsu de aru* (Yet Kakuei Tanaka is eternal). Tokyo: Kōdansha, 1986.

van Wolferen, Karel. *The Enigma of Japanese Power.* New York: Alfred A. Knopf, 1989.

Watanabe, Kensuke. *Ano hito: hitotsu no Ozawa Ichirō ron* (The man: One theory of Ichiro Ozawa). Tokyo: Asuka Shinsha, 1992.

Watanabe, Kōzō. *Seijika ni tsukeru kusuri* (Medicine to apply to politicians). Tokyo: Tōyō Keizai Shinpōsha, 1995.

Welfield, John. *An Empire in Eclipse: Japan in the Postwar American Alliance System.* London and Atlantic Highlands, N.J.: The Athlone Press, 1988.

Wilkinson, Thomas. *The Globalization of Japanese Labor, 1868–1955.* Amherst, Mass.: University of Massachusetts Press, 1965.

Woodall, Brian. *Japan Under Construction: Corruption, Politics, and Public Works.* Berkeley and Los Angeles: University of California Press, 1996.

Yamagishi, Akira. *"Renritsu" shikakenin* (The maker of the "coalition"). Tokyo: Kōdansha, 1995.

Yamamoto, Kōichi. *Tanaka Kakuei zen kiroku: mitchaku ni nen han, ni man katto kara no hōkoku* (A complete record of Kakuei Tanaka: A report from 20,000 photos taken while following him for two and a half years). Tokyo: Shūeisha, 1985.

Yanaga, Chitoshi. *Big Business in Japanese Politics.* New Haven: Yale University Press, 1968.

Yoshida, Kyūichi. *Yoshida Kyūichi chosaku shū 2: Nihon hinkonshi kaiteiban* (Collection of Kyuichi Yoshida's works, vol. 2: History of Japanese poverty, revised edition). Tokyo: Kawashima Shoten, 1993.

Acknowledgments

I must begin my acknowledgments with both an expression of gratitude and a disclosure. My wife, Louisa Rubinfien—who provided indispensable intellectual and moral support throughout the writing process—worked for seven years in Tokyo as an aide to Ichiro Ozawa, one of the main characters of this book. In that capacity, she translated Ozawa's *Blueprint for a New Japan,* which is cited frequently in this text. Though readers should be aware of these circumstances, I believe that this work meets the standards of journalistic objectivity.

I did most of my writing as a visiting scholar at Stanford University's Asia/Pacific Research Center. I am especially indebted to the center's director, Professor Dan Okimoto, who gave me a grant, an office, access to all of the Stanford community's resources, and, most generously, his constant guidance. The staff at A/PARC extended copious aid and made an arduous process a lot of fun.

Several people encouraged me to take on this project. In particular, John Bussey, *The Wall Street Journal*'s indefatigable Tokyo bureau chief at the time, gave me the confidence and motivation. *Journal* colleagues Paul Ingrassia and Joe White, who coauthored *Comeback,* about the auto industry, offered inspiration and advice.

I could not have completed my research without translations and other help from numerous assistants. A few deserve special mention. In Tokyo, Chieko Tsuneoka's first-rate journalistic instincts and perfectionism were essential for gathering my materials and shaping my thoughts. At Stanford, Jennifer Amyx consistently tracked down detailed answers to my most obscure questions. Kyoko Onoki in Japan, and Sakiko Adachi and Junko Waki in California, also devoted themselves to this endeavor.

Many people in Japan educated me and opened doors for me. Japanese journalists, notably from the *Asahi Shimbun,* contributed their time and expertise. I am most obliged to the *Asahi*'s Toru Hayano for teaching me about the intricacies of Niigata, the Tanaka faction, and national politics as a whole. Toshizo Oda of the *Niigata Nippo* provided tremendous assistance in navigating his, and Tanaka's, home region. Toshio Toyoda of Kodansha Ltd. and Shiro Tazaki of Jiji Press also offered invaluable suggestions. Toshiko Oguchi's language lessons became scintillating seminars on the country and its politics. Hiroshi Ishikawa, formerly of the Foreign Press Center, selflessly steered me, as he has other foreign journalists, toward useful sources. Takao Toshikawa helped demystify and enliven the complexities of Japanese politics. The national and home-district staffs of many Parliament members went to great lengths to set up interviews. Officials at the American Embassy in Tokyo kindly shared their knowledge and insights.

The staffs at several libraries patiently allowed me and my assistants to comb their archives. Bill Brooks at the American Embassy let me sift through and copy his translations of Japanese newspapers and magazines. I also owe debts of gratitude to the Foreign Correspondents Club of Japan librarians, and to those at the Hoover Institution's East Asian Collection at Stanford.

Dan Okimoto and Jim Raphael of Stanford took time out from their own work to read mine and to offer extensive comments. Mike Williams of *The Wall Street Journal* applied his fine editor's touch. As a result, this book is much better than it would have been; all remaining failings are the author's.

The original idea for this book came from my time as a Tokyo correspondent for *The Wall Street Journal* from 1989 to 1994. I am grateful to my editors and colleagues at the newspaper for providing me the opportunity to work in Japan, for giving me the time to write this book, and for taking me back upon its completion. During my stint in Japan with the *Journal,* I relied heavily upon Hiroko Fujita and Miho Inada, the news assistants who did not receive bylines but who made the bylines possible for those of us who did. Jim McDonald, one of the *Journal*'s computer gurus, went above and beyond the call of duty to assist me with technology crises during my leave of absence.

Alice Mayhew and Roger Labrie at Simon & Schuster masterfully directed the details, large and small, of this project. Andrew Wylie and Bridget Love offered the most timely, complete support an author could wish from agents.

Joseph and Mildred Schlesinger extended not just parental encouragement but their insights as scholars and authorities on American and comparative politics. The Rubinfiens generously proferred room, board, and a warm family atmosphere.

For the paperback edition, I owe yet another debt to Prof. Okimoto for helping arrange publication. I am grateful, too, to Zoe Pagnamenta of the Wylie Agency and Muriel Bell of Stanford University Press for making this edition possible.

Washington, D.C., 1998

Index

Library of Congress Cataloging-in-Publication Data

Schlesinger, Jacob M.

Shadow shoguns : the rise and fall of Japan's postwar political machine / Jacob M. Schlesinger.

p. cm.

Includes bibliographical references and index.

ISBN 0-8047-3457-7 (pbk. : alk. paper)

1. Political culture—Japan. 2. Political corruption—Japan. 3. Bureaucracy—Japan. 4. Business and politics—Japan. 5. Japan—Politics and government—1945– I. Title.

[JQ1681.S35 1999]

306.2'0952'09045—dc21 99–17347